DVD DEMYSTIFIED

OTHER MCGRAW-HILL BOOKS OF INTEREST

DVD
Demystified
The Guidebook for DVD-Video and DVD-ROM

Jim Taylor

McGraw-Hill
New York • San Francisco • Washington, D.C. • Auckland • Bogotá
Caracas • Lisbon • London • Madrid • Mexico City • Milan
Montreal • New Delhi • San Juan • Singapore
Sydney • Tokyo • Toronto

Library of Congress Cataloging-in-Publication Data

Taylor, Jim.
    DVD demystified : the guidebook for DVD-video and DVD-ROM / Jim
Taylor.
        p.   cm.
    Includes index.
    ISBN 0-07-064841-7 (softcover : set)
    1. DVD technology.   I. Title.
TK7882.C56T39   1997
621.388'332—dc21   97-27827
                                                                    CIP

McGraw-Hill

*A Division of The **McGraw·Hill** Companies*

        4 5 6 7 8 9 0   DOC/DOC   9 0 2 1 0 9 8

P/N 064846-8
PART OF
ISBN 0-07-064841-7 (PBK)

*The sponsoring editor for this book was Steve Chapman, and the production supervisor was
Sherri Souffrance. It was set in Vendome by North Market Street Graphics.*

Printed and bound by R. R. Donnelley & Sons Company.

McGraw-Hill books are available at special quantity discounts to use as premiums
and sales promotions, or for use in corporate training programs. For more information, please write to the Director of Special Sales, McGraw-Hill, 11 West 19th Street,
New York, NY 10011. Or contact your local bookstore.

 This book is printed on recycled, acid-free paper containing a minimum of
50% recycled de-inked fiber.

To Mom and Dad, who cultivated my deep sense of curiosity and wonder and illuminated the path of science and technology—the most curious and wondrous of subjects.

CONTENTS

Contents

Contents

Contents

Contents

Contents

FOREWORD

"What is DVD, anyway?" This seemingly simple question can cause anyone who is knowledgeable on the subject of DVD to cringe. The question is much like "What is digital audio?" or "How does television work?" in that there is simply no meaningful short answer. But unlike those examples, there have been no comprehensive reference materials to recommend on DVD—until now.

The book you are about to read is an extensive analysis of the historical, technical, and practical aspects of DVD. Far more than the traditional listing of technical traits and numbers, *DVD Demystified* also presents a wealth of thoughts and opinions on issues surrounding the format, including a chapter on the perceived limitations of DVD. And in addition to the coverage of how consumers will use DVD, there is a discussion on applications for DVD-Video and DVD-ROM in the industrial world. You will also find comparisons with other disc and tape formats, and even a novel section to help you decide whether to buy a DVD-Video player or not.

The author, Jim Taylor, is particularly qualified to demystify DVD, not only because of his extensive experience with video and multimedia technologies but because he does not represent the DVD format in any official capacity. In fact, his background as a battle-scarred technology *user* provides a perspective sorely needed by other potential users and interested parties who want an unbiased review of this remarkable but bewildering new format.

The group of companies that is now known as the DVD Forum had at one time proposed that the "V" in DVD should stand for "versatile", in apparent recognition of the many ways the format can be put to use. Although few people seemed to applaud the "Digital Versatile Disc" as a catchy name, it does begin to describe the essence of DVD as the first packaged media format to embrace and standardize virtually all uses of digital storage from its inception. To illustrate this, consider the following attributes of DVD.

DVD is powerful. As you will discover, DVD has the potential to affect almost everyone in any industry. It is an inexpensive, robust, and portable communications medium that can contain a huge amount of information unthinkable only a few years ago. A single two-sided disc can contain *fourteen times* the amount of information of a CD-ROM disc while occupying exactly the same physical space. It is a publishing medium that can deliver dazzling quality video, audio, and multimedia content to many thousands of people at a cost unmatched by any other mechanism—online or otherwise. It is also an archive medium that can safely store vast amounts of data and images critical to the mission of any organization.

DVD is complex. DVD comprises many diverse technological elements. It represents the combined visions and creative efforts of many talented engineering, manufacturing, artistic, and business people from organizations around the world. Multiple technologies, including laser optics, electronics, audio/video compression, data processing, and optional disc manufacturing have been combined to create the format. As a result, there are several different kinds of DVD discs, all with different capabilities, capacities, and underlying technical mechanisms. There are video versions for different television standards around the world, read-only and recordable versions for computer data, and even a forthcoming audio-only version.

DVD is exciting. Many people have predicted that DVD will be the "next big thing" for the consumer electronics and computer industries. It can enable innovative, nonlinear ways to present motion picture content. It can deliver many hours of stunning quality video images and thundering sound in home theater systems and, for those so inclined, even on computers. Its higher data rate can greatly expand the quality and realism of multimedia program delivery—all on a relatively cheap, durable disc less than five inches in diameter.

But powerful, complex, and exciting formats do not automatically succeed just because they are brilliant examples of technology. To take advantage of all that DVD has to offer, one should first understand what it is and how it works—this book will help you with that. But it is just as important to discover how DVD can be used to add genuine value in the real world. Recent history warns us loudly not to get carried away with the "gee-whiz" aspects of new technology, because it is valuable only if it can help solve real problems and make life more rewarding for those who will use it. Cellular telephones, compact discs, pagers, videocassette recorders, and fax machines are just a few examples of technologies that succeeded because they met these basic requirements. On the other hand, it is just as easy to think of other technologies and formats that failed because they apparently did not have what it takes. Only time, coupled with the creativity and hard work of those who believe in DVD's potential, will determine which category it will ultimately end up in.

But enough philosophy and on to the fun stuff. If you work (or play) with DVD or just have a general interest in the format, you should acquire and read this book. Along the way, I would encourage you to imagine creative and innovative ways that DVD might be enjoyed and put to use. But beware—once people find out that you know about DVD, be prepared to hear "what is DVD anyway?" a lot more frequently . . .

Andrew W. Parsons

ACKNOWLEDGMENTS

My heartfelt thanks to those who encouraged and supported me in writing this book.

Many wonderful people spent time reading and commenting on my drafts: Kilroy Hughes, Dana Parker, Julia Taylor, Jerry Pierce, Steve Taylor, Robert Lundemo Aas, Chad Fogg, Roger Dressler, Tristan Savatier, Ralph LaBarge, Van Ling, Andy Parsons, and Leo Backman. This book is much richer because of them.

Thanks also to Peter Biddle at Microsoft, John Cook at Apple, Dave Schnuelle at THX, Mike Schmit at CompuCore, Geoffrey Tully, and others who took time to explain many things.

I'm grateful to the helpful members of the alt.video.dvd Internet newsgroup for posting enlightening comments, for asking so many questions, and for putting up with my questions. I'm grateful as well to the IMA DVD SIG members who have shared their knowledge.

I'm indebted to all the generous people who made the sample disc possible: Skip Griffin, Jamie Cave, and David Newcomb at NB Digital, Randy Berg and Mark Lang at Rainmaker, Sandy Benedetto and Linda Toleno at Pioneer, Kim Yost and Susan Griffin at THX, Gene Radzik at Dolby, Scott Epstein at SHORT, Bryan Rusenko at Crest National, and Vini Bancalari at Elite Entertainment.

My thanks to Joe Clark at Videodiscovery for his support and understanding. Thanks to Steve Chapman at McGraw-Hill for answering yes more often than no. Special thanks to Fleischman and Arthur, who have been solidly supportive.

And last, thanks to Microsoft for my mantra.

ABOUT THE AUTHOR

Jim Taylor is the Director of Information Technology at Videodiscovery, Inc. He is also a primary member of the Interactive Multimedia Association's DVD Special Interest Group. The author of several articles on DVD and a contributor to the Optical Video Disc Association's DVD Guidebook, he is often quoted as an industry expert on DVD issues. Jim Taylor is based in Seattle, Washington.

1

Introduction

What Is DVD?

DVD is the future. Viewed through the prism of time, it's only one potential future out of myriad possibilities. But this particular possibility looks quite promising—chances are excellent that DVD will be in your future, supplying video, audio, and computer software. DVD embodies the grand unification theory of entertainment and business media: if it fulfills the hopes of its creators, DVD will replace audio CDs, videotapes, laserdiscs, CD-ROMs, and even video game cartridges and many business publications.

DVD stands for *digital video disc, digital versatile disc,* or nothing, depending on whom you ask. Put simply, DVD is the next generation of compact disc technology. Improvements in technology allowed engineers to make the tightly packed microscopic pits that store data on an optical disc even more microscopic and even more tightly packed. A DVD is the same size as the familiar CD—12 centimeters (about 4½ inches) wide—but it holds up to 25 times more and is up to 9 times faster.

NOTE   *In essence, DVD is a bigger, faster compact disc.*

But DVD is much more than CD on steroids. Its increased storage capacity allows it to hold high-quality video, which up until now has been too massive to store in digital form. The result is a small, shiny disc that holds high-quality video as well as higher-than-CD-quality audio. A basic DVD can contain a movie over two hours long. A double-sided, double-layer DVD holds eight or more hours of video. And if you leave off the video and drop the audio quality a bit, a DVD will hold an audio book over 50 hours long.

DVD has many other tricks to woo both the weary couch potato and the multimedia junkie alike, such as a widescreen picture, six-channel surround sound, multilingual audio tracks, selectable subtitles, multiple camera angles, karaoke features, seamless branching, navigation menus, instant fast forward/rewind, and more.

Just as audio CD has its computer counterpart in CD-ROM, DVD has DVD-ROM, which shatters the limitations of CD-ROM. DVD-ROM holds from 4.4 to 16 gigabytes of data—25 times as much as a 650-megabyte CD-ROM—and sends it to the computer at least four times faster than a double-speed CD-ROM drive.

DVD is—or will be—inexpensive. The first generation of DVD-ROM drives are more expensive than CD-ROM drives but, as the technology improves and production quantities increase, the drives are expected to drop quickly to the same low prices. The first generation of DVD-Video players are as expensive as high-end VCRs, but mass production of DVD-ROM drives and plummeting costs of audio/video decoder chips will drive the price of players to the same level as VCRs and CD players. DVD discs are produced with most of the same equipment used for CDs, and because they're stamped instead of recorded they can be produced cheaper and faster than tapes.

DVD has the potential to bring about a significant change in the world of video entertainment and multimedia. It's the first high-quality interactive medium to be affordable to the mass market. Until now, the high-impact visuals of television, videotape, and movies have been linear and unchanging, while the fluid and responsive environment of computer multimedia has suffered from unimpressively tiny video windows with fuzzy, jerky motion. Many artists with the vision to do extraordinary things with an interactive environment have shunned CD-ROMs because their creative standards would be compromised. As a result, they've been constricted to the plodding straight and narrow of traditional linear video presentation designed to force-feed the masses. This doesn't mean that DVD should close the door on beginning-to-end storytelling, only that it can open a new door for different approaches. DVD is a fresh digital canvas onto which artists can expand their abilities and sketch their nonlinear visions in both time and space to be recreated on television screens and computer screens alike as a different experience for each participatory viewer.

DVD-Video versus DVD-ROM

This book will tell you practically everything you need to know about DVD, but if you take away only a few tidbits, one of them should be that DVD-Video is not the same as DVD-ROM. Just as CD audio and CD-ROM are different applications of the same technology, DVD is really two separate things: (1) an audio/video storage medium, and (2) a computer data storage medium. You use a *DVD player*—like a VCR or a CD player—to play back video and audio from a DVD (often called DVD-Video). You use a *DVD-ROM drive*—like a CD-ROM drive—to read computer data from a DVD-ROM. As computers become true multimedia systems, this distinction will begin to disappear; but until then, it's important to understand the difference.

NOTE   *DVD-Video is not the same as DVD-ROM.*

Technically, DVD is three or more separate things: DVD-ROM, DVD-Video, DVD-Audio, and other possible specialized formats. The DVD-Audio format was far from finalized when this book was written in early 1997, but it conceivably could be different enough from DVD-Video that the discs might not be playable on existing DVD-Video players and DVD-ROM—equipped computers.

Will DVD Succeed?

Many pundits predict that DVD will be a flop, joining the neglected ranks of other consumer electronics innovations such as quadraphonic sound, the 8-track tape, the Timex-Sinclair computer, and the digital compact cassette. *Failure,* of course, is in the eye of the pronouncer, but it's essentially impossible for DVD to fail. DVD on the computer side (DVD-ROM) is as close to a sure seller as wine and cheese in France. DVD on the consumer entertainment side (DVD-Video and DVD-Audio) is much less of a sure thing, but should it fail, it will be the most spectacular bomb in the history of computer electronics. Dozens of companies are behind DVD-Video, more than have ever before backed a major new product launch. Toss in another hundred or so companies that have announced DVD-ROM products of one kind or another, and it's easy to see that DVD can go a long way on inertia alone.

See the "DVD Myths" section of Chap. 3 for additional discussion of this point.

What Does DVD Portend?

Motion video is one of the most deeply affecting creations of humankind. It combines the ethereal effects of sound and music, the realistic impact of photography, the engrossing drama of theatrical plays, and the variety of visual arts, and weaves them all together with the ageless appeal of the storyteller. We are endlessly attempting to improve the richness of this medium, with which we replay and reshape our impressions and visions of the world. DVD is one small step in that quest, but a very critical one. It's a milestone in the ascendancy of things digital.

DVD is one of the final nails in the coffin of analog technology. Our representation of the world is changing from analog forms such as vinyl records, film, and magnetic tape, to digital forms such CDs, computer graphics, and now DVD. The advantage of information in digital form is that it can be easily manipulated and processed by computer; it can be compressed for cheaper and faster storage or transmission; it can be stored and duplicated without generational loss; its circuitry does not drift with heat or age; noise and distortion can be separated from the signal; and it can be transmitted over any distance without degrading. As the Internet becomes the dominant paradigm for the way we receive, send, and work with information, DVD will play a vital role. It will take many, many years before the Internet is able to easily carry the immense amounts of data needed for television and movies, music, interactive multimedia, and even virtual worlds. Until then, DVD is positioned to be the primary vehicle for delivering these information streams. And, there will always be a need to archive information so that it's still quickly accessible. DVD and its evolutionary successors fit the bill.

Some people believe DVD heralds the convergence of computers and entertainment media. They feel that a technology such as DVD that works as well in the family room as in the office is another reason that the TV and the computer will merge into one. Perhaps. Or, perhaps the computer will always be a separate entity with a separate purpose. How many people want to write in a word processor or work on a spreadsheet while sitting on the couch in front of the TV with a cordless keyboard on their lap—especially if the kids want to watch Animaniacs or play Ultra Mario instead? Whatever the case, it is inevitable that consumer electronics will gain more of the capabilities of computers and computers will integrate more of the features of televisions and stereo systems. The line is blurring, and DVD is rubbing a very big eraser across it.*

---

*Perhaps in this age of digital art, it's more appropriate to say that DVD is rubbing a very large *smudge tool* across the line.

Who Needs to Know About DVD?

The number of people who will feel the effect of DVD is truly astonishing. A large part of this astonished multitude requires a working knowledge of DVD, including its capabilities, strengths, and limitations. This book provides most of this knowledge.

A remarkably diverse range of fields will be affected by DVD.

Music and Audio

Because audio CD is established and fulfills most needs of music listeners, DVD will not have much of an effect in this area. As of early 1997, the DVD-Audio format is not specified, but the DVD-Video format already includes higher-than-CD-quality audio as well as surround sound audio. All DVD players will also play audio CDs.

DVD will give a slight boost to karaoke, since it includes special karaoke audio modes to remove the vocals or add vocal backup tracks. And more importantly, DVD's subtitle feature breaks the language barrier with up to 32 different sets of lyrics in any language, complete with bouncing balls or word-by-word (or symbol-by-symbol) highlighting.

DVD is also a boon for audio books and other spoken-word programs. Over 50 hours of stereo audio can be stored on one side of a single disc—a disc which is cheaper to produce and more convenient than cassette tapes or multidisc CD sets.

Music Performance Video

In spite of the success of MTV and the virtual prerequisite that a music group cut a video in order to be heard, music performance video has not done as well as expected in the videotape or laserdisc markets. Perhaps it's because you can't pop a video in the player and continue to read or work around the house. But it's possible that DVD will prove to be the golden key that unlocks the gates for music performance. With high-quality, long-playing video and multichannel surround sound, DVD music video should appeal to a range of fans from opera to ballet to New Age to acid rock.

A common argument against the success of video is that it's not as collectible as music. Music can be listened to over and over, while most movies only bear watching a few times. Music can play in the background without disrupting everyday tasks, but movies require devoted watching. However, music combined with video is more collectible than music alone. And more playable than movies. Research shows that televisions are often left tuned to music channels such as MTV with no one in the room. Six percent of the top-selling video titles are music videos. Music albums on DVD can improve their fan appeal by including such added tidbits as live performances, backstage footage, outtakes, video liner notes, musician biographies, documentaries, and interviews.

One of the first targets for DVD-Video player sales will be the replacement CD player market. CD players inevitably break or are upgraded, and shoppers looking for a new player may be persuaded to spend a little more to get something that can also play movies. The natural convergence of the audio and video player will bolster the success of combined music and video titles.

Movies

DVD has the potential to significantly raise the quality and enjoyability of home entertainment. According to the Consumer Electronics Manufacturers Association (CEMA), there will be over 16 million American homes with a home theater* system by the end of 1997, all of them ripe for DVD-Video. The obvious question is how many people will be interested in replacing their VCR with a more expensive DVD player that can't even record? But as the prices drop, the players will become attractive as additions to home theater systems or as replacements for aging CD players.

Training and Productivity

DVD will probably become the platform of choice for video training. Low cost of hardware and discs, widespread use of players, availability of authoring systems, and a profusion of knowledgeable DVD developers and producers will make DVD ideal for industrial training, teacher training, sales presentations, home education, and any other application where full audio and video are needed for effective instruction.

Videos for teaching skills from accounting to TV repair to dental hygiene, from tai chi to guitar to flower arranging can become vastly more

---

*Defined as a 25-inch or larger TV, HiFi VCR or laserdisc player, and a surround-sound system with at least four speakers.

effective by taking advantage of the crisp video, multiple soundtracks, selectable subtitles, graphics, menus, branching, and other advanced interactive features of DVD. Consider an exercise video that randomly selects different routines each day or lets you choose the mood, the tempo, and the muscle groups to focus on. Or, a first aid training course that slowly increases the level of the lessons and the complexity of the practice sessions. An auto-mechanic training video that allows you to view a procedure from different angles at the touch of a remote control. A cookbook that helps you select recipes via menus and indexes and then shows a skilled chef leading you through every step of the preparation. All this on a familiar compact disc which never wears out and never has to be rewound or fast-forwarded.

DVD is cheaper to produce and much cheaper and easier to distribute than videotape. Other products such as laserdisc, CD-i, and even Video CD have done well in training applications but require expensive or specialized players. Once DVD becomes established, players will be available in homes, offices, and even be built into average computers. Training applications of DVD will be able to make the most of this ubiquity.

Education

Laserdiscs have been a success in education almost since day one. Teachers quickly saw the advantage of rapid access to thousands of pictures and high-impact motion video sequences. They were willing to invest in laserdisc players after seeing the effectiveness of laserdisc-based instruction in the classroom. By 1996, there were over 200,000 laserdisc players in schools in the United States. Most of these are enhanced with laser barcode technology to provide quick and easy access to video by scanning a bar code printed in a textbook or on a student worksheet. Computer multimedia has begun to replace laserdisc in the classroom, but the ease of popping in a laserdisc and pressing play or scanning a few bar codes may never be matched by computers and CD-ROMs with their complicated cables and software setups and their daunting troubleshooting requirements.

CD-i, Video CD, and multimedia CD-ROMs have attempted to replace laserdisc but they all lack the picture quality and clarity that's so important for full-class presentations. The excellent image quality, high storage capacity, and low cost of DVD make it a worthy successor to laserdisc, especially if it is combined with simple and foolproof bar codes. Pioneer, the leader in educational laserdisc technology, makes combination DVD/

laserdisc players which could allow schools to take advantage of DVD technology and still make the most of their investment in laserdiscs.

And, even if DVD-Video is not widely adopted in education, DVD-ROM will be. CD-ROM has infiltrated all levels of schooling from home to kindergarten to college and will soon segue to DVD-ROM as CD-ROM drives are upgraded and new computers with built-in DVD-ROM drives are purchased, enabling truly interactive applications with the sensory impact and realism that can best stimulate and inspire inquisitive minds.

Computer Software

CD-ROM is becoming the computer software distribution medium of choice. To reduce manufacturing costs, many software companies have begun shipping CD-ROMs in place of expensive and unwieldy piles of floppy disks. Yet some applications are too large even for the hundreds of megabytes of space on a CD-ROM. These include software libraries containing dozens of programs which can be unlocked by paying a fee and receiving a special code, specialized databases with hundreds of millions of entries, and massive software products such as network operating systems and document collections. Phone books that used to fill six or more CD-ROMs now fit onto a single DVD-ROM. Companies that distribute monthly updates of large CD-ROM sets could ship free DVD-ROM drives to their customers and pay for them within a year with the savings on production costs alone.

Computer Multimedia

Many multimedia producers are stifled by the narrow confines of CD-ROM and yearn for the wide open spaces and liberating speed of DVD-ROM. The 1997 edition of Microsoft's Encarta encyclopedia has already overflowed onto two CD-ROMs but could expand for years more without filling up one DVD-ROM.

In addition to space, DVD brings along high-quality audio and video. Many new computers have hardware or software decoders that can be used to play DVD movies on a computer. These DVD-enabled computers will be even more effective for realistic simulations, games, education, and "edutainment." DVD will soon make blocky, quarter-screen computer video a distant, unhappy memory.

Video Games

The capacity to add high-quality, real-life video and full surround sound to three-dimensional game graphics is very appealing to video game manufacturers. Some past attempts to combine video footage with interactive games has been met with yawns, but the technology will improve until it finally clicks. Major game publishers, Nintendo, Sega, Sony, and 3DO have made announcements of support for DVD, although a few of them seem to have backed off from immediate plans. A combination video game/CD/DVD player could be very appealing.

Video games that make extensive use of full-screen video and even multimedia games traditionally available only for computers will start to appear in DVD-Video editions that will play on any home DVD player and on DVD-Video—enabled computers. Many of these games currently require as many as six or more CDs, but will fit with room to spare on a DVD-Video or DVD-ROM.

Information Publishing

The Internet is a wonderfully effective and efficient medium for information publishing, but it lacks the bandwidth needed to do justice to large amounts of data rich with graphics, audio, and motion video. DVD, with storage capacity vastly superior to CD-ROM plus standardized formats for audio and video, is perfect for publishing and distributing information in our ever more knowledge-intensive and information-hungry world.

Organizations can use DVD-Video and DVD-ROM to quickly and easily disseminate reports, training material, manuals, detailed reference handbooks, document archives, and much more. Portable document formats such as Adobe Acrobat, WordPerfect Envoy, and even HTML are perfectly suited to publishing text and pictures on DVD-ROM. Recordable DVD will soon be available and affordable for custom publishing of discs created on the desktop.

Marketing and Communications

DVD-Video and DVD-ROM are well suited to carry information from businesses to their customers. A DVD-Video can hold an exhaustive product catalog able to elaborate on each product with full-color illustrations, video clips, demonstrations, and more, at a fraction of the cost of printed catalogs. Bulky, inconvenient product information videotapes can be replaced with thin discs containing on-screen menus guiding the viewer on how to use the product and allowing easy and instant access to any section.

The massive storage capacity of DVD-ROM can be exploited to put entire software product lines on a single disc which can be sent out to thousands or millions of prospective customers in inexpensive mailings. The disc can include demo versions of each product, with protected versions of the full product that can be unlocked by placing an order over the phone or the Internet.

And More...

- *Picture archives.* Photo collections, clip art, and clip media have long since exceeded the capacity of CD-ROM. DVD-ROM allows more content or higher quality, or both.

- *Set-top boxes and digital receivers.* Savvy designers are already at work combining DVD players with the boxes required for interactive TV, digital satellite, digital cable, and other forms of digital video. All these systems are based on the same underlying digital compression technology and can benefit from shared components.

- *Hybrid Internet.* Many announcements have been made of products combining the multimedia capabilities of DVD-ROM and DVD-Video with the timeliness and interactivity of the Internet. Data-intensive media such as audio, video, and even large databases don't travel well over the Internet. This bottleneck is unlikely to improve in the near future, and DVD is a perfect candidate on which to offload the lion's share of the content.

- *Home productivity and "edutainment."* The eventual low cost of DVD will slide it into the niche between home computers and video games. DVD-Video can be used for reference products such as encyclopedias, fact books, travelogues, and cookbooks; training material such as music tutorials, arts and crafts lessons, and home improvement series; and education products such as documentaries, historical recreations, nature films, and more, all with accompanying text, photos, sidebars, quizzes, and so on.

About This Book

DVD Demystified is an introduction and reference for anyone who wants to understand DVD. It is not a production guide, nor is it a detailed technical handbook, but it provides almost all the information that most anyone interested in DVD needs to know.

Chapter 2, "The World Before DVD," provides a historical context and background. Many of the best analysts and business leaders predict technology trends by extrapolating from prior technologies. This chapter takes a historical stroll through the developments leading up to DVD and the first moments after its birth. If you enjoy crystal ball gazing for the DVD market, you will benefit from this chapter.

Chapter 3, "Technical Overview," covers the basic features of DVD-ROM and DVD-Video, including concepts such as aspect ratios and digital compression. This chapter is a slightly technical introduction for nontechnical readers, but should be useful for technical readers alike.

Chapter 4, "Technical Details," delves deeper into the fine points brought up in Chap. 3. This chapter is not essential to understanding DVD, but may be fascinating and instructive for anyone desiring a better grasp of the technology.

Chapter 5, "What's Wrong with DVD," explores the shortcomings of DVD and how these might be overcome as the technology develops.

Chapter 6, "DVD Comparison," examines the relationships between DVD and other consumer electronics technologies and computer storage media, including advantages and disadvantages of each, plus discussions of compatibility and interoperability.

Chapters 7, 8, and 9, "DVD-Video at Home," "DVD-Video in Business," and "DVD for Computers," discuss how DVD applies to each of these areas and what effect it might have.

The last chapter, "The Future of DVD," is a quick peek into the crystal ball to see what possibilities lie ahead for DVD.

Units and Notation

DVD is a casualty of an unfortunate collision between the conventions of computer storage measurement and the norms of data communications measurement. The SI (*Système International d'Unités*) prefixes of k (thousands), M (millions), and G (billions) usually take on slightly different meanings when applied to bytes, in which case they are based on powers of 2 instead of powers of 10 (see Table 1.1).

TABLE 1.1

Meanings of
Prefixes

Prefix	Name	Common use	Computer use	Difference (%)
k or K	Kilo	1,000 (10^3)	1,024 (2^{10})	2.4
M	Mega	1,000,000 (10^6)	1,048,576 (2^{20})	4.9
G	Giga	1,000,000,000 (10^9)	1,073,741,824 (2^{30})	7.4
T	Tera	1,000,000,000,000 (10^{12})	1,099,511,628 (2^{40})	10

The problem is that there are no universal standards for unambiguous use of these prefixes. One person's 4.70G bytes is another one's 4.38G bytes, and one person's 1.353 MB/s is another's 1.385 MB/s. Can you tell which is which?*

The laziness of many engineers who mix notations such as *Kb/s, kbps,* and *kb/s* with no clear distinction and no definition merely compounds the problem. It may seem trivial, but at larger denominations the difference between the two usages—and the resulting potential error—becomes significant. There is almost a 5 percent difference at the mega level, and a 7.4 percent difference at the giga level. Things will only get worse down the road when there's a 10 percent difference at the tera level.

Since computer data and disk space, including that of CD-ROMs, is usually measured in megabytes and gigabytes (as opposed to millions of bytes and billions of bytes), this book uses 1024 as the basis for measurements of *data size* and *data capacity,* with notations of *KB, MB,* and *GB.* (Note the large *K.*) In cases where it's necessary to be consistent with published numbers based on the alternate usage, the words *thousand, million,* and *billion* are used or the abbreviations *k bytes, M bytes,* and *G bytes.* (Note the small *k* and the spaces.)

Computer data storage transfer rates are customarily measured in bytes/sec. Therefore this book uses 1024 as the basis for measurements of *byte rates,* with notations of *KB/s* and *MB/s.*

Since data transmission rates are generally measured in thousands and millions of bits, this book uses 1000 as the basis for measurements of *bit rates,* with notations of *kbps* and *Mbps.* (Note the small *k.*) See Table 1.2 for a listing of notations.

---

*The first is the typical data capacity given for DVD, measured in magnitudes of 1000. The second is the real data capacity of DVD, measured using the conventional computing method in magnitudes of 1024. The third is the standard data transfer rate of DVD-ROM measured in computer units of 1024 bytes/second. The fourth is DVD-ROM data transfer rate in thousands of bytes/second. If you don't know what any of that means, don't worry—by Chap. 4, it should all make sense.

TABLE 1.2

Notations Used
in This Book

Notation	Meaning	Magnitude	Common variations
b	Bit	(1)	
B	Byte	(8 bits)	
kbps	Thousand bits per second	10^3	Kbps, kb/s, Kb/s
KB	Kilobyte	2^{10}	Kbytes
KB/s	Kilobytes per second	2^{10}	
Mbps	Million bits per second	10^6	mbps, mb/s, Mb/s
MB	Megabyte	2^{20}	Mbytes
MB/s	Megabytes per second	2^{20}	
GB	Gigabyte	2^{30}	Gbytes

Keep in mind that when translating from bits to bytes there is a factor of 8, and when converting from bit rates to data capacities in bytes there is a factor of 1000/1024.

Other Conventions

WIDESCREEN.   When the term *widescreen* is used in this book, it generally means an aspect ratio of 16:9 (see Chap. 3 for an explanation of aspect ratios). The term *widescreen* as traditionally applied to movies has meant anything wider than television, from 1.66:1 to 2.7:1. But since the 16:9 ratio has been chosen for DVD, digital television, and widescreen TVs, it's expected that it will become the commonly implied ratio of the term *widescreen*.

DVD FORMAT NAMES.   The term *DVD* is often applied both to the DVD family as a whole and specifically to the DVD-Video format. This book follows the same convention for simplicity and readability but only when unambiguous. When a clear distinction is needed, the terms *DVD-V* or *DVD-Video*, *DVD-A* or *DVD-Audio*, *DVD-ROM* (for read-only), *DVD-R* (for record-once), and *DVD-RAM* (for rewritable) are used.

TELEVISION SYSTEMS.   There are basically two incompatible television systems in common use around the world, which are supported by corresponding formats used by DVD-Video. One system uses 525 lines scanned at 60 fields/second with NTSC color encoding and is used in Japan and North America. The other system uses 625 lines scanned at 50 fields/second with PAL or SECAM color encoding and is used in the rest of the world. This book generally uses the technically correct terms of *525/60* (simplified from 525/59.94) and *625/50,* but also uses the terms NTSC and PAL in the generic sense.

COLORSPACE. DVD uses the standard ITU-R BT.601 component digital video colorspace of $Y'C_bC_r$ nonlinear luma and chroma signals. Some DVD video playback systems include analog component video output in $Y'/B'-Y'/R'-Y'$ format (more accurately $Y'P_bP_r$). When a technical distinction is not critical or is clear from the context, this book uses the general term *YUV* to refer to the component video data in nonlinear color-difference format. This book also uses the general term *RGB* to refer to nonlinear R'G'B' video.

Many of these terms and concepts are explained in Chap. 3.

The World Before DVD

A Brief History
of Audio Technology

In 1877, Thomas Edison recorded and played back the words "Mary had a little lamb" on tinfoil, presaging a profound change in the way we record events. Instead of relying on written histories and oral retellings, we began to capture audible information in a way that enabled us to replay the events later. Since then, we have worked continuously to improve the verisimilitude of recording. See Fig. 2.1.

By the 1890s, 12-inch shellac gramophone discs that could play up to 4½ minutes of sound at 78 rpm had become popular. Radio followed soon after, with the first commercial broadcast in 1920. Acoustical recording (where sound vibrations were directly converted to wavy grooves in a wax disc) was replaced in the early 1920s by electrical recording (where sound vibrations were first converted to electrical impulses which could be amplified and mixed before being used to drive an electromechanical cutting head). Performers no longer had to cluster around a large horn which gave too much emphasis to the most powerful instruments and the loudest voices. Electrical technology was also applied to sound reproduction, resulting in the birth of the loudspeaker.

Recording technology took a major leap in 1948 when the long-playing record (LP) was introduced by Columbia Records. New *microgroove* technology allowed 25 to 30 minutes of sound to fit on a 12-inch disc turning at the slow speed of 33⅓ rpm. Columbia's LP was developed under the direction of Peter Goldman, who went on to develop the first commercial closed-circuit color television system. A year after the LP appeared, RCA Victor introduced a similar 7-inch disc which turned at 45 rpm and played for about 8 minutes. These two new record types quickly replaced the unwieldy 5-minute, 78-rpm records.

Magnetic recording appeared in the laboratory in the 1890s, but did not become an actual product until about 1940. The first systems recorded onto a thin wire. Wire is still used today for airline black boxes but elsewhere has been replaced by polyester tape with a thin coating of magnetic particles. A major advantage of storing electrical sound impulses using the alignment of magnetic particles is that the recording process is as easy as the reproduction process, and the same head can be used for recording and playback.

Up to this point, sound recording had been *monophonic,* meaning it was recorded as a single-point source. The first patent on stereo sound was issued in 1931, but commercial *stereophonic* tape systems were not developed until 1956, with stereo phonographs following in 1958. These sys-

Figure 2.1
Timeline of audio technology.

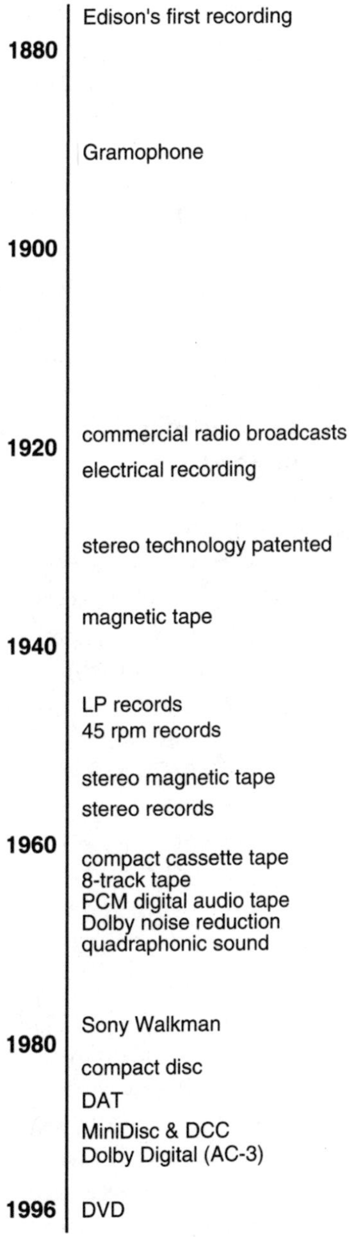

	Edison's first recording
1880	
	Gramophone
1900	
1920	commercial radio broadcasts
	electrical recording
	stereo technology patented
	magnetic tape
1940	
	LP records
	45 rpm records
	stereo magnetic tape
	stereo records
1960	compact cassette tape
	8-track tape
	PCM digital audio tape
	Dolby noise reduction
	quadraphonic sound
1980	Sony Walkman
	compact disc
	DAT
	MiniDisc & DCC
	Dolby Digital (AC-3)
1996	DVD

tems added a spatial component to the sound by storing a second channel, giving the reproduction a much greater sense of realism. Stereo technology debuted to an apathetic reception; many people felt that the slight improvement was not worth the added complexity, and some claimed that stereo recording would never be practical for mainstream application. This was soon proven shortsighted as engineers became accustomed to the new technology and artists began to take advantage of it.

The natural step beyond stereo was four-channel audio. Quadraphonic systems appeared in early 1970, but in addition to technical problems there were three incompatible standards which confused and divided the marketplace and doomed the entire movement to quick extinction.

Cassette tapes were introduced by Philips in 1963, originally as a business dictation device which subsequently became popular for music. Prerecorded tapes were released in 1966 and steadily encroached on the sales of LPs. Eight-track (and less-successful 4-track) audio tapes emerged in 1965 to enjoy a brief spurt of success mainly in automobile sound systems. Dolby noise reduction appeared in 1969 and did much to reduce the problem of tape hiss. The theories and techniques behind noise reduction were steadily refined and today are the basis of the Dolby Digital surround-sound system used by DVD.

By 1982, music sales on cassette surpassed vinyl. An attempt was again made to create a 4-channel system, this time for cassette tapes, but no one was able to agree on a standard and the benefits didn't seem to outweigh the technical complexity of extending the existing cassette format.

Philips again led the development of consumer electronics technology when it partnered with Sony to introduce Compact Disc Digital Audio in 1982. Digital audio recording is based on *sampling:* converting electrical signal levels measured over 40,000 times per second into discrete numbers represented by binary digits of zero and one which are stored as pulses. This pulse-code modulation (PCM) technology was invented in 1937 and was applied to communication theory by C. E. Shannon in 1949. The first digital PCM audio tape recorder was developed 1967 at the NHK Technical Research Institute in Japan. PCM is used by most digital audio systems, including CD, DAT, laserdisc, and DVD. The advantages of reproducing sound digitally include exceptional frequency response (the rendition of frequencies covering the entire range of human hearing from 20 to 20,000 Hz), excellent dynamic range (the reproduction of very soft to very loud sounds with little or no extraneous noise), and no generational loss from copying. The improvement in quality over LP records (arguments of audio purists notwithstanding) plus other advantages such as longer playing time, smaller size, near-instant track access, no wear from being played, and better resistance to dust and scratches led CD sales to pass LP sales around 1988.[*]

---

[*]It may seem reasonable that a similar comparison can be made to support the prediction that DVD will replace VHS videotape. However, the analogy must be tempered since VHS doesn't share the many deficiences of LP records such as breakable discs, fragile tone arms, no protection from abuse by children, crackles and pops from dust and scratches, a tendency to skip or repeat, and very high cost for high-fidelity sound.

Of course, a major drawback to audio CD is that it does not record. All attempts to produce a recordable successor to CD have failed to become significant consumer successes. Digital audio tape (DAT), Philips's digital compact cassette tape (DCC), Sony's MiniDisc, and other technologies have languished for many reasons including high cost, incompatibility with existing standards, limited manufacturer support, and politics—which come to the fore when the ability to make perfect digital copies increases the importance of copyright protection.

Sony and Philips continued their work on the compact disc format, mostly for computer and multimedia applications. That part of the story is covered later in this chapter.

Many other companies are busy developing new audio storage techniques, each in the hopes that its technology will become the successor to tape or CD. These include magnetic cards, solid-state electronic cards, superdense miniature discs, and DVD-Audio. Although DVD does little to advance the art of digital audio other than providing slightly higher quality and multichannel surround sound, many people have high hopes for the recordable version. Once available, and with its expected industrywide support, recordable DVD may finally bring consumer audio recording completely into the digital realm. Unfortunately, the issues of copy protection and their associated political baggage will also enter the picture.

A Brief History of Video Technology

It's unknown when the principle of persistence of vision was first discovered (see Fig. 2.2). Since it can be seen by waving a burning stick in the darkness it has undoubtedly been known since prehistoric times. The phenomenon, caused by the brain holding an image for a fraction of a second after the optical stimulus is removed, means that a series of still images viewed in rapid succession blur together into a single moving image. About 170 years ago, revolving picture toys with strange names such as zoetrope, phenakistiscope, thaumatrope, praxinoscope, and fantascope (see Fig. 2.3) began to capitalize on this particular feature of human perception, which is what makes modern motion picture and video technology possible.

It was also discovered that quickly flickering light appears to be continuous. At low light levels, the flicker threshold—or *fusion frequency*—is around

Figure 2.2
Timeline of video
technology.

1820	revolving picture toys
	photographs
1840	
	color photographs
1860	
	Muybridge's photographs
1880	Nipkow's scanning disc, Eastman's celluloid film
	Kinetograph
1900	
	mechanical TVs
1920	
	talking pictures, Farnsworth's electronic TV
	Baird's video disc, Technicolor
	commercial TV broadcasts in Germany and England
1940	
	cable TV, professional videotape
	color added to TV
1960	Ampex helical scan, color videotape
	Cinemascope
	PAL and SECAM adopted
	Sony Betamax, JVC VHS
	Dolby Stereo added to movies, video stores
1980	laserdisc
	HiFi VCRs, stereo TV broadcasts
	S-VHS, 8 mm
	HiVision, VideoCD
1996	digital satellite (DBS)
	digital videotape (DV), DVD
	HDTV (DTV)

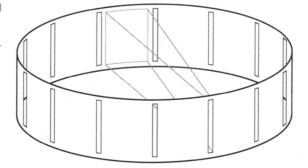

Figure 2.3
Revolving picture toy.

50 times a second.* Early experimenters discovered that a continuous stream of images merely caused blurring as the eye attempted to track their motion. Absence of the image, thus producing the flicker effect, turned out to be as important as the image. The technique of showing a sequence of still images thus emerged. Most moving image toys used slots through which the image was momentarily viewable. Many years later it was discovered that the eye employs high-frequency tremors to create snapshots as part of its image acquisition mechanism. By rapidly jerking back and forth, the eye creates multiple still images which it then passes on to the brain for processing.

Captured Light

Early motion picture toys used drawings, which were intriguing but fell short of the real thing. The first attempts at capturing a direct visual representation of reality began about the same time, in the 1820s, with Niépce and Daguerre's photographic plates. Photography steadily improved but remained motionless for almost 60 years. In 1877, photographer Eadweard Muybridge captured images of a moving horse as it tripped strings attached to 12 cameras in sequence.[†] He realized that the motion could be recreated by placing the photographs on a rotating wheel and projecting light through them. This led to another string of oddly named magic

---

*Fusion frequency depends greatly on the ambient light level. In a dark movie theater, a flicker rate of 48 times a second (twice for each frame) is sufficient. European PAL television flickers at 50 times a second (50 Hz), which is just at the limit for home viewing and is noticeable by some people, especially in well-lit environments or with bright video images. American NTSC television, at 60 Hz, is generally adequate for most environments. Many computer monitors flicker at 72 Hz or higher in order to abate eye strain and mental fatigue in brightly lit offices.

†Muybridge had been hired by the governor of California in an attempt to win a bet that all four of a horse's hooves left the ground during a gallop. Muybridge's success left the governor $25,000 richer.

lantern gadgets such as the zoopraxiscope, phantasmagoria, chrono-photographe, and zoogyroscope. Unfortunately, the early recording process was very cumbersome, requiring that dozens of cameras be painstakingly set up. In 1882, Étienne-Jules Marey was inspired by Muybridge's work to create a single camera, patterned after a rifle, which exposed 12 images in one second on a rotating glass plate. This was a great improvement, but made for a very short viewing time and did not bode well for popcorn sales. It wasn't until seven years later that the celluloid roll film developed by George Eastman—the founder of Kodak—was used by Thomas Edison's engineers to create the Kinetograph camera and the Kinetoscope viewing box for movies lasting up to 15 seconds. Lessons from the past were apparently missed by these and other pioneers, who tried to use continuous film motion only to rediscover that intermittent motion was required. Edison's lead engineer, William Dickson, shot the first film in the United States, *Fred Ott's Sneeze*.

The Lumière brothers were the first to project moving photographic pictures to a paying audience in 1895. Their first film, no less inspired than Dickson's, was *Workers Leaving the Lumière Factory.* The motion picture industry was born and began to steadily improve the technology and the content. Many methods of adding sound were tried, some less dismal than others, and by 1927, Warner Bros. (one of the modern-day contributors to the development of DVD) and Fox had developed a practical synchronized sound technology. Within two short years, most films had soundtracks. After the limited success of two-color film in the 1920s, three-color film was introduced by Technicolor in 1932, although it took another 25 years before most films were in color. At about the same time, in an effort to improve the movie theater experience and battle the threat of television, movies were made almost twice as wide. Cinemascope was introduced in 1953 with the biblical epic *The Robe*. Some widescreen systems used more than one projector, but the most successful early widescreen systems were based on anamorphic lenses which had been invented by Dr. Henri Chretien for tank periscopes in World War I. These lenses squeezed the image sideways to fit in a standard film frame, then unsqueezed it during projection. The same technique is still occasionally used for movies and is now used by DVD for widescreen video; the squeezing and unsqueezing is done by computers rather than glass lenses.

Less successful improvements to movies were attempted, such as 1960's Smell-O-Vision and many variations of three-dimensional images. Another failure, Sensurround, recently reappeared in a new form as a niche home theater product: transducers which attach to the frame of your couch to add extra kick to explosions and low-frequency sounds.

More recent advances in motion picture film technology include stereo audio and 70mm film—twice the width of standard 35mm film. Prestige formats such as IMAX and OmniMax use 70mm film with large square frames to achieve presentations of breathtaking impact.

In 1976, Dolby Laboratories made an affordable surround-sound system using standard film soundtracks and, in 1992, released multichannel Dolby Digital (AC-3). In 1993, the movie *Jurassic Park* debuted the exceptional sonic realism of DTS (Digital Theater Systems) which uses an optical synchronization track on the film coupled with multichannel digital audio from a compact disc. The primary multichannel audio system of DVD-Video is Dolby Digital. DTS is a mostly unsupported option.

Jurassic Park was also a tour de force in computer-generated images (CGI). Movie production is now entering the era where entire scenes are generated inside a computer, never being touched by light to trace the images in silver halide crystals on a negative.

Dancing Electrons

About the same time as Muybridge was stretching strings across racetracks, scientists across the world were envisioning television. Once again, the new ideas were christened with fanciful names derived from familiar technology such as radioscope, phonoscope, cinematophone, radiovision, telephone eye, and the jaw-breaking chronophotographoscope. The word *television* is credited to science writer Hugo Gernsback[*] who published pop science journals beginning in 1908.

Many early television ideas were developed almost simultaneously around the world and involved mechanical systems which transmitted each individual picture element on a separate connection. These were dropped in favor of rapidly scanning the image a line at a time, once again relying on persistence of vision. In 1884, Paul Nipkow applied for a patent in Germany on his image scanning design which used a rotating disc with holes arranged in a spiral, essentially an updated version of the Phenakistoscope. Television technology slowly improved, still based on clumsy mechanical designs, until the first experimental broadcasts were made in the 1920s. Meanwhile, a 14-year-old Utah farm boy named Philo Farnsworth was looking at plowed furrows and dreaming of deflecting beams of electrons in similar rows. Six

---

[*]Hugo Gernsback may be familiar to science fiction fans as the eponym of the Hugo Award. His name may also be familiar to readers of *Popular Electronics* magazine, produced by Gernsback Publications.

years later, on January 7, 1927, he submitted the patent applications which established him as the inventor of the all-electronic television.

The first nonexperimental television broadcasts began in 1935 in Germany and included coverage of the 1936 Olympics in Berlin. The German system had only 180 lines. In Britain, John Baird steadily improved a mechanically scanned television system from 50 lines to 240 and the BBC used it for experimental broadcasts. Improved "high-definition" commercial broadcasts using a 405-line system were begun by the BBC in Britain in 1936, although they were shut down three years later by World War II (with a sign-off broadcast of a Mickey Mouse cartoon) and didn't return until 1946 (with a repeat of the same cartoon). In the United States, NBC demonstrated television to entranced crowds at the 1939 World's Fair and RCA's David Sarnoff declared that 10,000 sets would be sold before the end of the year. But at a price equivalent to more than $2500 and with sparse programming from scattered transmitters, only a few thousand were sold. NBC began commercial broadcasts on July 1, 1941. CBS also switched from experimental to commercial broadcasts about the same time.

About 10,000 televisions were scattered around the United States in 1946, and when World War II production restrictions were lifted, another 10,000 were soon sold. Three years later, there were over 1 million sets, and after only two more years, in 1951, there were over 10 million. The NTSC color television system was implemented in 1954, and widespread purchase of color television sets began in 1964. The NTSC system piggybacked color information onto the black and white signal so that the millions of existing sets would still work with new broadcasts. NTSC was adopted by Japan in 1960.

Meanwhile, television in Britain after World War II experienced the same rapid growth as in the United States. In 1967, when it came time to implement color television, Britain adopted the PAL system which had been developed in Germany. PAL was technologically superior to NTSC, but it was incompatible with existing British television sets and had to be gradually phased in over many years. In 1967, France and the Soviet Union settled on the SECAM system. In 1968, the number of televisions passed 78 million in the United States and 200 million worldwide. By 1972, half of all American homes had a television set. At the end of the 1970s, almost every country had adopted one of the three standards, as television began to saturate the planet. NTSC is still the most widely used system, PAL is common in most of Europe, and SECAM holds a distant third.

As television was gaining a foothold, Community Antenna TV (CATV, the first version of cable television) was founded in rural Pennsylvania by a shopkeeper who built an antenna on a hill to improve reception in his store and then began connecting up the receivers of his customers and neighbors. From its beginnings in 1949, cable TV's promise of more channels and better reception has attracted millions of customers and, in just under 40 years, over half the television homes in the United States were connected to cable.

The first television signal was beamed via satellite across the Atlantic Ocean in 1962, and in 1975, satellites were put in use to distribute programming to cable TV centers. Satellite dishes were eventually made available to consumers and ironically became a competitor to cable TV, especially with the advent of DBS (direct broadcast satellite), which uses the same digital video compression system as DVD.

Metal Tape and Plastic Discs

Visual information is hundreds of times more dense than audio information. Sound waves are simple vibrations which the human ear can detect from about 20 per second to over 20,000 per second (20 Hz to 20 kHz). Visible images, on the other hand, are formed from complex light waves which the eye can detect within the range of 430 to 750 trillion Hz. Clearly, recording a video signal is a much bigger challenge than recording audio.

For magnetic tape, raising the speed at which the tape moves past the head increases the amount of information that can be recorded in a given period of time, but the amount of tape required quickly becomes preposterous. Nevertheless, in 1951, Bing Crosby Enterprises demonstrated a commercial videotape recorder which used tape travelling at 100 inches per second (almost 6 miles per hour) across 12 heads. A few similarly cumbersome and very expensive systems were developed for television studios, but their high price tags barred them from wider use. The eureka factor didn't arrive for another 10 years until engineers at Ampex hit upon the idea of moving the head past the tape in addition to moving the tape past the head. A revolving head can record nearly vertical stripes on a slow-moving tape, greatly increasing the recording efficiency (see Fig. 2.4). The first *helical scan* videotape recorder appeared in 1961 and color versions followed within a few years.

Videotape recording was first used only by professional television studios. A new era for home video was ushered in when Philips and Sony

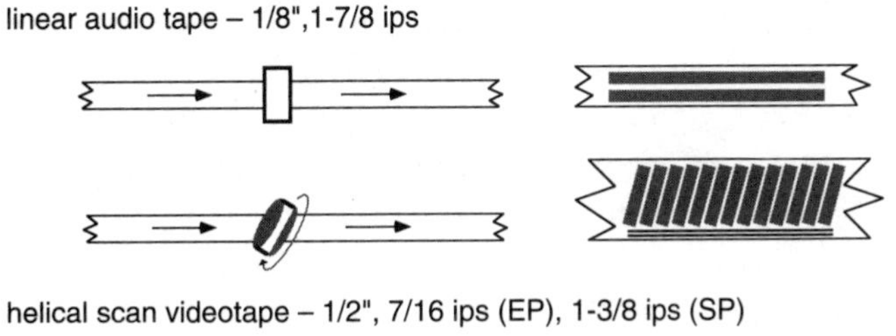

Figure 2.4
Tape head
comparison.

linear audio tape – 1/8",1-7/8 ips

helical scan videotape – 1/2", 7/16 ips (EP), 1-3/8 ips (SP)

produced black-and-white, reel-to-reel videotape recorders in 1965, but at $3000, they didn't grace many living rooms. Sony's professional ¼-inch U-matic video cassette tape appeared in 1972, the same year as the video game Pong. More affordable color video recording reached home consumers in 1975 when Sony introduced the Betamax videotape recorder. The following year JVC introduced VHS, which was slightly inferior to Betamax but won the battle of the VCRs because of extensive licensing agreements with equipment manufacturers and video distributors. The first Betamax VCR cost $2300 (over $6700 adjusted for inflation), and a one-hour blank tape cost $16 (over $46 in today's dollars). The first VHS deck was cheaper at $885 (equivalent to more than $2500), and Sony quickly introduced a new Betamax model for $1300; but both systems were out of the financial reach of most consumers for the next few years.

MCA/Universal and Disney studios sued Sony in 1976 in an attempt to prevent home copying with VCRs. Eight years later, the courts upheld consumer recording rights by declaring Sony the winner. Studios are fighting the same battle today with DVD but have switched to trying to change the technology before the law.

In 1978, Philips and Pioneer introduced videodiscs, which had actually been demonstrated in rudimentary form in 1928 by John Baird. The technology had improved in 50 years, replacing wax discs with polymer discs and delivering an exceptional analog color picture by using a laser to read information from the disc. The technology got a big boost from GM which bought 12,000 players to use for demonstrating cars. In 1979, videodisc systems became available to the home market when MCA joined the laserdisc camp with its DiscoVision brand. A second videodisc technology called Capacitance Electronic Disc (CED), introduced just over two years later, used a diamond stylus that came in direct contact with the disc—as with a vinyl record. CED went by the brand name SelectaVision and was initially more successful, but eventually failed because of its technical flaws. CED was abandoned in 1984 after less than 750,000 units were sold, leaving laserdisc to overcome the resulting stigma. For years, laserdisc was the Mark Twain of video technology, with many exaggerated reports of its demise as customers and the media confused it with the defunct CED. Adding to the confusion was the addition of digital audio to laserdisc, which in countries using the PAL television system required the relaunch of a new incompatible version. Laserdisc persevered, but because of its lack of recording, high price of discs and players, and inability to show a movie without breaks (a laserdisc can't hold more than one hour per side), it was never more than a niche success catering to videophiles and penetrating less than 2 percent of the consumer market. Laserdisc systems did achieve modest success in education and training, especially after

Pioneer's bar-code system became a popular standard in 1987 and enabled printed material to be correlated to random-access visuals.

In spite of the exceptional picture quality of both laserdisc and CED, they were quickly overwhelmed by the eruption of VHS VCRs in the late 1970s, which started out at twice the price of laserdisc players but quickly dropped below them. The first video rental store in the United States opened in 1977 and the number rapidly grew to 27,000 in the late 1990s. Direct sales to customers, known as *sellthrough*, began in 1980. Today the home video market is a $16 billion business in the United States alone. Over 87 percent of households have at least one VCR, creating a market of over a hundred million customers who, in 1996, rented about 3 billion tapes and bought over 580 million tapes. There are now over 25,000 VHS titles available in the United States, compared to 9000 on laserdisc.

In the late 1980s, a new video recording format based on 8mm tape with metal particles was introduced. The reduced size and improved quality were not sufficient to displace the well-established VHS format, but 8mm and Hi-8 were quite successful in the camcorder market where smaller size is more significant.

Around this time, minor improvements were made to television, with stereo sound added in the United States in 1985, and later closed captions.

In 1987, JVC introduced an improved super VHS system called S-VHS. In spite of being compatible with VHS and almost doubling the picture quality, S-VHS was never much of a success because there were too many barriers to customer acceptance. Players and tapes were much more expensive, VHS tapes worked in S-VHS players but not vice versa, a special cable and an expensive TV with an s-video connector were required to take advantage of the improved picture, and S-VHS was not a step toward high-definition television (HDTV) which was receiving lavish attention in the late 1980s and was expected to appear shortly. It's interesting to note that DVD has many of the same strikes against it, even the specter of HDTV again.

The Digital Face-Lift

As television began to show its age, new treatments appeared in an attempt to remove the wrinkles. Major European broadcasters rolled out PALplus in 1994 as a stab at enhanced-definition television (EDTV) that maintains compatibility with existing receivers and transmitters. PALplus achieves a widescreen picture by using a letterboxed* image for display on conven-

---

Letterboxing is a technique of adding black bars at the top and bottom of a picture in order to preserve the originally wider aspect ratio. Aspect ratios and letterboxing are covered in Chap. 3.

tional TVs and hiding *helper lines* in the black bars so that a widescreen PALplus TV can display the full picture with extended vertical resolution.

Other ways of giving television a face-lift include improved definition televisions (IDTV) which double the picture display rate or use digital signal processing to remove noise and to improve picture clarity.

None of these measures are more than stopgaps while we wait for the old workhorse to be replaced by high-definition television (HDTV). HDTV was first demonstrated in the United States in 1981, and the process of revamping the boob tube reached critical mass in 1987 when 58 broadcasting organizations and companies filed a petition with the Federal Communication Commission (FCC) to explore advanced television technologies. The Advanced Television Systems Committee (ATSC) was formed and began oozing toward consensus as 25 proposed systems were extensively evaluated and either combined or eliminated.

In Japan, a similar process was underway but was unfettered by red tape. An HDTV system called HiVision, based on MUSE compression, was quickly developed and was put into use in 1991.* Ironically, the quick deployment of the Japanese system was its downfall. The MUSE system was based on the affordable analog transmission technology of its day, but soon the cost of digital technology plummeted while its capability skyrocketed. Back on the other side of the Pacific, the lethargic U.S. HDTV standards-making process was still in motion while video technology graduated from analog to digital. In 1993, the ATSC recommended that the new television system be digital. The Japanese government and the Japanese consumer electronics companies—which would be making the majority of high-definition television sets for use in the United States—decided to wait for the American digital television standard and adopt it for use in Japan as well. A happy by-product of HiVision is that the technology-loving early Japanese adopters served as guinea pigs, supporting the development of high-resolution widescreen technology and paving the way for HTDV elsewhere. A European HDTV system, HD-MAC, was even more short-lived; it was demonstrated at the Albertville Olympics but was abandoned shortly thereafter.

In 1992, the ATSC outlined a set of proposed industry actions for documenting a standard. In 1993, the three groups that had developed the four final digital systems: AT&T and Zenith; General Instrument and MIT; and Philips, Thomson, and the David Sarnoff Research Center formed a Grand Alliance and agreed to merge their best features into a final standard. The ATSC made its proposal for a Digital Television Standard (DTV) to the FCC

---

*The HiVision system uses 1125 video scan lines. In charmingly quirky Japanese marketing style, HiVision was introduced on November 25 so that the date (11/25) corresponded with the number of scan lines.

in November 1995. The motion picture industry and the computer industry had been aware of the proceedings but apparently had not bothered to become sufficiently involved. At the eleventh hour, they both began to complain loudly that they were not happy with the choice of widescreen aspect ratio or the computer-unfriendly parts of the proposal. In December of 1996, with this opposition in mind, the FCC approved all but the video format constraints (aspect ratios, resolutions, and frame rates) of the ATSC DTV proposal, putting these aside as a voluntary standard. This "Grand Compromise" freed broadcasters to begin implementation but wisely left the standard open for additional video formats. HDTV, originally promised for the early 1990s, is expected to finally conclude its long gestation period and emerge in 1998 to begin an even longer battle for ascendancy.

In the meantime, numerous new formats have been developed to store video digitally and convert it to a standard analog television signal for display. As with early videotape, the elephantine size of video is a problem. Uncompressed digital television video requires 124 million bits per second (Mbps).* Compare this to hard drives, which run at around 25 to 100 Mbps, high-speed T-1 digital telephone lines at 1.5 Mbps, and audio CD at a meager 1.4 Mbps. Obviously, some form of compression is needed. Many proprietary and incompatible systems have been developed, including Intel's DVI in 1988 (which had been developed earlier by the Sarnoff Institute). That same year, the Moving Picture Experts Group (MPEG) committee was created by Leonardo Chairiglione and Hiroshi Yasuda with the intent to standardize video and audio for compact discs. In 1992, the International Standards Organization (ISO) and the International Electrotechnical Commission (IEC) adopted the standard known as MPEG-1. Audio and video encoded by this method could be squeezed down to fit the limited data rate of the single-speed CD format. CD-i first used MPEG-1 video playback in 1992 to achieve near-VHS quality. This became Video CD, the precursor to DVD. Video CD has done quite well in markets where VCRs were not already established, selling 6 million players in Asia in 1996, but it has not fared as well in Europe and might qualify as an endangered species in the United States. MPEG-1 is also commonly used for transmitting video and audio over the Internet.

The MPEG committee extended and improved its system to handle high-quality audio/video at higher data rates. MPEG-2 was adopted as an international standard in 1994 and is used by many new digital video sys-

---

*124 Mbps is the data rate of active video at ITU-R BT.601 4:2:0 sampling with 8 bits, which provides an average of 12 bits per pixel ($720 \times 480 \times 30 \times 12$ or $720 \times 576 \times 25 \times 12$). The commonly seen 270 Mbps figure comes from studio-quality video at 4:2:2 sampling at 10 bits and includes blanking intervals. At higher 4:4:4 10-bit sampling, the data rate is 405 Mbps.

tems, including the ATSC's DTV. Direct broadcast satellite (DBS), with convenient 18-inch dishes and digital video, also appeared in 1994. With sales of over 3 million units by the end of 1996, DBS can be considered the most successful home entertainment product ever. DBS was introduced just as MPEG-2 was being finalized. Consequently, most early DBS systems used MPEG-1 but have since converted to MPEG-2. Digital video cassette tape (DV) appeared in 1996. With near-studio quality, it's aimed at the professional and "prosumer" market and is priced accordingly. New competitors to cable and satellite TV are also based on MPEG-2; these include *video dialtone* (video delivered over phone lines by the phone company), digital cable, and *wireless cable* (terrestrial microwave video transmission). MPEG-2 is also the basis of DVD-Video, augmented with the Dolby Digital (AC-3) multichannel audio system—developed as part of the original work of the ATSC. DVD-Video is intended for the home video market where it provides the highest resolution yet from a consumer format.

A Brief History of Data Storage Technology

Rewind almost 200 years. In 1801, Joseph-Marie Jacquard devised an ingenious method for weaving complex patterns using a loom controlled by punched metal cards. The same idea was borrowed over thirty years later by Charles Babbage as the storage device for his mechanical computer, the Analytical Engine.* Ninety years after Jacquard, Herman Hollerith used a similar system of punched cards for tabulating the U.S. census after getting the idea from watching a train conductor punch tickets. Fifty years later, the first electronic computers of the 1940s also employed punched cards and punched tape—using the difference between a surface and a hole to store information. The same concept is used in modern optical storage technology. Viewed through an electron microscope, the pits and lands of a CD or DVD would be immediately recognizable to Jacquard or Hollerith. (See Fig. 2.5.) But the immensity and variety of information stored on these miniature pockmarked landscapes would truly amaze

---

*Unlike Jacquard, whose system enjoyed widespread success, Babbage seemed incapable of finishing anything he started. He never completed any of his mechanical calculating devices, although his designs were later proven correct when they were turned into functioning models by other builders.

them. Hollerith's cards held only 80 characters of information and were read at a glacial few per second.*

The other primary method of data storage—magnetic media—was developed for the UNIVAC I in 1951. Magnetic tape improved on the storage density of cards and paper tape by a factor of about 50 and could be read significantly faster. Magnetic disks and drums appeared a few years later and improved upon magnetic tape, but cards and punched tape were still much cheaper and remained the primary form of data input until the late 1970s. In the 1970s, flexible floppy disks appeared; first unwieldy 8-inch behemoths, then smaller 5¼-inch disks, and finally, in 1983, 3½-inch diskettes small enough to fit in a shirt pocket. Each successive version held 2 or 3 times more data than its predecessor in spite of being smaller.

Optical media languished during the heyday of magnetic disks, never achieving commercial success other than for analog video storage: laser videodisc. It wasn't until the development of Compact Disc Digital Audio in the 1980s that optical media again proved its worth in the world of bits and bytes, setting the stage for DVD. (See Fig. 2.6.)

*Modern card readers of the 1970s still used only 72 to 80 character per card, but could read over 1000 cards per second.

Figure 2.5
Punched card and optical disc.

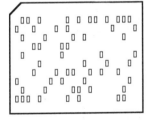 

Figure 2.6
Capacities and costs of data storage media.

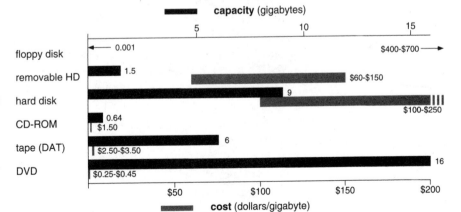

Other innovations of the 1980s included removable hard disk cartridges, high-density floppy disks from IOmega based on the Bernoulli principle, and erasable optical media based on magneto-optical technology. Magneto-optical disks use a laser to heat a polyphase crystalline material which can then be aligned by a magnetic field.

Innovations of CD

Sony and Philips reinvigorated optical storage technology when they introduced Compact Disc Digital Audio in 1982. This was known as the Red Book standard because of the red covers on the book of technical specifications. The first CD players cost around $1000 (over $1500 in 1996 dollars).

Three years later, a variation for storing digital computer data—CD-ROM—was introduced in a book with yellow covers. CD-ROM didn't take hold immediately, especially since the first drives cost over $1000. The first Microsoft CD-ROM conference in March of 1986 was attended by a sparse thousand people. But by 1992, the conference had metamorphosed into the Intermedia trade show and was attended by hundreds of thousands. As CD-ROM entered the mainstream, original limitations such as slow data rates and glacial access times were overcome with higher spin rates, bigger buffers, and improved hardware. CD-ROM became the pre-eminent instrument of multimedia and is becoming the standard for delivery of general software as well. (See Fig. 2.7.)

A clever variation on audio CDs called CD+G was developed around 1986. A CD+G disc uses six previously unused bits in each audio sector (subcode channels R through W) to hold graphic bitmaps. The player collects snippets of a graphic from each sector as it plays the audio, and after a few thousand sectors, it has accumulated enough to display a picture. CD+G was never widely supported and is available mostly on karaoke CD players and CD-i players.

CDV (CD-Video) was developed in 1986 as a hybrid of laserdisc and CD. Part of the disc contained five to six minutes of standard audio tracks and could be played on a CD player, while the other part contained about 20 minutes of analog video in laserdisc format. The standard was in a blue book but isn't considered part of the canon of colors. The CDV format has mostly disappeared.

After introducing CD-ROM, Sony and Philips continued to refine and expand the CD family. In 1986, they produced CD-i (Compact Disc Interactive, the Green Book standard), intended to become the standard for interactive home entertainment. CD-i incorporated specialized file formats and custom hardware with the OS-9 operating system running on the Motorola 68000 microprocessor. Unfortunately, CD-i was obsolete before it was finished, and the scant supporting companies dropped out early leaving Philips to stubbornly champion it alone. After consuming over a billion dollars in development and misguided marketing, CD-i is still limping along as a niche product. Philips, not one to give up easily, announced it would develop a DVD player that can accept a CD-i add-in card.

Some early CD-ROM producers developed their own file systems to organize the data on the disc, requiring a specific device driver. This forced users to either reboot and load a different driver or use multiple CD-ROM drives, one for each title. In the face of proliferating proprietary CD-ROM file formats, a group of industry representatives met in 1986 at the High Sierra Hotel and Casino near Lake Tahoe, Nevada, and proposed a common structure which became known as the High Sierra format. In 1988, the International Standards Organization adopted this format, with a few modifications, as the ISO 9660 CD-ROM file interchange standard. Unfortunately, it was a lowest-common-denominator solution designed to support MS-DOS, so it didn't properly support other systems such as the Apple Macintosh Hierarchical File System (HFS) and many UNIX systems. These operating systems could read ISO 9660 CDs but had to add their own incompatible extensions to make full use of the advantages of their native file systems. When Microsoft moved beyond DOS, it also rolled its own "Joliet" extensions.

In 1989, the CD-ROM Yellow Book standard was augmented with an updated format called CD-ROM XA (eXtended Architecture). XA was based on ideas developed for CD-i, including the interleaving of data, graphics, and ADPCM compressed audio. CD-ROM XA required newer hardware to read the mixed sector types on the disc and to take advantage of the interleaved streams. Most CD-ROM drives are now XA-compatible, but the interleaving features are almost never used. CD-ROM XA also introduced the so-called *bridge disc*, which is a type of disc with extra information that can be used in a CD-i player or a computer with a CD-ROM XA drive.

The Orange Book standard was developed in 1990 to support magneto-optical (MO) and write-once (WO) technology. MO has the advantage of being rewritable, but is incompatible with standard CD drives and has remained expensive. CD-WO has been largely superseded by Orange Book Part II: recordable CD (CD-R). CD-R can only be written to once, which is sufficient for many uses. The Orange Book also added *multisession* capabilities to allow CDs to be written to in chunks across different recording sessions. Recordable technology revolutionized CD-ROM production by enabling developers to create fully functional CDs for testing and for submission to disc replicators. As prices have dropped, CD-R has also become

Figure 2.7
The CD family tree.

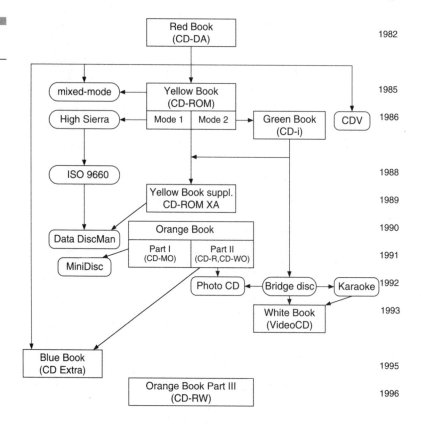

popular for business and even personal archiving. Although tape backup systems are cheaper, the familiarity of CD and the widespread availability of CD-ROM drives has made CD-R very appealing. Tape also lacks the quick random access of CD-R. Even though it's possible to use CD-R to record custom music CDs, the price of the CD-R drive plus blank discs and authoring software, along with the general difficulty of digitizing the source audio has kept the practice from becoming widespread. It will be interesting to see if this changes as CD-R (and DVD-R) becomes cheaper.

Around 1990, music CD singles became popular in Japan and the format was subsequently adopted for use with Sony's Data Discman. The 8-cm discs had a capacity of 200 megabytes and commonly held modified CD-ROM XA applications. The Data Discman and its cousin the Bookman had piddling success outside of Japan. Sony also developed the portable MMCD player based on an Intel 286 processor and an LCD display, which it concentrated on to the exclusion of CD-i. But, as with CD-i, heavy marketing failed to make the MMCD a success and Sony finally gave up around 1994.

Kodak and Philips developed the Photo CD format in 1992, based on the CD-ROM XA and Orange Book standards. Photo CDs are bridge discs which hold up to one hundred 35mm photographs written in one or more sessions. Special Photo CD players and CD-i players can show the pictures on a television, but the concept never appealed much to home photographers. Nevertheless, since multisession CD-ROM XA drives can read Photo CDs, the format is popular for professional photo production work and for stock photography libraries.

In 1991, Sony introduced the 8-cm MiniDisc, a portable music format based on the rewritable Orange Book's MO standard and using Sony's ATRAC compression. The poor audio quality of MiniDisc earned it a bad reputation, but it has since improved considerably and is now in over 10 percent of Japanese households and accounts for 30 percent of prerecorded music sales in Japan. MiniDisc had less success in other countries, and even the recent resurgence of support may be too late to save it if a recordable 8-cm DVD-Audio standard is developed.

MPEG-1 video from a CD was demonstrated by Philips and Sony on their CD-i system in 1991. About 50 movies were released in CD-i Digital Video format before a standardized version appeared as Video CD in 1993, based on proposals by JVC, Sony, and Philips and documented as the White Book specification. Not to be confused with CD-Video (CDV), Video CD uses MPEG-1 compression to store 74 minutes of near-VHS-quality audio and video on a CD-ROM XA bridge disc. Philips developed a $200 Video CD add-on for its CD-i players. Hardware and software were made available for computers to play Video CDs. Video CD 2.0 was finalized in 1994. The format has done very well in countries where VHS was not well established. Over 6 million Video CD players were sold in China alone in 1996.

By 1994, drive speeds—and resulting data transfer rates—had risen to quadruple speed. Once again, the price for the new drives was around $1000. Two years later, 8X CD-ROM drives appeared, but the introductory price was down to $400. Later the same year, 12X drives appeared for around $250. Tests began to show that in many cases data transfer rates were not much better than 6X drives because the high speeds increased errors and required repeated reads.

After CD-ROM—based multimedia reached mass-market potential, music artists began to look for ways to add multimedia to their music. The idea was to create a CD which would play in a music player but also include software for use on a computer. The various techniques are grouped under the moniker of *Enhanced CD*. The first attempts—in the late 1980s—used mixed-mode CDs which put computer data on the first track and music on the remaining tracks. The downside was that some CD players attempted to play the computer data is if it were music, producing noise that could damage speakers. Stickers on CDs warning of potential equipment damage were not felt to be a good way to increase sales, so more ingenious methods were pursued. A trick of placing the computer data at index zero (in the *pregap* area before the beginning of the music) worked well with most players, which begin at index one. It was still possible to use the rewind feature on some players to back up into the data, so clever implementations included an audio message warning the listener to stop the player before reaching the noise. Since CD-ROM drives begin at index zero, they are able to read the computer data. That is, they were until Microsoft released a new SCSI CD-ROM driver which began reading at index 1, thus skipping over the data intended for the computer.

By this time, Sony and Philips, with the help of Apple and Microsoft, were working on a more foolproof solution. The answer was *stamped multi-session*, which uses a feature of the Orange Book format—originally designed for recordable discs—to put one session of Red Book audio data on the CD followed by a session of Yellow Book computer data. Combining red, yellow, and orange normally produces extra-orange, but in this case blue covers were chosen for the book that documented the new CD Plus standard, released in 1995, which was almost immediately renamed to CD Extra because of threatened lawsuits by the owner of the CD Plus trademark. The CD Extra format is completely compatible with audio CD players but doesn't work on all computers. Many CD-ROM drives are multisession-capable, but only about 50 percent of multimedia PCs have the requisite multisession software drivers. Fortunately, computers are easier to upgrade than CD players, and sales of Enhanced CDs are expected to increase tenfold to over $750 million by the year 2000. Since the DVD-Audio specification will be built on top of the DVD-ROM standard, DVDs with both audio and computer data will be straightforward and compatible with all audio players and computers.

Erasable CD, part III of the Orange Book standard, did not appear until 1997. The standard was finalized in late 1996 and the official name of Compact Disc Rewriteable (CD-RW) was chosen in hopes of avoiding the disturbing connotations of *erasable*. Unfortunately, CD-RW requires new drive hardware to read it. None of more than 700 million existing CD-ROM drives and CD players are able to read CD-RW discs, so it remains to be seen how well this format does, especially since many view it as a short-lived interim before DVD-R and DVD-RAM (or DVD-RW) appear.

NOTE   *The compatibility of DVD players with the many variations of CD is detailed in Chap. 6.*

An erasable CD format called THOR was actually announced by Tandy in 1988, eight years before CD-RW, but this ambitious technology—with its familiar-sounding promise of storing music, video, and computer data—was plagued by technical problems and never made it out of the lab. Tandy later joined with Microsoft to create the CD-based VIS (Video Information System), which was mercifully short-lived.

Another notable failure was 1991's Commodore Dynamic Total Vision (CDTV), a consumer multimedia console along the lines of CD-i. CDTV employed a CD-ROM-equipped Amiga computer that hooked up to a TV. Proprietary standards and the decline of Commodore's business doomed CDTV to museum shelves.

Early DVD Development

Shortly after the introduction of CD and CD-ROM, prototypes of their eventual replacement began to be developed. Systems using blue lasers achieved four times the storage capacity, but these were based on large, expensive gas lasers, since cheap semiconductor lasers at that wavelength were not available. In 1993, ten years after the worldwide introduction of the compact disc, the prototypes began to approach reality. Nimbus first demonstrated a double-density CD proof-of-concept in January of 1993. Optical Disc Corporation followed suit in October. Philips and Sony announced that they had a similar project underway, and later Toshiba claimed it had been working on something similar since 1993. Some of these first attempts simply used CD technology with smaller pits to create discs that could hold twice as much data. Although this was far beyond original CD tolerances, the optics of most drives were good enough to read the discs; and it would even be possible to connect the digital output of a regular CD player to an MPEG video decoder. But it was recognized that CD technology tended to falter when pushed too far. Philips reportedly put its corporate foot down and said it would not allow CD patent licensees to market the technology since it couldn't guarantee compatibility. When all things were considered, it was better to develop a new system. (See Fig. 2.8.)

Hollywood Weighs In

The stage was set in September of 1994 by seven international entertainment and content providers, Columbia Pictures (Sony), Disney, MCA/Uni-

Figure 2.8
Timeline of DVD
development.

	Hollywood proposal
1995	Sony/Philps MMCD proposal
	SD Alliance proposal
	computer industry objectives announced
	UDF recommended
	reconciliation announced
1996	combined DVD standard announced
	product announced for Fall 1996
	Digital Recording Act attempted
	copy protection agreement (Macrovision) announced
	Philips/Sony unilaterally announce joint licensing
	specification version 1.0 released
	copy protection agreement (scrambling) announced
	players appear in Japan
1997	movie titles appear in Japan
	drives appear in Japan
	players appear in U.S.
	movie titles appear in U.S.
	drives appear in U.S.

versal (Matsushita), MGM/UA, Paramount, Viacom, and Warner Bros. (Time Warner), who called for a single, worldwide standard for the new generation of digital video on optical media. These studios formed the Hollywood Digital Video Disc Advisory Group and requested the following:

- Room for a full-length feature film, about 135 minutes, on one side of a single disc
- Picture quality superior to high-end consumer video systems such as laserdisc
- Compatibility with matrixed surround and other high-quality audio systems
- Ability to accommodate three to five languages on one disc

■ Copy protection

■ Multiple aspect ratios for widescreen support

■ Multiple versions of a program on one disc, with parental lockout

Preparations and proposals began, but two incompatible camps soon formed. Like antagonists in some strange mechanistic mating ritual, each side boasted of its prowess and attempted to line up the most backers. At stake was the billion-dollar home video industry as well as millions of dollars in patent licensing revenue.

Dissension in the Ranks

On December 16, 1994, Sony and its partner Philips independently announced their own standard: a single-sided, 3.7-billion-byte Multimedia CD (MMCD). The remaining cast of characters jointly proposed a different standard just over a month later on January 24, 1995. Their superdensity (SD-DVD) standard was based on a double-sided design holding 5 billion bytes per side.

The SD Alliance was led by seven companies: Hitachi, Matsushita (Panasonic), Mitsubishi, Victor (JVC), Pioneer, Thomson (RCA/GE), and Toshiba (business partner of Time Warner), and attracted about 10 other supporting companies, mostly home electronics manufacturers and movie studios.* Philips and Sony assembled a rival gang of about 14 companies, mostly peripheral hardware manufacturers.† Neither group had support from major computer companies. At this stage, the emphasis was on video entertainment, with computer data storage as a sideline goal.

Two days after the SD announcement, Sony head Norio Ohga told the press that Sony "may make concessions but we will not join," and indicated that Sony would hold out for a third standard incorporating more of its own specifications, even to the point of asking the Ministry of International Trade and Industry to arbitrate the unification. Sony and Philips held the lion's share of CD technology patents and hoped to include as many of them as possible in the new format. The companies in

---

*Other companies supporting SD-DVD included MCA (then owned by Matsushita), MGM/UA (owned by Turner), Nippon Columbia, Samsung, SKC, Turner Home Entertainment (independent at the time, now merged with Time Warner), WEA (Time Warner's giant CD-ROM manufacturing arm), and Zenith.

†Others backing the MMCD format included Acer, Aiwa, Alps, Bang & Olufson, Grundig, Marantz, Mitsumi, Nokia, Ricoh, TEAC, and Wearnes.

the SD Alliance, including Sony's arch rival Matsushita, planned to use their own newly patented technology and slow the flow of patent revenue to the competition.

Sony and Philips played up the advantages of MMCD's single-layer technology such as lower manufacturing costs and CD compatibility without the need of a dual-focus laser, but the SD Alliance was winning the crucial support of Hollywood with its dual-layer system's longer playing time. On February 23, Sony played catch-up by announcing a two-layer, one-side design licensed from 3M that would hold 7.4 billion bytes.

The Referee Shows Up

The scuffling continued, and the increasing emphasis on data storage by consumer electronics companies began to worry the computer industry. At the end of April 1995, five computer companies, Apple, Compaq, HP, IBM, and Microsoft, formed a technical working group that met with each faction and urged them to compromise. The computer companies flatly stated that they did "not plan to choose between these proposed new formats" and provided a list of nine objectives for a single standard.

- One format for both computers and video entertainment
- A common file system for computers and video entertainment
- Backward compatibility with existing CDs and CD-ROMs
- Forward compatibility with future writeable and rewriteable discs
- Cost similar to current CD media and CD-ROM drives
- No mandatory caddy or cartridge
- Data reliability equal to or better than CD-ROM
- High data capacity, extensible to future capacity enhancements
- High performance for video (sequential files) and computer data

Sony refused to budge and a month later said there would be "no adjustment in its DVD standards." Norio Ohga said "a split on the standard is unavoidable because we are in a world of democracy." He rejected the possibility of a third standard and defended his decision on the grounds of "liberalism and democracy." Both sides invited the other to give in, Toshiba inviting "Sony/Philips to engage in serious discussion to resolve this issue," and Sony pronouncing that "we would, of course, be happy to discuss our proposal with all interested parties." Meanwhile, the

SD group announced on May 11 that Matsushita had developed a transparent bonding technology that allowed both substrates to be read from a single side. It then tried to stack the deck by announcing the development of recordable SD technology.

On August 14, 1995, the computer industry group, now up to seven with the addition of Fujitsu and Sun, concluded that the most recent versions of the two formats essentially met all of their requirements except the first one: that there be a single, unified standard. In order to best support the requirements for a cross-platform file system and read-write support, they recommended adoption of the Universal Disk Format (UDF) developed by the Optical Storage Technology Association (OSTA). OSTA had already agreed to refine the UDF standard for interchange compatibility between read-only and nonsequential read-write applications for both television products and computers and had held the first of a set of technical meetings on July 25. IBM reportedly told Sony and Philips that it intended to settle on the higher-capacity SD format and gave them a few weeks to come up with a compromise. Faced with the hazard of no support from the computer industry or the possibly worse prospect of a standards war reminiscent of Betamax versus VHS, the two DVD camps announced at the Berlin IFA show that they would discuss the possibility of a combined standard. The companies officially entered into negotiations on August 24. The computer companies expressed their preference that the MMCD data storage method and dual-layer technology be combined with SD's bonded substrates and better error correction method.

Reconciliation

At the end of August 1995, Philips and Sony proposed a new MCD combined format to the SD Alliance. Conflicting reports appeared in the press, some saying a compromise was imminent, others claiming that officials from Sony and Toshiba had denied both the compromise news and the rumors that MMCD would be standardized for computer data applications while SD would be used for video. On September 15, 1995, the SD Alliance announced that "considering the computer companies' requests to enhance reliability" it was willing to switch to the Philips/Sony method of bit storage in spite of a capacity reduction from 5 billion byes to 4.7 billion. It complained that circuit designs would have to be changed and that "reverification of disc manufacturability" would be required, but conceded that it could be done. It didn't concede the naming war, however, proposing that the SD name be retained. Sony and Philips made a similar conciliatory announcement, and thus, almost a year after they began, the hostilities officially ended.

Henk Bodt, executive vice president of Philips, said that the next step was to publish in October a comprehensive specification. Mr. Bodt made some notable predictions, stating that the new players would be "substantially more expensive" than VHS players, at around $800. He also thought that issues of data compression would probably make recordability realistic only in the professional field. "Certainly I don't think that these players will replace the video cassette recorder."

On September 25, 1995, OSTA announced establishment of the UDF file system interchange standard, a vast improvement over the old ISO 9660 format, finally implementing full support for modern operating systems along with recording and erasing. Work on support for application of the UDF format to DVD was still underway.

Seeing an opportunity to make its own recommendations, the Interactive Multimedia Association (IMA) and the Laser Disc Association (LDA, which later changed its name to OVDA—Optical Video Disc Association) held a joint conference on October 19 to determine requirements for "innovative video programming" based on years of experience with laserdisc and CD-ROM.* The general consensus was that better video and audio were insufficient and DVD movie players required interactivity to be of more interest to the worldwide mass market. The group recommended that baseline interactivity be required in all DVD-Video players and also recommended that the design allow optional addition of proven features such as player control using printed bar codes, on-the-fly seamless branching under program control, and external control. Some of the group's recommendations, such as random access to individual frames, graphic overlay, and multiple audio tracks, were mostly supported by the tentative DVD standards, but the remaining recommendations were largely ignored.

On October 30, 1995, OSTA announced the completion of an appendix to the UDF file system specification that described the restrictions and requirements for DVD media formatted with UDF. This simplified version, which became commonly known as MicroUDF, allowed DVD-

---

*At this meeting, your humble yet foresighted author predicted that DVD would not appear in the United States in meaningful numbers before 1997. It turned out that DVD did not appear in the United States in any numbers at all before 1997.

Video players to implement low-cost circuitry for locating and reading movie files.

Undeterred by the prospect of retooling its standard, Toshiba announced on November 7 a prototype SD-ROM drive and claimed that its data transfer rate of 9 times CD-ROM speed had not yet been achieved with CD-ROM technology.

The two DVD groups continued to hammer out a consensus which was finally announced on December 12, 1995. The new format covered the basic DVD-ROM format and video standards, taking into account the recommendations made by movie studios and the computer industry.* A new alliance was formed—the DVD Consortium—consisting of Philips and Sony, the big seven from the SD camp, and Time Warner. When all was said and done, Matsushita held 25 percent of the approximately 4000 patents, Pioneer and Sony each had 20 percent, Philips, Hitachi, and Toshiba were left with 10 percent of the pie, Thomson had 5 percent, and the remaining members—Mitsubishi, JVC, and Time Warner—held negligible slivers. (See Fig. 2.9.)

---

*The SD physical format of two 0.6-mm bonded substrates was selected, with both Matsushita's dual-layer system (one on each substrate) from the SD format and 3M's dual-layer technology (a second photopolymer layer on a single substrate) from the MMCD format. Toshiba's 8/15 modulation was replaced by MMCD's more reliable EFMPlus 8/16 modulation. SD's more robust Reed-Solomon Product Code error correction was chosen with 32K blocks instead of 23K blocks. The maximum pit length was reduced from 2.13 to 1.87 µm for higher data density and the scanning velocity was raised from 3.27 to 3.49 m/s. These last two changes resulted in the channel bit rate improving from SD's 25.54 Mbps to 26.16 Mbps and helped compensate for the increased modulation. (See Table A.8 for more details.)

Figure 2.9
The DVD patent pie.

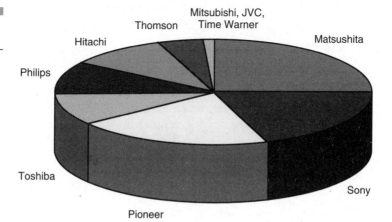

Recent DVD Development

In January of 1996, companies began announcing their DVD plans for the new year. Philips targeted late 1996 for its hardware release. Most other companies pegged a slightly earlier fall release. Thomson stunned everyone by announcing that its player would be available by summer for $499—$100 less and months sooner than the rest.*

The road ahead looked smooth and clear until the engineers in their rose-colored glasses, riding their forecast-fueled marketing machines, crashed headlong into the protectionist paranoia of Hollywood.

As the prospect of DVD solidified, the movie studios began to obsess about what would happen when they released their family jewels in pristine digital format with the possibility that people could make high-quality videotape copies or even perfect digital dubs. Rumors began to surface that DVD would be delayed because of copyright worries, but Toshiba and others confidently stated that everything was on track for the planned fall release. On March 29, the Consumer Electronics Manufacturers Association (CEMA) and the Motion Picture Association of America (MPAA) announced that they had agreed to seek legislation that would protect intellectual property and consumers' rights concerning digital video recorders. They hoped their proposal would be included in the Digital Recording Act of 1996 that was about to be introduced in the U.S. Congress.

Their recommendation was intended to

- Allow consumers to make home video recordings from broadcast or basic cable television

- Allow analog or digital copies of subscription programming, with the qualification that digital copies of the copy could be prevented

- Allow copyright owners to prohibit copying from pay-per-view, video-on-demand, and prerecorded material

The two groups hailed their agreement as a landmark compromise between industries which had often been at odds over copyright issues. They added that they welcomed input from the computer industry, and input they got! A week later a very upset industry group fired off a "list

---

*Almost exactly a year later, Thomson reannounced its RCA-brand players at $599 and $699 for limited spring 1997 release, with full availability delayed until fall. The Thomson-designed players were built by Matsushita.

of critiques" of the technical specifications that had been proposed by Hollywood and the consumer electronics companies. The Information Technology Industry Council (ITI), a group of 30 computer and communications companies including Apple, IBM, Intel, Motorola, and Xerox, was less than thrilled with the MPAA and CEMA attempting to unilaterally dictate hardware and software systems to keep movies from being copied onto personal computers. "No way will we simply accept it as is," said IBM's Dr. Alan Bell, chair of the Copy Protection Technical Working Group, in reference to the proposal. The computer industry said it preferred voluntary standards for copy protection and objected to being told exactly how to implement things. "Any mandatory standard that was legislated and then administered by a government body is anathema to the computer industry," said an ITI spokesperson, who also pointed out that legal protection for copyrights "should cover all digital media including records, movies, images and texts," rather than focusing on motion pictures as MPAA and CEMA had proposed. The ITI announced it would have a counter proposal ready for an April 29 meeting, recognizing that it was "an important issue to Hollywood, and we don't want to take money out of the studios' pockets."

Turbulence

The news media was filled with reports of DVD being "stalled," "embattled," and "derailed." A few weeks later, on May 20, Toshiba's executive vice president Taizo Nishimuro was reported to have said that a copy protection deal between the computer industry's Technical Working Group and the DVD Consortium would be signed at a June 3 meeting. But apparently the agreement had only been that all three parties would refrain from introducing copy protection legislation before the June 3 meeting, and Toshiba officials later denied the reports of any sort of settlement. In spite of all this, executives at Thomson said they were confident the issues would be resolved and that they were ready for launch as early as summer.

As DVD progress was being attacked by the popular press, standardization efforts were having their own problems. Sony threw a monkey wrench into the process by proposing a completely new DVD-Audio format, Direct Stream Digital (DSD). Sony claimed its single-bit format was not tied to specific sampling frequencies and sizes, thus eliminating downsampling and oversampling, and resulting in less noise. The ARA did not agree and continued to push for PCM. Then, in the May 1996 issue of *CD-ROM Professional*, guest columnist Hugh Bennet publicized a serious flaw that had apparently gone unrecognized or was being ignored by DVD engineers. The dye used in recordable CD media (CD-R) did not reflect the smaller-wavelength laser light used in DVD, thus rendering the discs invisible. He pointed out that more than 2 million CD recorders were expected to be in use by the end of 1996 and that the recorders were expected to have written between 75 and 100 million CD-R discs by then. A new Type II CD-R that would work with CD and DVD had been proposed but would take years to supersede the current format, leaving millions of CD-R users out in the cold when it came time to switch to DVD readers.

Glib Promises

At a June 1996 DVD conference, participants glossed over the technical difficulties and downplayed the copy-protection schism, expecting a solution to be announced before the end of the month. Toshiba executive Toshio Yajima said, "It was a misunderstanding between industries." Sixty executives from the three sides were committed to meeting once a week to resolve the copyright protection disputes. At the same conference, one of DVD's most ardent cheerleaders, Warner Home Video president Warren Lieberfarb, told attendees in his keynote speech that 250 movie titles would be ready for a fall launch. Lieberfarb also gave projections that player sales would be from 2.8 million to 3.7 million units in the first year. Other first-day speakers were equally optimistic and everyone was assured that the fall launch was on schedule, that the 10 companies of the DVD Consortium had agreed to establish a one-stop agency for licensing, and that the preliminary DVD 0.9 specification book was immediately available for a paltry $5000. A few days into the conference, Thomson admitted that prospects for a fall rollout of its player were only "50/50," and Toshiba let it be known that it would delay its product launch until October.

Attendees at the conference were even less sanguine. Many thought December would be a more realistic target date, even though it would be too late for the Christmas buying spree. An industry executive was quoted as saying "What the DVD industry needs is a healthy dose of realism. Somebody ought to just stand up and announce that it's a '97 product, and all this speculation would come to an end." But over the next few months, realism didn't make much of an appearance and speculation refused to leave the stage.

Sliding Deadlines and Empty Announcements

On June 25, Toshiba announced that the 10 companies in the consortium had agreed to integrate standardized copy protection circuits in their players, including a regional management system to control the distribution and release of movies in different parts of the world. Many people took this to mean that the copy protection issue had been laid to rest, not understanding that this copy protection agreement dealt only with analog copying by using the Macrovision signal modification technology to prevent recording on a VCR. The manufacturers, still clutching their dreams of DVD players under Christmas trees and hoping to keep enthusiasm high, conveniently failed to mention that Hollywood was holding out for digital copy protection as well.

On July 11, Matsushita announced it would begin shipping DVD players in Japan in September, with machines reaching the United States in October. Matsushita blamed copyright protection and licensing issues for the delay. Again, more pragmatic viewpoints appeared, such as that of Jerry Pierce, director of MCA's Digital Video Compression Center, who flatly stated that "the DVD launch will be in 1997." By this time Philips—the most conservative of the bunch—had moved its release date to spring of 1997. Matsushita also said its DVD-ROM drives for PCs would not be introduced until early 1997, but that within two to three years every PC would have a DVD drive.

At the end of July, over a month after a copy protection settlement was to have been made, the DVD Consortium—the hardware side of the triangle—agreed to support a copy-protection method proposed by Matsushita. The Copy Protection Technical Working Group—representing all three sides of the triangle—agreed to look into the proposal, which used content encryption to prevent movie data from being directly copied using a DVD-ROM drive and bus authentication to keep it from being copied while traveling from the computer to the monitor.

Not unexpectedly, licensing discussion had by now fallen apart. On August 2, Philips made a surprise announcement that it had been authorized by Sony to begin a licensing program for their joint DVD technology. "In an effort to avoid further undesirable delays, Philips and Sony have decided to move forward in the best interest of the DVD system and its future licensees." They called on other companies to join in pooling patents, but Thomson, for one, declined. Many less-than-responsible journalists had a field day, reporting that the DVD standard had been sabotaged or that Philips and Sony were trying to steal patent revenue from the other companies.

By the end of August, there was still no copy protection agreement. At the gigantic CeBIT Home exhibition in Hanover, Germany, Jan Oosterveld of Philips explained that key issues such as copy protection, regional coding, and software availability were unresolved. "The orchestra is assembled, the musicians have their positions, but they have not decided which tune they will play and how much time they need to rehearse and tune their instruments," he said. He elaborated that copy protection was complicated by export and import restrictions and that key technology was still not available to non-Japanese companies. The regional control issue—on the table for almost a year—still "created confusion on how the world should be divided." The software supply for DVD-ROM drives also looked bleak, with only 12 companies working on DVD-ROM titles. Oosterveld reiterated that the music industry was expected to take the lead with DVD-Audio and that there was no decision on whether to use phase-change or magneto-optical technology for DVD-RAM. In spite of this, Philips was optimistic that by the year 2000 around 10 percent of all optical drives, or 25 million out of 250 million, would be based on DVD. Compared to other predictions, this was rather pessimistic, but given Philips's slightly better track record at forecasting, it may be the most realistic.

At the same time, Sakon Nagasaki of Matsushita told the press that completion of the DVD specification and resolution of the encryption problem were two separate issues, saying that encryption "is a problem in the United States, not in Japan." Matsushita announced that it could not wait any longer for a copy protection agreement and that its two movie player models would be available in Japan on November 1 for 98,000 and 79,800 yen, and that if a copy protection agreement was reached, the players would be introduced a few weeks later in the United States for $599 and $699.* Although Sony announced that it was delaying the release of its players until spring, Hitachi, Pioneer, and Toshiba followed Matsushita's lead and promised players before Christmas.

A few weeks later, on September 12, 1996, Toshiba announced its first home PCs and reaffirmed its commitment—despite ongoing copyright protection issues—to bring out DVD-Video and DVD-ROM players, stating that PC makers "should have the first units with our implementation of the copyright protection toward the end of September, and we think we can start shipping those units in volume by mid-November."

The following week was the IMA Expo, with a special focus on DVD. The glowing news from Toshiba was that every DVD-ROM PC would

---

*When they were finally released in March of 1997, the price of the DVD-A100 was unchanged but the DVD-A300 had risen by $50 to $749.95.

have hardware or software to play DVD movies, DVD-RAM would be ready within a year, and DVD-ROM would be such a success that Toshiba would no longer be making CD-ROM drives in the year 2000. Estimates from International Data Corporation (IDC) placed DVD-ROM drive sales at 10 million in 1997 and 70 million in 2000. During the Expo, Pioneer announced November 22 as the release date in Japan of a combination laserdisc and DVD player at 133,000 yen and a DVD-only player at 83,000 yen, plus two other DVD karaoke players. U.S. prices were expected to be $1200 and $750. By this time, the DVD Consortium had managed to fit most of the world into six geographical regions for release control purposes, but Mexico, Australia, and New Zealand were still bouncing from region to region. According to Warner Advanced Media there were supposedly 30 DVD-ROM software titles in development for early 1997. Matsushita representatives at the Expo were privately admitting that their players would not be out in the United States until February.

About this time, the supposedly final 1.0 version of the $5000 DVD-ROM and DVD-Video technical specifications appeared. A few features such as NTSC closed-caption support had been dropped, and a complex country-specific ratings system had reverted to a simpler version from the earlier spec. Copy protection details had been left for a later appendix.

Pioneer announced on September 27 that beginning in the latter half of October it would sell a mix-and-match system of DVD players and receivers, bringing its total to five models placed on sale in 1996. European introduction of the mix-and-match models was planned for spring 1997 with the United States to follow in the summer.

On October 5, 1996, Samsung announced that November 1 would be the debut date of its DVD player in Korea and cited predictions of a global market for DVD players at 400,000 before the end of 1996. The affiliated Samsung Entertainment Group expected to release at least 10 DVD movie titles by the end of the year, with more than 100 in 1997 and over 500 in the year 2000. Samsung also expected to commercialize its DVD-ROM drive by the end of 1996.

Hopes for a DVD-Audio specification before the end of 1996 dwindled. Philips announced it would team up with Sony to develop bitstream-based Direct Stream Digital (DSD) technology for DVD.

Real Progress and Real Product

Then the big news finally arrived: the Copy Protection Technical Working Group announced on October 29, 1996, that a tentative agreement had been reached. The modified copy protection technology developed by Matsushita and Toshiba would be licensed through a nonprofit entity. On the same day, Pioneer confessed that it would delay U.S. shipment of DVD players until January, pushing back the December release date it had announced just the day before. At this point only Toshiba and Matsushita were still promising to make DVD hardware available in December, although most of the press and even more of the public were confused as to release dates in Japan versus the United States.

Matsushita and Toshiba delivered DVD players in Japan as promised. News reports from November 1 described a dismal rainy day with lackluster player sales and a handful of discs, mostly music videos. A student was quoted as saying, "Pre-recorded discs are not particularly appealing, but it would be great if you can record your favorite films on the disc as many times as you want," which undoubtedly didn't help convince the studios to rush their movies onto DVD.

The PR machines didn't rest, with Fujitsu claiming on November 6 that it was the first company to market a DVD-ROM—equipped computer, Toshiba stating on November 7 that it expected rewritable DVD-RAM to be available within a year or soon thereafter, and Matsushita announcing on November 11 the development of the world's first DVD-Internet Linkage System for playing video from an Internet Web page through the use of a DVD-ROM drive. Toshiba's news on November 18 was more down to earth: postponement of its DVD player release in the United States until late January or early February.

Most other announcements were put on hold for Comdex, the huge computer technology exhibition in Las Vegas. At Comdex, there were dozens of announcements of hardware and software, including the expected release of Toshiba's DVD-ROM drive worldwide in January 1997. Intel CEO Andy Grove's keynote speech included a DVD demo of *Space Jam* using Compcore's software-only playback system.

November came and went with no sightings of DVD players for sale in North America. On December 2, Akai announced its own DVD player to be launched in Japan at the end of January and worldwide in April.

By December 13, 1996, Toshiba's Precia PC, which was to have been rolled out in Japan in November, had been pushed back to January. Toshiba blamed it on bureaucratic problems with copy protection chips. "We're hoping it's resolved any day now, but we've been hoping for that for two or three weeks," went the now-too-familiar refrain. Other sources claimed the real reason for the delays was that the Japanese government had barred Toshiba from releasing hardware to the United States because of concerns over the export of encryption technology. The U.S. delivery date for Toshiba's DVD-equipped PCs slipped to March.

Things began to look up on December 20 when Warner Home Video began sales in Japan of four major movie titles: *The Assassin, Blade Runner, Eraser,* and *The Fugitive,* with another four announced for January release.

By this time, the delay was being blamed on lack of titles rather than copy protection issues, but in the first week of January 1997, at the Consumer Electronics Show in Las Vegas, DVD finally began to look like a real product. At least six studios announced the release of over 60 DVD-Video titles for the March/April time frame: New Line Home Video, Warner Home Video, Sony's Columbia TriStar Home Video, Sony Music Entertainment/Sony Wonder, MGM Home Entertainment, and Philips' Polygram. Perennial favorites *Casablanca* and *Singin' in the Rain* were announced by two studios each.

Also at the Consumer Electronics Show, DVD players were demonstrated or announced by Akai, Denon, Faroudja, Fisher, JVC, Meridian, Mitsubishi, Panasonic, Philips/Magnavox, Pioneer, RCA, Samsung, Sony, Toshiba, Yamaha, and Zenith, most with a U.S. release date between March and summer. This brought the lineup of player manufacturers to at least 20, including others who had previously announced DVD movie plans: Goldstar, Hitachi, Hyundai, and Sharp. Compared to typical industry support of new launches—even now-ubiquitous products such as telephone, television, VCR, and compact disc—this was an astonishing endorsement which flew in the face of the predictions of gloom and doom for DVD as a consumer video product.

And on the computer side, where most people expected DVD to be a slam dunk, there were now over 45 companies developing hardware or support software: Alliance Semiconductor, Apple, AST, ATI Technologies, C-Cube, CEI, Cirrus Logic, Compaq, Compcore Multimedia, Creative Technology, Diamond Multimedia, Digital, Elektroson, Fujitsu, Hitachi, Hyundai, IBM, Innovacom, Intel, JVC, LSI, Matrox, Matsushita, Mediamatics, Microsoft, Mitsubishi, Motorola, Number 9, NEC, Oak Technology, Packard Bell, Philips, Pioneer, S3, Samsung, SGS-Thomson, Software Architects, Sony, STB Systems, TDK, Toshiba, Trident Microsystems, Truevision, Wired, Yamaha, and Zoran, plus more than 20 publishers who had announced DVD-ROM software titles: 2 Way Media, Activision, Byron Preiss/Simon & Schuster, Creative Multimedia, Digital Directory Assistance, Discovery, Electronic Arts, Graphix Zone, Grolier, GT Entertainment, Interactual Technologies, IVS, Japan Travel Bureau, The Learning Company (SoftKey), Mechadeus, Multicom, Pro CD, Sega, Sumeria, SuperZero, Tsunami, Warner Advanced Media, and Xiphias.

Players from Panasonic and Pioneer finally began to appear in the United States in February as more movies and music performance videos were announced from Lumivision, Warner Bros. Records, and others. Eager customers bought the players, only to discover that no titles were scheduled to appear before the end of March. Warner, the primary supplier, limited its release to seven test cities. Pioneer announced that its $11,500 DVD-R recorder would be available, complete with $40 to $50 blank discs, around June of 1997. Computer makers geared up for both hardware and software DVD-Video playback, but once again the copy protection issue settled on the scene like a wet blanket: decryption/descrambling licenses were available for hardware but not yet allowed for software. The studios were unconvinced that DVD players implemented in software would completely protect their assets. They were right, of course, but that didn't mollify the computer makers and software developers who were counting on cheap software playback.

The two final competing DVD-RAM standards were merged and an official format was announced on April 14. The approval procedure was allegedly changed so that members of the original SD camp could steamroll their combined proposal over the objections and abstentions of Sony and Philips. The fresh veneer of cooperation was cracking, revealing the possibility of a competing recordable DVD format from Philips. Toshiba, which apparently announced the arrangement before it was approved, made almost comical claims that DVD-RAM drives would be available before the end of 1997 for only $350. More sober predictions targeted 1998 and prices of $800 or more. At about the same time, Pioneer revealed that its DVD-R drive would cost $6000 more than originally expected, raising the price to about $17,000. Creative Labs' DVD-ROM upgrade kit with hardware DVD-Video playback appeared in April, but showed signs of a rushed release. Other DVD-ROM products failed to make their already delayed debuts, and both Apple and Microsoft pushed back release dates for DVD support. There were still no movie decryption licenses allowed for software playback, and industry observers began to doubt that DVD-ROM computers would be available in more than miniscule numbers before 1998. This was increasingly irksome to those who simply wanted a DVD-ROM data drive and had no interest in using their computers to play movies. Many in this group began hoping for a quick and early death to DVD-Video so they could get on with the real business of DVD-ROM.

On the home video front, a few of the major studios were keeping their wait-and-see stance. Some sources claimed that the studios were pressuring the hardware makers for a kickback. Meanwhile, rumors spread of a pay-per-view version of DVD called Zoom TV, supposedly under development for use by the holdout studios such as Disney. Home consumers who heard the rumors were less than thrilled at the prospect of having their movie-viewing habits held hostage to the vagaries of telephone systems and remote authentication servers. Amidst the litany of boredom and frustration, one of the few bright spots was the initial success of disc sales. By the end of April, less than one month after the release of the first 40 or so DVD titles in the United States, over 50,000 copies had been sold, exceeding most expectations. The title wave of DVD had begun to swell. Over 30,000 players had been bought in the first 15 weeks of U.S. sales, and over 150,000 players had been sold in Japan since DVD's introduction six months earlier. Initial bad reviews of in-store demos were supplanted by glowing reports from early purchasers who made side-by-side comparisons of DVD to laserdisc and proclaimed DVD the clear winner.

DVD had finally embarked, late and lacking some of its early luster, on the long and rocky road to acceptance.

CHAPTER **3**

Technical Overview

This chapter deals mostly with the fundamentals of DVD, with an emphasis on DVD-Video. Chapter 4 covers the more technical aspects of DVD-ROM and DVD-Video.

DVD Myths

Numerous myths have sprung up around DVD. Apparently some people had nothing better to do while waiting for it to appear than sit around and misconstrue its characteristics. This section deals with some of the most common misperceptions of DVD.

"DVD Is Revolutionary"

DVD is evolutionary, not revolutionary. The printing press was revolutionary. Television was revolutionary. Even CD can be considered revolutionary: a completely new way of storing digital audio and computer data on a compact optical disc. But DVD isn't much more than the evolution of CD and the refinement of Video CD. It adds digital video and other features, but there is nothing radically different between DVD and VHS, between DVD and laserdisc, or between DVD-ROM and CD-ROM.

"DVD Will Fail"

Many arguments have been put forth in an attempt to show that DVD will suffer the same fate as other short-lived new technologies. But on closer inspection, none of these arguments hold water. There is a possibility that DVD-Video will never be more than a niche market, similar to laserdisc, but the success of DVD-ROM is virtually secured. The ever expanding needs of computer data and multimedia require a capacious medium for storage and distribution. CD-ROM is the undisputed king of the realm, and DVD-ROM is the crown prince—the guaranteed successor, since nothing else provides a similarly compatible improvement.

The window of opportunity for new technology grows smaller all the time, as evidenced by such not-quite-failures as S-VHS, DAT, DCC, and MiniDisc. But none of these can be compared to DVD, which has a mainstream computer counterpart holding open the door to acceptance. In fact, DAT is arguably the most successful of these other products only because it's used for computer data backup.

DVD-Video players share most of the same physical and mechanical components with DVD-ROM drives. As DVD-ROM is widely adopted in the computer market, the economies of scale will drive the cost down dramatically. Within just a few years, the drive units will probably cost less than $40 in quantity to equipment manufacturers. At the same time, audio/video decoding chips will feed an ever increasing demand in digital satellite receivers, digital cable boxes, and computers. Unlike most new products, which must recoup their investment while building up to economical production levels, DVD-Video will essentially be subsidized by related technologies.

DVD-Video has more backing than any new entertainment product in the history of consumer electronics. The annual sales income of the 10 primary DVD companies alone is over $340 billion, more than the gross domestic product of many countries. Staggering amounts of money have been spent to develop DVD, and even more is being spent to market it. For example, Matsushita allocated over $17 million to promote its Panasonic brand players in America alone. Toshiba and Philips have likewise embarked on multimillion dollar U.S. campaigns. In the first few months of 1997, dealers began clearing out their stock of laserdiscs and laserdisc players in premature anticipation of DVD, indicating that part of the mindshare battle had already been won.

If for some reason DVD-Video fails to catch the interest of home consumers and businesses, it will almost surely succeed on its second try: the next generation of high-density DVD will be much more compelling when HDTV and PC-TV replace standard television, and the resulting difference between old media and high-density DVD is screamingly apparent.

"DVD Is Better Because It's Digital"

There is nothing inherent to digital formats that magically makes them better than analog formats. The celluloid film used in movie theaters is analog, yet no one would say that DVD is better than film. Japan's Hi-Vision television has much higher video quality than DVD, but it's analog. And the quality of digital video from CD-ROMs is certainly nothing to write home about.

There are certain advantages to the way DVD stores audio and video in digital form, not the least of which is the ability to use compression. And the quality and flexibility of DVD stands out when compared to similar analog products. But it's a mistake to make the generalization that anything digital must be superior to anything analog.

"DVD Video Is Poor Because It's Compressed"

Much ado is made of the "digital artifacts" that supposedly plague DVD-Video. While it's true that digital video can appear blocky or fuzzy, a properly compressed DVD will exhibit few or no discernible artifacts. Many early discs, especially demonstration discs, were created with hardware or software that was partially finished or not fully tested. There is much room for improvement in compression techniques; video encoders are steadily improving, producing better pictures within the same compression constraints. The improvements will benefit all existing players—no hardware upgrade is required. Minor glitches and quality problems will quickly disappear as compression engineers improve their craft.

The term *artifact* refers to anything that wasn't in the original picture. Artifacts can be from film scratches, film-to-video conversion, analog-to-digital conversion, noise reduction, digital encoding, digital decoding, digital-to-analog conversion, NTSC or PAL video encoding, antitaping alterations, composite signal crosstalk, connector problems, electrical interference, waveform aliasing, signal filters, television picture controls, and much more. Many people blame all kinds of visual deficiencies on the MPEG-2 encoding process. Occasionally this blame is accurately placed, but usually it's not. Only those with training or experience can tell for certain where a particular artifact came from. The most recognizable digital artifacts appear as small dots called *mosquitoes* or as small squares, but even these aren't necessarily from the digital encoding process. If an artifact can't be duplicated in repeated playings of the same sequence, then it's not a result of MPEG encoding.

"DVD Compression Doesn't Work for Animation"

It's often claimed that animation, especially hand-drawn cell animation such as cartoons and Japanese anime, does not compress well with MPEG-2 or even that it ends up larger than the original. Other people claim that animation is so simple that it compresses better. Neither is generally true.

Supposedly the *jitter* between frames caused by differences in the drawings or in their alignment causes problems. Modern animation techniques produce very exact alignment, so there is usually no variation between object positions from frame to frame unless it's an intentional effect. Even when objects change position between frames, the motion estimation feature of MPEG-2 can easily compensate for it.

Because of the way MPEG-2 compresses video, it can have difficulty with the sharp edges common in animation. This loss of high-frequency information can show up as "ringing" or blurry spots along high-contrast edges. This is called the *Gibbs effect*. However, at the data rates commonly used for DVD, this problem does not occur. The complexity of sharp edges tends to balance out the simplicity of broad areas of a single color.

"DVD Discs Are Too Fragile to Be Rented"

The Blockbuster Video chain allegedly made a stance early on that it would not rent DVDs unless the format included a protective caddy. But the designers of DVD, having learned from experience to hate CD-ROM caddies, and not wishing to more than double the cost of discs by requiring a caddy or protective shell, politely ignored such requests.

Since then, many Blockbuster stores have begun renting discs, Blockbuster has joined with Sony to demonstrate DVD in selected rental outlets, and Sony is packaging free Blockbuster rental coupons with its players. West Coast Entertainment, another large video rental chain, also made an early DVD rental commitment. Obviously, these companies have some concern for the durability of DVDs in a rental environment, but do not think it prevents renting.

DVDs are, of course, liable to scratches, cracks, dirt, and fingerprints. But these occur at the surface of the disc where they are out of focus to the laser. Damage and imperfections may cause minor channel data errors that are easily corrected. A common misperception is that a scratch will be worse on a DVD than on a CD because of higher areal density and because the audio and video are compressed. DVD data density is about seven times that of CD-ROM, so it's true that a scratch will affect more data. But DVD error correction is more than 10 times more effective than CD error correction. This improved reliability more than makes up for the density increase. It's also important to realize that MPEG-2 and Dolby Digital compression are partly based on removal or reduction of imperceptible information, so decompression doesn't expand the data as much as might be assumed. For example, video might be compressed to one-tenth its original size, but might only be decompressed to nine-tenths, with the remaining one-tenth permanently removed. Major scratches on a disc may cause uncorrectable errors that will cause an I/O error on a computer or show up as a momentary glitch in DVD-Video picture, but there are many schemes for concealing errors in MPEG video.

Consider that laserdiscs, music CDs, and CD-ROMs are likewise subject to scratches, but many video stores and libraries rent them. DVD manufacturers are fond of taking a disc and rubbing it vigorously with sand-paper, then placing it in a player where it plays perfectly.

Videocassettes have their own share of reliability problems: deterioration from repeated play, susceptibility to heat and magnetic fields, broken tape, and broken parts. On balance, DVD is not likely to perform significantly worse in a rental environment than tapes.

"DVD Holds 4.7 To 18 GB"

As mentioned in the introduction, the abbreviation *GB* when referring to storage capacity usually stands for *gigabytes*, which are measured in powers of 2, not powers of 10. A DVD holds 4.4 to 15.9 gigabytes, which is the same as 4.7 to 17 billion bytes. In some cases, proponents seem to have even taken the liberty of rounding 17 up to 18.

See the capacities section later in this chapter (pg. 79).

"DVD Lets You Watch Movies As They Were Meant to Be Seen"

This refers to DVD's widescreen feature. However, almost all movies have a wider shape than widescreen TVs. So, even though movies will look much better on a widescreen TV, they will still have to be formatted to fit the less-oblong shape. For many movies this will not be noticeable, but it can require visible black bars to adjust to the very wide shape of some movies.

See the aspect ratios section of this chapter (pg. 79) for more information.

"DVD Crops Widescreen Movies"

This myth comes from a confusion between original movie aspect ratio and DVD's widescreen picture aspect ratio. The widescreen mode of DVD uses a wider picture shape than standard televisions. This wider picture can be displayed full-screen on a widescreen television or formatted to fit a standard television. The widescreen picture is about the same proportional width as most movies, but some movies are wider. It's these movies that are the source of confusion. In almost all cases they are *letter-*

boxed to fit the entire original width within DVD's widescreen picture shape.

See the aspect ratios section of this chapter (pg. 79) for more information.

"DVD Will Replace Your VCR"

Not in the twentieth century it won't. DVD-Video in its initial form does not record. Recordable DVD formats—DVD-R and DVD-RAM—will become available in late 1997 and 1998 but are intended solely for the computer market and will start out at four-digit prices. Even after the cost of DVD recorders and recordable discs drops, additional expensive hardware will be required to compress the audio and video to fit on the disc.

See Chap. 5, "What's Wrong with DVD," for details.

"You Can Play DVD Movies on Your Computer"

You can lead a DVD-ROM drive to your computer but you can't make it drink. You can only play DVD-Video movies on your computer if you have the right stuff. A very fast computer, such as a 266-MHz Pentium MMX with accelerated video hardware (such as AGP), needs only special software to play DVD-Videos. Slower computers require additional DVD playback hardware and must run faster than 100 MHz to handle the load. All systems must include controller software to read the DVD-Video navigation information on the disc. The computer's operating system may require new software drivers to read DVD-ROMs. And each hardware and software component must be licensed to decrypt copy-protected movies.

See Chap. 9, "DVD for Computers."

"DVD Is a Worldwide Standard"

If only it were so. DVD is still closely tied to the NTSC and PAL television formats. Most NTSC DVD players cannot play PAL discs, and some PAL DVD players will not play NTSC discs. Most computers will be able to play both. Even worse, DVD includes regional codes which can prevent a disc from being played on players sold in other countries.

See Chap. 5, "What's Wrong with DVD," for more explanation, and Chap. 4, "Technical Details," for the minutiae.

"DVD Can Hold 133 Minutes of Video"

The oft-quoted length of 133 minutes is apocryphal. It's simply a rough estimate based on an average 3.5-Mbps video track and three 384-kbps audio tracks. (Typical subtitles are negligibly small.) If there's only one audio track, the average playing time goes up to 159 minutes. The video rate is highly variable—a standard 4.4-gigabyte DVD can actually hold over 9 hours of MPEG-1 video and audio. Admittedly the quality is low, but the point is that the only constant is 4.4 gigabytes (and a maximum video data rate of 9.8 Mbps). All the rest is variable. Even 4.4 is constant only for a single-sided, single-layer discs. A dual-layer disc with an 8-gigabyte capacity holds over 4 hours of video, and a double-sided, dual-layer disc holds over 8 hours. Using MPEG-1, a double-sided, dual-layer disc can contain a mind-numbing 33 hours of video, which would also be butt-numbing if you tried to watch all of it in one sitting.

It's said that the figure of 133 minutes was originated by the press. The original SD proposal achieved approximately 142 minutes of playing time, but by adopting 8/16 modulation from the MMCD format they sacrificed 6.3 percent of disc capacity. Supposedly, a clever but clueless journalist applied 6.3 percent to 142 and the meaninglessly exact figure of 133 minutes has stuck ever since.

It's recommended that anyone talking or writing about DVD-Video make things easier for themselves and their audience by simply stating that a disc holds over two hours of video. If more precision is required, the nice round figure of two hours and fifteen minutes (135 minutes) is just as accurate.

It should be noted that all of this applies only to DVD-Video. A DVD-ROM can hold any sort of digitized video to be played back on an endless variety of computer hardware or software. If someone develops a revolutionary new holographic wavelet compression system, then perhaps a DVD-ROM could hold three hours of film-quality video. Or perhaps not. The point is that it's important to differentiate between the deliberate restrictions of DVD-Video and the wide-open digital expanse of DVD-ROM.

"Early Units Can't Play Dual-Layer or Double-Sided Discs"

Dual-layer compatibility is required by the DVD specification. All DVD-Video players and DVD-ROM drives, even the very first ones sold, can read dual-layer discs.

All players and drives will also read double-sided discs—as long as you flip them over. None of the first generation of DVD players and drives are able to read both sides of a disc, but such capabilities may eventually appear. The combination laserdisc/DVD players from Pioneer (DVL-90 and DVL-700) can play both sides of a laserdisc, but not both sides of a DVD.

"DVD-Video Runs at 4.692 Mbps"

This figure is about as meaningless as 133 minutes. The figure of 4.692 Mbps is supposedly the average data rate for a DVD-Video. Table 3.1 shows how it is calculated.

What if there is only one subpicture track? Then the pristine sum is off by an egregious 0.03 kbps (or so, since 10 kbps is only an average). And if there is only one audio track and one subpicture track, the so-called average data rate goes all the way up to 3.894, an error of more than two-tenths!

Sarcasm aside, what usually happens is that the content is compressed to fit the capacity of the disc. If the movie is 110 minutes long and has two audio tracks, the video bit budget can be set at a much higher 4.9 Mbps to achieve better quality. Or a two-and-a-half-hour movie might be compressed slightly more than usual if the disc producer determines that the video quality is acceptable.

The probable genesis for this number was that it was calculated from the required 133 minutes of length (which was calculated from the original 135) by figuring out what video data rate was left over after accounting for the audio. Then the subpicture tracks were thrown in to even things up.

"DVD Video Has a Burst Rate of 9.8 Mbps"

The maximum video data rate of DVD is limited to 9.8 Mbps by the DVD-Video specification. The maximum combined rate of video, audio,

TABLE 3.1

How to Create a Meaninglessly Exact Number

Bit rate	Count	Total (Mbps)
3.5 Mbps average video	1	3.500
384 kbps audio	3	1.152
10 kbps average subpicture	4	0.040
		4.692

and subtitles is limited to 10.08 Mbps. The average data rate is almost always lower, usually between 4 and 5 Mbps. Some people assume that DVD is therefore unable to sustain a continuous rate of 9.8 Mbps or higher. This is not the case. All DVD players and drives can maintain an internal data rate of at least 11.08 Mbps. DVD-Video players have a 1 Mbps overhead for navigation data. A movie compressed to a constant bit rate of 10.08 Mbps would play for 62 minutes.

Single-speed DVD-ROM drives can sustain a transfer rate of 11.08 Mbps, with burst rates as high as 100 Mbps or more, depending on the data buffer and the speed of the drive connection. DVD-ROM drives with higher spin rates are accordingly faster.

Bells and Whistles

The creators of DVD realized that in order to succeed, DVD had to be more than just a roomier CD or a more convenient laserdisc. Hollywood started the ball rolling by requesting a digital video consumer standard that would hold a full-length feature film, had better picture quality than existing high-end consumer video with widescreen aspect ratio support, contained multiple versions of a program and parental control, supported high-quality surround audio with soundtracks for at least three languages, and had built-in copy protection. Then the computer industry added its requirements of a single format for computers and video entertainment with a common, cross-platform file system, high performance for both movies and computer data, compatibility with CDs and CD-ROMs, compatible writeable and rewriteable versions, no mandatory caddy or cartridge, and high data capacity with reliability equal to or better than CD-ROM. Later on, Hollywood decided that it wanted a copy protection and a locking system to control release across different geographical regions of the world.

The designers threw in a few more features, such as multiple camera angles and graphic overlays for subtitling or karaoke, and DVD was born. Unlike CD, where the computer data format was cobbled on top of the digital music format, the digital data storage system of DVD-ROM is the base standard. DVD-Video is built on top of DVD-ROM using a specific set of file types and data types. A DVD-ROM can contain digital data in almost any conceivable format, as long as a computer or other device can make use of it. DVD-Video, on the other hand, requires simple and inexpensive video players, so its capabilities and features are strictly defined.

Over Two Hours of High-Quality Digital Video

Over 95 percent of Hollywood movies are shorter than 2 hours and 15 minutes, so 135 minutes was picked as the goal for a digital video disc. Uncompressed, this much video could take up 255 gigabytes.* DVD uses MPEG-2 compression to fit high-resolution digital video onto a single disc. The MPEG-2 encoding system compresses video in two ways: spatially, by reducing areas of repetitive detail and removing information that's not perceptible; and temporally, by reducing information that doesn't change over time. Reducing the video information by a factor of almost 50 allows it to fit in less than 5 gigabytes. Unfortunately, compression can introduce artifacts such as blockiness, fuzziness, and video noise. But the variable data rate of DVD allows extra data to be allocated for more complex scenes. Carefully encoded video is almost indistinguishable from the original studio master.

As mentioned earlier, the 135-minute length (or the absurdly precise 133-minute length) is a rough guideline based on estimates of average video compression and number of audio tracks. The length of a movie that can fit on a standard DVD depends entirely on how many audio tracks there are and how heavily the video is compressed. Many other factors come into play, such as the frame rate of the source video (24, 25, or 30 frames per second), the quality of the original (soft video is easier to compress than sharp film grain, and clean video is easier to compress than noisy or dirty video), and the complexity (slow, simple scenes are easier to compress than rapid motion, frequent changes, and intricate detail).

In any case, the average Hollywood movie easily fits on one side of a DVD. This overcomes one of the big objections to laserdisc, that you had to flip the disc over—or wait for the player to flip it over—after each hour of playing time.

Widescreen Movies

Television and movies shared the same rectangular shape until the early 1950s when movies began to get much wider. Television has stayed unchanged until recently. Widescreen TVs are slowly appearing, and DVD

---

*Digital studio masters generally use 4:2:2 10-bit sampling, which at 270 Mbps eats up over 32 megabytes every second.

is bound to cause a huge jump in demand. Movies can be stored on DVD in widescreen format to be shown on widescreen TVs close to the width envisioned by the director. DVD includes techniques to show these widescreen movies on regular televisions, and straddles old and new television, since HTDV is a widescreen format. These different aspect ratios are discussed in detail later in this chapter.

Multiple Surround Audio Tracks and Foreign Languages

The DVD-Video standard provides for up to eight sound tracks to support multiple languages and supplemental audio. Each of these audio tracks can include surround sound with 5.1 channels of discrete audio.* DVD surround-sound audio uses Dolby Digital (AC-3) encoding or MPEG-2 audio encoding. The 5.1-channel digital tracks can be downmixed with Dolby Surround encoding for compatibility with regular stereo systems and Dolby Pro Logic audio systems. There's also an option for better-than-CD-quality linear PCM audio. Almost all DVD players include digital audio connections for high-quality output.

The usefulness of multiple audio tracks was discovered when digital audio was added to laserdiscs, leaving the old analog tracks free. Visionary publishers such as Criterion used the analog tracks to include audio commentary from directors and actors, musical sound tracks without lyrics, foreign language audio dubs, and other fascinating or obscure audio tidbits.

Most DVD players allow the owner to select a preferred language so that the appropriate menus, language track, and subtitle track can be automatically selected when available. In many cases, the selection also determines the language used for the player's on-screen display.

Subtitles and Karaoke

Video can be supplemented with one of 32 *subpicture* tracks for subtitles, captions, and more. Unlike existing closed captioning or teletext systems, DVD subpictures are graphics that can fill the screen. The graphics can appear anywhere on the screen and can create text in any alphabet or

---

Discrete means that each channel is stored and reproduced separately rather than being mixed together (as in Dolby Surround) or simulated. The *.1* refers to a low-frequency effects (LFE) channel that connects to a subwoofer. MPEG-2 and SDDS audio allow 7.1 channels, but this feature is unlikely to be used for home products.

symbology. Subpictures can be karaoke song lyrics complete with bouncing balls, Monday Night Football—style motion diagrams, pointers and arrows, highlights and overlays, and much more. Subpictures are limited to a few colors at a time but the graphics and colors can change with every frame, which means subpictures can be used for simple animation and special effects.

For example, the transparency effect can be used to dim down areas of the picture and make other areas stand out. The same video can be shown with or without this highlighting effect. This can be used to great effect for educational video and documentaries. Other options include covering parts of a picture for quizzing, drawing circles and arrows, and even creating overlay graphics to simulate a camcorder, night-vision goggles, or a jet fighter cockpit.

Seamless Branching

A major drawback of almost every previous video format, including laserdiscs, Video CD, and even computer-based video such as QuickTime, is that any attempt to switch to another part of the video causes a break in play. DVD-Video finally achieves completely seamless branching. For example, a DVD can contain additional director's cut scenes for a movie but jump right over them without a break to recreate the original theatrical version.

This opens up endless possibilities for mix-and-match variety. At the start of a movie the viewer could choose to see the extended director's cut, alternate ending number four, and the punk rock club scene rather than the jazz club scene, and the player would jump around the disc indistinguishably stitching scenes together. It's even possible for a disc to tell the player to randomly select alternate sequences so the experience will be different every time.

Of course, this requires significant additional work by the director or producer. Many mass-market releases will probably skip this option at first, leaving it to small, independent producers with more creative energy to expend.

Different Camera Angles

A by-product of seamless branching is a feature for viewing scenes from different angles. A movie could be filmed with multiple cameras so the viewer can switch at will between up to nine different viewpoints. A classic sports event on DVD could let the viewer have complete control over instant replays.

This feature presents a major paradigm shift which could be as significant as the way sound changed motion pictures. The storytelling opportunities are fascinating to contemplate. Imagine a movie about a love triangle, which can be watched from the point of view of each main character; a murder mystery with multiple solutions; a scene which can be played at different times of day, different seasons, or different points in time. Music videos can include shots of each performer, allowing viewers to focus on their current favorites or to pick up instrumental techniques. Classic sports videos can be designed so that armchair quarterbacks have complete control over camera angles and instant replay shots. Exercise videos might allow viewers to choose their preferred viewpoints. Instructional videos can provide close-ups, detail shots, and picture insets containing supplemental information. The options are endlessly diverse and merely require new tools and new approaches to filmmaking and video production.

The disadvantage of this feature is that each camera angle requires that additional footage be created and stored on the disc. A program with three camera angles available the entire time can only be one-third as long.

Parental Lock

Parents can lock a movie rating into their DVD player with a password so that it won't play objectionable pieces or even entire discs. Studios can release multiple-ratings versions of a movie on a single disc. The seamless branching feature will automatically select the appropriately rated versions of scenes or skip over scenes as necessary, with no visible pause or break. However, given the additional work required to create such discs, there may not be much enthusiasm or return on investment for producing them.

Menus

In order to provide access to some of these advanced features, the DVD-Video standard includes on-screen menus. The video can stop at any point for interaction with the viewer, or there can be selectable hot spots on live video. Menus are used to select from multiple programs, choose different versions of program content, navigate through multilevel or interactive programs, activate features of the player or the current disc, and more.

For example, a movie disc may have a main menu from which you can choose to watch the movie, view supplemental information, or watch a "making of" featurette. Selecting the movie option may bring up another menu from which you can choose to hear the regular sound track, foreign language sound track, or director's commentary. Selecting the supplemental information option from the main menu may bring up another menu with options such as production stills, script pages, storyboards, and outtakes.

Interactivity

In addition to menus, DVD-Video can be even more interactive when the creator of the program takes advantage of the rudimentary control language. DVD-Video can be programmed for simple games, quizzes, branching adventures, and so on. DVD brings a new level of personal control to video programs. While it's not apparent just how much control the average couch potato is interested in, there is a certain appeal to directing the path and form of a presentation. "Choose your own ending" books will graduate to video and an entire new genre of nonlinear cinema could be embraced by the creative community.

For example, a music video disc could provide an editing environment where the viewers can choose music, scenes, and so on to create their own custom version. An instructional video can include comprehension check questions. If the wrong answer is chosen, a special remedial segment can be played to further explain the topic.

Customization

As mentioned, DVD players can be customized with a parental lock. Many other features are permanently selectable. Indicating a preferred language lets the DVD player automatically select the appropriate movie scenes, language soundtrack, subtitle track, and even menus in the proper language. Preferred aspect ratio—widescreen, letterbox, or pan & scan—can also be set.

If you were studying French, for example, you could set your preferences to watch movies with French dialog and English subtitles (assuming that the additional soundtrack and subtitle track have been incorporated on the disc).

Instant Access

Consumer surveys indicate that one of the most appealing features of DVD is that you never have to rewind it. Or fast forward it. It's truly amazing how important time and convenience can be to consumers, but consider our penchant for microwave ovens, electric pencil sharpeners, and escalators. A DVD player can obligingly jump to any part of a disc—program, chapter, or time position—in less than a few seconds.

Special Effects Playback

In addition to near-instantaneous search, most DVD players include features such as perfect freeze-frame, frame-by-frame advance, slow motion, double speed, and high-speed scan. Most DVD players will scan backward at high speed, but because of the nature of MPEG-2 video compression most can't play at normal speed in reverse or step a frame at a time in reverse. This is only possible on advanced players which have more sophisticated video processors.

Durability

Unlike tape, DVDs are impervious to magnetic fields. A DVD left on a speaker or placed too near a motor will be unharmed. Discs are also much less sensitive to extremes of heat and cold. Since they are read by a laser which never touches the surface, the discs will not wear out; even your favorite one that you play six times a week or the kids' favorite one that they play six times a day. DVDs are susceptible to scratching but their sophisticated error correction technology can recover from any minor damage. Most people have few problems with scratched CDs, and DVDs are even more reliable.

Programmability

Some DVD players are viewer-programmable, similar to CD players. Chapters can be selected for playback in specified order. So, if a certain part of a horror movie is too much for a squeamish viewer, the player might be programmed to skip it. Or, you can rearrange the sequence of tracks in a music video to your own taste. You can even drive your friends crazy by having the catchiest song reappear at strategically annoying points.

Availability of Features

Obviously, most of DVD's features require extra work by the producer of the disc. Adding additional scenes, multiple language tracks, subtitles, ratings information, menus, branch points, and more, demands additional effort and expense. The extent to which movie producers support these features will depend largely on how much customers demand them and how much they are willing to pay for them. In the laserdisc market, a thriving special edition industry has emerged, titillating videophiles with restored footage, outtakes, director's commentaries, production photos, and "making of" documentaries. These special editions require hundreds of hours of extra work by dedicated or obsessed professionals, and they generally sell for about $120—three times the cost of the regular edition. It's expected that similar special edition DVDs will be produced, but it's too early to tell how much of this will trickle down to regular releases and what effect on prices it will have.

Beyond DVD-Video Features

DVD discs can contain much more than the limited selection supported by home DVD-Video players. Computer software such as screen savers or pictures can be added. Once the DVD format becomes supported by home video game systems and Internet Web/TV boxes, a single disc could contain a movie; the video game version; computerized text of the book complete with pictures, annotation, and hyperlinks; and even a link to an Internet Web site with more information along with an on-line merchandise order form. Multipurpose players will appear, such as a video game console that's also a DVD-Video player or a combination of digital cable set-top box, Internet box, and video player.

Bits and Bytes and Bears

This section provides a brief overview of a few selected aspects of DVD physical format and data format.

Pits and Error Correction

Data is stored on optical discs in the form of microscopic pits (see Fig. 3.1). The discs are stamped in a molding machine from molten polycarbonate, then coated with a reflective layer. As the disc spins, the pits pass under a laser beam and are detected according to the change in intensity of the beam. These changes happen very fast (over 300,000 times per second) and create a stream of off/on bits: a digital signal. Half of the information in this signal is used to arrange (*modulate*) the data in sequences and patterns designed to be accurately readable as a string of pulses. About 13 percent of the remaining digital signal is extra information for correcting errors. Errors can occur for many reasons such as imperfections on the disc, dust, scratches, a dirty lens, and so on. A human hair can be as wide as 150 pits, so even a speck of dust or a minute air bubble can cover a large number of pits. However, the laser beam focuses past the surface of the disc, so the spot size at the surface is much larger and is hardly affected by anything smaller than a few millimeters. This is similar to the way dust on a camera lens is not visible in the photographs because the dust is out of focus. As the data is read from the disc, the error correction information is separated out and checked against the remaining information. If it doesn't match, the error correction codes are used to try to correct the error.

The error correction process is like a number square, where you add up columns and rows of numbers (see Fig. 3.2). You could play a game with these squares where a friend randomly changes a number and challenges you to find and correct it. If the friend gives you the sums along with the numbers, you can add up the rows and columns and compare your totals against the originals. If they don't match, then you know that something's wrong—either a number has been changed or the sum has been changed.* If a number has been changed, then a corresponding sum in

---

*It's possible for more than one number to be changed in such a way that the sum still comes out correct. However, the DVD encoding format makes this an extremely rare occurrence.

Figure 3.1
DVD pits.

Figure 3.2
Number squares.

3	5	8
4	1	3
7	7	2

original data

3	5	8	16
4	1	3	8
7	7	2	16
14	13	13	40

sums calculated

3	5	8	16
1	1	3	8
7	7	2	16
14	13	13	40

4 changed to 1,
data and sums
transmitted

3	5	8	16	16
1	1	3	8	5
7	7	2	16	16
14	13	13	40	37
11	13	13	37	

new sums calculated,
mismatches found

3	5	8
4	1	3
7	7	2

corrected by
adding difference
(14 - 11 or 8 - 5)

the other direction will also be wrong. The intersection of the incorrect row and incorrect column pinpoints the guilty number, and in fact, by knowing what the sums are supposed to be, you can calculate what the original number was. The error correction scheme used by DVD is a bit more complicated than this, but operates on the same general principle.

It's always possible that so much of the data is corrupted that error correction fails. In this case, the player must try reading that section of the disc over again. In the very worst cases, such as an extremely damaged disc, the player will be unable to correctly read the data after multiple attempts. At this point, a movie player will continue on to the next section of the disc, causing a brief glitch in the picture. A DVD-ROM drive, on the other hand, can't do this. Computers will not tolerate missing or incorrect data, so the DVD-ROM drive must signal the computer that an error has occurred so that the computer can request that the drive either try again or give up.

Layers

One of the clever innovations of DVD is the use of layers to increase storage capacity. The laser that reads the disc can be focused at two different levels and actually looks through the top layer to read the layer beneath. The top layer is coated with a semireflective material which allows the laser to read through it when focused on the bottom layer. When the player reads a disc, it starts at the inside edge and moves toward the outer edge, following a spiral path. If unwound, this path would stretch 11.8 kilometers (7.3 miles), three times around the Indianapolis 500 Speedway. When the laser reaches the end of the first layer, it quickly refocuses onto the second layer and starts reading in the opposite direction—from the outer edge toward the inner. Refocusing can happen in less than a few hundred milliseconds, so quickly that there is no discernible break in the video or data. Since the disc feeds data into a buffer faster than the player displays it, there is time for the laser pickup to move or refocus.

The DVD standard does not actually require compatibility with existing CDs. However, manufacturers recognize the vital importance of backward-compatibility. If the hardware were unable to read CDs, DVD wouldn't have a snowball's chance in Hollywood of surviving. The difficult part is that the pits on a CD are at a different level than that of a DVD (see Fig. 3.3). In essence, a DVD player must be able to focus a laser at three different distances. There are various solutions to this problem, including using lenses that switch in and out and holographic lenses that are actually focused at more than one distance simultaneously. An additional difficulty is that CD-R discs don't properly reflect the 635- to 650-nm wavelength laser required for DVD, so DVD-ROM drives intended to read recordable CDs must include a second 780-nm laser or other trick.

The remaining task of being CD-compatible merely requires another chip or two for reading CD-format data. However, the CD family is quite large and includes some odd characters, not all of which fit well with DVD. The prominent members of the CD family are audio CD, Enhanced CD (or CD Plus), CD-ROM, CD-R, CD-RW, CD-i, Photo CD, CDV, and Video CD. It would be technically possible to support all of these, but most of them require specialized hardware. Therefore, most manufacturers choose to support only the most common or easy-to-support versions. Some, such as Enhanced CD and Video CD, are easy to support with existing hardware. Others, such as CD-i and Photo CD, require additional hardware and interface, so they are not commonly supported. But since the data on a CD can be read by any DVD system, conceivably any CD format

Figure 3.3
DVD layers.

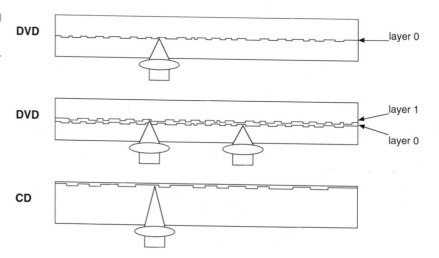

could be supported. DVD-ROM drives will support more CD formats than DVD-Video players, partly because some are designed for computer applications, and partly because specialized CD systems can be simulated with computer software.

See Chap. 6, "DVD Comparison," for details of the different CD formats and the compatibility of DVD-Video and DVD-ROM with each.

Variations of DVD

Believe it or not, there are about 20 variations of DVD with even more to come. DVDs come in numerous physical incarnations as well as data format variations (see Table 3.2).

There are two sizes of discs: 12 cm (4.7 inches) and 8 cm (3.1 inches), both 1.2 mm thick. These are the same diameters and thickness as CD, but

TABLE 3.2

Variations of DVD

Physical format			Video	Audio	Data	Game
				Application		
Read-only	12 cm	SS/SL*	C[†]	E[‡]	C	F[§]
		SS/DL	C	E	C	F
		DS/SL	C	E	C	F
		DS/DL	C	E	C	F
	8 cm	SS/SL	C	E	C	F
		SS/DL	C	E	C	F
		DS/SL	C	E	C	F
		DS/DL	C	E	C	F
Write-once	12 cm	SS/SL	E	E	C	
		DS/SL	E	E	C	
	8 cm	SS/SL	E	E	C	
		DS/SL	E	E	C	
Rewritable	12 cm	SS/SL	E	E	C	
		DS/SL	E	E	C	
	8 cm	SS/SL	E	E	F	
		DS/SL	E	E	F	

*SS = single side; DS = double side; SL = single layer; DL = dual layer.
[†]C = currently defined (as of July 1997).
[‡]E = expected to be defined.
[§]F = future possibility.

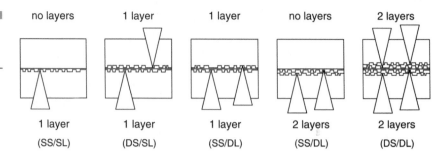

Figure 3.4
Configurations of
layers and sides.

DVDs are made of two 0.6-mm substrates glued together. This makes them more rigid than CDs so they spin with less wobble and can be tracked more reliably by the laser. A DVD can be single-sided or double-sided. A single-sided disc is a stamped substrate bonded to a blank substrate. A double-sided disc is two stamped substrates bonded back to back. To complicate matters, each side can have one or two layers of data. This is part of what gives DVD its enormous storage capacity. A double-sided, dual-layer disc has data stored on four separate planes.

There are five common configurations of layers and substrates:[*]

- Single-layer substrate bonded to dummy substrate (1 side, 1 layer)
- Two single-layer substrates bonded together (2 sides, 1 layer each)
- Two single-layer substrates with transparent bond (1 side, 2 layers)
- Dual-layer substrate bonded to dummy substrate (1 side, 2 layers)
- Two dual-layer substrates bonded together (2 sides, 2 layers each)

See Fig. 3.4. Also see Chap. 4 for more details on dual-layer construction.

A single-sided, single-layer DVD holds 4.38 gigabytes of data, 7 times more than a CD-ROM, which holds over 650 megabytes.[†] A double-sided, dual-layer DVD holds 15.9 gigabytes, which is 25 times what a CD-ROM holds. See Table 3.3.

NOTE *It takes about 2 gigabytes to store 1 hour of average MPEG-2 video.*

---

[*]It's possible to create a disc with one layer on one side and two layers on the other, but this doesn't seem to be a popular configuration.

[†]The loose tolerance of the CD standard allows tracks to be placed more tightly together, so that CDs can actually hold 750 megabytes or more.

TABLE 3.3

Capacities of DVD

Type	Width (cm)	Number of sides	Number of layers/side	Data* (gigabytes)	Approximate playing time† (hours)
CD-ROM	12	1	1	0.64 (0.68)	¼‡
DVD-5	12	1	1	4.38 (4.70)	2¼
DVD-9	12	1	2	7.95 (8.54)	4
DVD-10	12	2	1	8.75 (9.40)	4½
DVD-18	12	2	2	15.90 (17.08)	8
	8	1	1	1.36 (1.46)	¾
	8	1	2	2.48 (2.66)	1¼
	8	2	1	2.72 (2.92)	1½
	8	2	2	4.95 (5.32)	2½

*Data capacities are shown as reference values in gigabytes, followed by billions of bytes. Actual capacities can be slightly larger if the track pitch is reduced.

†Assuming an average aggregate data rate near 4.7 Mbps. Actual playing times can be much longer or shorter. (See Tables A.2 and A.4.)

‡Assuming that the data from the CD is transferred at average video data rate, about 4 times faster than a single-speed CD-ROM drive.

Pegs and Holes: Understanding Aspect Ratios

The standard television picture is restricted to a specific shape: a third again wider than it is high. This *aspect ratio* is designated as 4:3, or 4 units wide by 3 units high, also expressed as 1.33.* This rectangular shape is a fundamental part of the NTSC and PAL television systems—it cannot be changed without redefining the standards.†

*There's no special meaning to the numbers 4 and 3. They are simply the smallest whole numbers that can be used to represent the ratio of width to height. An aspect ratio of 12:9 is the same as 4:3. This can also be normalized to a height of 1, but the width becomes the repeating fraction 1.33333..., which is why the more accurate 4:3 notation is generally used. But for comparison purposes, it's useful to use the normalized form of 1.33:1 or 1.33 for short.

†The next generation of television—known as HDTV, ATV, DTV, and so on—has a 16:9 picture that's much wider than current television. But the new format is incompatible with existing equipment.

The problem is that movies are wider than television screens. Most movies are 1.85 (about 5.5:3). Extrawide movies in Panavision or Cinemascope format are around 2.35 (about 7:3). So, the trick is to somehow fit a wide movie shape into a not-so-wide television shape. (See Fig. 3.5.)

Fitting a movie into television is like the old conundrum of putting a square peg in a round hole, but in this case it's a rectangular peg. Consider a peg that's twice as wide as a square hole (Fig. 3.6). There are essentially three ways to get the peg in the hole:

1. Shrink the peg to half its original size or make the hole twice as big (Fig. 3.7)

Figure 3.5
TV shape versus movie shapes.

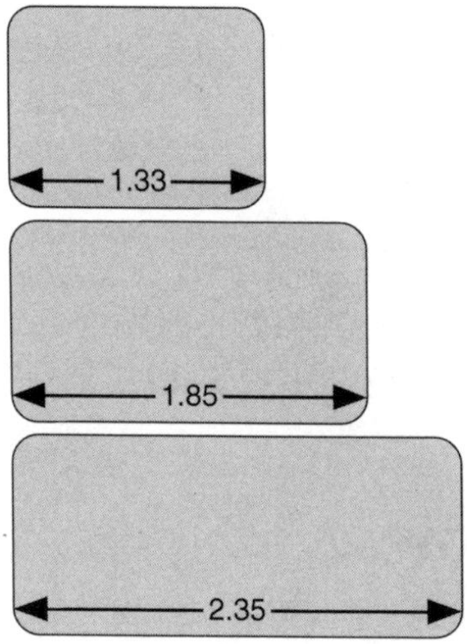

Figure 3.6
Peg and hole.

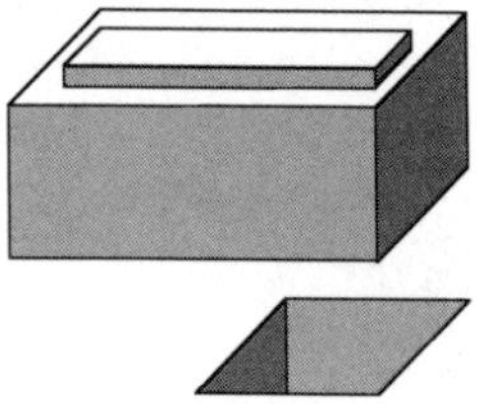

Figure 3.7
Shrink the peg.

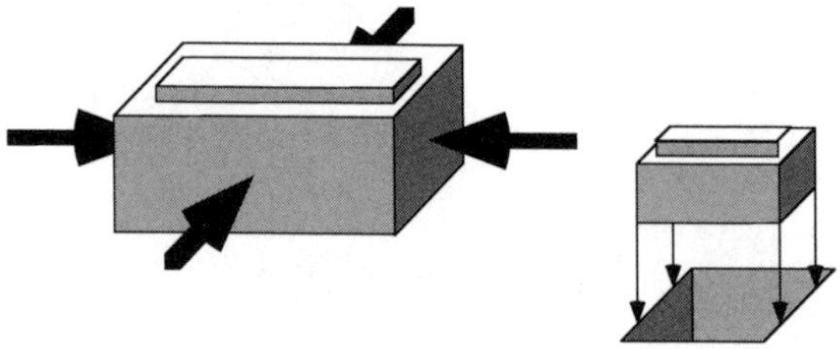

2. Slice off part of the peg (Fig. 3.8)

3. Squeeze the sides of the peg until it's the same shape as the hole (Fig. 3.9)

Now, think of the peg as a movie and the hole as a TV. The first two peg-and-hole solutions are commonly used to show movies on television. Quite often you'll see horizontal black bars at the top and bottom of the picture. This means that the width of the movie shape has been matched to the width of the TV shape, leaving a gap at the top and the bottom. This is called *letterboxing*. It doesn't refer to postal pugilism, but rather the process of putting the movie in a black box with a hole the shape of a standard paper envelope. The black bars are called *mattes*.

At other times, you might see the words "This presentation has been formatted for television" at the beginning of a movie. This indicates that a *pan & scan* process has been used, where a TV-shaped window over the film image is moved from side to side, or up and down, or zoomed in and out. (See Figs. 3.10 and 3.11.) It's more complicated than just chopping off a little from each side: sometimes the important part of the picture is all on one side or mostly on the other side, sometimes there is more picture on the film above or below what is shown in the theater, so the artist who transfers the movie to video must determine for every scene how much of each side should be chopped off or how much additional picture from above or below should be included in order to preserve the action and story line. For the past 20 years or so, most films have been shot with a *soft matte*. The cinematographer has two rectangles in the viewfinder, one for

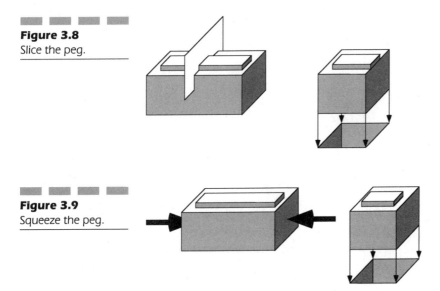

Figure 3.8
Slice the peg.

Figure 3.9
Squeeze the peg.

Figure 3.10
Pan & scan transfer.

← 1.33

← 1.85

← (1.78)

1.85 (or wider) and one for 4:3 (see Fig. 3.10). He or she composes the shots to look good in the 1.85 rectangle while making sure that no crew, equipment, or raw stage edges are visible above or below in the 4:3 area. For presentation in the theater, a *theatrical matte* is used to mask off the top and bottom, either when the film is printed or with an aperture plate on the projector. When the movie is transferred to video for 4:3 presentation, the full frame is available for the pan & scan (& zoom) process.* In many cases, the director of photography or even the director approves the transfer to ensure that the intention and integrity of the original filming is maintained. Full control over how the picture is reframed is very important. For example, when the mattes are removed, close-up shots become medium shots, and the frame might need to be zoomed in to recreate the intimacy of the original shot. In a sense, the film is being composed anew for the new aspect. The pan & scan process has the disadvantage of losing some of the original picture, but is able to make the most of the 4:3 television screen and is able to enlarge the picture to compensate for the smaller size and lower resolution as compared to a theater screen.

The third peg-and-hole solution has been used for years to fit widescreen movies onto standard 35mm film. As filmmakers tried to enhance the theater experience with ever wider screens, they needed some way to

---

*Contrast this to *hard matte* filming, where the top and bottom are physically—and permanently—blacked out to create a wide aspect ratio. Movies filmed with anamorphic lenses also have a permanently wide aspect ratio, with no extra picture at the top or bottom.

Figure 3.11
Soft-matte filming.

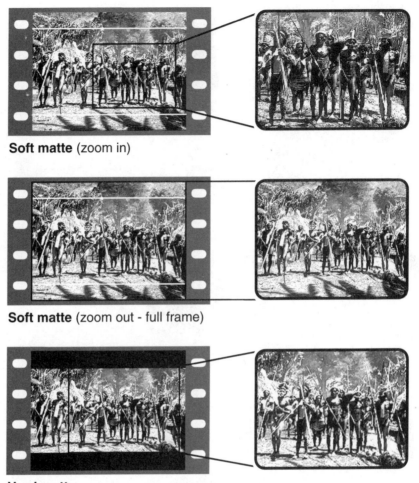

Soft matte (zoom in)

Soft matte (zoom out - full frame)

Hard matte

get the image on the film without requiring new wider film and new projectors in every theater. They came up with the *anamorphic* process, where the camera is fitted with an anamorphic lens that squeezes the picture horizontally, changing its shape so it fits in a standard film frame. The projector is fitted with a lens that unsqueezes the image back to its original width when it's projected. (See Fig. 3.12.) It's as if the peg were accordion-shaped so that it can be squeezed into the square hole and then pop back into shape after it is removed. You may have seen this distortion effect at the end of a Western movie where John Wayne suddenly becomes tall and skinny so that the credits will fit between the edges of the screen.

Figure 3.12
The anamorphic
process.

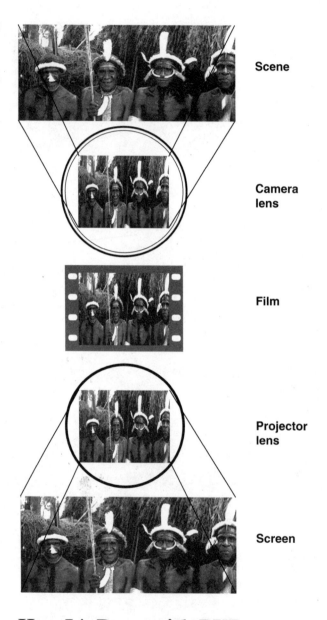

Scene

Camera
lens

Film

Projector
lens

Screen

How It's Done with DVD

DVD mixes and matches all of the preceding techniques. Three standard methods are targeted for 4:3 displays, while a newer format is intended for widescreen displays. The four options provided by DVD are as follows.

1. *Full frame ("the peg fits the hole").* Most material shot for television is already in 4:3 format.

2. *Pan & scan ("chop off the sides").* This is the traditional "fill the frame" way of showing video on a standard TV. When the film is converted to video, the transfer artist (also called *colorist* or *telecine artist*) uses a variety of techniques to make the picture fill the screen and best follow the story, including zooming in and out and scanning up, down, left, and right. The zoom technique is often used with soft-matte movies to preserve the nuances of close-ups.

3. *Letterbox ("shrink and matte").* This is the alternate way of showing widescreen video on a standard TV, preferred by videophiles and popularized by laserdiscs. The original theatrical image is boxed into the 4:3 frame by adding mattes to the top and bottom of the picture.

4. *Wide-screen ("accordion squeeze").* One of the advantages of DVD-Video for home theater systems is widescreen support. DVD supports wide images by using a 16:9 (1.78) aspect ratio which is anamorphically squeezed into a 4:3 TV shape before being stored on the disc. (The 4:3 ratio can be expressed as 12:9, so in order to get from 16:9 to 12:9, the width needs to be reduced by 25 percent, from 16 down to 12.) New widescreen televisions have a wider scanning pattern to display the full 16:9 shape. DVD players can also display widescreen video on a standard 4:3 TV.* There are three ways to do this, including two options similar to those performed during video transfer, but in this case they are performed by the player.

   - *Automatic letterbox.* All DVD players can add letterbox mattes when displaying widescreen video on a 4:3 display. The player actually squeezes the image vertically by 25 percent (the same amount it was squeezed horizontally in the anamorphic process) so that its proper proportions are restored.

   - *Automatic pan & scan.* *Center of interest* information can be included with the widescreen video to tell the player which part to extract. The player chops off the indicated amount from each side, then unsqueezes the remaining picture to create a 4:3 image for the TV.

   - *Lie to the player.* A DVD player has no way to know what kind of TV you have, so you can tell it to send a 16:9 picture to a 4:3 TV. You will see the direct anamorphic picture, making Hardy look like Laurel. You're not supposed to do this, but just as there are no "mattress tag police" there are no "aspect ratio police" who will come and take your player away.

---

*Anamorphic video is not unique to DVD. There are a few anamorphic laserdiscs and even rare anamorphic videotapes. The problem is that they can only be viewed properly on a widescreen TV. Unlike DVD players, standard laserdisc players and VCRs are unable to adapt anamorphic video for standard TVs.

Options 1, 2, and 3 are illustrated in Fig. 3.13. Option 4 is illustrated in Fig. 3.14.

HOW IT WASN'T DONE WITH DVD. There are other possible solutions for dealing with widescreen video that could have been used. DVD could have stored the full-width, undistorted image, but this would have

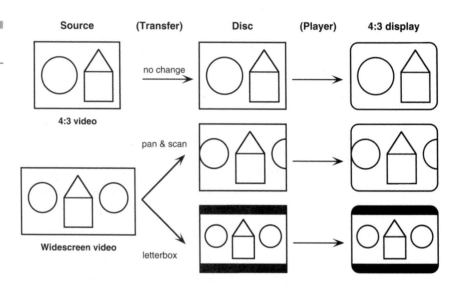

Figure 3.13
Standard 4:3 display.

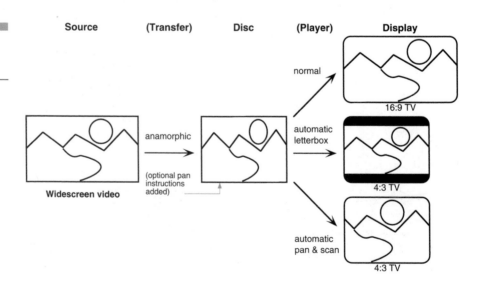

Figure 3.14
Wide-screen
16:9 display

used up more storage space* and would have required reducing the amount of video on a disc or reducing the video quality.

Another option would have been to always letterbox the video before storing it on DVD. The problem with this approach is that vertical information would have been lost and storage space that could have held picture information would have been used to hold black mattes instead.

Variable anamorphic squeeze could also have been used. The wider the video, the more it would be squeezed. The advantage to this approach is that every pixel of video storage space would be used to hold video. The problem is that more expensive circuitry would be required to handle multiple squeeze ratios.

The designers of DVD chose the reasonable compromise of using the anamorphic technique to fit the most amount of information into the standard television image space, and they settled on the standard 16:9 wide aspect ratio (see the "Why 16:9?" section which follows). Having the DVD player shrink the anamorphic picture vertically for letterbox display on a 4:3 TV gives the same result (and the same information loss) as shrinking and letterboxing the picture before storing it on the disc, yet preserves more picture information for widescreen TVs.

Widescreen TVs

Widescreen TVs are quite flexible in the way they deal with different input formats. They can display 4:3 video with black bars on the side—a kind of sideways letterbox—and they also have display modes which enlarge the video to fill the entire screen.

Wide mode stretches the picture horizontally (see Fig. 3.15). This is sometimes called *full* mode. This is the proper mode to use with anamorphic video, but it makes everything look short and fat when applied to 4:3 video. Some widescreen TVs have a *parabolic* or *panorama* version of wide mode which uses nonlinear distortion to stretch the sides more and the center less, thus minimizing the apparent distortion. This mode should not be used with anamorphic DVD output or very strange fun-house mirror effects will occur.

Expand mode proportionally enlarges the picture to fill the width of the screen, thus losing the top and bottom (see Fig. 3.16). This is sometimes

---

*Thirty-three percent more, to be exact, since 1.78 is 33 percent larger than 1.33. Even more data would be needed to store movies in their original aspect ratio. Most movies have an aspect ratio of 1.85, which would require 39 percent more data. Panavision and Cinemascope movies with a 2.35 ratio would require 76 percent more data.

Figure 3.15
Wide (full) mode
on a widescreen TV.

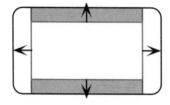

Figure 3.16
Expand (theater)
mode on a
widescreen TV.

called *theater* mode. Expand mode is for use with letterboxed video, since it effectively removes the mattes. If used with standard 4:3 picture, this mode causes a Henry VIII "off with their heads" effect.

NOTE *Expand mode should only be used when the video is permanently letterboxed, as on a laserdisc, a letterbox-only DVD, or other nonanamorphic source. Letting the player letterbox a widescreen DVD for display on a widescreen TV in expand mode gives you a much worse picture than using direct anamorphic output to the widescreen TV in wide mode. What happens is that information is lost when the picture is squeezed vertically by the player for letterboxing. This loss is then amplified when the picture is expanded by the TV. (See Fig. 3.20d.)*

Most widescreen TVs also have other display modes which are variations of the three basic modes.

When DVD contains widescreen video, the different output modes of the player can be combined with different widescreen TV display modes to create a confusing array of options. Figures 3.17 through 3.20 show how the different DVD output modes look on a regular TV and on a widescreen TV. Note that there is one OK way to view widescreen video on a regular TV (Fig. 3.20), but that a very large TV or a widescreen TV is required to do it justice. Also note that there is only one good way to view widescreen video on a widescreen TV, and that is with widescreen (anamorphic) output to wide mode (Fig. 3.18c).

Clearly, it's very easy to display the wrong picture in the wrong way. In some cases, the equipment is smart enough to help out. The player can send a special signal embedded in the video blanking area or via the s-video connector to the widescreen TV, but everything must be set up properly:

Figure 3.17
Standard 4:3 video
to 4:3 TV and
widescreen TV.

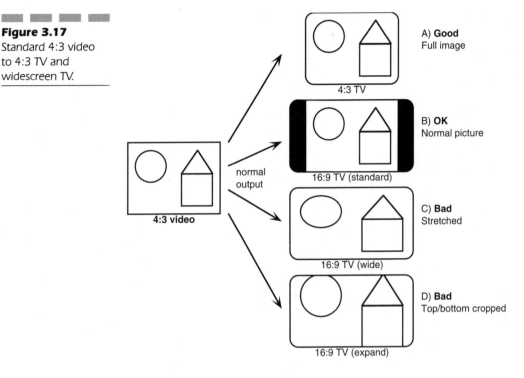

A) **Good**
Full image

4:3 TV

B) **OK**
Normal picture

16:9 TV (standard)

C) **Bad**
Stretched

16:9 TV (wide)

D) **Bad**
Top/bottom cropped

16:9 TV (expand)

4:3 video

normal output

Figure 3.18
Widescreen 16:9
video in normal
mode to 4:3 TV
and widescreen TV.

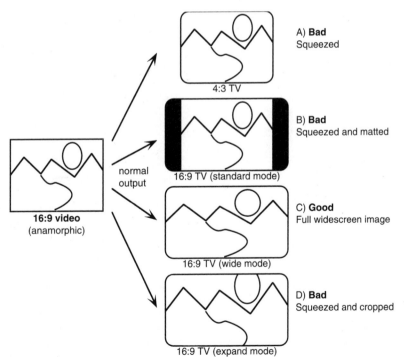

A) **Bad**
Squeezed

4:3 TV

B) **Bad**
Squeezed and matted

16:9 TV (standard mode)

C) **Good**
Full widescreen image

16:9 TV (wide mode)

D) **Bad**
Squeezed and cropped

16:9 TV (expand mode)

16:9 video
(anamorphic)

normal output

Figure 3.19
Widescreen 16:9
video in pan & scan
mode to 4:3 TV and
widescreen TV.

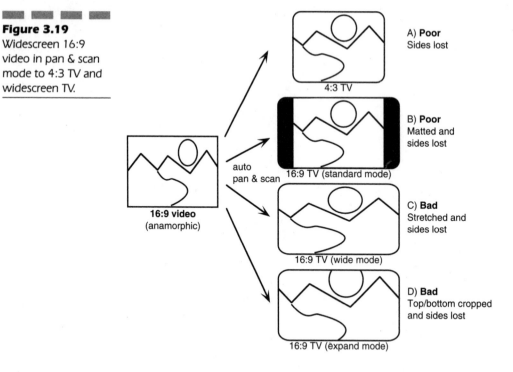

A) **Poor**
Sides lost

4:3 TV

B) **Poor**
Matted and
sides lost

16:9 TV (standard mode)

C) **Bad**
Stretched and
sides lost

16:9 TV (wide mode)

D) **Bad**
Top/bottom cropped
and sides lost

16:9 TV (expand mode)

16:9 video
(anamorphic)

auto
pan & scan

Figure 3.20
Widescreen 16:9
video in letterbox
mode to 4:3 TV and
widescreen TV.

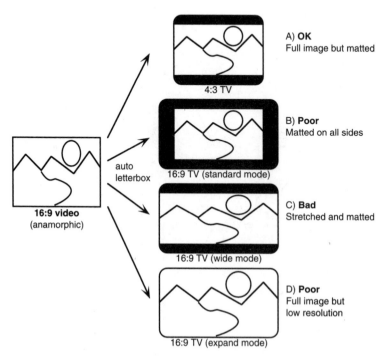

A) **OK**
Full image but matted

4:3 TV

B) **Poor**
Matted on all sides

16:9 TV (standard mode)

C) **Bad**
Stretched and matted

16:9 TV (wide mode)

D) **Poor**
Full image but
low resolution

16:9 TV (expand mode)

16:9 video
(anamorphic)

auto
letterbox

1. Connect the DVD player to the widescreen TV with an s-video cable.
2. Set the widescreen TV to s-video in (using the remote control of the front-panel input selector).
3. Set the TV to *automatic* or *normal* mode.
4. Set the DVD player to 16:9 output mode (using the on-screen setup feature with the remote control or with a switch on the back of the player).

If everything is working right, and the TV is equipped to recognize widescreen signaling, it will automatically switch modes to match the format of the video.

Aspect Ratios Revisited

To review, video comes out of a DVD-Video player in basically four ways:

1. Full frame (4:3 original)
2. Pan & scan (widescreen original)
3. Letterbox (widescreen original)
4. Anamorphic (widescreen original)

All four can be displayed on any TV, but the fourth is specifically intended for widescreen TVs. This may seem straightforward, but it gets much more complicated. The problem is that very few movies are in 16:9 (1.78) format. The previous discussions dealt with 16:9 widescreen in a general case. But until 16:9 cameras become more wide-spread, there will be very little video created in 16:9 format.

Most movies are usually 1.85 or wider, although European movies are often 1.66. DVD only supports aspect ratios of 4:3 and 16:9 because those are the two most common television shapes. Movies that are a different shape must be made to fit, which brings us back to pegs and holes. In this case, the hole is DVD's 16:9 shape (which is either shown in full on a widescreen TV or formatted to letterbox or pan & scan for a regular TV). There are essentially four ways to fit a 1.85 or wider movie peg into a 1.78 hole.

1. *Letterbox to 16:9.* When the movie is transferred from film, black mattes are added to box it into the 16:9 shape. These mattes become a permanent part of the picture. The position and thickness of the mattes depend on the shape of the original:
   a. For a 1.85 movie, the mattes are very small. On a widescreen TV or in automatic pan & scan on a regular TV (where the player is

extracting a vertical slice from the letterboxed picture), the mattes are hidden in the *overscan* area.* On a standard TV in automatic letterbox mode (where the player is letterboxing an already letter-boxed picture), the thin permanent mattes merge imperceptibly with the thick player-generated mattes.

b. For a 2.35 movie, the permanent mattes are much thicker. In this case, the picture has visible mattes no matter how it is displayed. When the picture is letterboxed by the player, the permanent mattes merge with the player-generated mattes to form extra-thick mattes on the television. These mattes are the same size as if the movie had been originally letterboxed for 4:3 display (as with a laserdisc).

c. For a 1.66 movie, thin mattes are placed on the sides instead of at the top and bottom and will generally be hidden in the overscan area.

2. *Crop to 16:9.* For 1.85 movies, slicing 2 percent from each side is suffi-cient and probably won't be noticeable. The same applies to 1.66 movies, except that about 3 percent is sliced off the top and off the bottom. But to fit a 2.35 movie requires slicing 12 percent from each side. This procrustean approach throws away a quarter of the picture and is not a likely to be a popular solution.

3. *Pan & scan to 16:9.* The standard pan & scan technique can be used with a 16:9 window (as opposed to a 4:3 window) when transferring from film to DVD. For 1.85 movies, the result is essentially the same as cropping and is hardly worth the extra work. For wider movies, pan & scan is more useful, but the original aspect ratio is lost, which goes against the spirit of a widescreen format. When going to the trouble of supporting DVD's widescreen format, it seems silly to pan & scan inside it, but if the option is there, someone is bound to use it.

4. *Open the soft matte to 16:9.* When going from 1.85 to 16:9, a small amount of picture from the top and bottom of the soft matte area can be included. This sticks close to the original aspect ratio without requiring a matte, and the extra picture will be hidden in the over-scan area on a widescreen TV or when panned & scanned by the DVD player. Even wider movies are usually shot full frame, so the soft matte area can be included in the transfer. (See Fig. 3.21.)

Overscan refers to covering the edges of the picture with a mask around the screen. Overscan was originally implemented to hide distortion at the edges. Television technology has improved to the point where overscan isn't usually necessary, but it is still used. Most tele-visions have an overscan of about 4 to 5 percent. Anyone producing video intended for tele-vision display must be mindful of overscan, making sure that nothing important is at the edge of the picture. It should be noted that when DVD-Video is displayed on a computer there is usually no overscan and the entire picture is visible.

Figure 3.21
Opening the matte
for 1.85 to 16:9.

No standard has yet emerged for converting films to widescreen DVD, but methods 1 and 4 are the most likely candidates. Many directors are opposed for artistic reasons to the pan & scan process, especially if done mechanically by the player. They may choose to make their movies on DVD viewable only in widescreen or letterbox format. Or they may choose to do a full-frame transfer in 4:3 format. This brings up the issue of different transfers, which will be discussed after a brief digression into why 16:9 is the widescreen aspect ratio of choice.

WHY 16:9? The 16:9 ratio has become the standard for widescreen. Most widescreen televisions are this shape, it's the aspect ratio used by almost all high-definition television standards, and it's the widescreen aspect ratio used by DVD. You may be wondering why this ratio was chosen, since it does not match television, movies, computers, or any other format. But that is exactly the problem, there is no standard aspect ratio (see Fig. 3.22).

Figure 3.22
Common aspect
ratios.

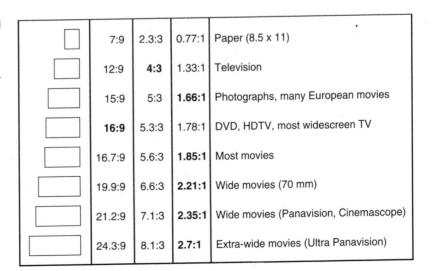

	7:9	2.3:3	0.77:1	Paper (8.5 x 11)
	12:9	**4:3**	1.33:1	Television
	15:9	5:3	**1.66:1**	Photographs, many European movies
	16:9	5.3:3	1.78:1	DVD, HDTV, most widescreen TV
	16.7:9	5.6:3	**1.85:1**	Most movies
	19.9:9	6.6:3	**2.21:1**	Wide movies (70 mm)
	21.2:9	7.1:3	**2.35:1**	Wide movies (Panavision, Cinemascope)
	24.3:9	8.1:3	**2.7:1**	Extra-wide movies (Ultra Panavision)

Current display technology is limited to fixed physical sizes. A television picture tube must be built in a certain shape. A flat-panel LCD screen must be made with a certain number of pixels. Even a video projection system is limited by electronics and optics to project a certain shape. These constraints will remain with us for decades until we progress to new technologies such as scanning lasers or amorphous holographic projectors. Until then, a single aspect ratio must be chosen for a given display. The cost of a television tube is based roughly on diagonal measurement (taking into account the glass bulb, the display surface, and the electron beam deflection circuitry), but the wider a tube is, the harder it is to maintain *uniformity* (consistent intensity across the display) and *convergence* (straight horizontal and vertical lines). Therefore, too wide a tube is not desirable.

The 16:9 aspect ratio was chosen in part because it's an exact multiple of 4:3. That is, $\frac{4}{3} \times \frac{4}{3} = \frac{16}{9}$. The clean mathematical relationship between 4:3 and 16:9 makes it easy to convert between the two. Going from 4:3 to 16:9 merely entails adding one horizontal pixel for every three (3→4) and going from 16:9 to 4:3 requires simply removing one pixel from every four (4→3).* This makes the scaling circuitry for letterbox and pan & scan functions much simpler and cheaper. It also makes the resulting picture cleaner.

The 16:9 aspect ratio is also a reasonable compromise between television and movies. It's very close to 1.85 and it's close to the mean of 1.33 and 2.35. That is, $\frac{4}{3} \times \frac{4}{3} \times \frac{4}{3} \approx 2.35$. Choosing a wider display aspect ratio, such as 2:1, would have made 2.35 movies look wonderful but would have required huge mattes on the side when showing 4:3 video (as in Fig. 3.17*b*, but even wider).

Admittedly, the extra space could be used for *picture outside picture* (POP, the converse of PIP), but it would be very expensive extra space. To make a 2:1 display the same height as a 35-inch television (21 inches) requires a width of 42 inches, giving a diagonal measure of 47 inches. In other words, to keep the equivalent 4:3 image size of 35-inch television you must get a 47-inch 2:1 television. Figure 3.23 shows additional widescreen display sizes required to maintain the same height of common television sizes.

Figure 3.24 demonstrates the area of the display used when different image shapes are letterboxed to fit it (i.e., the dimensions are equalized in

---

*In each case, a weighted scaling function is generally used. For example, when going from 4 to 3 pixels, three-quarters of the first pixel is combined with one-quarter of the second to make the new first; one-half of the second is combined with one-half of the third to make the new second; and one-quarter of the third is combined with three-quarters of the fourth to make the new third. Similar weighted averages can be used when going from 4 to 3. (See Figs. 4.33 and 4.35.)

Figure 3.23
Display sizes at equal heights.

Diagonal size (width x height)

4:3	16:9	2:1
27" (22 x 16)	33" (29 x 16)	36" (32 x 16)
32" (26 x 19)	39" (34 x 19)	43" (38 x 19)
35" (28 x 21)	43" (37 x 21)	47" (42 x 21)
42" (34 x 25)	51" (45 x 25)	56" (50 x 25)
50" (40 x 30)	61" (53 x 30)	67" (60 x 30)
57" (46 x 34)	70" (61 x 34)	76" (68 x 34)
65" (52 x 39)	80" (69 x 39)	87" (78 x 39)
82" (66 x 49)	100" (87 x 49)	110" (98 x 49)
98" (78 x 59)	120" (105 x 59)	131" (118 x 59)

Figure 3.24
Relative image sizes for letterbox display.

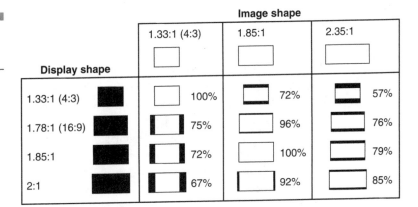

Display shape	Image shape		
	1.33:1 (4:3)	1.85:1	2.35:1
1.33:1 (4:3)	100%	72%	57%
1.78:1 (16:9)	75%	96%	76%
1.85:1	72%	100%	79%
2:1	67%	92%	85%

the largest direction to make the smaller box fit inside the larger box).* The 4:3 row makes it clear how much smaller a letterboxed 2.35:1 movie is: only 57 percent of the screen is used for the picture. On the other hand, the 2:1 row makes it clear how much expensive screen space goes unused by a 4:3 video program or even a 1.85:1 movie. The two middle rows are quite similar, so the mathematical relationship of 16:9 to 4:3 gives it the edge.

In summary, the only way to support multiple aspect ratios without mattes would be to use a display that can physically change shape—a

*If you wanted to get the most for your money when selecting a display aspect ratio, you would need to equalize the diagonal measurement of each display since the cost is roughly proportional to the diagonal size. This approach is sometimes used when comparing display aspect ratios and letterboxed images, and it has the effect of emphasizing the differences. The problem is that wider displays end up being shorter (for example, a 2:1 display normalized to the same diagonal as a 4:3 display would be 4.47:2.25, which is 12 percent wider but 25 percent shorter). In reality, no one would be happy with a widescreen TV that was shorter than their existing TV. Therefore it's expected that a widescreen TV will have a larger diagonal measurement and will cost more.

"mighty morphin' television." Since this is currently impossible (or outra-geously expensive), 16:9 is the most reasonable compromise. That said, the designers of DVD could have improved things slightly by allowing more than one anamorphic distortion ratio. If a 2.35 movie were stored using a 2.35 anamorphic squeeze, then 24 percent of the internal picture would not be wasted on the black mattes and the player could automatically gen-erate the mattes for either 4:3 or 16:9 displays. This was probably not done because of the extra cost and complexity it would add to the player. The limited set of aspect ratios presently supported by the MPEG-2 standard (4:3, 16:9, and 2.21:1) may have also had something to do with it.

The Transfer Tango

Of course, the option still remains to transfer the movie to DVD's 4:3 aspect ratio instead of 16:9. At first glance, there may seem to be no advantage in doing this, since 1.85 movies are so close to 16:9 (1.78). It seems simpler to do a 16:9 transfer and let the player create a letterbox or pan & scan version. But there are disadvantages to having the player automatically format a widescreen movie for 4:3 display: the vertical resolution suffers by 25 per-cent, the letterbox mattes are visible on movies wider than 1.85, and the player is limited to lateral motion. In addition, many movie people are averse to what they consider as surrendering creative control to the player. Therefore, most DVD producers will choose to create a pan & scan transfer in the studio. Here, they have the freedom to use the full frame or zoom in for closer shots, which is especially handy when a microphone or a piece of the set is visible at the edge of the shot. The auto pan & scan feature of the player generally will be used only when the movie is true widescreen (filmed with a hard matte or anamorphic lens or computer-generated in wide format) so that the only freedom of motion is side to side.

Many directors are violently opposed to the pan & scan butchery of their films. Director Sydney Pollack sued a Danish television station for airing a pan & scan version of his *Three Days of the Condor* which was filmed in 2.35 Cinemascope. Pollack feels strongly that the pan & scan ver-sion infringed his artistic copyright. He believes that "The director's job is to tell the film story, and the basis for doing this is to choose what the audience is supposed to see, and not just generally but exactly what they are to see." Some directors such as Stanley Kubrick will accept only the original aspect ratio. Others such as James Cameron, who closely super-vise the transfer process from full-frame film, feel that the director is responsible for making the pan & scan transfer a viable option by recom-posing the movie to make the most of the 4:3 TV shape.

A pan & scan transfer to 4:3 makes the "I didn't pay good money for my 30-inch TV just to watch black bars" crowd happy. But a letterbox transfer to 16:9 is still needed to appease the videophiles who demand the theatrical aspect ratio and to keep the "I paid good money for my widescreen TV" crowd from revolting. Ordinarily this would mean two separate products, but not with DVD. The producer of the disc can put the 4:3 version on one side (or one layer) and the letterboxed 16:9 version on the other. This doubles the premastering cost and slightly increases the mastering and replication costs, but at production runs of at least 100,000 copies, this adds less than a few dollars to the unit cost. On the other hand, the widescreen letterbox transfer may be reserved for a special edition and sold as a separate product at a higher price.

As widescreen TVs and HDTVs slowly replace traditional TVs, 4:3 transfers will become less common and even letterboxed 4:3 transfers will become more appreciated. In Japan and Europe, widescreen TVs already outsell standard TVs, and letterboxed video is more popular.

Summary

Putting everything together (ignoring the option of cropping during transfer) gives the following variations to the four basic output formats:

1. 4:3 full frame (4:3 original)
   a. Direct transfer
2. 4:3 pan & scan (wide original)
   a. Pan & scan transfer
   b. Automatic pan & scan done by player
      (1) On direct transfer (16:9 original)
      (2) On pan & scan transfer (not 16:9 original)
      (3) On letterbox transfer (not 16:9 original)
3. 4:3 letterbox (wide original)
   a. Letterbox transfer
   b. Automatic letterbox done by player
      (1) On direct transfer (16:9 original)
      (2) On pan & scan transfer (not 16:9 original)
      (3) On letterbox transfer (not 16:9 original)
4. 4:3 anamorphic (wide original)
   a. Direct transfer (16:9 original)
   b. Pan & scan transfer (not 16:9 original)
   c. Letterbox transfer (not 16:9 original)

This may be more clear in the form of Table 3.4.

TABLE 3.4

Combinations of Output Formats and Video Transfers

	4:3 original	16:9 original		Non-16:9 original	
	Stored in 4:3	Stored in 4:3	Stored in 16:9	Stored in 4:3	Stored in 16:9
Full frame (1)	Direct transfer (a)	n/a	n/a	n/a	n/a
Pan & scan (2)	P&S transfer from full frame (a)	P&S transfer (a)	Auto P&S by player (b1)	P&S transfer (a)	Auto P&S by player on P&S transfer (b2) or on LB transfer (b3)
Letterbox (3)	LB transfer from inside soft matte (a)	LB transfer (a)	Auto LB by player (b1)	LB transfer (a)	Auto LB by player on P&S transfer (b2) or on LB transfer (b3)
Anamorphic (4)	Anamorphic transfer from 16:9 soft matte (a)	n/a	Anamorphic transfer (a)	n/a	P&S transfer to anamorphic (b) or LB transfer to Anamorphic (c)

Note: Labels in parentheses refer to the preceding outline.

All of these variations are possible, but only a few of them will be regularly used, such as 1a, 2a, 3a, and 4c. The automatic pan & scan feature of DVD players will rarely be used; in many cases, both a 4:3 pan & scan version and a widescreen letterbox version will be included on a single disc. In other cases, where a new video transfer is deemed too expensive or the original film is no longer available, whatever existing transfer is available will be used, such as 4:3 pan & scan or 4:3 letterbox.

NOTE *Technical details of aspect ratios and related picture resolution are covered in Chap. 4.*

Birds Over the Phone: Understanding Video Compression

After CDs appeared in 1982, digital audio soon became a commodity. It took many years before the same transformation could begin to work its magic on video. The step up from digital audio to digital video is a doozy, for in one second of television there is about 250 times as much information as in one second of CD audio. But in spite of its larger capacity, DVD is not even close to 250 times more spacious than CD-ROM. The trick is to reduce the amount of video information without significantly reducing the quality of the picture. The solution is digital compression.

In a sense, you employ compression in daily conversations. Picture yourself talking on the phone to a friend. You are describing the antics of a particularly striking bird outside your window. You might begin by depicting the scene, then mentioning the size, shape, and color of the bird. But when you begin to describe the bird's actions, you naturally don't repeat your description of the scene or the bird. You take it for granted that your friend remembers this information so you only describe the action—the part that changes. If you had to continually refresh your friend's memory of every detail, you would have very high phone bills. The problem with TV is that it has no memory; the picture has to be refreshed, literally. It's as if the TV were saying "There's a small tree with a 4-inch green and black bird with a yellow beak sitting on a branch. Now there's a small tree with a 4-inch green and black bird with a yellow beak hanging upside down on a branch. Now there's a small tree with a 4-inch green and black bird with a yellow beak hanging upside down on a branch trying to eat some fruit," and so on, only in much more detail, redescribing the entire scene 30 times a second. In addition, a TV individually describes each piece of the picture even when they're all the same. It would be as if you had to say, "The bird has a black breast and a green head and a green back and green wingfeathers and green tailfeathers and..." (again, in much more meticulous detail) rather than simply saying, "The bird has a black breast and the rest is green."

This kind of conversational compression is second nature to us, but for computers to do the same thing requires complex programming.

The simplest form of digital video compression takes advantage of spatial redundancy—areas of a single picture that are the same. Computer pictures are made up of a grid of dots, each one a specified color. But many of the dots are the same color. So, rather than storing, say, a hundred red dots, you store one red dot and a count of 100. This reduces the amount of information from 100 pieces to 3 (a marker indicating a run of similar colored dots, the color, and the count) or even 2 (if all information is stored as pairs of color and count). (See Fig. 3.25.) This is called *run-length compression*. It's a form of *lossless* compression, meaning that the original picture can be reconstructed perfectly with no missing detail. Run-length compression is great for simple pictures and computer data, but doesn't reduce a large, complex picture enough for most purposes.

DVD-Video uses run-length compression for subpictures, which contain captions and simple graphic overlays. The legibility of text in subpictures is critical, so it's important that no detail be lost. DVD limits subpictures to four colors at a time, so there are lots of repeating runs of colors, mak-

Figure 3.25
Run-length com-
pression example.

Figure 3.25
Run-length compression example.

ing them perfect candidates for run-length compression. Compressed sub-picture data makes up less than one-half of 1 percent of a typical DVD-Video program.

In order to reduce picture information even more, *lossy* compression is required. In this case information is permanently removed. The trick is to remove detail that won't be noticed. Many such compression techniques, known as *psychovisual* encoding systems, take advantage of a number of aspects of the human visual system.

1. The eye is more sensitive to changes in brightness than color.

2. The eye is unable to perceive brightness levels above or below certain thresholds.

3. The eye can't distinguish minor changes in brightness or color. This perception is not linear. In other words, certain ranges of brightness or color are more important visually than others. For example, variegated shades of green such as leaves and plants in a forest are more easily discriminated than various shades of dark blue such as in the depths of a pool.

4. Gentle gradations of brightness or color (such as a sunset blending gradually into a blue sky) are more important to the eye and more readily perceived than abrupt changes (such as pinstriped suits or confetti).

The human retina has three types of color photoreceptor cells, called *cones.*[*] Each is sensitive to different wavelengths of light which roughly correspond to the colors red, green, and blue. Because the eye perceives color as a combination of these three stimuli, any color can be described as a combination of these primary colors.[†] Televisions work by using three electron

---

[*] *Rods,* another type of photoreceptor cell, are only useful in low-light environments to provide what is commonly called night vision.

[†] You may have learned that the primary colors are red, yellow, and blue. Technically, these are magenta, yellow, and cyan, and usually refer to pigments rather than colors. A magenta ink absorbs green light, thus controlling the amount of green color perceived by the eye. Since white light is composed of equal amounts of all three colors, removing green leaves red and blue, which together form magenta. Likewise, yellow ink absorbs blue light and cyan ink absorbs red light. Reflected light, such as that from a painting, is formed from the character of the illuminating light and the absorption of the pigments. Projected light, such as that from a television, is formed from the intensities of the three primary colors. Since video is projected, it deals with red, green, and blue colors.

beams to cause different phosphors on the face of the television tube to emit red, green, or blue light, abbreviated to *RGB*. Television cameras record images in RGB format, and computers generally store images in RGB format.

RGB values are a combination of brightness and color. Each triplet of numbers represents the intensity of each primary color. But as just noted, the eye is more sensitive to brightness than to color. Therefore, if the RGB values are separated into a brightness component and a color component, the color information can be more heavily compressed. The brightness information is called *luminance* and is often denoted as Y.* Luminance is essentially what you see when watching a black-and-white TV. Luminance is the range of intensity from 0 percent (black) through 50 percent (gray) to 100 percent (white). A logical assumption is that each RGB value would contribute one-third of the intensity information, but the eye is most sensitive to green, less sensitive to red, and least sensitive to blue, so a uniform average would yield a yellowish green image instead of a gray image.† Consequently, it's necessary to use a weighted sum corresponding to the spectral sensitivity of the eye, which is about 70 percent green, 20 percent red, and 10 percent blue. See Fig. 3.26.

The remaining color information is called *chrominance* (denoted as C), which is made up of *hue* (the proportion of color, the redness, orangeness, greenness, etc.) and *saturation* (the purity of the color, from pastel to vivid). But for the purposes of converting from RGB, it's easier to use *color difference* information rather than hue and saturation. In other words, the color information is what's left after the luminance is removed. By subtracting the luminance value from each RGB value, three color difference signals are created, R-Y, G-Y, and B-Y. Only three stimulus values are needed, so only two color difference signals need be included with the luminance signal. Since green is the largest component of luminance, it has the smallest difference signal. (G makes up the largest part of Y, so G-Y results in the smallest values.) The smaller the signal, the more it is subject to errors from noise, so B-Y and R-Y are the best choice. The green color information can be recreated by subtracting the two difference signals from the Y signal (roughly speaking).

---

*The use of Y for luminance seems to come from the XYZ color system defined by the Commission Internationale de L'Eclairage (CIE). The system uses three-dimensional space to represent colors, where the Y axis is luminance and X and Z axes represent color information.

†Luminance from RGB can be a difficult concept to grasp. It might help to think of colored filters. If you look through a red filter you will see a monochromatic image composed of shades of red. The image would be the same if it were changed to a different color, such as gray. Since the red filter only passes red light, anything that's pure blue or pure green won't be visible. To get a balanced image, you would use three filters, change the image from each one to gray, and average them together.

Figure 3.26
Color and luminance
sensitivity of the eye.

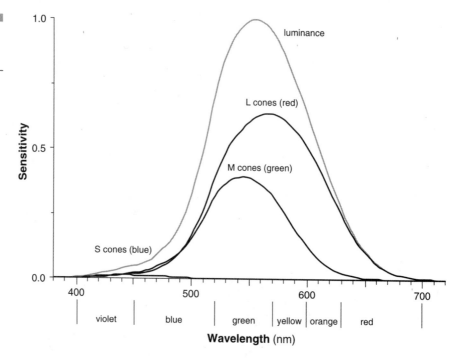

Different weightings are used to derive Y and color differences from RGB, such as YUV, YIQ, and YC_bC_r. DVD uses YC_bC_r. Details of these variations are beyond the scope of this book.

As mentioned earlier, the sensitivity of the eye is not linear, and neither is the response of the phosphors used in television tubes. Therefore, video is usually represented with corresponding nonlinear values, and the terms *luma* (Y′) and *chroma* (C′) are used. These are denoted with the prime symbol as Y′, C′, and the corresponding R′G′B′. Details of nonlinear functions are also beyond the scope of this book, which occasionally uses the general terms luminance and chrominance for simplicity.

Compressing Single Pictures

An understanding of the nuances of human perception led to the development of compression techniques which take advantage of certain characteristics. Just such a development is *JPEG compression,* which was produced by the Joint Photographic Experts Group and is now a worldwide standard. JPEG separately compresses Y, B-Y, and R-Y information, with more compression done on the latter two to which the eye is less sensitive.

To take advantage of another human vision characteristic—less sensitivity to complex detail—JPEG divides the image into small blocks and applies a *discrete cosine transform* *(DCT)*, a mathematical function that changes spatial intensity values to spatial frequency values. This describes the block in terms of how much the detail changes and roughly arranges the values from lowest frequency (represented by large numbers) to highest frequency (represented by small numbers). For areas of smooth colors or low detail (low spatial frequency), the set of numbers will be large. For areas with varying colors and detail (high spatial frequency), the set of values will be close to zero. A DCT is an essentially *lossless transform,* meaning that an inverse DCT function can be performed on the resulting set of values to restore the original values. In practice, integer math and approximations are used, causing some loss at the DCT stage. Ironically, the numbers are bigger after the DCT transform. The solution is to *quantize* the DCT values so they become smaller and repetitive.

Quantizing is a way of reducing information by grouping it into chunks. For example, if you had a set of numbers between 1 and 100 you could quantize them by 10. That is, divide by 10 and round to the nearest integer. The numbers from 5 to 14 would all become 1s, the numbers from 15 to 24 would become 2s, and so on, with 1 representing 10, 2 representing 20, and so forth. Instead of individual numbers such as 8, 11, 12, 20, and 23, you end up with "3 numbers near 10" and "2 numbers near 20." Obviously, quantizing causes a loss of detail.

Quantizing the DCT values means that the result of the inverse DCT will not exactly reproduce the original intensity values, but the result is close and can be adjusted by varying the quantizing scale to make it finer or coarser. More importantly, since the DCT function includes a progressive weighting that puts bigger numbers near the top left corner and smaller numbers near the lower right corner, quantization and a special zigzag ordering result in runs of the same number, especially zero. This may sound familiar. Sure enough, the next step is to use run-length encoding to reduce the number of values. A variation of run-length coding is used, which stores a count of the number of zero values, followed by the next nonzero value. The resulting numbers are used to look up symbols from a table. The symbol table was developed using Huffman coding to create shorter symbols for the most commonly appearing numbers. See Figs. 3.27 and 3.29.

The result of these transformation and manipulation steps is that the information which is thrown away is least perceptible. Since the eye is less sensitive to color than to brightness, the RGB values are transformed to luminance and chrominance so that less chrominance data can be stored.

Figure 3.27
Block transforms
and quantization.

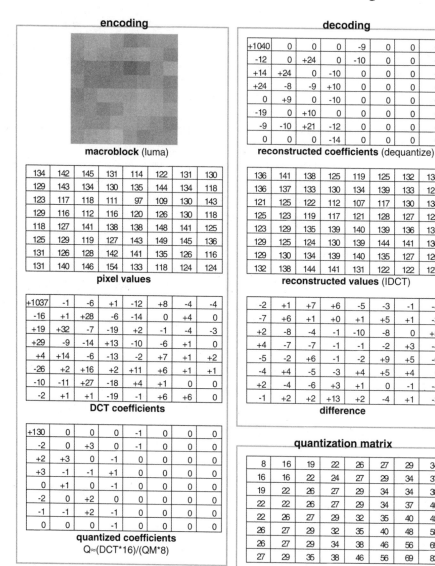

encoding

macroblock (luma)

pixel values

134	142	145	131	114	122	131	130
129	143	134	130	135	144	134	118
123	117	118	111	97	109	130	143
129	116	112	116	120	126	130	118
118	127	141	138	138	148	141	125
125	129	119	127	143	149	145	136
131	126	128	142	141	135	126	116
131	140	146	154	133	118	124	124

DCT coefficients

+1037	-1	-6	+1	-12	+8	-4	-4
-16	+1	+28	-6	-14	0	+4	0
+19	+32	-7	-19	+2	-1	-4	-3
+29	-9	-14	+13	-10	-6	+1	0
+4	+14	-6	-13	-2	+7	+1	+2
-26	+2	+16	+2	+11	+6	+1	+1
-10	-11	+27	-18	+4	+1	0	0
-2	+1	+1	-19	-1	+6	+6	0

quantized coefficients
Q≈(DCT*16)/(QM*8)

+130	0	0	0	-1	0	0	0
-2	0	+3	0	-1	0	0	0
+2	+3	0	-1	0	0	0	0
+3	-1	-1	+1	0	0	0	0
0	+1	0	-1	0	0	0	0
-2	0	+2	0	0	0	0	0
-1	-1	+2	-1	0	0	0	0
0	0	0	-1	0	0	0	0

decoding

reconstructed coefficients (dequantize)

+1040	0	0	0	-9	0	0	0
-12	0	+24	0	-10	0	0	0
+14	+24	0	-10	0	0	0	0
+24	-8	-9	+10	0	0	0	0
0	+9	0	-10	0	0	0	0
-19	0	+10	0	0	0	0	0
-9	-10	+21	-12	0	0	0	0
0	0	0	-14	0	0	0	0

reconstructed values (IDCT)

136	141	138	125	119	125	132	134
136	137	133	130	134	139	133	121
121	125	122	112	107	117	130	138
125	123	119	117	121	128	127	122
123	129	135	139	140	139	136	131
129	125	124	130	139	144	141	136
129	130	134	139	140	135	127	120
132	138	144	141	131	122	122	127

difference

-2	+1	+7	+6	-5	-3	-1	-4
-7	+6	+1	+0	+1	+5	+1	-3
+2	-8	-4	-1	-10	-8	0	+5
+4	-7	-7	-1	-1	-2	+3	-4
-5	-2	+6	-1	-2	+9	+5	-6
-4	+4	-5	-3	+4	+5	+4	0
+2	-4	-6	+3	+1	0	-1	-4
-1	+2	+2	+13	+2	-4	+1	-3

quantization matrix

8	16	19	22	26	27	29	34
16	16	22	24	27	29	34	37
19	22	26	27	29	34	34	38
22	22	26	27	29	34	37	40
22	26	27	29	32	35	40	48
26	27	29	32	35	40	48	58
26	27	29	34	38	46	56	69
27	29	35	38	46	56	69	83

And since the eye is less sensitive to high-frequency color or brightness changes, the DCT and quantization process removes mostly the high-frequency information. JPEG compression can reduce a picture to about one-fifth the original size with almost no discernible difference, and to about one-tenth with only slight degradation.

Compressing Moving Pictures

Motion video adds a *temporal* dimension to the spatial dimension of single pictures. Another worldwide compression standard, *MPEG*, from the Moving Pictures Experts Group, was designed with this in mind. MPEG is similar to JPEG but also reduces redundancy between successive pictures of a moving sequence.

Just as your friend's memory allows you to describe things once and then only talk about what's changing, digital memory allows video to be compressed in a similar manner by first storing a single picture and then only storing the changes. For example, if the bird moves to another place, you can tell your friend that the bird has moved without needing to describe the bird over again.

MPEG compression uses a similar technique, called *motion compensation, motion estimation,* or *motion prediction.* Since motion video is a sequence of still pictures, many of which are very similar, each picture can be compared the pictures next to it. The MPEG encoding process breaks each picture into blocks, called *macroblocks,* then hunts around in neighboring pictures for similar blocks. Then, instead of storing the entire block, the system stores a much smaller *vector* describing how far the block moved

TABLE 3.5

Differences between MPEG-1 and MPEG-2

MPEG-1	MPEG-2 (MP@ML)
Progressive frames only	Progressive or interlaced frames
No control of field display	Repeat_first_field flag for display rate conversions
Fixed bit rate (officially)	Variable bit rate
No aspect ratio information	Aspect ratio can be specified
Integer pixel grid	Half-sample resolution for motion vectors
Linear macroblock quantization	Additional nonlinear quantization
One DCT scan order	Alternate scan pattern
8-bit DCT quantization	8-, 9-, or 10-bit quantization
1 chroma sample sited between 4 luma samples	Chroma samples colocated horizontally with luminance samples (vertical samples still between lines)
Fixed picture window	Pan & scan syntax added
Little information about source video	Source information such as color primaries, video type, field sequence, and subcarrier phase

(or didn't move) between pictures. Vectors can be encoded in as little as one bit, so that backgrounds and other elements that don't change over time are compressed extremely efficiently. Large groups of blocks that move together, such as large objects or the entire picture panning sideways, are also efficiently compressed.

MPEG uses three kinds of picture storage methods. *Intra* pictures are like JPEG pictures, in which the entire picture is compressed and stored with DCT quantization. This creates a reference frame from which successive pictures are built. These *I frames* also allow random access into a stream of video and in practice occur about twice a second. *Predicted* pictures, or *P frames*, contain motion vectors describing the difference from the closest previous I frame or P frame. If the block has changed slightly in intensity or color (remember, these are separated into three channels and compressed separately) then the difference (*error*) is also encoded. If something entirely new appears which doesn't match any previous blocks, such as a person walking into the scene, then a new block is stored in the same way as in an I frame. If the entire scene changes, as in a cut, the encoding system is usually smart enough to make a new I frame. The third storage method is a *bidirectional* picture, or *B frame*. The system looks both forward and backward to match blocks. This way if something new appears in a B frame, it can be matched to a block in the next I frame or P frame.

Experience has shown that two B frames between each I or P frame work well. A typical second of MPEG video at 30 frames/second looks like I B B P B B P B B P B B P B B I B B P B B P B B P B B P B B (see Fig. 3.28). Obviously, B frames are much more complex to create than P frames, requiring time-consuming searches in both the previous and subsequent I or P frame. For this reason, some MPEG encoders only create I and P frames. Likewise, I frames are easier to create than P frames which require searches in the subsequent I or P frame. Therefore, the simplest encoders only create I frames. This is less efficient but is often required for very inexpensive real-time encoders which must process 30 or more frames a second.

MPEG-2 encoding can be done in real time (where the video stream enters and leaves the encoder at display speeds), but it's difficult to pro-

Figure 3.28
Typical MPEG picture sequence.

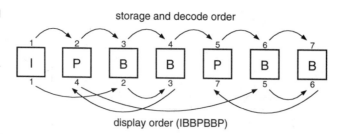

storage and decode order

display order (IBBPBBP)

duce quality results, especially with *variable bit rate* (*VBR*). Variable bit rate allows varying numbers of bits to be allocated for each frame depending on the complexity. Less data is needed for simple scenes, while more data can be allocated for complex scenes. This results in a lower average data rate and longer playing times, but provides room for data peaks to maintain quality. DVD encoding is usually at variable bit rates and is almost never done in real time, so the encoder has plenty of time for macroblock matching, resulting in much better quality at lower data rates. Good decoders make one pass to analyze the video and determine how to compress each frame, then make a second pass to do the actual compression. The human operator often tweaks minor details between the two passes. Most low-cost MPEG encoding hardware or software for personal computers uses only I frames, especially when capturing video in real time. This results in a simpler and cheaper decoder, since P and B frames require more computation and more memory to decode. Some of these systems can later reprocess the I frames to create P and B frames.

MPEG can also encode still images as I frames. The menus of DVD-Video, for example, are I frames.

The result of the encoding process is a set of data and instructions. (See Fig. 3.29.) These are used by the decoder to recreate the video. The amount of compression (how coarse the quantizing was, how large a motion estimation error is allowed) determines how closely the reconstructed video resembles the original. MPEG decoding is *deterministic*—a given set of input data should always produce the same output data. Decoders which properly implement the complete MPEG decoding process will produce the same numerical picture, even if they are built by different manufacturers.* This doesn't mean that all DVD players will produce the same video picture. Far from it, since there are many other factors involved such as filtering, conversion from digital to analog, connection type, cable quality, and display quality. Advanced decoders may include extra processing steps such as block filtering and edge enhancement. Also, many software MPEG decoders take shortcuts to achieve sufficient performance. Software decoders may skip frames and use mathematical approximations rather than the complete but time-consuming transformations. This results in lower-quality video than from a fully compliant decoder.

Encoders, on the other hand, can and do vary widely. The encoding process has the greatest effect on the final video quality. The MPEG stan-

---

*Technically, the inverse discrete cosine transform (IDCT) stage of the decoding process is not strictly proscribed and is allowed to introduce small statistical variances. This should never account for more than an occasional least-significant bit of discrepancy between decoders.

Figure 3.29
MPEG video compression example.

DC	symbols
130	01 0

run codes (zeros, value)	symbols (from lookup table)
1,-2	0011 01
0,+2	1100
3,+3	0000 0001 1100 0
0,+3	0111 0
0,+3	0111 0
1,-1	0101
2,-1	0010 11
1,-1	0101
0,-1	101
0,-1	101
0,+1	100
0,-2	1101
0,-1	101
2,+1	0010 10
7,-1	0000 1001
0,+1	100
0,-1	101
2,+2	0000 1110
9,-1	1111 0001
1,-1	0101
EOB	0110

bytestream (14 bytes: 22 symbols)
46 E0 0E 1C E5 2D 6D 9B 4A 09 94 3B C5 58

compression
4.6:1 (64:14)

134	142	145	131	114	122	131	130
129	143	134	130	135	144	134	118
123	117	118	111	97	109	130	143
129	116	112	116	120	126	130	118
118	127	141	138	138	148	141	125
125	129	119	127	143	149	145	136
131	126	128	142	141	135	126	116
131	140	146	154	133	118	124	124

pixel values

+130	0	0	0	-1	0	0	0
-2	0	+3	0	-1	0	0	0
+2	+3	0	-1	0	0	0	0
+3	-1	-1	+1	0	0	0	0
0	+1	0	-1	0	0	0	0
-2	0	+2	0	0	0	0	0
-1	-1	+2	-1	0	0	0	0
0	0	0	-1	0	0	0	0

quantized coefficients

	1	5	6	14	15	27	28
2	4	7	13	16	26	29	42
3	8	12	17	25	30	41	43
9	11	18	24	31	40	44	53
10	19	23	32	39	45	52	54
20	22	33	38	45	51	55	60
21	34	37	47	50	56	59	61
35	36	48	49	57	58	62	63

zig-zag scan sequence

dard proscribes a *syntax* defining what instructions can be included with the encoded data and how they are applied. This syntax is quite flexible and leaves much room for variation. The quality of the decoded video depends very much on how thoroughly the encoder examines the video and how clever it is about applying the functions of MPEG to compress it. In a sense, MPEG is still in its infancy, and there remains much to be learned about efficient encoding. DVD video quality will steadily improve as encoding techniques and equipment get better. The decoder chip in the player won't change—it doesn't need to be changed—but the improvements in the encoded data will provide a better result. This can be likened to reading aloud from a book. The letters of the alphabet are data organized according to the syntax of language. The person reading aloud from the book is similar to the decoder—the reader knows every letter and is familiar with the rules of pronunciation. The author is similar to the encoder—the writer applies the rules of spelling and usage to encode thoughts as written language. The better the author, the better the results. A poorly written book will come out sounding bad no matter who reads it,* but a well-written book will produce eloquent spoken language.

It should be recognized that random artifacts in video playback (aberrations that appear in different places or at different times when the same video is played over again) are not MPEG encoding artifacts. They may indicate a faulty decoder, errors in the signal, or something else independent of the MPEG decoding process. It's impossible for fully compliant, properly functioning MPEG decoders to produce visually different results from the same encoded data stream.

MPEG (and most other compression techniques) are *asymmetric*, meaning the encoding process does not take the same amount of time as the decoding process. It's more effective and efficient to use a complex and time-consuming encoding process, since video is generally encoded only once before being decoded hundreds or millions of times. High-quality MPEG encoding systems can cost upward of a million dollars, but since most of the work is done during encoding, decoder chips cost less than $50 and decoding can even be done in software.

Some analyses indicate that a typical video signal contains over 95 percent redundant information. By encoding the changes between frames, rather than reencoding each frame, MPEG achieves amazing compression. The difference from the original is generally imperceptible even when compressed by a factor of 10 to 15. DVD-Video data is typically compressed to approximately one-thirtieth its original size.

Birds Revisited: Understanding Audio Compression

Audio takes up much less space than video, but uncompressed audio coupled to compressed video uses up a large percentage of the available bandwidth. Compressing the audio can result in a small loss of quality, but if the resulting space is used instead for video it may significantly improve

---

*Obviously, it would sound better if read by James Earl Jones than by Ross Perot. But the analogy holds if you consider the vocal characteristics to be independent of the translation of words to sound. The brain of the reader is the decoder, the diction of the reader is the post-MPEG video processing, and the voice of the reader is the television.

the video quality. In essence, applying compression equally to audio and video is more effective.

Just as MPEG compression takes advantage of characteristics of the human eye, modern audio compression relies on an understanding of the human ear. This is called *psychoacoustic* or *perceptual* coding.

Picture, again, your telephone conversation with a friend. Imagine you live near an airport, so that when a plane takes off, your friend cannot hear you over the sound of the airplane. In a situation like this, you quickly learn to stop talking when a plane is taking off, since your friend won't hear you. The airplane has *masked* the sound of your voice. At the opposite end of the loudness spectrum from airplane noise is background noise, such as a ticking clock. While you are speaking, your friend can't hear it, but if you stop, then the background noise is no longer masked.

The hairs in your inner ear are sensitive to sound pressure at different frequencies (pitches). When stimulated by a loud sound they are incapable of sensing softer sounds at the same pitch. Because the hairs for similar frequencies are near each other, a stimulated audio receptor nerve will interfere with nearby receptors and cause them to be less sensitive. This is called *frequency masking.*

Human hearing ranges roughly from low frequencies of 20 Hz to high frequencies of 20,000 Hz (20 kHz). The ear is most sensitive to the frequency range from about 2 to 5 kHz, which corresponds to the range of the human voice. Because aural sensitivity varies in a nonlinear fashion, sounds at some frequencies mask more neighboring sounds than at other frequencies. Experiments have established certain *critical bands* of varying size that correspond to the masking function of human hearing.

Even sounds within the range of hearing can't be sensed when they fall below a certain loudness (or *amplitude*). This *sensitivity threshold,* as with everything else, is not linear. In other words, the threshold is at louder or softer points at different frequencies. The overall threshold varies a little from person to person—some people have better hearing than others. The threshold of hearing is adaptive; the ear can adjust its sensitivity in order to pick up soft sounds when not overloaded by loud sounds. This characteristic causes the effect of *temporal masking* in which you are unable to hear soft sounds for up to 200 milliseconds after a loud sound, and even for up to 2 or 3 milliseconds before a loud sound.*

---

*How can masking work backward in time? The signal presented by the ear to the brain is a composite built up from stimuli received over a period of about 200 milliseconds. A loud noise effectively overrides a small portion of the earlier stimuli before it can be accumulated and sent to the brain.

Perceptual Coding

DVD uses two audio compression systems: Dolby Digital (AC-3) coding and MPEG audio coding. Both use mathematical models of human hearing based on the threshold of hearing, frequency masking, and temporal masking to remove sounds that you can't hear. The resulting information is compressed to about one-third to one-tenth the original size with little to no perceptible loss in quality.

Digital audio is *sampled* by taking snapshots of an analog signal thousands of times a second. Each sample is a number that represents the amplitude (strength) of the waveform at that instance in time. Perceptual audio compression takes a block of samples and divides them into frequency bands of equal or varying widths. Bands of different widths are designed to match the sensitivity ranges of the human ear. The intensity of sound in each band is analyzed to determine two things: (1) how much masking it causes in nearby frequencies, and (2) how much noise the sound can mask within the band. Analyzing the masking of nearby bands means that the signal in bands which are completely masked can be ignored. Calculating how much noise can be masked in each band determines how much compression can be applied to the signal within the band. Quantization involves dividing and rounding, which can create errors known as *quantization noise*. For example, the number 32 quantized by 10 gives 3.2 rounded to 3. When reexpanded, the number is reconstructed as 30, creating an error of 2. These errors can manifest themselves as audible noise.

After masked sounds are ignored, remaining sounds are quantized as coarsely as possible so that quantization noise is either masked or is below the threshold of hearing. The technique of noise masking is related to *noise shaping* and is sometimes called *frequency-domain error confinement*.

Another technique of audio compression is to compare each block of samples with the previous and following blocks to see if any can be ignored on account of temporal masking—soft sounds near loud sounds—and how much quantization noise will be temporally masked. This is sometimes called *temporal-domain error confinement*.

Digital audio compression can also take advantage of the redundancies and relationships between channels, especially when there are 6 or 8 channels. A strong sound in one channel can mask weak sounds in other channels, information that is the same in more than one channel need only be stored once, and extra bandwidth can be temporarily allocated to deal with a complex signal in one channel by slightly sacrificing the sound of other channels.

MPEG-1 Audio Coding

MPEG-1 digital audio compression carries either monophonic or stereo audio. It divides the signal into frequency bands (typically 32) of equal widths. This is easier to implement than the slightly more accurate variable widths.

MPEG-1 has three *layers*, or compression techniques, each more efficient but more complicated than the last. Layer II is the most common and is the only one allowed by DVD. Layer II compression typically uses a sample block size of 23 milliseconds (1152 samples).

MPEG-2 Audio Coding

MPEG-2 digital audio compression adds multiple channels and provides a mode for backward-compatibility with MPEG-1 decoders. This backward-compatible mode is required for DVD. Five channels of audio are *matrixed* into the standard left/right stereo signal which is encoded in the normal MPEG-1 format. Matrixing is the process of mixing multiple audio channels into two channels according to a defined mathematical relationship. This relationship can then be used to later reconstruct a total of four channels (left, right, center, and surround).* The advantage of matrixing is that the two-channel audio can still be played on standard stereo audio systems. MPEG provides predetermined matrixing formulas depending on the intended audience for the stereo audio signal. One is a conventional stereo signal, and another is designed to deliver a signal that is compatible with Dolby Surround decoding to recreate a center channel and left/right surround channels. Additional discrete channel separation information, plus the low-frequency channel, are put in an *extension stream* so that an MPEG-2 audio decoder can recreate six separate signals. For eight channels, an additional layer is provided in another extension stream. The extension streams are compressed in a way that reduces redundant information shared by more than one channel. Because of the need to be backward-compatible with MPEG-1 decoders, the center and surround channels that are matrixed into the two MPEG-1 channels are duplicated in the extension stream. This allows the MPEG-2 decoder to

---

*A signal containing two main channels with additional channels matrixed onto them is often referred to as L_t/R_t, with the *t* standing for *total*. A pure stereo signal that does not carry phase-shifted audio intended for a decoder is sometimes identified as L_0/R_0.

subtract these signals from the matrixed signals, leaving the original left and right channels. This duplication of information adds an overhead of approximately 32 kbps, making the backward-compatible mode somewhat inefficient.

The hierarchical structure of MPEG-1 plus extension streams means that a two-channel MPEG decoder need only decode a two-channel data stream, and a six-channel MPEG decoder need only process a six-channel data stream. The eight-channel MPEG decoder is the only one that must decode the entire contents of an eight-channel stream. Therefore, an MPEG-1 decoder "sees" only the MPEG-1—compatible data to produce stereo audio, while an MPEG-2 decoder combines it with the first layer of extension data to produce 5.1-channel audio or, with both layers of extension data, to produce 7.1-channel audio. This clever technique provides an advantage to MPEG-2 over other encoding schemes, since cheap MPEG-1 decoders can be used when necessary. But the cost of MPEG-2 decoders will soon drop to the same level as MPEG-1. There are several drawbacks to the backward-compatibility scheme, in addition to the inefficiency of matrixed channel duplication. The original two-channel MPEG-1 encoding process was not developed with matrixed audio in mind, and therefore may remove surround-sound detail. The matrix-canceling process tends to expose coding artifacts; that is, when the signal from a matrixed channel is removed, the remaining signal may no longer mask the same neighboring frequencies or noise as the original signal, thus unmasking the noise introduced by formerly appropriate levels of quantization. This problem can be partially mitigated with special processing by the encoder, but this makes the encoding process less efficient with a resulting loss in quality at a given bit rate.

MPEG-2 includes a non-backward-compatible process, originally labeled *NBC* but now known as *AAC* (*Advanced Audio Coding*). This coding method deals with all channels simultaneously and is thereby more efficient, but it was not developed in time to be supported by DVD.

MPEG-2 allows a variable bit rate in order to handle momentary increases in signal complexity. Unfortunately, this turns out to be difficult to deal with in practice since audio and video are usually processed separately, and with two variable rates there is a danger of simultaneous peaks pushing the combined rate past the limit. This can be controlled by limiting the peak rate, but at the expense of possibly reducing audio quality in difficult passages. Another drawback of variable rate is that the higher allowed maximum rate requires a larger memory buffer for decoding, thus increasing hardware cost.

Dolby Digital Audio Coding

Dolby Digital audio compression (known as *AC-3* in standards documents) provides for up to 5.1 channels of discrete audio. One of the advantages of Dolby Digital is that it analyzes the audio signal to differentiate short, transient signals from long, continuous signals. Short sample blocks are then used for short sounds and long sample blocks are used for longer sounds. This results in smoother encoding without the block boundary effects that can occur with fixed block sizes. For compatibility with existing audio/video systems, decoders can downmix multichannel programs to ensure that all the channels are present in their proper proportions for optimum mono, stereo, or Dolby Pro Logic reproduction. In addition, dynamic range control is provided to further optimize audio reproduction depending on listening equipment or conditions.

Dolby Digital uses a frequency transform—somewhat like the DCT transform of JPEG and MPEG—and groups the resulting values into frequency bands of varying widths to match the critical bands of human hearing. Each transformed block is converted to a floating-point frequency representation which is allocated a varying number of bits from a common pool according to the importance of the frequency band. The result is a constant bit rate data stream.

Dolby Digital also includes dynamic range information, so that different listening environments can be compensated for. Original audio mixes, such as movie sound tracks, which are designed for the wide dynamic range of a theater, can be encoded to maintain the clarity of the dialogue and to enable emphasis of soft passages when played at low volume in the home.

Dolby Digital was developed from the ground up as a multichannel coder designed to meet the diverse and often contradictory needs of consumer delivery. It also has a significant lead over other multichannel systems in both marketing and standards adoption. At the end of 1996, over 100,000 Dolby Digital decoders were entrenched in living rooms, compared to essentially no MPEG-2 audio decoders, no SDDS decoders, and very few DTS decoders. Dolby Digital has been chosen for the U.S. DTV standard and is likely to be used for digital satellite systems and most other digital television systems.

Effects of Audio Encoding

Audio compression techniques result in a set of data that is processed in a specific way by the decoder. The process is flexible, so that improvements in the encoder result in improved quality without changing the decoder. As understanding of psychoacoustic models improves, the perceptual encoding systems can be made better.

With small amounts of compression, around 7 to 1 or less for today's encoders and even higher for future encoders, perceptual encoding removes only the imperceptible information and provides decoded audio which is virtually indistinguishable from the original. At higher levels of compression, and depending on the nature of the audio, *bit starvation* may cause identifiable effects of compression. These include a slightly harsh or gritty sound, poor reproduction of transients, loss of detail, and less-pronounced separation and spaciousness.

Both Dolby Digital and MPEG-2 on DVD are usually compressed at a factor of about 12 to 1. Most tests place the quality of Dolby Digital and MPEG-2 audio neck and neck, just short of sounding as good as the original uncompressed source. These tests have shown that the audio quality is completely acceptable to the average listener.

The Pin-Striped TV: Interlaced versus Progressive Scanning

One of the biggest problems facing early television designers was to display images fast enough to achieve smooth motion. Early video hardware was simply not fast enough to provide the required flicker fusion frequency of around 50 or 60 frames per second. The ingenious solution was to cut the amount of information in half by alternately transmitting every other line of the picture (see Fig. 3.30). The engineers counted on persistence of vision to make the two pictures blur into one when viewed. For a 525-line signal, first the 262 (and a half) odd lines are sent and displayed, followed by the 262 (and a half) even lines. This is called *interlaced*

Figure 3.30
Interlaced scan and progressive scan.

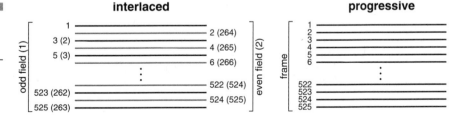

scanning. Each half of a frame is called a *field.* For the NTSC system, 60 fields are displayed per second, resulting in a rate of 30 frames per second. For the PAL system, there are 50 fields per second, resulting in a rate of 25 frames per second.

The alternate approach, *progressive scan,* displays every line of a complete frame. Progressive scan requires twice the frequency in order to achieve the same refresh rate. Progressive scan monitors are more expensive and are generally used for computers. High-definition television (HDTV) also includes progressive scanning.

Progressive scan provides a much superior picture, since there are many disadvantages to interlaced scanning. Small details, especially thin horizontal lines, only appear in every other field. This causes a disturbing flicker effect, which you can often see when someone on TV is wearing stripes. A common practice in video production is to filter the video to eliminate details smaller than two scan lines. This improves the stability of the picture but cuts the already poor resolution in half. The flicker problem is especially noticeable when computer video signals are converted and displayed on a standard TV. Interlaced scanning also causes problems when the picture is paused. If objects in the video are moving, they end up in a different position in each field. When two fields are shown together in a freeze-frame, the picture appears to shake. One solution to this problem is to show only one field, but this cuts the picture resolution in half. You may have seen this effect on a VCR: when the tape is paused, much of the detail disappears.

DVD-Video can be stored in progressive and interlaced formats.* Signals from video cameras are already in interlaced format and are usually stored as a combination of interlaced and progressive blocks, depending on the motion between fields. Film, which is inherently progressive, is usually stored on DVD as frames along with information to tell the player how to split and repeat the frames as fields. Since film is originally at 24 frames per second, displaying it at NTSC rates of 60 video fields per second requires a process called *3:2 pulldown,* where one film frame is shown as three fields and the following film frame is shown as two fields ([3 + 2] × 12 = 60). (See Fig. 3.31.) Unfortunately, this causes motion artifacts, since two

---

*In MPEG-2 encoding, the decision between progressive and interlaced format can be made all the way down at the macroblock level. The DVD-Video specification limits MPEG-2 video to nonprogressive sequences, which can include both progressive and interlaced frames. Interlaced frames can further include both progressive and interlaced macroblocks. Since progressive macroblocks are more efficient (using one motion vector instead of two), even an interlaced source is typically encoded by using more than 50 percent progressive macroblocks.

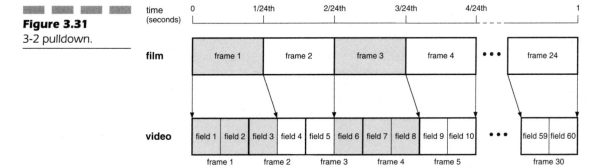

Figure 3.31
3-2 pulldown.

of every five television frames contain fields derived from two different film frames. Displaying film at PAL rates of 50 video fields per second is usually achieved by showing each film frame as two fields and playing it 4 percent faster. This is sometimes called *2:2 pulldown*. The MPEG-2 decoders in DVD players can automatically perform these pulldown techniques, but only by following instructions encoded with the video. Therefore, a film on DVD must be encoded for the intended display rate: either NTSC or PAL, but not both.

One advantage of MPEG-2 video on DVD is that computers and future players can deinterlace it and display it on progressive-scan HDTV screens, with considerably better quality than today's interlaced screens.

CHAPTER

4

Technical Details

This chapter covers the details of DVD-ROM and DVD-Video. A basic understanding of terms and concepts from Chap. 3 is assumed.

DVD-ROM is the foundation of DVD: the physical layer and the file system layer. DVD-Video is an application of DVD-ROM and is also an application of MPEG-2 and Dolby Digital. That is, the DVD-Video format defines subsets of other standards to be applied in practice for audio and video playback. DVD-ROM can contain any desired digital information, but DVD-Video is limited to certain data types designed for audio and video reproduction. The DVD-Video data types are matched to NTSC and PAL television formats, since NTSC and PAL televisions are the primary target systems.

When the DVD-Audio specification is defined, it will also be a specialized application of DVD-ROM. Variations of DVD for video games and other defined areas may also beget application standards based on DVD-ROM.

DVD Specification

The official specification for DVD is documented in a series of five books. The books are available from Toshiba only under a nondisclosure agreement and after payment of a $5000 fee. (See App. C for contact information.)

The first two books, DVD-ROM and DVD-Video, were released in version 1.0 in August of 1996, but more than six months later were still lacking sections on regional management and copy protection. As of April 1997, the DVD-R and DVD-RAM standards were being finalized. The DVD-Audio specification is on indefinite hold.

Book A: DVD-ROM

Book B: DVD-Video

Book C: DVD-Audio

Book D: DVD-R (write-once)

Book E: DVD-RAM (rewritable)

Book A defines the physical specifications of DVD, including disc specifications and physical data format, as well as the file system (UDF and UDF Bridge). Books B and C define the video and audio applications. Books D and E define extensions to the physical specification and the file system.

Additional parts of the various applications of DVD are covered by other standards documents. See the "Standards" sections at the end of the "DVD-ROM" and "DVD-Video" sections of this chapter.

DVD-ROM

Physical Structure

Table 4.1 lists the physical characteristics of DVD.

MASTERING AND STAMPING.   DVDs are made from polycarbonate, acrylic, polyolefine, or similar material which is stamped from the molten material by using a mold.

The physical format of a DVD disc is close to that of a CD. In fact, most of the production process is the same as for a CD. More care needs to be taken to properly replicate the tinier pits in thinner substrates, and two substrates need to be bonded together, but for discs with only one data layer per substrate, the process can be accomplished with only minor modification to existing CD replication machinery.

Mastering refers to the process of creating the physical stamping molds used in the replication process. (See Fig. 4.1.) The formatted data signal is used to modulate the cutting laser of a laser beam recorder machine (LBR), which creates pits in a glass disc with a photoresist coating. The laser does

Figure 4.1
Mastering
and stamping.

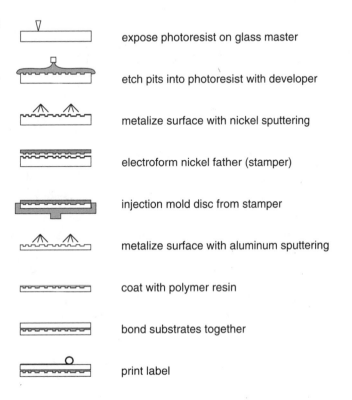

expose photoresist on glass master

etch pits into photoresist with developer

metalize surface with nickel sputtering

electroform nickel father (stamper)

injection mold disc from stamper

metalize surface with aluminum sputtering

coat with polymer resin

bond substrates together

print label

TABLE 4.1

Physical
Characteristics
of DVD

Thickness	1.2 mm (+0.3/−0.06) (2 bonded substrates)
Substrate thickness	0.6 mm (+0.043/−0.030)
Spacing layer thickness	55 μm (±15)
Mass (12 cm)	13 to 20 g
Mass (8 cm)	6 to 9 g
Diameter	120 or 80 mm (±0.30)
Spindle hole diameter	15 mm (+0.15/−0.0)
Clamping area diameter	22 to 33 mm
Inner guardband diameter	33 to 44 mm
Burst cutting area diameter	44.6 (±0.8) to 47 (±0.10) mm
Lead-in diameter	45.2 to 48 mm
Data diameter (12 cm)	48 (+0/−0.4 mm) to 116 mm
Data diameter (8 cm)	48 to 76 mm
Lead-out diameter	70 to 117 mm (approximately 2 mm wide, 1 mm min.)
Outer guardband diameter	117 to 120 mm or 77 to 80 mm
Reflectivity	45 to 85% (SL), 18 to 30% (DL)[*]
Readout wavelength	650 or 635 nm (red laser)
Polarization	Circular
Numerical aperture	0.60 (objective lens)
Optical spot diameter	0.58 to 0.60 μm
Refractive index	1.55 (±0.10)
Tilt margin (radial)	±0.8°
Track spiral (outer layer)	Clockwise
Track spiral (inner layer)	Clockwise or counterclockwise
Track pitch	0.74 μm (±0.01 avg.)
Pit length	0.400 to 1.866 μm (SL), 0.440 to 2.054 μm (DL)
Data bit length (avg.)	0.2667 μm (SL), 0.2934 μm (DL)
Channel bit length (avg.)	0.1333 μm (SL), 0.1467 μm (DL)
Correctable burst error	6.0 mm (SL), 6.5 mm (DL)
Maximum local defects	100 μm (air bubble), 200 μm (black spot)
Rotation	Counterclockwise (to readout surface)
Rotational velocity[†]	570 to 1630 rpm (574 to 1528 rpm in data area)
Scanning velocity[†]	3.49 m/s (SL), 3.84 m/s (DL) (±0.03)
Environmental temperature	−25 to 70°C

[*]SL = single layer, DL = dual layer.
[†]Reference value for a single-speed drive.

not actually cut the glass, but rather exposes sections of the photosensitive coating. The coating is then developed and sent through an etching process which creates a conductive layer. The glass master can then be used in an electrochemical plating process to create the stamping master, or *father*. The stamping master, usually made of nickel, contains a mirror image of the pits that are to be created on the disc. The raised bumps on the stamper are pressed into the liquid plastic during the injection molding process to create the pits. In some cases, the father is used to create *mother* discs, which can then be used to create multiple stampers. Masters can also be made using a dye polymer and metallization process.

NOTE *The term* mastering *is often misused to refer to the authoring or premastering process.*

DISC LAYOUT: SUBSTRATES AND LAYERS. A DVD disc is composed of two bonded plastic substrates (see Fig. 4.2). Each substrate can contain one or two layers of data. The first layer, called layer 0, is closest to the side of the disc from which the data is read. The second layer, called layer 1, is further from the readout surface. A disc is read from the bottom, so layer 0 is below layer 1. The layers are spaced very close together: the distance between layers is less than one-tenth of the thickness of the substrate (less than one-twentieth of the thickness of the disc).

In the case of a single layer, the stamped surface is covered with a thin reflective layer of aluminum by a *sputtering* process. This creates a metallic coating between 60 and 100 angstroms thick. For two layers, the laser must

Figure 4.2
Disc structure.

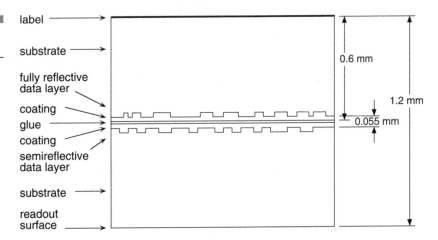

be able to reflect from the first layer when reading it, but also focus through it when reading the second layer. Therefore, the first layer has a semitransparent coating. The first layer is about 20 percent reflective, while the second layer is about 70 percent reflective. The top metallic layer is optionally given a protective coating before being bonded to the other substrate.

The confusing part is that there are two ways to make a single-sided, dual-layer disc. The first method, developed by Matsushita, puts one layer on each substrate, separated by a very thin, transparent adhesive film. The second method, developed by 3M, puts one layer on a substrate, then adds a second layer to the same substrate using a photopolymer (2P) material.

A dual-layer disc can be made in two different ways. (See Fig. 4.3.)

1. One layer on each side:
   a. Stamp outer data layer into first substrate
   b. Add semireflective coating
   c. Stamp inner layer "upside down" on second substrate
   d. Add fully reflective coating
   e. Flip second substrate over and glue with transparent adhesive to first

2. Two layers on one side:
   a. Stamp outer data layer into first substrate
   b. Add semireflective coating
   c. Cover with molten transparent material (UV resin)
   d. Stamp inner layer into the transparent material
   e. Add fully reflective coating
   f. Glue on blank substrate

Clearly the first method is simpler. The second method is required for double-sided, dual-layer discs, which have four layers. These discs are slightly thicker than other discs.

In either case, the result is essentially the same, since the data layers end up at the proper distance from the outer surface. In the first case, the laser focuses through the first side and through the transparent glue onto the layer at the inner surface of the second side. In the second case, the laser focuses through the added transparent material onto the layer at the inner surface of the first side.

BONDING.   There are currently two methods used to bond DVD substrates: hot-melt and UV. Each has different variations.

The hot-melt method rolls a thin coat of melted adhesive onto each substrate, then presses them together with a hydraulic ram. Once the glue has set, a strong bond is formed which remains stable at temperatures up to 70°C (150°F). The hot-melt bonding technique is currently cheaper than the UV technique.

Figure 4.3
Dual-layer
construction.

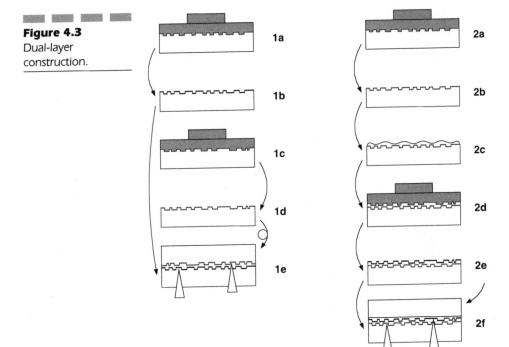

The UV method uses a lacquer which is spread across the bonding surface by spinning the disc (radial bonding) or by silk-screening (cationic bonding). The lacquer is hardened by ultraviolet light. This forms an extremely strong bond which is unaffected by temperature.

Similar bonding techniques are used with MO discs and laserdiscs. Laserdiscs sometimes suffer from deterioration of the aluminum layer, which is colloquially referred to as *laser rot* even though it has nothing to do with the laser beam. Laserdiscs are molded from PMMA, which absorbs about 10 times more moisture than the polycarbonate used in DVDs and can lead to oxidation of the aluminum. The flexibility of laserdiscs allows movement along the bond, which can also damage the aluminum layer. Laser rot problems were more prevalent several years ago when the interaction between the materials that make up a disc was not as well understood as it is today. Since DVDs are molded from improved materials and are more rigid than laserdiscs, they should not be susceptible to laser rot.

BURST CUTTING AREA. A section near the hub of the disc, called the *burst cutting area* (*BCA*) can optionally be used by production systems for individualizing discs. A strong laser is used to cut a series of stripes, somewhat like a bar code, to store up to 188 bytes of information such as ID codes or serial numbers. This information can be used for inventory purposes or by storage systems such as disc jukeboxes to quickly identify discs. See Fig. 4.4.

OPTICAL PICKUPS. A critical component of DVD units is the *optical pickup,* which houses the laser (or lasers), optical elements, and associated electronic circuitry. The optical pickup is mounted on an arm which physically positions it under the disc, moving in and out to read different tracks.

Because of the requirement to read DVDs (which have data layers recorded at two different distances from the surface of the disc) as well as CDs (which have the data recorded at yet a third level), many different techniques have been developed for controlling focus depth. This is also complicated by the fact that CD-R discs require a different wavelength laser than is needed to read DVD discs.

Holographic pickups use aspherical lenses with annular rings that can focus reflected laser light from two different depths: one for DVD and one for CD. These pickups are unable to read CD-R discs.

Twin-lens pickups use two different lenses designed to focus at DVD or CD depth. The appropriate lens is physically moved into the path of the

Figure 4.4
Burst cutting area.

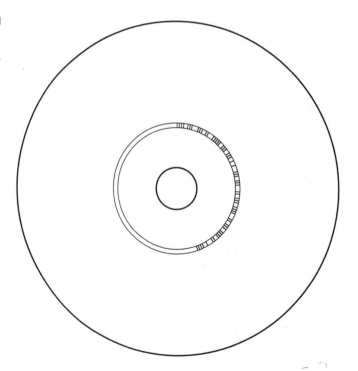

laser beam by a magnetic actuator. These pickups are unable to read CD-R discs.

Twin-laser pickups use two separate laser and lens assemblies, with one laser wavelength tuned for CD and CD-R, and the other for DVD. In some cases, these pickups include holographic lenses.

In all cases, the focusing control is used to change the focus depth between DVD layers, which are spaced about 55 µm apart. The DVD data layers are approximately 0.55 mm from the surface of the disc, and the CD data layer is approximately 1.15 mm deep.

DVD players use semiconductor red laser diodes at 635- or 650-nm wavelength. These components typically costs less than $10 in quantity.

Data Format

Table 4.2 lists the data storage characteristics of DVD.

TABLE 4.2

Data Storage
Characteristics
of DVD

Modulation	8/16 (EFMPlus)
Sector size (user data)	2048 bytes
Logical sector size	2064 bytes (2048 + 12 header + 4 EDC)
Recording sector size	2366 bytes (2064 + 302 ECC)
Unmodulated physical sector	2418 bytes (2366 + 52 sync)
Physical sector size	4836 (2418 × 2 modulation)
Error correction	Reed-Solomon product code (208,192,17) × (182,172,11)
Error correction overhead	15% (13% of recording sector: 308/2366)
ECC block size	16 sectors (32,768 bytes user data, 37,856 bytes total)
Format overhead	16% (37,856/32,768)
Maximum random error	≤280 in 8 ECC blocks
Channel data rate*	26.16 Mbps
User data rate*	11.08 Mbps
Capacity (per side, 12 cm)	4.38 to 7.95 gigabytes (4.70 to 8.54 billion bytes)
Capacity (per side, 8 cm)	1.36 to 2.48 gigabytes (1.46 to 2.66 billion bytes)

*Reference value for a single-speed drive.

DATA STORAGE AND ERROR CORRECTION. Each user sector of 2048 bytes is scrambled with a bit-shifting process to help spread the data around for error correction. Sixteen extra bytes are added to the beginning: 4 bytes for the sector ID (3 bytes for the sector number), 2 bytes for ID error detection, 6 bytes of copy protection information; and 4 bytes of payload error detection code are added to the end. This makes a data sector of 2064 bytes. (See Fig. 4.5.) Each data sector is arranged into 12 rows of 172 bytes, and the rows of 16 data sectors are interleaved together (spreading them apart to help with burst errors) into error correction code blocks (192 rows of 172 bytes). (See Fig. 4.6.) For each of the 172 columns of the ECC block, a 16-byte outer-parity Reed-Solomon code is calculated, forming 16 new rows at the bottom. For each of the 208 (192 + 16) rows of the ECC block, a 10-byte inner-parity Reed-Solomon code is calculated and appended. The ECC block is then broken up into recording sectors by taking a group of 12 rows and adding 1 row of parity codes. This spreads the parity codes apart for further error resilience. Each recording sector is 13 rows (12 + 1) of 182 bytes (172 + 10).

Each recording sector is split down the middle and 1-byte sync codes are inserted in front of each half-row. (See Fig. 4.7.) The data is processed with 8/16 modulation (doubling each byte to 16 bits). This creates a physical sector of 4836 bytes which is written out row by row to the disc as channel data. Data is written using NRZI format (nonreturn to zero, inverted), where each transition from pit to land represents a one, and the lack of a transition represents zeroes.

The 8/16 modulation process replaces each byte with a 16-bit code selected from a set of tables (or a four-state machine). These codes have been carefully chosen to minimize low-frequency (DC) energy, and they also incorporate sync and merge characteristics. The codes guarantee at least 2 and at most 10 zeroes between each group of ones. 8/16 modulation

Figure 4.5
Data sector.

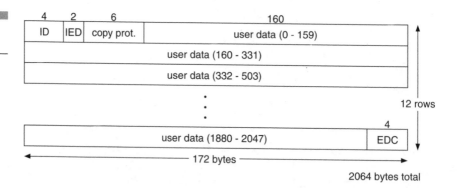

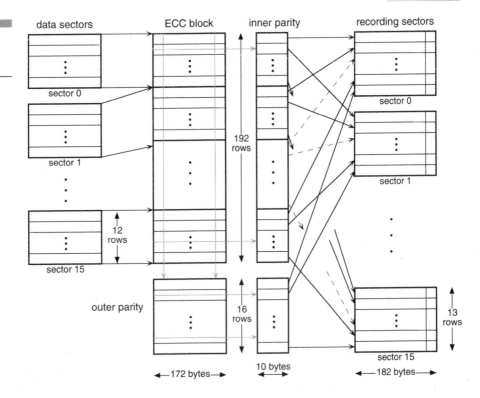

Figure 4.6
ECC block and
recording sectors.

is sometimes called *EFMPlus*. This is a very odd name, since *EFM* is the
method used for channel data modulation on CDs and stands for *eight-to-
fourteen modulation*. Apparently the *plus* is meant to add two to the second
number.

The additional error detection and correction information takes up
approximately 13 percent of the total data: 308 bytes out of 2366 bytes for
each sector. Six error detection bytes are included with the sector data (2
for the ID and 4 for the complete sector). There are 302 bytes for RS parity
codes (120 for the 12 rows, 172 for the 172 columns, and 10 for the 13th row
of column codes). The *product code* part of the error correction system
refers to calculating parity codes on top of parity codes, where the rows of
outer parity cross the columns of inner parity codes. This creates an extra
level of detection and correction. RS-PC can reduce a random error rate
from 2×10^{-2} (one error in 200) to less than 1×10^{-15} (one error in 1
quadrillion, or 1 million-billion). This is an error correction efficiency
approximately 10 times that of CD.

Unlike one-dimensional error correction systems such as CIRC, which
treat the data as a continuous stream, RS-PC works on relatively small

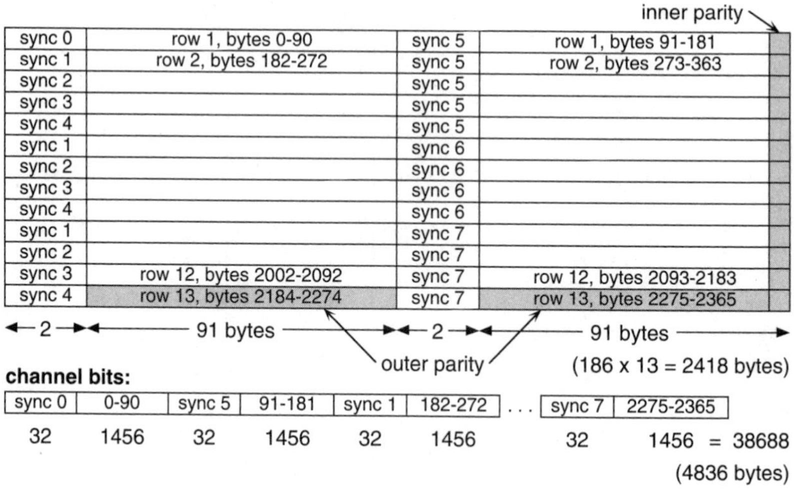

Figure 4.7
Physical sector.

			inner parity
sync 0	row 1, bytes 0-90	sync 5	row 1, bytes 91-181
sync 1	row 2, bytes 182-272	sync 5	row 2, bytes 273-363
sync 2		sync 5	
sync 3		sync 5	
sync 4		sync 5	
sync 1		sync 6	
sync 2		sync 6	
sync 3		sync 6	
sync 4		sync 6	
sync 1		sync 7	
sync 2		sync 7	
sync 3	row 12, bytes 2002-2092	sync 7	row 12, bytes 2093-2183
sync 4	row 13, bytes 2184-2274	sync 7	row 13, bytes 2275-2365

← 2 → ← 91 bytes → ← 2 → ← 91 bytes →

outer parity   (186 x 13 = 2418 bytes)

channel bits:

sync 0	0-90	sync 5	91-181	sync 1	182-272	. . .	sync 7	2275-2365
32	1456	32	1456	32	1456		32	1456 = 38688

(4836 bytes)

blocks of data which are more appropriate for computer data. A disadvantage of RS-PC is that the matrix structure requires twice the buffer size, but due to the ever falling cost of memory this is no longer a critical issue.

The maximum correctable burst error length is approximately 2800 bytes, corresponding to physical damage of 6 mm in length (6.5 mm for dual layers). In comparison, the CIRC structure of CD can only correct burst errors of approximately 500 bytes, corresponding to 2.4 mm of physical damage.

DATA FLOW AND BUFFERING.   Raw *channel data* is read off the disc at a constant 26.16 Mbps. The 16/8 demodulation process reduces the data by half to 13.08 Mbps. After error correction, the *user data stream* runs at a constant 11.08 Mbps. (See Fig. 4.10.)

The track is broken into sectors of 2048 bytes (2 kilobytes). A 37,856-byte ECC block is made up of 16 sectors; 5088 bytes of this is overhead: 4832 bytes of RS-PC error correction, 96 bytes of sector error detection and correction, and 160 bytes of ID and copy protection info. Because error correction is applied to an entire block, data must be read from the disc in complete blocks.

DVD-ROM drives, sometimes referred to as *DVD logical units*, transfer data in 2048-byte units. An internal cache parcels out these units from an ECC block. This presents a special problem for recordable drives which receive data in 2048-byte chunks but must write it to the drive in 37,856-byte chunks. Drives must implement an internal process for maintaining an ECC block which can be read, modified to add a new sector's-worth of data, then rewritten. This read-modify-write process may use an internal cache rather than writing to the disc.

Unlike CD, DVD has no specially defined low-level data formats for audio or video. There is also no TOC or subchannel data. There is only the concept of general data.

DISC ORGANIZATION.   A DVD contains data written in a continuous spiral track. The track in layer 0 travels from the inner to the outer part of the disc. If layer 1 exists, its track can travel in either direction. Opposite track path (OTP) is designed for continuous data from layer to layer. The laser pickup assembly begins reading layer 0 at the center of the disc, starting with the lead-in area; when it reaches the outside of the disc it enters the middle area and refocuses to layer 1, then reads back toward the center of the disc until it reaches the lead-out area. Parallel track path (PTP) is designed for special applications where it's advantageous to switch between layers. In this case, each layer is treated separately and each has its own lead-in and lead-out area (there is no middle area). (See Fig. 4.8.)

The lead-in area contains information about the disc. See Table 4.3. The descrambling keys are also contained in the lead-in area.

The middle area and lead-out area each provide a guide to the readout system that it has reached the middle of a two-layer extent or the end of a layer.

The rotational velocity of the disc varies: the farther from the center the laser pickup is, the slower the disc spins. This creates a constant linear velocity (CLV) so that the data density remains the same across the entire surface. Accordingly, there are more data sectors per revolution further from the center of the disc.

Figure 4.8
Disc organization.

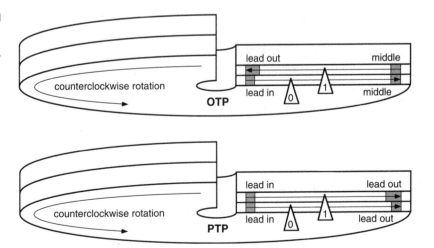

Physical data		
Book type	4 bits	DVD-ROM, DVD-R, ...
Book version	4 bits	1.0, ...
Disc size	4 bits	80 mm, 120 mm
Minimum data rate	4 bits	2.52, 5.04, 10.08 (Mbps)
Number of layers	2 bits	1, 2
Track path	1 bit	PTP, OTP
Layer type	4 bits	Read, write-once, write-many
Linear density	4 bits	0.267, 0.293 (µm/data bit)
Track density	4 bits	0.74 µm/track
Starting sector number	3 bytes	030000h
Ending sector number (main)	3 bytes	
Ending sector number (layer 0)	3 bytes	
BCA flag	1 bit	doesn't exist, exists
Copyright data		
Copyright protection system	1 byte	doesn't exist, exists
Region management flags	1 byte	1 bit per region (8)
Encryption data	2048 bytes	
Manufacturing data	2048 bytes	1 per layer
Content provider information	28,672 bytes	

File Format

Data sectors on a DVD-ROM can essentially contain any type of data in any format. Officially, the OSTA UDF file format standard is mandatory. UDF defines specific ways in which the ISO 13346 volume and file structure standard is applied for specific operating systems.

UDF limits ISO 13346 by making multivolume and multipartition support optional, defining filename translation algorithms and defining extended attributes such as MacOS file/creator types and resource forks. UDF provides information specific to DOS, OS/2, Macintosh, Windows 95, Windows NT, and UNIX. On top of the UDF limitations, the DVD-ROM standard requires that the logical sector size and logical block size be 2048 bytes.

UDF includes an appendix defining additional restrictions for DVD-Video. See the "File format" section of the "DVD-Video" section, which follows, for details.

DVD-ROM PREMASTERING. The premastering process for a DVD-ROM is very similar to the premastering process for a CD. The computer directory structure and data files are written to a UDF, UDF Bridge (UDF/ISO 9660), or other format disc image. Some premastering systems allow the disc image to be used to simulate an actual disc. The disc image is copied to DLT or DVD-R for creating a one-off test disc or for mastering and replication.

The DVD-Video premastering process is described in a later section.

Improvement over CD

The storage capacity of a single-layer DVD is seven times higher than a CD. This is accomplished by a combination of smaller physical bit size, slightly larger data area, and improved logical channel coding. (See Table 4.4.)

Standards

File system: *OSTA Universal Disc Format Specification: 1996* (Appendix 6.9) "OSTA UDF Compliant Domain" of *ISO/IEC 13346:1995 Volume and file structure of write-once and rewritable media using non-sequential recording for information interchange.* (*Note: ECMA 167, 2d edition, 1994,* is equivalent to ISO/IEC 13346:1995.)

TABLE 4.4

Incremental Improvements of DVD over CD-ROM

Factor	DVD	CD	Gain
Smaller pit length	0.400 μm	0.833 μm	2.08×
Tighter tracks	0.74 μm	1.6 μm	2.16×
Slightly larger data area	8759 mm^2	8605 mm^2	1.02×
More efficient modulation	16/8	17/8	1.06×
More efficient error correction	13% (308/2366)	34% (1064/3124)	1.32×
Less sector overhead	2.6% (62/2418)	8.2% (278/3390)	1.06×
Total increase			~7×

File system: *ISO 9660:1988 Information processing—Volume and file structure of CD-ROM for information interchange* (*Note:* Equivalent to *ECMA 119, 2d edition, 1987.*)

Device interface: *SFF 8090* ATAPI/SCSI (Mt. Fuji)

Physical connection:

—*ANSI X3.131-1994: Information Systems—Small Computer Systems Interface-2 (SCSI-2)*

—*ANSI X3.277-1996: Information Technology—SCSI-3 Fast-20*

—*ANSI X3.221-1994: Information Systems—AT Attachment Interface for Disk Drives* (EIDE/ATA)

—*ANSI X3.279-1996: Information Technology—AT Attachment Interface with Extensions (ATA-2)*

DVD-Video

The DVD-Video standard is an application of DVD-ROM intended to provide high-quality audio and video in a format supported worldwide by consumer electronics manufacturers, movie studios, video publishers, and computer makers.

DVD-Video provides 1 stream of MPEG-2 variable bitrate video; up to 8 streams of Dolby Digital multichannel audio, MPEG-2 multichannel audio, or linear PCM audio; and up to 32 streams of full-screen subpicture graphics, supplemented with navigation menus, still pictures, seamless branching, parental management, and rudimentary interactivity.

The DVD-Video format is designed for playback on all standard NTSC and PAL television displays via analog video connections and should also be playable in standard resolution on upcoming digital and high-definition televisions via a digital connection.

DVD-Video incorporates multichannel digital audio for compatible digital audio systems and also provides digital or analog audio to support all standard stereo audio systems. (See Fig. 4.9.)

DVD-Video can also be played on compatible computer systems. See Chap. 9 for details.

Data Flow and Buffering

Raw *channel data* is read off the disc at a constant 26.16 Mbps. The 16/8 demodulation process cuts it in half to 13.08 Mbps. After error correction,

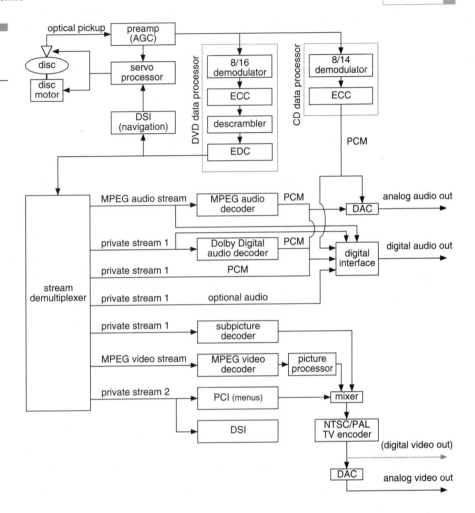

Figure 4.9
DVD-Video player block diagram.

the *user data stream* goes into the track buffer at a constant 11.08 Mbps. Data search information (DSI) is copied from the data stream before it reaches the track buffer. The track buffer feeds the *program stream* data out at a variable rate of up to 10.08 Mbps. The program stream contains five kinds of packetized elementary streams (PES): video, audio, subpicture, presentation control information (PCI), and data search information (DSI). PCI and DSI together constitute DVD system overhead. The maximum combined rate of the remaining three streams is 10.08 Mbps, with a per-stream limit of 9.8 Mbps. (See Fig. 4.10.)

The MPEG-1 or MPEG-2 video stream is a standard MPEG elementary stream. MPEG-1 or MPEG-2 audio, if any, is also presented as a standard MPEG audio stream. An MPEG private stream is used to hold PCI

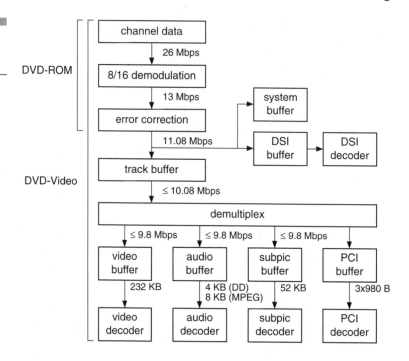

Figure 4.10
DVD data flow
block diagram.

and DSI, and a second private stream holds subpicture and all other audio data.

The video stream is limited to 9.8 Mbps but must be lower to allow for audio. MPEG-1 video is limited to 1.856 Mbps.

A PCM audio stream is limited to 6.144 Mbps (sufficient for 8 channels at 16/48 sampling), Dolby Digital is limited to 448 kbps, MPEG-1 audio is limited to 384 kbps, the MPEG-2 audio extension stream is limited to 528 kbps (giving a combined limit of 912 kbps), DTS is limited to 1536 kbps, and SDDS is limited to 1280 kbps. See Tables 4.5 and 4.6 and Figs. 4.11 and 4.12.

File Format

In order to limit the computing requirements for a home consumer DVD player, additional constraints were applied to the OSTA UDF file format. This constrained format is outlined in Appendix 6.9 of the UDF standard and is commonly referred to as *MicroUDF.* Constraints include the following:

- A DVD player is recommended to support UDF. ISO 9660 will eventually be phased out.

TABLE 4.5

Stream Data Rates

	Minimum (kbps)	Typical (kbps)	Maximum (kbps)	Combined maximum
MPEG-2 video	1500	3500	9800	n/a
MPEG-1 video	1150	1150	1856	
PCM	768	1536	6144	
Dolby Digital	64	384	448	9800
MPEG-1 audio	64	192	384	
MPEG-2 audio	64	384	912	
Subpicture	n/a	10	3360	9800

- One logical volume per side, one partition, and one file set.
- Individual files must be less than or equal to 1 gigabyte in length.
- Each file must be a contiguous extent.
- File and directory names must use only 8 bits per character.
- Short allocation descriptors only.
- Fields such as OS and implementation use must be zero.
- No symbolic links (aliases) can be used.
- ICB strategy 4.
- No multisession format is allowed.
- No boot descriptor is allowed.
- A specific directory (VIDEO_TS) must be present and must contain a specific file (VIDEO_TS.IFO).

These constraints apply only to the directory and files which the DVD player needs to access. There can be other files and directories on the disc which are not intended for the DVD player and do not meet the preceding listed constraints. Such directories and files must be placed on the disc following the DVD-V data and are ignored by DVD players (unless the DVD player employs extensions to the DVD-Video standard). This allows many kinds of data and applications to coexist with DVD-Video data.

The DVD-Video specification proscribes a directory and set of files within the UDF file format. All files are stored in one directory (VIDEO_TS). In the future, DVD-Audio information will be stored in a homologous directory (AUDIO_TS). An optional, root-level directory

TABLE 4.6

Playing Times for
Various Data Rates

Video average	Audio (no. of tracks)	Total[1]	SS/SL[2]	SS/DL	DS/SL	DS/DL
	Data rate (Mbps)		Playing time per disc in minutes (hours)			
3.5	1.152 (3)[3]	4.69	133 (2.2)	242 (4.0)	267 (4.4)	485 (8.0)
3.5	0.768 (2)[3]	4.31	145 (2.4)	264 (4.4)	290 (4.8)	528 (8.8)
3.5	0.384 (1)[3]	3.92	159 (2.6)	290 (4.8)	319 (5.3)	580 (9.6)
3.5	3.072 (8)[3]	6.61	94 (1.5)	172 (2.8)	189 (3.1)	344 (5.7)
3.5	1.536 (1)[4]	5.08	123 (2.0)	224 (3.7)	246 (4.1)	448 (7.4)
8.9	1.152 (3)[3]	10.08	62 (1.0)	112 (1.8)	124 (2.0)	225 (3.7)
9.7	0.384 (1)[3]	10.08	62 (1.0)	112 (1.8)	124 (2.0)	225 (3.7)
7.0	0.768 (2)[3]	7.81	80 (1.3)	145 (2.4)	160 (2.6)	291 (4.8)
6.0	0.768 (2)[3]	6.81	92 (1.5)	167 (2.7)	184 (3.0)	334 (5.5)
5.0	0.768 (2)[3]	5.81	107 (1.7)	196 (3.2)	215 (3.5)	392 (6.5)
4.0	0.768 (2)[3]	4.81	130 (2.1)	236 (3.9)	260 (4.3)	473 (7.8)
3.0	0.768 (2)[3]	3.81	164 (2.7)	299 (4.9)	329 (5.4)	598 (9.9)
2.0	0.192 (1)[5]	2.23	280 (4.6)	510 (8.5)	561 (9.3)	1020 (17.0)
1.15[6]	0.192 (1)[5]	1.38	453 (7.5)	823 (13.7)	906 (15.1)	1647 (27.4)
1.15[6]	0.064 (1)[7]	1.25	499 (8.3)	908 (15.1)	999 (16.6)	1816 (30.2)

[1]Total data rate includes 4 subpicture streams (0.04 Mbps).
[2]SS = single side (4.7G), DS = double side (8.5G), SL = single layer (9.4G), DL = dual layer (17G).
[3]5.1-channel Dolby Digital audio
[4]16-bit/48-kHz PCM audio
[5]2-channel Dolby Digital or MPEG audio
[6]MPEG-1 video
[7]1-channel Dolby Digital or MPEG audio

(JACKET_P) can contain identifying images for the disc in three sizes, including thumbnails for graphical directories of disc collections.

The required VIDEO_TS.IFO file contains the video manager title set (main menu) information (VMGI). Additional .IFO files hold other title set information (VTSI), with backup copies in .BUP files. For each title on the disc, there can be up to 10 .VOB files that hold one or more video object set blocks (see the "Physical data structure" section that follows; see Figs. 4.13 and 4.14).

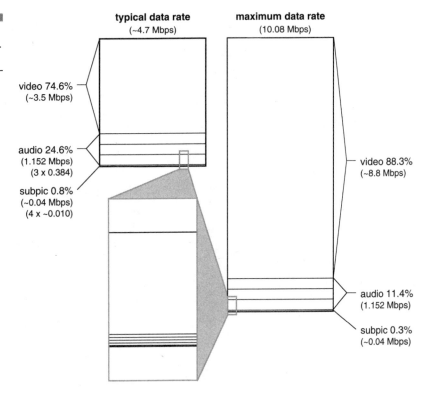

Figure 4.11
Relative sizes of DVD-Video data streams.

typical data rate
(~4.7 Mbps)

maximum data rate
(10.08 Mbps)

video 74.6%
(~3.5 Mbps)

audio 24.6%
(1.152 Mbps)
(3 x 0.384)

subpic 0.8%
(~0.04 Mbps)
(4 x ~0.010)

video 88.3%
(~8.8 Mbps)

audio 11.4%
(1.152 Mbps)

subpic 0.3%
(~0.04 Mbps)

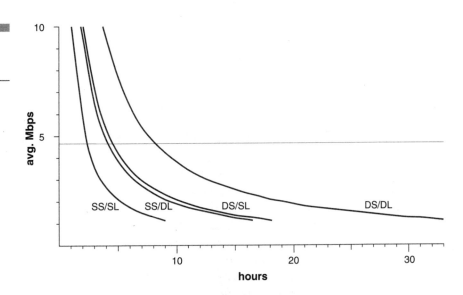

Figure 4.12
Data rate versus playing time.

avg. Mbps

SS/SL   SS/DL   DS/SL   DS/DL

hours

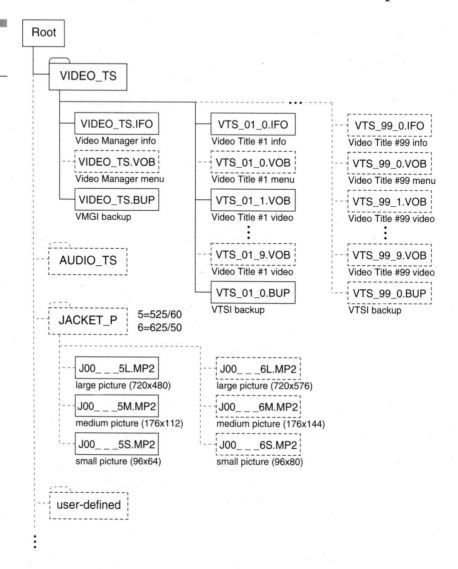

Figure 4.13
DVD-Video file structure.

Navigation and Presentation Overview

DVD-Video players (and software DVD-Video navigators) include a presentation engine and a navigation manager. The presentation engine uses the information in the presentation data stream from the disc to control what is shown. The navigation engine uses information in the navigation data stream from the disc to provide a user interface, create menus, control branching, and so on. In a general sense, the user input determines the path of the navigation manager, which controls the presentation engine to create the display. See Fig. 4.15.

Figure 4.14
DVD-Video volume
layout.

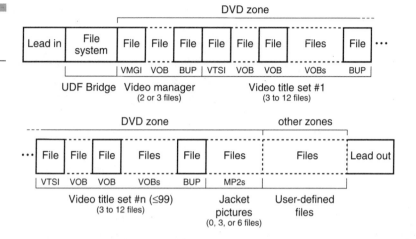

Navigation data includes information and a command set that provides rudimentary interactivity. Menus are present on almost all discs to allow content selection and feature control. DVD-Video content is broken into *titles* (movies or albums), and *parts of titles* (chapters or songs). For example, a disc containing four television episodes could make each episode a title. A disc with a movie, supplemental information, and a theatrical preview might be organized into three titles, with the long movie title arrayed in chapters. A disc can have up to 99 titles, but in many cases there will be only one. Most discs have a main menu for the entire disc, from which titles are selected. Each title can also provide a title menu. Depending on

Figure 4.15
Navigation and
presentation model.

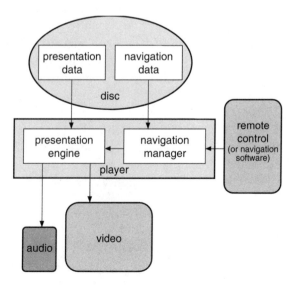

the complexity of the title, additional menus can be provided at any point.

Each menu has a still or moving background and on-screen *buttons*. Remote-control units have four arrow keys for selecting on-screen buttons, plus numeric keys, a select or enter key, a title key, a menu key, and a return key. Additional remote functions may include freeze, step, slow, fast, scan, next, previous, audio select, subtitle select, camera angle select, play mode select, search to program, search to part of title (chapter or scene), search to time, and search to camera angle. Any of these features can be disabled by the producer of the disc. Additional features of the navigation and command set are covered in the navigation and presentation sections that follow.

Material for camera angles, seamless branching, and parental control is interleaved together in chunks. The player jumps from chunk to chunk, skipping over unused angles, branches, or scenes to stitch together a seamless video presentation. These chunks are not multiplexed as individual streams of video and audio,* but are separately interleaved (see Fig. 4.16). The interleaved chunks have no direct effect on the bit rate but they do reduce the maximum allowable rate, since the track buffer must be able to continue supplying data while intervening chunks are skipped over. Adding one camera angle for the duration of a title roughly doubles the amount of space it requires (and cuts the playing time in half).

Data Structures

DVD data is organized into a complex structure representing the physical location of data on the disc. Since data may be shared among different titles and programs, logical data structures are overlaid on the physical structure. The logical structures contain navigation information and determine the presentation order of information, which is independent of the physical order.

PHYSICAL DATA STRUCTURE. The physical data structure determines the way data is organized and placed on the disc. The standard specifies that data must be stored sequentially—physically contiguous—according to the DVD-Video physical structure. The top line of Fig. 4.17

---

*Everything turns out to be interleaved if you dissect it far enough. At the MPEG packet level, the different program streams are interleaved, but the player sees them as individual streams coming out of the demultiplexer.

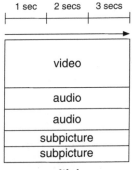

Figure 4.16
Multiplexing versus interleaving.

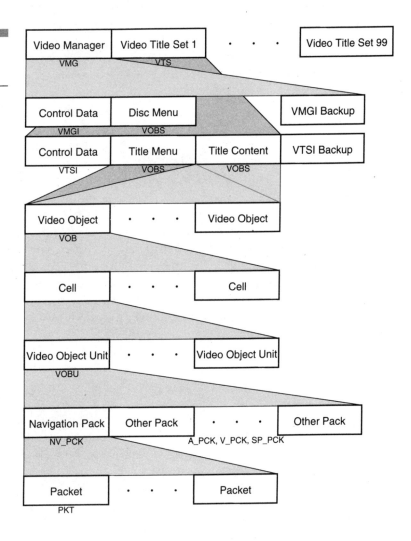

Figure 4.17
Physical data structure.

represents the order in which data is stored on the disc. The structure is hierarchical: each block can be broken up into component blocks, which can be further subdivided, as illustrated in Fig. 4.17.

The primary block is a *video title set* (*VTS*), which contains internal information about the title, followed by *video object sets* (*VOBSs*). The first video object set may be an optional menu, followed by video object sets which contain the actual title content. In general, the terms *title* and *video title set* mean the same thing. *Video title set* refers to the physical collection of data, and *title* refers to the logical construct (a movie, an episode, a collection of songs, and so on). (See Figs. 4.18 and 4.19.)

The main menu of the disc is called the *video manager* (*VMG*) and is a special case of a video title set. If this menu is present, it's the first thing the viewer sees after inserting the disc. Alternately, there can be a special *autoplay* piece which automatically begins playback of the disc.

Data at the VOBS level includes attributes for video, audio, and subpicture. See Tables 4.7, 4.8, and 4.9. The language of audio and subpictures can be identified with ISO 639 codes (see Table A.20) and can also be identified as commentary, simplified audio, and so forth.

Each video object set is composed of one or more *video objects* (*VOBs*). The granularity of the video object level is designed to group or interleave blocks for seamless branching and camera angles. A video object is part or all of an MPEG-2 program stream. (See Fig. 4.20.)

A video object is one or more *cells*. A cell is a group of pictures or audio blocks and is the smallest addressable chunk. A cell can be as short as a second or as long as a movie. Cell IDs are relative to the video object in which they reside, so a cell can be uniquely identified with its cell ID and video object ID. Note that the player may need to get additional presentation information about the cell from the PGC (defined later). (See Fig. 4.21.)

Each cell is further divided into *video object units* (*VOBUs*). (See Fig. 4.22.) In spite of its name, a video object unit does not always contain video. A

TABLE 4.7		
	Compression mode	MPEG-1 or MPEG-2
VOBS Video Attributes	TV system	525/60 or 625/50
	Aspect ratio	4:3 or 16:9
	Display mode permission*	Letterbox, pan & scan, both
	4:3 source is letterboxed	Yes or no

*When 16:9 aspect ratio is presented on a 4:3 display.

TABLE 4.8	Audio coding mode[*]	AC-3, MPEG-1/MPEG-2, MPEG + extension, LPCM, DTS, or SDDS
VOBS Audio Attributes	DRC (dynamic range)	On, off
	Quantization (PCM)	16, 20, or 24 bits
	Sampling rate (PCM)	48 or 96 kHz
	Number of channels[*]	1 to 8
	Film/camera mode (625/50)	Film or camera
	Application mode	Surround, karaoke, or unspecified
	Code	ISO 639 language code or unspecified
	Code extension	Unspecified, caption, for visually impaired, director comments 1, director comments 2

[*]VOBSs containing menus can use only 2-channel PCM audio.

TABLE 4.9	Coding mode	2-bit RL (no other options)
VOBS Subpicture Attributes	Code	ISO 639 language code or unspecified
	Code extension	Unspecified, normal caption, large caption, children's caption, forced caption, director caption, large director caption, director caption for children
	Channel mixing info	Contents, mixing phase, mixed flag, mix mode

video object unit is an integer number of video fields and is from 0.4 to 1 second long, unless it's the last VOBU of a cell, in which case it can be up to 1.2 seconds long. Analog protection system (APS) data is stored at the video object unit level and specifies if analog protection is off or is one of three types. See the section "Analog protection system" for details.

Finally, at the bottom of the heap, video object units are broken into *packs* of *packets*. The format of packs and packets is compliant with the MPEG standard. Packs include system clock reference information for timing and synchronization. Each packet identifies which stream it belongs to and carries a chunk of data for that stream. Packs are stored in recording order, interleaved according to the different streams that were multiplexed together. Different packs contain data for navigation, video, audio, and subpicture. See Figs. 4.23 and 4.24.

TABLE 4.10

Limits of Physical
Units

Unit	Maximum
Video Title Set (VTS)	99 per disc
Video Object Set (VOBS)	99 per VTS
Video Object (VOB)	
Cell	
Video Object Unit (VOBU)	
Pack (PCK)	
Packet (PKT)	

Figure 4.18
VTS structure.

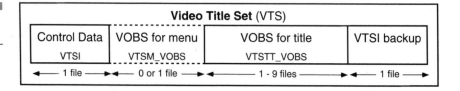

Figure 4.19
VOBS structure.

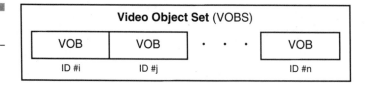

PRESENTATION DATA STRUCTURE. The presentation data structure is overlaid on the physical data structure. (See Figs. 4.25 and 4.30.) The top level comprises titles. Each title contains up to 999 *program chains* (*PGCs*). A program chain contains 0 to 99 *programs* (PGs), which are ordered collections of pointers to cells.* The physical data and the logical presentation data structure converge at the cell level. The PGC links cells together and indicates in what order the programs and cells are to be played. Programs within a PGC can be flagged for sequential play, random play (programs are randomly selected and may repeat), or shuffle play (programs are played in random order without repeats). Individual cells may be used by more than one program chain, which is how parental management and seamless branching are accomplished: different program chains define different sequences through mostly the same material. (See Figs. 4.25 and 4.30.)

---

*A PGC with no programs (no VOBs) contains only navigation commands.

Figure 4.20
VOB structure.

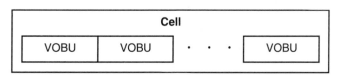

Video Object (VOB)

Cell	Cell	• • •	Cell
ID #1	ID #2		ID #n

Figure 4.21
Cell structure.

Cell

VOBU	VOBU	• • •	VOBU

Figure 4.22
VOBU structure.

Video Object Unit (VOBU)

Navigation Pack	Video Pack	Audio Pack	Video Pack	• • •	Video Pack	Subpicture Pack
NV_PCK	V_PCK	A_PCK	V_PCK		V_PCK	SP_PCK

required (1 only) — optional (repeated in any order)

Figure 4.23
Pack structure.

Pack

start code	system clock	program mux rate	stuffing length	stuffing	packet 1	• • •	packet n
4 bytes	6 bytes	3 bytes	1 byte	0-7 bytes			

pack header (14 bytes) — 2034 bytes
2048 bytes

Figure 4.24
Packet structure.

Packet

start code	stream ID	packet length	misc. (incl. substream ID)	packet-dependent data (PCI, DSI, video, audio, subpic)
3 bytes	1 byte	2 bytes	3-24 bytes	

The presentation data structure includes additional groupings within levels. The groupings provide additional organization and include leading and/or trailing information. (See Fig. 4.26.) Groupings include *parental blocks,* which are used for parental management; *angle blocks* for multiple camera angles; *interleaved blocks* for seamless branching; and so on.

There's also the *part of titles* (PTT) construct, commonly called a *chapter* or a *scene.* It's best to think of a part of title as a marker or branch point. For a multi-PGC title, the user may take different paths from PGC to PGC, so that "chapter 2" via one path might be made of up different PGCs than "chapter 2" via another path. (See Fig. 4.27.)

Figure 4.25
Presentation
data structure.

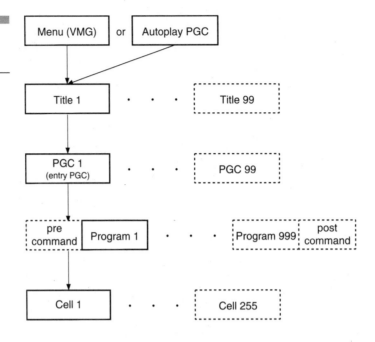

There are three types of titles: a monolithic title meant to be played straight through (One_Sequential_PCG_Title), a title with multiple PGCs for varying program flow (Multi_PCG_Title), and a title with multiple PGCs which are automatically selected according to the parental restriction setting of the player (Parental_Block_Title). See Figs. 4.28 and 4.29.

NAVIGATION DATA STRUCTURE. As with presentation data, the navigation data structure is a logical hierarchy overlaid on the physical data structure. Navigation data is grouped into four categories: control, search, user interface, and navigation commands. (See Fig. 4.31.)

TABLE 4.11

Limits of
Logical Units

Unit	Maximum
Title	99 per disc
Program chain (PGC)	999 per title, 16 per parental block
Part of title (PTT)	999 per title
Program (PG)	99 per PGC
Cell pointer	255 per PGC

GANDER MOUNTAIN
MERRILLVILLE #185

LC 1/3 GLO GRN
048515100259   1.47 T
LC 1/3 GLO GRN
048515100259   1.47 T
LC 1/4 GLO GRN
048515140262   1.47 T
LC 1/4 GLO GRN
048515140262   1.47 T
PRO-PK WALL HK RED#6
043193373988   2.79 T
BULLET WEIGHTS1/16
089186100100   0.99 T

SUBTOTAL $9.66
Sales Tax 5% $0.48
TOTAL $10.14
CASH $11.00
CHANGE $0.86

Receipt required for all
Returns and Exchanges

ITEMS 6   Jonathan B.
10-07-99   17:02:44
0185 20 004275   5470

THANK YOU FOR SHOPPING AT
GANDER MOUNTAIN

HUNT FISH CAMP

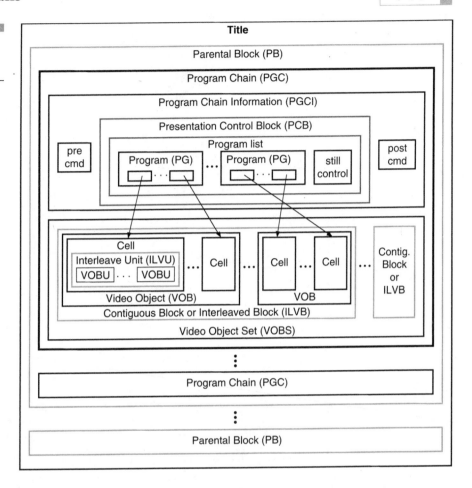

Figure 4.26
Presentation data
structure groupings.

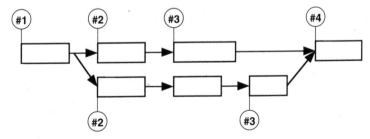

Figure 4.27
Example of part
of title markers.

CONTROL INFORMATION. Control information describes the data. This includes information such as format (NTSC or PAL), aspect ratio, language, audio and subpicture selection, and moral codes for parental management.

These are described elsewhere in more detail.

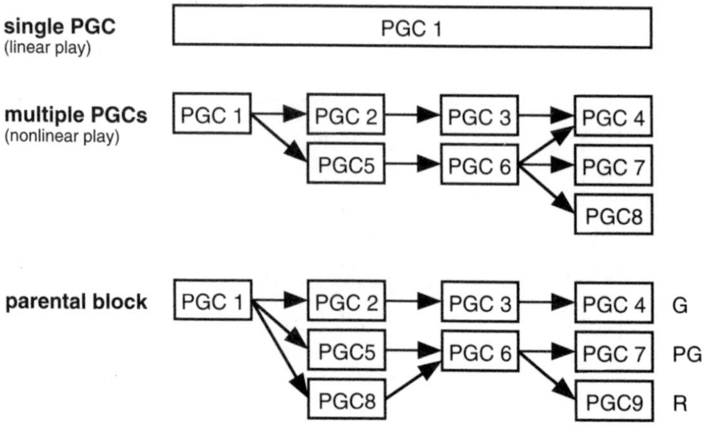

Figure 4.28
Title structures.

Figure 4.28
Title structures.

Figure 4.29
Example presentation
structures.

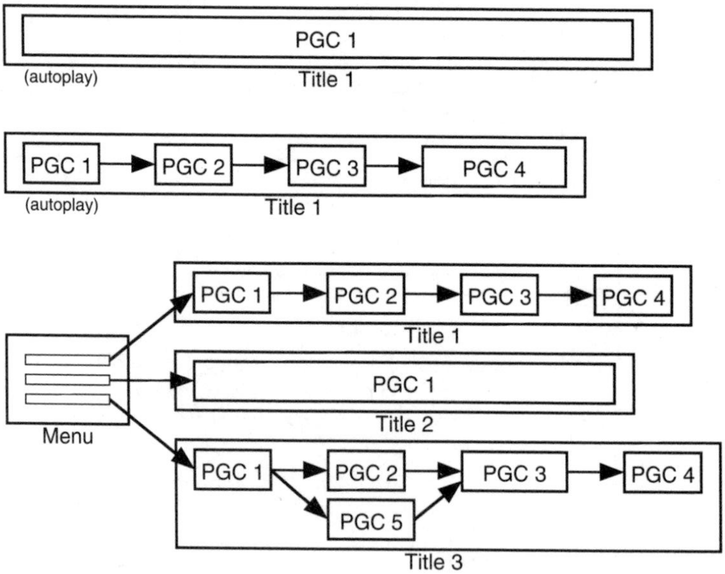

Figure 4.29
Example presentation structures.

SEARCH DATA. The search data creates a navigational structure which can be steered through with the remote control or by program control (see the following section entitled "Navigation commands").

There are seven search types, described in Table 4.12, which are associated with a key or combination of keys on the remote control. These searches are associated with a PGC: the search map is stored in the PGCI. Additional search types are provided for parts of titles (chapters), time, angles, and VOBUs (for trick play modes such as slow and fast).

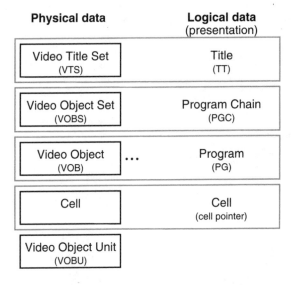

Figure 4.30
Relationship of presentation data to physical data.

If no search data is present for a particular search type, the player is unable to provide that function. It's possible to create a disc which plays from beginning to end and cannot be interrupted by the user (other than by stopping or ejecting the disc).

NAVIGATION COMMANDS. Navigation commands provide DVD's branching and other interactive features. Each PGC can optionally begin with a set of precommands, followed by cells which can each have one optional command, followed by an optional set of postcommands. In total, a PGC cannot have more than 128 commands; but since commands are stored in a table at the beginning of the PGC and referenced by number, they can be used many times within the PGC. Cell commands are executed after the cell is presented.

The commands are similar to computer CPU instruction words and are in fact instructions to the processing unit of the player. Each command is up to 8 bytes long and can consist of one, two, or three instructions. Instructions include

- *Math operations:* add, subtract, multiply, divide, modulo, random
- *Logical (bitwise) operations:* and, or, xor
- *Comparison:* equal, not equal, greater than, greater than or equal to, less than, less than or equal to
- *Register operations:* load (set), move, swap
- *Flow control:* goto, link, jump, exit, etc.

Figure 4.31
Navigation data
structure.

Control
- format (NTSC/PAL)
- language
- audio selection
- subpicture selection
- parental management
- karaoke
- display mode and aspect

Navigation
- general parameters
- system parameters
- navigation timer
- buttons

Search
- PGCI search (jump to menu)
  - Title (disc menu; VMG)
  - Root (title menu; VTS)
  - Audio (title audio menu)
  - Subpicture (title subpicture menu)
  - Angle (title angle menu)
  - Part of Title (title chapter menu)
- Presentation data search
  - Part of Title (chapter skip)
  - Time
  - Angle
  - VOBU (trick play)

There are 24 system registers which hold information such as language code, audio and subpicture settings, and parental level (see Table 4.13). Some of these registers can be set by commands, allowing programs to control presentation of audio, video, subpicture, camera angles, and so on. There are 16 general 16-bit registers for such uses as keeping score or tracking status. A countdown timer is also provided. A potentially serious design limitation is that the registers are cleared when control is returned to a title menu. However, this occurs only at initial access, when menu_call is executed in stop state or when title play, part of title play, or time play is executed.

TABLE 4.12

Search Types

Search type	Example (remote control)
PGCI search	
Title (disc menu; VMG)	TITLE
Root (title menu; VTS)	MENU
Audio (title audio menu)	TITLE+AUDIO
Subpicture (title subpicture menu)	TITLE+SUBTITLE
Angle (title angle menu)	TITLE+ANGLE
Part of title (title chapter menu)	TITLE+CHAPTER
Data search	
Part of title (chapter skip)	CHAPTER+8+ENTER
Time	TIME+1+2+0+0+ENTER
Angle	ANGLE

TABLE 4.13

*Player System
Registers*

0	Menu language code	12	Parental management country code
1	Audio stream number	13	Parental level
2	Subpicture stream number	14	Video setting
3	Angle number	15	Audio setting
4	VTS number	16	Audio language code setting
5	Title number	17	Audio language extension code
6	PGC number	18	Subpicture language code setting
7	Part of title number	19	Subpicture language extension code
8	Highlighted button number	20	Reserved
9	Navigation timer	21	Reserved
10	PGC jump for navigation timer	22	Reserved
11	Karaoke audio mixing mode	23	Reserved

BUTTONS. Information to create menu buttons is included in the command data. Up to 36 highlightable, rectangular buttons can be positioned on the screen. In the case of widescreen content (with anamorphic, auto letterbox, or auto pan & scan modes), only 18 buttons are allowed per screen when two modes are used, and only 12 buttons are allowed per screen when all three modes are used.

Menu buttons are tightly coupled to subpictures. The foreground and background pixel types are used to draw the buttons on the video background (which can be still or motion video). Invisible buttons can be created by setting the pixel contrast to 0.

The remote control is used to highlight buttons by jumping from one to another. Each button includes information for four directional links to determine which button on the screen is selected when the corresponding arrow keys are pressed on the remote control. This creates a complex web of links between buttons that may or may not correspond to their physical arrangement. When a button is selected (highlighted), the four color and contrast values are changed to those defined for the *select state*. The selected button is activated by pressing the enter or select key on the remote control. Alternately, any button can be activated by pressing the corresponding number keys on the remote control. When the button is activated, its pixels are momentarily displayed in a new set of color and contrast values defined for the *action state*. See the following "Subpicture" section for details about pixels and subpicture format.

Each button has one command associated with it. This is generally a flow control command that links to a title or a PGC. PGCs are not required to contain programs (physically, they are not required to contain VOBs) and can simply be a set of precommands and postcommands. PGCs can be linked together, allowing a button to trigger an arbitrarily large sequence of commands.

Video Format

See Table 4.14 for a listing of DVD-Video format details.

VIDEO STREAM. DVD-Video is based on a subset of MPEG-2 (ISO/IEC 13818) Main Profile at Main Level (MP@ML). Constant and variable bit rates (CBR and VBR) are supported. MPEG-2 Standard Profile at Main Level (SP@ML) is also supported. DVD adds additional restrictions. These are detailed in Table 4.15. DVD-Video also supports MPEG-1 video at constant and variable bit rates.

TABLE 4.14

DVD-Video Format

Multiplexed data rate	Up to 10.08 Mbps
Video data	1 stream
Video data rate	Up to 9.8 Mbps (typical average 3.5)
TV system	525/60 (NTSC) or 625/50 (PAL)
Video coding	MPEG-2 MP@ML/SP@ML VBR/CBR or MPEG-1 VBR/CBR
Coded frame rate	24 fps* (film), 29.97 fps[†] (525/60), 25 fps[†] (625/50)
Display frame rate	29.97 fps[†] (525/60), 25 fps[†] (625/50)
MPEG-2 resolution	720×480, 704×480, 352×480 (525/60); 720×576, 704×576, 352×576 (625/50)
MPEG-1 resolution	352×240 (525/60); 352×288 (625/50)
MPEG-2 GOP maximum	36 fields (525/60), 30 fields (625/50)
MPEG-1 GOP maximum	18 frames (525/60), 15 frames (625/50)
Aspect ratio	4:3 or 16:9 anamorphic[‡]

*Progressive (decoder performs 3-2 or 2-2 pulldown).

[†]Interlaced (59.94 or 50 fields per second).

[‡]Anamorphic only allowed for 720 and 704 resolutions.

MPEG parameter	DVD	MP@ML
Display frame rate (525/60)	29.97	23.976, 29.97, 30
Display frame rate (625/50)	25	24, 25
Coded frame rate (525/60)	23.976, 29.97	23.976, 24, 29.97, 30
Coded frame rate (625/50)	24, 25	24, 25
Maximum data rate	9.8 Mbps	15 Mbps
Frame size (horizontal size × vertical size) (525/60)	720×480, 704×480, 352×480, 352×240	From 16×16 to 720×480
Frame size (horizontal size × vertical size) (625/50)	720×576, 704×576, 352×576, 352×288	From 16×16 to 720×576
Aspect ratio	4:3, 16:9	4:3, 16:9, 2.21:1
Display horizontal size	540 (4:3), 720 (16:9)	Variable
GOP maximum (525/60)	36 fields/18 frames (30/15 recommended)	No restriction
GOP maximum (625/50)	30 fields/15 frames (24/12 recommended)	No restriction
Audio sample rate	48 kHz	32, 44.1, 48 kHz
Packet size	2048 bytes (one logical block)	Variable
Color primaries and transfer characteristics (525/60)	4 (ITU-R BT.624 M), 6 (SMPTE 170 M)	1, 2, 4, 5, 6, 7, (8)
Color primaries and transfer characteristics (625/50)	5 (ITU-R BT.624 B or G)	1, 2, 4, 5, 6, 7, (8)
Matrix coefficients (RGB to YC_bC_r)	5 (ITU-R BT.624 B or G), 6 (SMPTE 170 M)	1, 2, 4, 5, 6, 7
Low delay	Not permitted	Permitted

TABLE 4.15

Differences between DVD and MP@ML

Still frames (encoded as MPEG-2 I-frames) are supported and can be displayed indefinitely. These are generally used for menus. Still frames can be accompanied by audio. The DVD-Video presentation data also allows automatic freeze frames at the end of video segments (a PGC, a cell, or a VOBU).

Before MPEG-2 compression, the video is subsampled from ITU-R BT.601 format at 4:2:0 sampling with 8 bits of precision, which allocates an average of 12 bits/pixel. The actual color depth of the samples is 24 bits (one byte for Y, one byte for C_b, and one byte for C_r), but the C samples are shared by four pixels. The uncompressed source data rate is 124.416 Mbps (720×480×12×30 or 720×576×12×25). For 24 fps film, the source is typically at video frame rates of 30 fps (a telecine pulldown process has added duplicate fields). The MPEG encoder performs an inverse telecine process to remove the duplicate fields. Therefore, it's appropriate to consider the uncompressed film source data rate to be 99.533 Mbps (720×480×12×24) or 119.439 Mbps (720×576×12×24).

The maximum video bitrate is 9.8 Mbps (but must be less to allow for audio). The "average" bitrate is 3.5 Mbps, but the rate depends entirely on the length of the original video, the quality and complexity of the video, the amount of audio, and so forth. The 3.5 Mbps average data rate is a 36:1 reduction from uncompressed video source (124 Mbps) or a 28:1 reduction from film source (100 Mbps). Video at around 9 Mbps is compressed at less than a 14:1 ratio.

Variable bitrate encoding allows more data to be allocated for complex scenes and less data to be used during simple scenes. By lowering the average data rate, longer amounts of video can be accommodated, but the extra headroom allows the encoder to maintain video quality when a higher data rate is needed. See Fig. 4.32 for an illustration.

SCANNING AND FRAME RATES. DVD-Video supports two display television systems of 525/60 (NTSC, 29.97 interlaced frames/sec) and 625/50 (PAL, 25 interlaced frames/sec). Internal coded frame rates are typically at 29.97 fps interlaced scan from NTSC video, 25 fps interlaced scan from

Figure 4.32

Example of variable bit rate video.

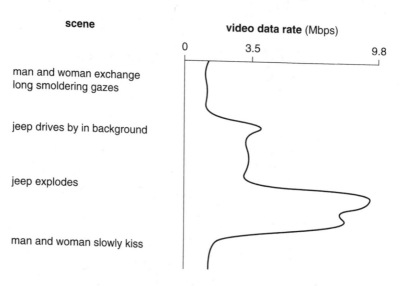

PAL video, and 24 fps progressive scan from film. In the case of 24 fps, the MPEG-2 encoder adds repeat_first_field flags to the data to make the decoder perform either 3-2 pulldown for 60 (59.94)-Hz displays or 2-2 pulldown for 50-Hz displays.

No current players convert from PAL video or film rates to NTSC display format or from NTSC video or film rates to PAL. However, many PAL DVD players are able to produce video in NTSC scanning format transcoded to PAL color format for display on televisions supporting the so-called 60-Hz PAL system.

Since DVD players and computers use standard MPEG-2 decoders, it's probably safe to assume that additional coded frame rates will work, as long as the MPEG-2 repeat_first_field and progressive_sequence flags are properly set to produce either 25 or 29.97 fps display rates.

RESOLUTION. DVD-Video supports numerous resolutions designed for the two television display systems. The lower resolutions are intended primarily for compatibility with MPEG-1 video formats. Most material will use a raster of 720×480 for 525/60 display and a raster of 720×576 for 625/50 display. The MPEG-2 display_horizontal_size value is set to 720 for 16:9 display mode and 540 for 4:3 display mode. See Table 4.16 for a listing of resolutions used in DVD-Video.

DVD pixels are not square. There are eight pixel aspect ratios (see Table 4.17) depending on the raster size and the picture aspect ratio. These ratios vary from the tallest of 0.909 to the widest of 2.909 (almost 3 times as wide as it is tall). Obviously, the pixels are wider for 16:9 anamorphic form than for normal 4:3 form. The 720- and 704-pixel rasters produce identical pixel aspect ratios because the 720-pixel version includes the overscan area (with a scanning line period of 53.33 microseconds), while the 704-pixel version is a tight scan (with a line period of 52.15 microseconds).

There is an alternate way of calculating pixel aspect ratios which divides the horizontal count by the vertical count, then divides the result by the picture aspect ratio. Confusingly, this gives a height/width aspect ratio rather than a consistent width/height aspect ratio. Table 4.17 includes values from the alternate method in parentheses as reciprocals and also adjusts them to match television scanning rates.

TABLE 4.16		16:9 aspect ratio allowed		16:9 aspect ratio not allowed	
DVD-Video	525/60 (NTSC)	720×480	704×480	352×480	352×240
Resolutions (Rasters)	625/50 (PAL)	720×576	704×576	352×576	352×288

TABLE 4.17

DVD-Video Pixel
Aspect Ratios

Resolution	4:3 display	16:9 display
720×480,* 704×480,† 352×240†	0.909 (1/1.095)	1.212 (1/0.821)
720×576,* 704×576,† 352×288†	1.091 (1/0.9157)	1.455 (1/0.687)
352×480†	1.818 (1/2.19)	2.424 (1/0.411)
352×576†	2.182 (1/1.831)	2.909 (1/0.343)

*Overscan.

†Exact scan.

Using the traditional (and rather subjective) television measurement of *lines of horizontal resolution per picture height* (*TV lines,* or *TVL*), DVD has a theoretical maximum of 540 lines on a standard TV (720/[4/3]) and 405 on a widescreen TV (720/[16/9]). Lines of horizontal resolution can also be approximated at 80 per MHz. DVD's MPEG-2 luma component is sampled at 6.75 MHz, which gives 540 lines. The actual observable lines of horizontal resolution may be closer to 500 on a standard TV due to low-pass filtering in the player. For comparison, video from a laserdisc player has about 425 lines of horizontal resolution, and video from a VHS VCR has about 230.

DVD resolution in pixels can be roughly compared to analog video formats by considering pixels to be formed by the intersections of active scan lines and lines of horizontal resolution adjusted for aspect ratio. Table 4.18 shows how the resolution of DVD compares to other formats, including the two high-definition formats of the U.S. ATSC proposal (labeled DTV3 and DTV4), which also correspond to the H0 and H1 levels of the Microsoft/Intel/Compaq "Digital TV Team" proposal. Also see Table A-17 for additional video resolution figures.

WIDESCREEN FORMAT. Video can be stored on a DVD in 4:3 or 16:9 aspect ratio. The 16:9 format is *anamorphic,* meaning the picture is squeezed horizontally to fit a 4:3 rectangle, then unsqueezed during playback. DVD players can produce video in essentially four different ways:

- 4:3 normal (for 4:3 or 16:9 displays)
- 16:9 letterbox (for 4:3 displays)
- 16:9 pan & scan (for 4:3 displays)
- 16:9 widescreen (anamorphic, for 16:9 displays)

TABLE 4.18

Resolution Comparison of Different Video Formats

Format	VCD* (16:9)	VCD (4:3)	VHS* (16:9)	VHS (4:3)	LD* (16:9)	LD (4:3)	DVD (16:9/4:3)	DTV3 (16:9)	DTV4 (16:9)
Horizontal pixels	352	352	333	333	567	567	720	1280	1920
Vertical pixels	180	240	360	480	360	480	480	720	1080
Total pixels	63,360	84,480	119,880	159,840	204,120	272,160	345,600	921,600	2,073,600
× VCD (16:9)‡		1.33†	1.89	2.52	3.22	4.30	5.45	14.55	32.73
× VCD (4:3)			1.42	1.89	2.42	3.22	4.09	10.91	24.55
× VHS (16:9)				1.33	1.70	2.27	2.88	7.69	17.30
× VHS (4:3)					1.28	1.70	2.16	5.77	12.97
× LD (16:9)						1.33	1.69	4.51	10.16
× LD (4:3)							1.27	3.39	7.62
× DVD (16:9/4:3)								2.67	6.00
× DTV3 (16:9)									2.25

*16:9 aspect ratios for VHS, LD, and VCD are letterboxed in a 4:3 picture.
†Comparisons between different aspect ratios are not as meaningful. These are shown in italics.
‡Comparisons at 1.85 or 2.35 aspect ratios are essentially the same as at 16:9 (1.78).

DVD-Video segments can be marked for the following display modes:

- 4:3 full frame
- 4:3 letterboxed (for automatically setting display mode on widescreen TV)
- 16:9 letterbox only (player not allowed to pan & scan)
- 16:9 pan & scan allowed (viewer can select pan & scan or letterbox on 4:3 TV)

NOTE   *See Chap. 3 for a comprehensive explanation of aspect ratios.*

Some players send a signal to the television indicating that the picture is in anamorphic widescreen form so that widescreen televisions can automatically adjust. In some cases, the player can also inform the television that the 4:3 picture was transferred to video in letterbox format so that the television can expand the picture to remove the mattes. In

Europe, the widescreen signaling system (WSS) may be used to convey this type of information (see Table 4.19). This standard is recommended for use by NTSC systems as well.

There is also a convention for signaling widescreen format by adding a 5V DC component to the chroma (C) line of the Y/C (s-video) output. This tells the widescreen equipment to expect video in anamorphic form. Most DVD players and many new video displays support this technique. Unfortunately, much of the existing equipment that the video signal might pass through on its way to the display is designed to filter out such DC "noise." New A/V receivers and video switchers are being designed to recognize the widescreen signal and either pass it through or re-create it at the output.

In anamorphic mode, the pixels are fatter (see Table 4.17). Because of the high horizontal resolution of DVD, the wider anamorphic pixels are not objectionably noticeable.

Video in anamorphic form causes no problems with line doublers, since they simply double the lines on their way to the widescreen display which then stretches out the lines.

LETTERBOX CONVERSION. For automatic letterbox mode the player uses a *letterbox filter* that creates mattes at the top and the bottom of the picture (60 lines each for NTSC, 72 for PAL). This leaves three-quarters of the height remaining, creating a shorter but wider rectangle for the image. In order to fit the shape of this shorter rectangle, the player squeezes the picture vertically by combining every four lines into three. Weighted averaging is typically used to give smooth results.

TABLE 4.19

Wide-screen
Signaling
Information

Aspect ratio	Range	Format	Position	Active lines
4:3 (1.33)	≤1.46	Full	Center	576 (480)
14:9 (1.57)	>1.46, ≤1.66	Letterbox	Top	504 (420)
14:9 (1.57)	>1.46, ≤1.66	Letterbox	Center	504 (420)
16:9 (1.78)	>1.66, ≤1.90	Letterbox	Top	430 (360)
16:9 (1.78)	>1.66, ≤1.90	Letterbox	Center	430 (360)
>16:9 (>1.78)	>1.90	Letterbox	Center	Undefined
14:9 (1.57)	>1.46, ≤1.66	Full*	Center*	576 (480)
16:9 (1.78)	>1.66, ≤1.90	Full (anamorphic)	n/a	576 (480)

*"Shoot and protect" 14:9, a soft-matte format intended to be displayed with top and bottom cropped on a 16:9 display.

This vertical downsampling compensates for the anamorphic horizontal distortion and results in the movie being shown in its full width but with a 25 percent loss of vertical resolution. See Figs. 4.33 and 4.34.

Initial reports indicate that some DVD players do a better job of letterbox filtering than others, perhaps by compensating for interlace jitter effects.

PAN & SCAN CONVERSION. For automatic pan & scan mode, a portion of the image is shown at full height on a 4:3 screen by following a *center of interest* offset that is encoded in the video stream according to the preferences of the people who transferred the film to video. The pan & scan *window* is 75 percent of the full width, which reduces the horizontal resolution from 720 to 540 (see Figs. 4.35 and 4.36), causing a 25 percent loss of horizontal resolution. Expanding the window by 33 percent compensates for the anamorphic distortion and achieves the proper 4:3 aspect ratio. The 540 extracted pixels on each line are interpolated by creating four pixels from every three, to scale the line back to the full width of 720. Weighted averaging is typically used to give smooth results.

Unlike letterbox conversion, which is new to DVD, pan & scan conversion is part of the MPEG-2 standard. Most MPEG-2 decoder chips include a pan & scan conversion feature. The offset is specified in increments of one-sixteenth of a pixel. DVD allows only horizontal adjustments; that is, MPEG-2 frame_center_vertical_offset must be 0, while frame_center_horizontal_offset can vary from –1440 to +1440 for 720-pixel frames and from –1312 to +1312 for 704-pixel frames.

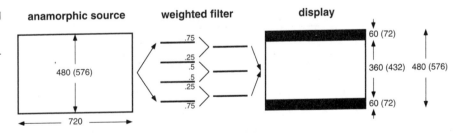

Figure 4.33
Letterbox conversion.

anamorphic source   weighted filter   display

480 (576)   720

.75   .25   .5   .5   .25   .75

60 (72)   360 (432)   480 (576)   60 (72)

Figure 4.34
Letterbox math.

$$\frac{\frac{4}{3}}{\frac{16}{9}} = \frac{1.33}{1.78} = 0.75 = 75\% = \text{"25\% reduction"}$$

$0.75 \times 480 = 360$

$0.75 \times 576 = 432$

Figure 4.35
Pan & scan
conversion.

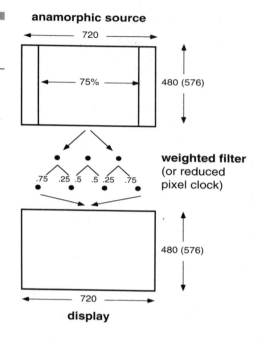

anamorphic source

720

75%   480 (576)

weighted filter
(or reduced
pixel clock)

.75 .25 .5   .5 .25 .75

480 (576)

720

display

Figure 4.36
Pan & scan math.

$$\frac{\frac{4}{3}}{\frac{16}{9}} = \frac{1.33}{1.78} = 0.75 = 75\% = \text{"25\% reduction"}$$

$$0.75 \times 720 = 540$$

$$\frac{\frac{16}{9}}{\frac{4}{3}} = \frac{1.78}{1.33} = 1.33 = 133\% = \text{"33\% increase"}$$

$$1.33 \times 540 = 720$$

It's also possible to stretch out the pixels by increasing the pixel clock in the TV encoder chip.

VIDEO INTERFACE. The MPEG video stream is decoded into 4:2:0 digital component format. This format can be sent directly from the player (with accompanying copy protection information) to a digital connection such as IEEE 1394/FireWire. However, in most cases the player is connected to an analog video display or recording system and requires that the signal be converted to analog form.

For analog component output, the digital signals are scaled and offset according to the desired output format(s) of YP_bP_r or RGB; blanking and sync information is added; and the digital values are converted to analog voltage levels.

For analog s-video and composite baseband video, the digital signal is sent through a TV encoder to produce an NTSC signal from 525/60 format data or a PAL or SECAM signal from 625/50 format data. Almost all TV encoders support both NTSC and PAL, but most NTSC players do not enable PAL video signal output. (See Fig. 4.37.)

See the "How to Hook Up a DVD Player" section of Chap. 7 for more information about audio connections.

See the "Digital Connections" section of Chap. 10 for information about future interface options.

Audio Format

DVD-Video supports three primary audio standards: Dolby Digital, MPEG-2, and linear PCM (LPCM). Additional audio formats such as DTS (Digital Theater Sound) or SDDS (Sony Dynamic Digital Sound) are optional and are provided for in the DVD-Video standard but aren't required. (See Table 4.20.)

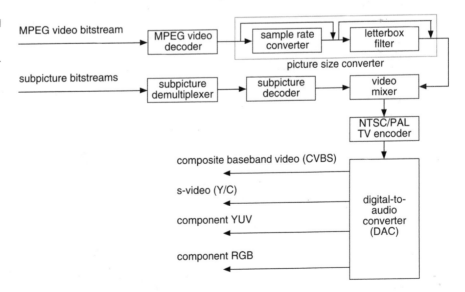

Figure 4.37
Video block diagram.

TABLE 4.20

DVD-Video Format, Audio Details

Audio	0 to 8 streams
Audio coding	Dolby Digital, MPEG-1, MPEG-2, LPCM (DTS, SDDS)
Audio bit rate	32 kbps to 6.144 Mbps, 384 typical

Dolby Digital and MPEG-2 can provide discrete, multichannel audio. This gives clean sound separation with full dynamic range from each speaker. The result is a more realistic soundfield in which sounds can travel left to right and front to back.

Discs containing 525/60 (NTSC) video are required to include at least one audio track in Dolby Digital or PCM format. After that, any combination of formats is allowed. Discs containing 625/50 (PAL/SECAM) video are required to have at least one track of MPEG or PCM audio. However, since Dolby Digital decoders greatly outnumber MPEG-2 audio decoders even in PAL and SECAM countries, many disc producers also include a Dolby Digital audio track on PAL discs. See Table 4.21.

TABLE 4.21

Audio Playing Times at Various Data Rates

		Playing time per disc (hours)							
		No video				+ Average 3.54 Mbps video			
Format	kbps	SS/SL*	SS/DL	DS/SL	DS/DL	SS/SL	SS/DL	DS/SL	DS/DL
DD mono (1 ch)	64	163.0	296.4	326.3	592.9	2.8	5.2	5.7	10.5
DD stereo (2 ch)	192	54.3	98.8	108.7	197.6	2.7	5.0	5.5	10.1
DD multi (5.1 ch)	384	27.1	49.4	54.3	98.8	2.6	4.8	5.3	9.6
DD maximum (5.1 ch)	448	23.2	42.3	46.6	84.7	2.6	4.7	5.2	9.5
2 DD multi (2 × 5.1 ch)	768	13.5	24.7	27.1	49.4	2.4	4.4	4.8	8.8
MPEG maximum (7.1 ch)	912	11.4	20.8	22.9	41.6	2.3	4.2	4.6	8.5
3 DD multi (3 × 5.1 ch)	1152	9.0	16.4	18.1	32.9	2.2	4.0	4.4	8.0
PCM 16/48 stereo (2 ch)	1536	6.7	12.3	13.5	24.7	2.0	3.7	4.1	7.4
PCM 20/48 stereo (2 ch)	1920	5.4	9.8	10.8	19.7	1.9	3.4	3.8	6.9
8 DD multi (8 × 5.1 ch)	3072	3.3	6.1	6.7	12.3	1.5	2.8	3.1	5.7
PCM 20/96 stereo (2 ch)	3840	2.7	4.9	5.4	9.8	1.4	2.5	2.8	5.1
PCM 24/96 stereo (2 ch)	4608	2.2	4.1	4.5	8.2	1.2	2.3	2.5	4.6
PCM 16/48 multi (8 ch)	6144	1.6	3.0	3.3	6.1	1.0	1.9	2.1	3.9

*SS = single side, DD = Dolby Digital, DS = double side, SL = single layer, DL = dual layer.

DOLBY DIGITAL AUDIO DETAILS. Dolby Digital (AC-3) is a multi-channel digital audio format, compressed using perceptual coding technology from original PCM with a sample rate of 48 kHz at up to 20 bits of precision. The Dolby Digital standard provides for other sampling rates of 32 and 44.1 kHz, but these are not allowed with DVD. Frequency response is 3 Hz to 20 kHz for the main five channels, and 3 to 120 Hz for the low-frequency effects (LFE) channel. See Table 4.22.

The bitrate is 64 to 448 kbps, with 384 being the normal rate for 5.1 channels. The typical bitrate for stereo (with or without Dolby Surround encoding) is 192 kbps. Monophonic audio is usually at 96 kbps for music or 64 kbps for voice.

There can be 1, 2, 3, 4, or 5 channels. The subwoofer (.1) channel can optionally be added to any combination. Dual mono is not allowed.

Dolby Digital supports two-channel Dolby Surround as the source in cases where only the Dolby Surround mix is available or where the disc producer doesn't want to remix from the multitrack masters. A DVD labeled as having Dolby Digital sound may use only the two main channels for surround audio or standard stereo. Even old movies with monophonic soundtracks are encoded with Dolby Digital on a DVD, but use only one or two channels.

All Dolby Digital decoders are required to perform a downmixing process to adapt 5.1 channels to 2 channels for stereo PCM and analog output. The downmixing process matrixes the center and surround channels onto the main stereo channels in Dolby Surround format for use by Dolby Pro Logic decoders.

When the audio is encoded, the downmixed output is auditioned by using a reference decoder. If the quality is not adequate, the encoding process can be tweaked, the 5.1-channel mix can be tweaked, or a separate Dolby Surround track can be added (in either Dolby Digital or PCM format). Most modern action movies require minor adjustments to the 5.1-channel mix to make sure the dialogue is audible. As long as the

TABLE 4.22		
Dolby Digital Audio Details	Sample frequency	48 kHz
	Sample size	Up to 20 bits
	Bitrate	64 to 448 kbps, 384 typical
	Channels (front/rear)*	1/0, 2/0, 3/0, 2/1, 2/2, 3/1, 3/2
	Karaoke modes	L/R, M, V1, V2

*LFE channel can be added to all variations.

adjustments don't detract from the 5.1-channel experience and don't undermine the original artistic intent, they are usually sufficient. Tests have shown that the downmixed audio output from the decoder is usually considered to be good enough.

Dolby Digital also provides dynamic range compensation. DVDs provide soundtracks with much wider dynamic range than most recorded media. This improves performance for a quality home theater setup, but may make dialogue and other soft passages too low to hear clearly on less-optimal audio systems. Information is added to the encoded data to indicate what parts of the sound should be boosted when the player's dynamic range compression setting is turned on.

See Chap. 3 for more details on Dolby Digital encoding.

MPEG AUDIO DETAILS. MPEG audio is multichannel digital audio, compressed using perceptual coding from original PCM format with sample rate of 48 kHz at 16 bits. MPEG-1 layer II and MPEG-2 backward-compatible (BC) are supported. The variable bitrate is 64 to 912 kbps, with 384 being the normal average rate. An MPEG-1 stream is limited to 384 kbps. See Table 4.23.

There can be 1, 2, 3, 4, 5, or 7 channels. The subwoofer (.1) channel is optional with any combination. The 7.1-channel format adds left-center and right-center channels, but is not intended for home use. Stereo channels are provided in an MPEG-1 layer II stream. Surround channels are

TABLE 4.23		
MPEG Audio Details	Sample frequency	48 kHz only
	Sample size	Up to 20 bits
	MPEG-1	Layer II only
	MPEG-1 bitrate	64 to 192 kbps (mono), 64 to 384 kbps (stereo)
	MPEG-2	BC (matrix) mode only
	MPEG-2 bitrate*	64 to 912 kbps
	Extension streams†	5.1-channel, 7.1-channel
	Channels (front/rear)‡	1/0, 2/0, 2/1, 2/2, 3/0, 3/1, 3/2, 5/2
	Karaoke channels	L, R, A1, A2, G

*MPEG-1 Layer II stream + extension stream(s).
†AAC (unmatrix, NBC) not allowed.
‡LFE channel can be added to all variations.

matrixed onto the MPEG-1 stream and duplicated in an extension stream to provide discrete channel separation. The LFE channel is also added to the extension stream. An additional extension layer can be added for 7.1 channels. The extension streams are carried by MPEG packets. This layering and packetizing process makes MPEG-2 audio backward-compatible with MPEG-1 hardware: an MPEG-1 decoder will see only packets containing the two main channels.

Stereo output includes surround channel matrixing for Dolby Pro Logic processors. The MPEG signal already has the center and surround channels matrixed onto the main stereo channels, so no special downmixing is required.

Since MPEG-2 decoders were unavailable at the introduction of DVD, first-generation PAL players contain only MPEG-1 decoders. Accordingly, most PAL players also include Dolby Digital decoders.

The MPEG-2 standard includes an AAC mode (advanced audio coding). In order for DVD-Video discs to be playable in players with only MPEG-1 decoders, the AAC mode is not allowed for the primary MPEG audio track, which must always be MPEG-1–compatible. The AAC mode was originally known as NBC (non-backward-compatible) and is also referred to as *unmatrix mode*.

See Chap. 3 for more details of MPEG audio encoding.

PCM AUDIO DETAILS. Linear PCM (pulse code modulation) is lossless, uncompressed digital audio. The same format is used on CDs. DVD-V supports sampling rates of 48 or 96 kHz with 16, 20, or 24 bits/sample. (Audio CD is limited to 44.1 kHz at 16 bits.) There can be from 1 to 8 channels in each track. See Table 4.24.

The maximum PCM bitrate is 6.144 Mbps, which limits sample rates and bit sizes with 5 or more channels (see Table 4.25). It's generally felt that the 96-dB dynamic range of 16 bits or even the 120-dB range of 20 bits combined with a frequency response of up to 22,000 Hz from 48-kHz sampling is adequate for high-fidelity sound reproduction. However, additional bits and higher sampling rates are useful in studio work, noise

TABLE 4.24 *PCM Audio Details*		
Sample frequency	48 or 96 kHz	
Sample size	16, 20, or 24 bits	
Channels	1, 2, 3, 4, 5, 6, 7, or 8	
Karaoke channels	L, R, V1, V2, G	

TABLE 4.25

Allowable PCM
Data Rates
and Channels

		Number of channels							
		1	2	3	4	5	6	7	8
kHz	**Bits**	Data rate (kbps)							
48	16	768	1536	2304	3072	3840	4608	5376	6144
	20	960	1920	2880	3840	4800	5760	n/a	n/a
	24	1152	2304	3456 ·	4608	5760	n/a	n/a	n/a
96	16	1536	3072	4608	6144	n/a	n/a	n/a	n/a
	20	1920	3840	5760	n/a	n/a	n/a	n/a	n/a
	24	2304	4608	n/a	n/a	n/a	n/a	n/a	n/a

shaping, advanced digital processing, and three-dimensional sound field reproduction.

DVD players are required to support all the variations of PCM, but most models subsample the 96-kHz rate down to 48 kHz, and some may not use all 20 or 24 bits. No first-generation players pass 96-kHz audio to the digital audio outputs.

OPTIONAL AUDIO DETAILS. DTS is an optional multichannel (5.1) digital audio format, compressed from PCM at 48 kHz. The data rate is from 64 to 1536 kbps. Channel combinations are (front/surround): 1/0, 2/0, 3/0, 2/1, 2/2, 3/2. The LFE channel is optional with all six combinations.

SDDS is an optional multichannel (5.1 or 7.1) digital audio format, compressed from PCM at 48 kHz. The data rate can go up to 1280 kbps.

KARAOKE MODES. The three standard audio formats support 5-channel karaoke modes, which have two channels for stereo (L and R) plus an optional melody channel (M) or a guide channel (G), and two optional vocal channels (V1 and V2). The karaoke modes are generally used only by specific DVD models with karaoke features.

Codes are included to identify audio segments such as master of ceremonies intro, solo, duet, male vocal, female vocal, climax, interlude, ending, and so on.

SDDS also supports karaoke modes, but they cannot be selected or mixed by standard players.

AUDIO INTERFACE. The digital audio signal from the currently selected audio track is sent to the audio subsection. Multichannel (Dolby Digital or MPEG-2) audio signals are directed to the digital audio output jacks for decoding by external equipment. The multichannel signals are also sent to the appropriate decoder where they are downmixed to two channels and converted to PCM signals. PCM signals from the decoder or directly from the disc are also routed to the digital audio output jacks for processing by external equipment with digital-to-analog converters. (See Figs. 4.38 and 4.39.) Some players also include built-in digital-to-analog audio converters and external jacks for discrete output from the decoder.

Some players provide PCM audio and multichannel audio signals on separate connectors; others provide dual-purpose connectors which must be switched between PCM and multichannel output. A standard extension to IEC 958, designed by Dolby and described in ATSC A/52, is used for Dolby Digital audio signals. This extension, with additions from Philips and others, is being formalized as IEC 1937.

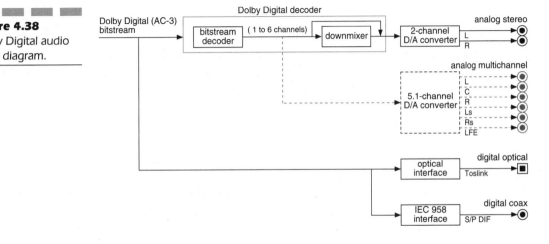

Figure 4.38
Dolby Digital audio block diagram.

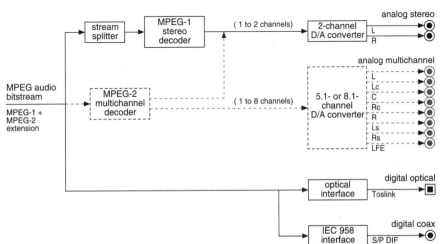

Figure 4.39
MPEG-2 audio block diagram.

PCM audio signals are also routed to a digital-to-analog converter for standard analog stereo output.

See the "How to Hook Up a DVD Player" section of Chap. 7 for more information about audio connections.

See the "Digital Connections" section of Chap. 10 for information about future interface options.

Subpicture

DVD-Video supports up to 32 subpicture streams that overlay the video for subtitles, captions, karaoke lyrics, menus, simple animation, and so on. These are part- to full-screen, run-length-encoded bitmaps limited to four pixel values. See Table 4.26. NTSC closed captions are also supported.

Each pixel is represented by two bits, allowing four types. The four pixel types are officially designated as background, pattern (foreground), emphasis-1, and emphasis-2, but are not strictly tied to these functions. The highlight functions are part of the button feature (described earlier). Each pixel type is associated with one color from a palette of 16 and one contrast, or transparency level. The 24-bit, YC_bC_r color palette entries provide selections from over 11 million colors. The transparency is set directly, from invisible (0), through 14 levels of transparency (1–14), to opaque (15).

The display area (starting coordinates, width, and height) can be specified, up to almost a full-screen rectangle (0,0,720,478 or 0,0,720,573).

TABLE 4.26 Subpicture Details	Data	0 to 32 streams
	Data rate	Up to 3.36 Mbps
	Unit size	53,220 bytes (up to 32,000 bytes of control data)
	Coding	RLE (maximum 1440 bits/line)
	Resolution*	Up to 720×478 (525/60) or 720×573 (625/50)
	Bits per pixel	2 (defining one of 4 types)
	Pixel types	Background, foreground, emphasis-1, emphasis-2
	Colors*	4 out of 16 (from 4-bit palette,[†] one per type)
	Contrasts*	4 out of 16[†] (one per type)

*Area, content, color, and contrast can be changed for each field.
[†]Color palette and contrast can be changed every PGC.

The display area and content (bitmap) can be changed for each frame or field. The color and contrast of the four pixel types can be changed for each frame or field; the palettes can be changed for each PGC.

The maximum data rate for a single subpicture stream is 3.36 Mbps, with a maximum size per frame of 53,220 bytes. Each run-length-encoded line can be up to 1440 bits (720 × 2). Associated display control sequences (DCSQs) can be up to 32,000 bytes. See Fig. 4.40.

The subpicture display commands (DCCs) are used to change the location, scroll position, transparency, and so on. A sequence of commands can be used to create effects such as color changes, moving highlights, fades, crawls, and so on.

Parental Management

Playback restrictions can be placed on a player by choosing a parental level from the settings menu. There are eight levels, each less restrictive of

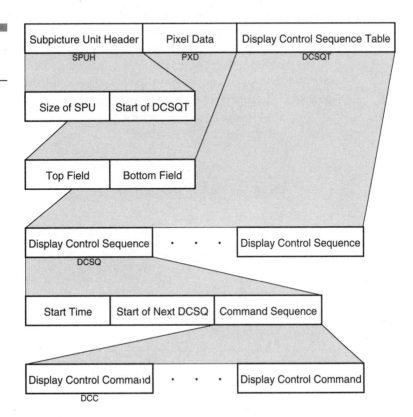

Figure 4.40
Subpicture unit structure.

content than the level below. The Motion Picture Association of America (MPAA) standard movie ratings are mapped to specific parental levels (see Table 4.27). Some players may be set to any of the eight levels; others limit the selection to the five MPAA levels; while others offer three levels: all titles, no adult titles, only children's titles. Most players include a password or code which can be used to prevent the level setting from being changed. However, resetting the player generally clears the password. DVD players are not required to support parental control.

Parental levels restrict either the playback of an entire disc or of certain scenes. Parental codes are placed on the disc in each parental block (a group of PGCs) so that the player can automatically select the proper path from scene to scene. This allows multiple ratings versions of a movie to be put on a single disc. For this to work, the video must be carefully broken into scenes. Objectionable scenes must be coded so that they can be skipped over, or alternate versions of the scenes must be provided and appropriately coded. Video, audio, and subpictures need to be orchestrated so that there is no discontinuity across scene splices. Obviously, this is a significant undertaking. It may take some time after the introduction of DVD before many discs are produced with multiple versions for different parental levels.

It's possible to also use parental levels to exert control beyond the scope of a single player. Players could be manufactured with a hardwired maximum parental level. For example, a country in the same region as countries with less restrictive morality laws could require that all players sold within that country be restricted to parental level 7 and also require that all discs sold in the country include parental codes to prevent playback of discs or scenes which are in violation of censorship regulations.

TABLE 4.27	**MPAA rating**	**Parental level**
MPAA Ratings		8
and Corresponding	NC-17	7
Parental Levels	R	6
		5
	PG-13	4
	PG	3
		2
	G	1

Seamless Playback

Seamless presentation allows multiple paths through mostly the same material by jumping from place to place without a break in the video (see Fig. 4.41). This is useful for movies with alternate endings, directors cuts, and so on. Seamless branching is accomplished in a manner similar to parental management. In fact, since commands exist to set the parental level, it's possible to use the parental features to control seamless branching.

Seamless branching can be accomplished within a PGC. Cells may be contiguous or noncontiguous, but the distance between them is restricted depending on the data rate. See Table 4.28. At higher data rates, the distance must be smaller so that the pickup head can jump to the new position and begin reading data before the track buffer runs out. Seamless branching (and camera angles) generally impose a combined stream data rate limit of 8 Mbps or lower. Also, video objects for seamless playback must be within a single PGC and on the same layer.

Seamless branching generally cannot be done on the fly in response to user interaction. Each path is encapsulated by a PGC, which contains cell pointers to link together the desired chunks of video. Each PGC must be created during the content authoring process and stored on the disc.

Camera Angles

Switching between camera angles is similar to seamless branching. The difference is that the switch can be accomplished on the fly by the viewer. This is usually done by pressing the angle key on the remote control. Another difference between angle switching and seamless (or parental) branching is that the alternate chunks of video must all be the same length and have identical audio tracks. The viewer can't switch to a different camera angle and have the action be out of sync (unless the video itself was not produced in sync).

Video objects, one for each angle, are interleaved into an *interleaved block* (*ILVB*). Interleaved blocks are required for camera angles and can optionally be used for parental branching and seamless branching. (See Fig. 4.42.)

Figure 4.41
Example of seamless playback.

version 1

version 2

TABLE 4.28

Allowable Distance between Cells for Seamless Playback

	Bitrate			
	8.5	**8**	**7.5**	**7**
Maximum jump sectors	5,000	10,000	15,000	20,000
Minimum buffer sectors	201	221	220	216

Regional Management

Motion picture studios want to control the home release of movies in different countries because theater releases aren't simultaneous. A movie may come out on video in the United States when it's just hitting screens in Europe. Therefore, the DVD standard includes codes which can be used to prevent playback of certain discs in certain geographical regions. Each disc contains a set of regional flags. If a flag is cleared, the disc is allowed to be played in the corresponding region; if the flag is set, the disc is not allowed to be played. Players are branded with the code of the region in which they are sold. The player will put up a message and refuse to play a disc which is locked out of the region. This means that discs bought in one country may not play on players bought in another country.

The use of regional codes is entirely optional. Discs with no region flags set will play on any player in any country. The codes are not an encryption system: there is just one bit of information on the disc that the player checks. In many cases, discs will be released without any region locks, but in other cases regional control is very important to the business model of movie distribution. Many studios sell exclusive foreign release rights to other distributors. If the foreign distributor can be assured that discs from other distributors won't be competing in its region, the movie studios can sell the rights for a better price. The foreign distributors are free to focus on their region of expertise, where they may better understand the culture and commercial environment.

The DVD standard specifies six regions, also called *locales*. Players and discs are identified by the region number that is usually superimposed on a world globe icon. If a disc plays in more than one region, it will have more than one number on the globe. The regions are roughly broken out as follows: (1) North America; (2) Japan and Europe; (3) Southeast

Figure 4.42
Example of camera angles.

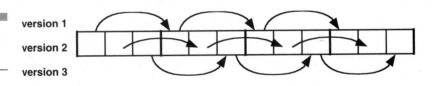

version 1

version 2

version 3

Asia; (4) Australia, New Zealand, and Central/South America; (5) Northwest Asia and North Africa; and (6) China. See Fig. 4.43 and Table 4.29 for details.

With all artificially imposed deterrents, a way around them is inevitably found. Many video game systems introduced in 1995 and 1996 included regional restrictions. Workarounds quickly appeared for buyers who were interested in games from other countries. Shortly after DVD players were released, Chinese and Hong Kong companies developed chips to defeat the regional code of some players. Certain Chinese-made players can play discs regardless of their regional codes. The movie studios in conjunction with the MPAA and consumer electronics companies are pursuing legislation to make such devices illegal in the United States.

Regional codes apply to DVD-ROM systems, but are ostensibly designed for DVD-Video, not computer software. Operating systems will check for regional codes before playing movies from a DVD-Video disc. Microsoft plans to add DVD regional management to versions of Windows and Windows NT planned for release in 1998. Apple likewise plans to add regional management support to QuickTime or the Mac OS near the end of 1997. Some DVD-ROM drives include regional identification codes, but this is not mandatory until CSS phase II begins in 1999. See Chap. 9 for more information on regional management in computers.

Copy Protection

DVD provides three forms of copy protection: antitaping protection, copyright information, and scrambling. All three forms of copy protection are optional for the producer of a DVD-Video disc and must be deliberately enabled by information contained on the disc.

TABLE 4.29	
DVD Regions	1 Canada, United States, Puerto Rico, Bermuda, the Virgin Islands, and some islands in the Pacific.
	2 Japan, Western Europe (including Poland, Romania, Bulgaria, and the Balkans), South Africa, Turkey, and the Middle East (including Iran and Egypt).
	3 Southeast Asia (including Indonesia, South Korea, Hong Kong, and Macao).
	4 Australia, New Zealand, South America, most of Central America, Papua New Guinea, and most of the South Pacific.
	5 Most of Africa, Russia (and former Russian states), Mongolia, Afghanistan, Pakistan, India, Bangladesh, Nepal, Bhutan, and North Korea.
	6 China and Tibet.

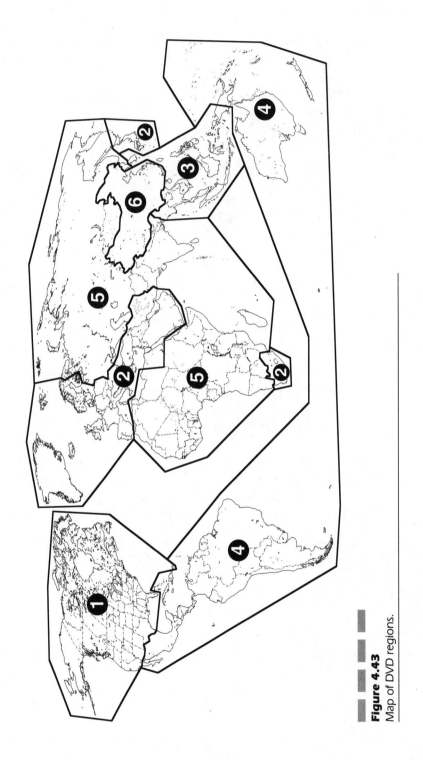

Figure 4.43
Map of DVD regions.

ANALOG PROTECTION SYSTEM. VHS and other analog videotape copying is prevented with a Macrovision 7.0 or similar circuit in the player. The general term is *APS* (*analog protection system*). Computer video cards with composite or s-video output may also use APS.

The Macrovision process provides two separate copy protection methods: Automatic Gain Control (AGC) and Colorstripe. Macrovision AGC technology has been in use since 1985 to protect prerecorded videotapes. It works by adding pulses to the vertical blanking sync signal in order to confuse the automatic-recording-level circuitry of a VCR, causing it to record a noisy, unstable picture. The Colorstripe technology was developed in 1994 for digital set-top boxes and digital video networks (it can't be applied to prerecorded tapes). The Colorstripe process produces a rapidly modulated colorburst signal that confuses the chroma processing circuitry in VCRs, resulting in horizontal stripes when the recording is played back.

AGC works on approximately 85 percent of consumer VCRs, and Colorstripe works on approximately 95 percent. The system is intended to affect only VCRs, but unfortunately may degrade the picture, especially with old or nonstandard television equipment. Macrovision creates severe problems for some line doublers. Effects of Macrovision may appear as stripes of color, repeated darkening and brightening, rolling or tearing, and black-and-white picture.

Macrovision protection is provided on the composite and s-video output of all commercial DVD players produced to date. Macrovision protection is not present on the component video outputs of first-generation DVD players, but, as of 1997, is required for new players (the AGC process only, since there is no colorburst in a component signal).

Just as with videotapes, some DVDs are Macrovision-protected and some aren't. The discs themselves tell the player whether to enable Macrovision AGC or Colorstripe. The producer of the disc decides what amount of copy protection to enable and pays Macrovision royalties accordingly. The copy protection information is present for each video object unit of the disc and can be set to off, AGC, Colorstripe, or AGC plus Colorstripe. This finely detailed selective control enables the disc producer to disable copy protection for scenes which may be adversely affected by the process.

Macrovision protection can be defeated with inexpensive video processing boxes that clean up the video signal. The Macrovision Corporation has been very aggressive in buying the patents for these technologies in order to force them off the market. Macrovision claims that no devices are yet available to defeat the Colorstripe process.

APS is not strictly required on video players or DVD-equipped computers, but those systems without it will not be licensed to play scrambled video (see the following).

COPY GENERATION MANAGEMENT.   Digital video copying—and some analog video copying—is controlled by information on each disc specifying if the data can be copied. This is a serial copy generation management system (CGMS) designed to prevent copies or to prevent copies of copies. The information is included in the analog and digital video signals. Obviously, the equipment making the copy has to abide by the rules.

The digital standards (CGMS/D) are not fully defined. The analog (CGMS/A) information is encoded into line 21 of the NTSC television signal so that digital recorders with analog inputs can recognize it.

The CGMS information indicates whether no copies, one copy, or unlimited copies can be made. If no copies are allowed, the recording device will not make a copy. If one copy is allowed, the recording device will make one copy and change the CGMS information to indicate that no copies can be made from the copy.

As with APS information, CGMS flags are present for each sector on the disc.

Some DVD devices are designed to check for no-copy flags on recordable media. If a no-copy flag is found, the disc is presumed to be an illegal copy and will not be played.

Obviously, CGMS does not prevent multiple copies being made from the original. However, it is the most fair and reasonable form of copy protection, in that it allows fair-use copies by consumers for their own personal use.

CONTENT SCRAMBLING.   Because of the potential for perfect digital copies, worried movie studios forced a deeper copy protection requirement into the DVD-Video standard. The Content Scrambling System (CSS) is a form of data encryption that prevents reading files directly from the disc. Occasional sectors are scrambled in such a way that the data can't be used to re-create a valid signal. The key required to descramble the data is hidden in an area of the disc which is not directly accessible from a DVD-ROM drive or other DVD reader.

All standard DVD players have a descrambling circuit that decrypts the data before displaying it. The process is similar to scrambled cable channels, except that the average consumer will never see the scrambled video and will have no idea that it has gone through a scrambling/descrambling process. The process does not degrade the data; it merely shifts it around and alters it so that the original values are unrecognizable and difficult to decipher. The descrambling process completely restores the data. The only case in which someone is likely to see a scrambled video signal is if they attempt to play it on a player or computer which does not support CSS, or if they attempt to play a copy of the data or the disc. Since the copy does not include the key, the video signal cannot be descrambled and appears garbled or blank.

No unscrambled digital output is allowed until work in progress for secure digital connections is finished. When digital recording devices become available, they may not be able to record scrambled video.

On the computer side, DVD-ROM drives and any hardware or software which decodes or displays video will exchange encryption keys. The scrambled data is then sent from the drive to the decoder to be descrambled and then MPEG decoded before being displayed. This means that many DVD-ROM drives and video display boards have extra hardware (and cost) in order to provide copy protection designed primarily to protect movies. Makers of equipment used to display DVD-Video (drives, chips, display boards, etc.) must license CSS. See Chap. 9 for more details.

CSS is not required of video players or DVD-equipped computers; systems without it will not be able to play scrambled movies.

RAMIFICATIONS OF COPY PROTECTION. These copy protection schemes are designed to guard against casual copying, which the studios claim causes billions of dollars in lost revenue. The people who developed the copy protection standards are the first to admit that it won't stop well-equipped pirates or even determined consumers. Video pirates have equipment that can easily make bit-by-bit copies of discs or create master copies for mass replication. Bit-by-bit copiers will also become available to computer owners who know where to look.

Technically, DVD-ROM systems can use CSS for computer data, even though it's designed for audio and video. Officially, the CSS system is supposed to be used for DVD-Video applications only, but it may be hard to draw the line on products that combine DVD-Video with computer data. Of course, since DVD-ROM can hold any form of computer data, any desired encryption scheme can be implemented independent of CSS.

See Chap. 9 for additional discussion of copy protection on computers and the potential ways of combining DVD-Video with computer multimedia.

Authoring and Premastering

Authoring refers to the process of designing and creating the content of a DVD-Video title. The more complex and interactive the disc, the more authoring is required. Authoring is done on an authoring system, which may be integrated with a premastering system. (See the following section, entitled "Production Systems," for details.)

The authoring process is similar to other creative processes such as making a movie, writing a book, or building an electronic circuit. It may include creating an outline, designing a flowchart, writing a script, sketching storyboards, filming video, recording and mixing audio, taking photographs, creating graphics or animation, designing a user interface, laying out menus, defining and linking menu buttons, writing captions, creating subpicture graphics, and then assembling, organizing, and synchronizing all the material.

The DVD authoring process also requires careful management of the *bit budget*. There are two axes of control: data rate and capacity. Within the resulting two-dimensional space, the author must balance title length, picture quality, number of audio tracks, quality of audio tracks, number of camera angles, amount of additional footage for seamless branching, and the not-quite-negligible subpictures. See Fig. 4.44.

Some definitions of authoring systems include audio and video compression, but this actually belongs to the premastering process.

Premastering is generally defined to include compression of audio and video; conversion of graphics to subpicture streams; generation of the DVD-Video navigation data and presentation control information streams; multiplexing the streams together; verifying compliance with the DVD specification; and writing the data to a UDF Bridge format disc image. Once a title has been premastered, it's ready for simulation, emula-

Figure 4.44
DVD authoring
bit budget.

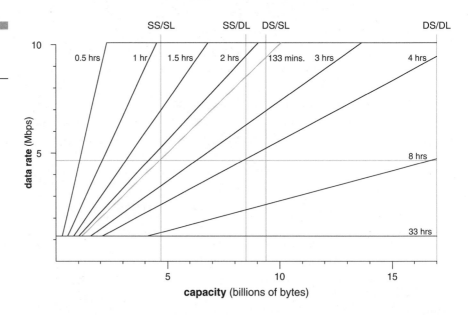

tion, or testing with a one-off copy, and then sending out on DLT or DVD-R for mastering and replication.

Production Issues

Videotape, laserdisc, and CD-ROM can't be compared to DVD in a straightforward manner. There are basically three stages of costs: production, premastering, and mastering/replication.

DVD production costs are not much higher than for existing media, unless the extra features of DVD-Video such as multiple sound tracks, camera angles, and so on are employed.

Premastering costs are proportionately the most expensive part of DVD. Video and audio must be encoded, menus and control information have to be authored and encoded, it all has to be multiplexed into a single data stream, and finally encoded in low-level format. Typical fees for compression at the beginning of 1997 were $120/min for video, $20/min for audio, $6/min for subtitles, plus formatting and testing at about $30/min. A ballpark estimate for producing a two-hour DVD movie is about $30,000. Those who want to do the work themselves can purchase authoring and encoding systems, which range in price from $100,000 to over $2 million. These prices will drop very rapidly in the next few years to where DVDs can be produced on desktop computer systems using additional hardware costing less than $20,000.

In comparison, videotapes don't have premastering or mastering costs to speak of, and they run about $2.40 for replication. CDs cost about $1000 to master and $0.50 to replicate. Laserdiscs cost about $3000 to master and about $8 to replicate. DVDs currently cost a few thousand dollars to master and about $2.40 to replicate. Since DVD production is based mostly on the same equipment used for CD production, the mastering and replication costs will quickly drop to CD levels.

Double-sided or dual-layer discs cost slightly more to replicate, since a data layer must be stamped on the second substrate (and transparent glue must be used for dual layers). Double-sided, dual-layer discs are more difficult to produce and more expensive.

PRODUCTION SYSTEMS.   Production systems are required for DVD-Video authoring and for DVD-ROM and DVD-Video premastering.

Movie studios, in conjunction with DVD hardware partners, developed proprietary production systems to develop content before the introduction of DVD. At the introduction, only one authoring system was commercially available: *Scenarist DVD,* created by Daikin and distributed by Sonic Solutions. A few compression and premastering systems were commercially available from companies including Daikin/Sonic Solutions, Minerva, Innovacom, and Zapex. These systems ranged from $80,000 to $200,000. Dozens of DVD production systems are under development. Within four years of the introduction of DVD, many desktop DVD-Video and DVD-ROM development systems may be available for $20,000 or less.

Standards

DVD is based on or has borrowed from dozens of standards developed over the years by many organizations.

SYSTEM STANDARDS

File system: *OSTA Universal Disc Format Specification:1996* (Appendix 6.9) "OSTA UDF Compliant Domain" of *ISO/IEC 13346:1995 Volume and file structure of write-once and rewritable media using non-sequential recording for information interchange* (Note: *ECMA 167, 2nd Edition, 1994* is equivalent to ISO/IEC 13346:1995)

File system: *ISO 9660:1988 Information processing—Volume and file structure of CD-ROM for information interchange* (Note: Equivalent to *ECMA 119, 2nd Edition, 1987*)

MPEG-2 system: *ISO/IEC 13818-1:1996 Information technology—Generic coding of moving pictures and associated audio information: Systems* (ITU-T H.222.0) (program streams only, no transport streams)

CD: *IEC 908 (1987-09) Compact disc digital audio system* (Red Book)

CD-ROM:

   —*ISO/IEC 10149:1995 Information technology—Data interchange on read-only 120 mm optical data disks (CD-ROM)* (Yellow Book) (Note: Equivalent to *ECMA 130, 2nd Edition, June 1996*)

   —Philips/Sony Orange Book part-II Recordable Compact Disc System

   —Philips/Sony Orange Book part-III Recordable Compact Disc System

VIDEO STANDARDS

MPEG-1 video: *ISO/IEC 11172-2:1993 Information technology—Coding of moving pictures and associated audio for digital storage media at up to about 1.5 Mbit/s—Part 2: Video*

MPEG-2 video: *ISO/IEC 13818-2:1996 Information technology—Generic coding of moving pictures and associated audio information: Video* (ITU-T H.262)

NTSC video:
> —*SMPTE 170M-1994 Television—Composite Analog Video Signal— NTSC for Studio Applications*
> —*ITU-R BT.470-4 Television Systems*

PAL video: *ITU-R BT.470-4 Television Systems*

Source video: *ITU-R BT.601-5 Studio encoding parameters of digital television for standard 4:3 and widescreen 16:9 aspect ratios*

PAL widescreen signaling:
> —*ETS 300 294 Edition 2:1995-12 Television Systems; 625-Line Television: Wide Screen Signalling (WSS)*
> —*ITU-R BT.1119-1 Widescreen signalling for broadcasting. Signalling for widescreen and other enhanced television parameters*

NTSC widescreen signaling and analog copy generation management system (CGMS-A): *EIAJ CPX-1204*

PAL analog copy generation management system (CGMS-A): *ITU-R BT.1119-1 Widescreen signalling for broadcasting. Signalling for widescreen and other enhanced television parameters*

Film/camera mode: *ETS 300 294 Edition 2:1995-12*

AUDIO STANDARDS

Dolby Digital audio: *AC-3 (ATSC A/52 1995)*

MPEG-1 audio: *ISO/IEC 11172-3:1993 Information technology—Coding of moving pictures and associated audio for digital storage media at up to about 1,5 Mbit/s—Part 3: Audio*

MPEG-2 audio: *ISO/IEC 13818-3:1995 Information technology—Generic coding of moving pictures and associated audio information—Part 3: Audio*

Digital audio interface:
> —*IEC 958 (1989-02) Digital audio interface* (Type II—Consumer)
> —*IEC 958-2 (1994-07) Digital audio interface—Part 2: Software information delivery mode*
> —IEC 1937 (draft as of 1997) (also ATSC A/52 Annex B: AC-3 Data Stream in IEC 958 Interface)

Optical digital audio: *EIAJ CP-340*

Recording codes: *ISO 3901:1986 Documentation—International Standard Recording Code (ISRC)*

OTHER STANDARDS

Language codes: *ISO 639:1988 Code for the representation of names of languages* (see Table A.20)

Country codes: *ISO 3166:1993 Codes for the representation of names of countries* (see Table A.21)

Text information:
— *ISO/IEC 646:1991 Information technology—ISO 7-bit coded character set for information interchange*
— *ISO 8859-1:1987 Information processing—8-bit single-byte coded graphic character sets—Part 1: Latin alphabet No. 1*
— *ISO 8859-2:1987 Information processing—8-bit single-byte coded graphic character sets—Part 2: Latin alphabet No. 2*
— *ISO/IEC 2022:1994 Information technology—Character code structure and extension techniques*
— *JIS, Shift-JIS, and others*

Digital interconnect: *IEEE 1394-1995 IEEE Standard for a High Performance Serial Bus* (FireWire)

Packaging

Manufacturers are worried that customers might assume a DVD will play in their CD player since it looks the same as a CD. Accordingly, many manufacturers and retailers would like the packaging to be different. The Video Software Dealers Association (VSDA) recommends a package 5⅛ inches wide, 7⅜ inches high and between ⅛ inches and ⅝ inches deep, which is as wide as a CD jewel box and as tall as a VHS cassette box. Time Warner is promoting a Snapper package (related to the plastic and paper eco CD packages) which is a similar same shape. See Fig. 4.45.

There is no official requirement for DVD package size and many companies are planning to use standard CD jewel cases. It remains to be seen if any package other than the jewel case becomes standard, especially for DVD-ROM.

Recordable DVD

DVD-R

DVD-R is the record-once version of DVD-ROM, similar in function to CD-R. Data can only be written permanently to the disc. It's expected that DVD-R will drop to prices of under $500 for recorders and under $5 for blank discs within several years of its introduction, leading to its widespread adoption for multimedia development, video editing, information

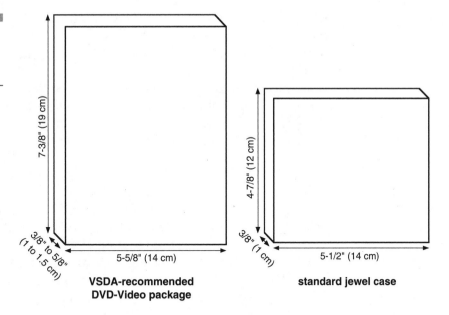

Figure 4.45
VSDA-recommended package and standard jewel case.

VSDA-recommended
DVD-Video package

standard jewel case

publishing, and data archiving. The success of DVD-R depends in part on the success of DVD-RAM. If the price of drives and disks drops as quickly, DVD-RAM will eclipse its less flexible older sibling.

Version 0.9 of the DVD-R specification was released in July 1997, with the final version expected in August. Recorders were expected to appear in late summer or early fall at initial prices of over $15,000.

DVD-R uses an organic dye polymer technology like CD-R. The dye is used to coat a carefully wobbled groove molded into the polycarbonate substrate. The dye is backed with a reflective metallic layer—usually gold for high reflectivity. The groove guides the laser beam of the DVD-R recorder as it "burns" pits into the photosensitive dye layer, and the wobble provides a self-regulating clock signal. These discs can then be read by standard DVD readers.

A single side holds only 3.68 gigabytes (3.95 billion bytes). This will eventually be enlarged to at least 4.38 gigabytes (4.7 billion bytes) to match the capacity of a single-layer DVD-ROM. DVD-R discs can be double-sided, but there are no plans to make dual-layer DVD-R discs, which are impossible to achieve with current dye polymer technology.

DVD-RAM

DVD-RAM is the erasable, recordable version of DVD-ROM, similar in function to CD-RW. It's difficult to predict how rapidly the technology will mature and how quickly prices will drop to the point that it's available to average consumers.

In April of 1997, two competing DVD-RAM proposals were combined into the preliminary standard: phase change technology using combined land and groove recording with track wobble and pre-embossed sector headers, holding 2.40 gigabytes (2.58 billion bytes) per side. As with DVD-R, the format was expected to be finalized in August 1997. Drives were expected to be commercially available in late 1997 or early 1998 for about $1000.

Because the DVD-RAM format requires a defect management list which was not in the original specification, DVD-RAM discs are not expected to be readable by first-generation DVD players and DVD-ROM drives. Of course, it's a moot point since DVD-RAM discs are encased in plastic shells like their magneto-optical cousins.

Because of differences not provided for in the original specification, DVD drives and players built before 1998 cannot read DVD-RAM discs. New units with a tiny amount of additional circuitry are required to handle defect management, reflectivity differences, and minor format variations.

Single-sided DVD-RAM discs optionally come in cartridges. There are two types of cartridges: type 1 is sealed, type 2 allows the disc to be removed. Double-sided DVD-RAM discs are only available in sealed cartridges.

What's Wrong with DVD

DVD-ROM is a well-designed update of CD and CD-ROM. Storage space and speed are much improved and many of the shortcomings of the original format have been rectified. DVD-Video, on the other hand, is a collection of compromises in which commercially and politically motivated restrictions far outweigh technical limitations. It's unfortunate that in an overzealous attempt to protect their intellectual property, Hollywood studios have crippled the very format which could have given it the best venue of expression outside of a theater.

Perhaps the biggest shortcoming of DVD-Video is ease of piracy. Ironically, the superior digital quality of DVD has proven to be its Achilles' heel. The ease with which unscrupulous or unthinking people might be able to make a perfect digital copy has caused too many sleepless nights on the part of studio executives. The thought of discs, legal or not, spreading across the entire world is also an apparent concern. The reaction has been to add restrictive regional codes and an analog copy protection system that can degrade the picture. These restrictions have also complicated the otherwise simple use of DVD-ROM in computers.

Regional Management

Movies are not released all over the world at the same time. A major motion picture might come out on video in the United States—months after its theatrical release—at the same time it's being shown on theater screens for the first time in Europe or Japan. Movie distributors are worried that if video copies of a movie were available before official release it would reduce the success of the movie in the theaters. Also, different distribution rights and licenses are established in different countries. For example, Disney might own distribution rights in the United States, but Studio Ghibli might own them in Japan.

Because of this, studios and distributors want a way to control distribution. Every DVD player has a code which identifies the geographical region in which it was sold. Discs intended for use only in certain countries have codes stored on them that identify which regions are allowed and which are not allowed. A DVD player will not play a disc which is not permitted to be played in that region.

This regional management system wreaks havoc with the import markets. An otherwise legally imported disc may not work because of its regional codes. A worse problem is that discs and players purchased in one country may not work when taken to another. If someone in Japan moves to the United States and takes a DVD player along, that person may not be able to play movies purchased in the United States, especially new releases. Likewise, if that person buys a new DVD player in the United States, he or she may not be able to play some of the discs brought from Japan.

The regional locks are optional: any disc can be designed to play in all players. But it's clear that most new movie releases will include regional locks, and many other movie releases may also be geographically circumscribed.

Most DVD-ROM drives, as well as computer software and operating systems, check for regional codes before playing movies from DVD-Video. It's possible for computer software on DVD-ROM to use regional codes as well, but this is officially frowned on.

Details of the regional management system are covered in more detail in Chap. 4.

Copy Protection

The movie industry claims that over $350 million is lost each year to casual illegal copying. Surveys of video rental outlets show that more than half believe that their business is hurt by consumers who make copies of rental tapes. It's debatable how many illegal copies would have been purchased or rented had they been uncopyable. The industry's own data shows that 14 percent of consumers who are thwarted by videotape copy protection subsequently rent or buy a legitimate copy, and video retailers believe that copy-protected tapes increase their revenue by 18 percent. Regardless of the effectiveness of copy protection schemes, DVD includes a number of them.

Every DVD player must include Macrovision or similar analog copy protection technology to deter copying of DVD onto videotape. Macrovision adds pulses to the video signal that confuse the recording circuitry of VCRs and render a tape copy unwatchable, supposedly without affecting the picture when played on a television. However, some equipment, especially line doublers and high-end televisions, is unable to cleanly display video which has been altered by the Macrovision process.

Analog and digital copying of DVD-Video is controlled by information specifying if the video can be copied, and if it can be copied only once or unlimited times. Future recording equipment must respect this information. The *copy once* setting is intended to allow consumers to make copies for personal use, but not allow copies of the copies, since the copy is marked for *no copies*.

Digital copying is also prevented by scrambling critical sectors on the disc. Video data which has been copied from a disc using a DVD-ROM drive will not play without the descrambling keys and algorithm that were hidden on the original disc. And the video data itself stays scrambled until just before being decoded and displayed, so it can't be easily intercepted and copied within the computer.

Even the people who designed the copy protection techniques (the DVD Copy Protection Technical Working Group) freely admit that they don't expect copy protection to slow down professional thieves. Anyone equipped with the proper equipment to defeat Macrovision or make a bit-by-bit digital copy of a disc can get around the copy protection barriers. Rather, the targets of these measures are people who make a copy or two for friends. The stated goal is "to keep the honest people honest."

Movie studios and consumer electronics companies want to make it illegal to defeat DVD copy protection. A cochair of the legal group of the copy protection committee stated, "In the video context, the contemplated legislation should also provide some specific assurances that certain reasonable and customary home recording practices will be permitted, in addition to providing penalties for circumvention." It's not at all clear how this might be "permitted" by a player before more intelligent digital copy protection mechanisms are developed.

All copy protection systems are optional for DVD publishers. Therefore, it's expected that those who care about video quality will choose not to enable the Macrovision process. Descrambling is also optional, so there will be DVD-ROM drives and possibly even DVD-Video players that simply will not be able to play scrambled movies.

DVD-Video Baggage on Computers

Given the ability of many computers to play movies from a DVD-Video, DVD's regional management and copy protection requirements apply. A license is required of manufacturers of hardware or software involved in the playback of scrambled movies. The hardware and software must ensure that descrambled files can't be copied, that digital outputs contain proper copy protection information, and that analog outputs are protected by Macrovision or a similar process.

The upside is that these safeguards assure Hollywood that its property will not be plundered and spread illegally from computer to computer. The downside is that the majority of law-abiding computer owners are inconvenienced and may pay slightly more because of these protection measures. This is especially irritating to those who have no interest in watching movies on their computer screens.

See Chap. 9 for more details of copy protection and regional management issues on computers.

NTSC versus PAL

Because DVD-Video is based on standard MPEG-2 digital video, it should be a worldwide standard capable of working with both NTSC and PAL television systems, allowing discs produced anywhere in the world to be played anywhere else in the world. Sadly, this is not the case. Partly in an attempt to limit the widespread distribution of discs, two internal formats are used, based on the 525/60 (NTSC) television system and 625/50 (PAL) television system. Two different surround audio standards are also used, Dolby Digital and MPEG-2 audio. Movies intended for distribution in the United States, Japan, and other countries using the NTSC system are encoded at 30 frames per second along with Dolby Digital audio, while movies intended for release in Europe and in countries using the PAL standard are encoded at 25 frames per second along with MPEG-2 audio. Therefore, countries with NTSC televisions require NTSC DVD playback hardware, and countries with PAL televisions require PAL DVD playback hardware. Movies are stored at 24 frames per second, but field repeat information makes the movie play at only one of the two display rates.

Since NTSC is the dominant standard, many DVD players released in PAL countries will play both kinds of discs as long as the right kind of television is connected—either a PAL television for PAL discs or an NTSC television for NTSC discs, or a *multistandard* television that is capable of displaying both PAL and NTSC. Multistandard players produce a PAL signal from a PAL disc and an NTSC signal from an NTSC disc. It's up to the television to automatically adjust.

It's technically possible to create a player that can play any disc when connected to any television by converting the video from one format to the other, but this requires expensive electronics in order to make the video look good. No such *standards-converting* players have been announced, and manufacturers are under pressure from movie studios not to develop them.

To take advantage of DVD's full surround sound, NTSC players require a built-in Dolby Digital audio decoder or a decoder in the audio system they are connected to. PAL countries ostensibly require MPEG-2 audio decoders, but since many studios plan on releasing PAL discs with both MPEG-2 audio and Dolby Digital audio tracks, this may not be a critical requirement.

The restrictions of television systems do not apply to computer monitors. Properly equipped computers can play movies from both NTSC and PAL discs, and most will also be able to decode both Dolby Digital and MPEG-2 audio.

Not Better Enough

Part of the reason for the success of compact disc was that the technology was not overly advanced. Technical difficulties in production and playback were minimized, tolerances could be easily met, and costs could be kept low. DVD has taken the same approach, which will go far toward helping it become cheap and widespread, but it also means that the bar was not raised terribly high. HDTV is just around the corner, and DVD could have been the first format to fully support it. There will undoubtedly be a second generation of DVD designed for HDTV, but in a way it's a shame that the designers didn't try harder to achieve more in the first generation.

DVD also has limited interactive capabilities. Perhaps this was a conscious decision so as not to undermine the support of video game companies, but it's a crippling limitation. This point is discussed in more detail later in this chapter.

No Recording Yet

Recordable DVD isn't expected until fall 1997 at the earliest. But this doesn't mean that home DVD recorders will appear. DVD-ROM has two recordable variations, DVD-R (record once) and DVD-RAM (erase and record many times), which are intended for storing computer data. DVD-R and DVD-RAM technologies are expensive. The drives will initially cost over $1000 and will not drop in price as quickly as DVD-ROM drives. Discs are expected to be priced between $40 and $50 when first introduced, but should drop quickly once demand goes up.

As for DVD-Video recording, the complexity of compressing video and audio is still beyond the reach of home technology and beyond the pocketbook of home consumers. The minimum requirement for reproducing audio and video on DVD is an MPEG-1 audio/video stream. Basic

DVD control codes are also needed. To use DVD to full capacity requires other streams such as MPEG-2 video, Dolby Digital audio or MPEG-2 audio, and subpicture. It's difficult enough to encode the video and audio, combine them with the control codes, and write the whole thing to disc, let alone do it in real time at 30 frames per second. Even if sufficient quality could be achieved in real time, it would be too expensive. Prices for DVD production systems are dropping from millions of dollars to thousands of dollars, but they won't drop below the essential $500 range for home use until several years after DVD's introduction.

A possible alternative is that the first home DVD recorders will require a source of already-compressed digital video such as direct broadcast satellite (DBS) or digital cable. This approach, called *bitstream recording*, is taken by D-VHS, a potential competitor. In this case, the cost of audio and video encoders is eliminated, and the video will generally be of higher quality since it's compressed by professional encoders during production or transmission. However, the incoming encoded video must be in a form that can be decoded by the DVD player, or there must be a bitstream output on the player that can be connected to an external decoder or a display with a built-in decoder.

Some people believe that recordable DVD-Video will never be practical for consumers to record TV shows or home videos since digital tape is more cost-effective. On the other hand, digital tape lacks many of the advantages of DVD such as seamless branching, instant rewind/fast forward, instant search, and durability, not to mention the appeal of shiny discs. So, once the encoding technology is fast and cheap enough, and the blank discs are also cheap enough, recordable DVD may be a reality. But that reality is at least beyond the turn of the century.

Recordable DVD may also face competition from digital videotape. However, DV is not currently intended for mass-market prerecorded video, and D-VHS can only record already-digitized video signals. See the "Digital Videotape" section of Chap. 6 for more information.

No Audio Standard Yet

No standard for the DVD-Audio disc format was ready when DVD was introduced. In fact, since the DVD-Video standard includes very high quality audio, and since existing audio CDs can be used in DVD players, there is no big hurry to define an audio standard. It may take another year or two, if indeed it ever happens. One potential drawback is that the DVD-Audio standard could be incompatible with existing DVD players.

The music industry has not reached a consensus on what to do with the greater bandwidth of DVD. Some want higher sampling rates, but there is almost no evidence that sample rates above 48 kHz improve the perceptible quality of music (although DVD-Video already supports 96-kHz sampling). Some want more bits per sample, but there is little evidence that this will perceptibly improve upon properly noise-shaped 16-bits. Others want surround sound, and while there is a consensus that this can be better than stereo there is no consensus on how best to record in surround sound (which is no surprise since there is no real consensus on how best to record in stereo). Others would prefer multitrack audio, so that individual instruments or vocals can be emphasized or isolated, but this would increase the complexity of DVD-Audio players by requiring integrated multitrack audio mixers.

Sony is pushing for its Direct Stream Digital (DSD) format, with the support of Philips. Other organizations such as Acoustic Renaissance for Audio (ARA) prefer a lossless compressed PCM format that's more appropriate for studio work and archiving.

Some factions are pushing for the smaller 8-cm (CD-single) form factor, while others prefer the more popular 12-cm size. The audio industry also favors *legacy* discs which would play on one side in existing CD players, and on the other side in DVD players. There are technical difficulties in doing this, but it may be possible.

The music industry is also requesting an *embedded signaling* or *digital watermark* copy protection feature. This applies a digital signature to the audio in the form of supposedly inaudible noise so that new equipment can recognize copied audio and refuse to play it. Audiophiles claim this degrades the audio. A similar system was attempted with digital audio tape (DAT), but was abandoned.

Inefficient Audio

It's generally recognized that MPEG-2 audio is inefficient in MPEG-1 compatibility mode, which is required for DVD-Video. Parts of the audio signal must be duplicated to achieve full channel separation, thus creating an overhead of about 10 percent. (See Chap. 3 for details.) MPEG-2 provides a non-backward-compatible format (AAC), but since this system was not finalized when DVD was introduced, and since MPEG-2 decoders were not available, DVD-Video discs intended for PAL players are saddled with a less-than-optimal algorithm in order to support MPEG-1 decoders.

Other ideas for improving the general efficiency of multiple audio tracks were considered. Alternate language sound tracks contain the same music and sound effects, differing only in the dialogue. It could be possible to store all dialogue tracks in mono or stereo form and have the player use a two-track decoder to mix them together. The problem is that dialogue is not isolated to one or two tracks. Using a mono or nondiscrete dialogue track could detract from the audio presentation. Another possibility is differential encoding, which allows additional speech tracks to be encoded relative to the main sound track containing music and special effects, rather than recoding an entire track for each language. This results in a lower data rate for additional language tracks. These ideas have the benefit of reducing data rate (and thus increasing either quality or playing time), but the added complexity may not be worth it.

No Reverse Gear

Because of the way MPEG-2 compressed video builds frames by using the differences from previous frames, it's impossible to play in reverse without a very large buffer to store a set of previous frames in, or without a very complex high-speed process of jumping back and forth on the disc to build frames in reverse order. RAM for video buffers is very expensive, so currently no DVD players can play backward at normal speed.

Some players can move backward through a disc by skipping between key frames. Attempting to display these frames at the proper time intervals results in jerky playback with delays of about ½ second between each frame. Smooth playback can only be achieved by showing the frames at 12 to 15 times normal speed.

Only Two Aspect Ratios

DVD is limited to 4:3 and 16:9 aspect ratios, even though MPEG-2 allows a third aspect ratio of 2.21:1. Better yet would be the ability to support any aspect ratio. Because of the necessity for a standard physical shape, televisions essentially come in two ratios: 4:3 and 16:9; but if the player or TV were able to unsqueeze anamorphic source of any ratio, it would provide better resolution since pixels would not be wasted on letterbox mattes. Letterbox mattes would still need to be generated by the player or the display, but high-resolution displays would be able to make the most of every pixel of the anamorphic signal.

The obvious disadvantage to this feature is that variable-geometry picture scaling circuitry is more expensive than the fixed-geometry scaling of DVD players and existing wide-screen TVs.

See Chap. 3 for aspect ratio details.

Inadequate Interactivity

The ability of DVD-Video players to process and react to user control is extremely limited. There is little beyond the bare basics of menus and branching. Features such as navigation, user input, score display, indexes, searching, and the like are possible with DVD-Video but must have each permutation anticipated and put in place when the disc is produced. Any video displayed by a player has to be created ahead of time, unlike other systems such as CD-i or video game consoles which can generate graphics and text on the fly.

Consider, for example, a DVD-Video quiz game designed for a standard DVD player. Commands on the disc can program the player to keep track of the player's score, but there is no way to directly display the score. Instead, a set of screens must be created ahead of time to cover all the possible results. To give a score to within 5 percent, 21 screens are needed (0%, 5%, 10%,...90%, 100%). Given the amount of work required to create the screens and to design the code for displaying them, it's more likely that a compromise of 3 or 4 screens would be used, giving a coarse result such as "bad," "fair," "good," and "great." This type of compromise is likely to pervade all attempts at interactivity in DVD-Video.

Searches or lookups can only be done with DVD-Video in a hierarchical or sequential manner. For example, to look up a word in a small 1000-word glossary, the first screen would list the 26 letters of the alphabet (DVD allows up to 36 buttons on a screen). After the first letter was selected, additional screens of words would be displayed. Ten or more screens might be required to list all the words beginning with a common letter. The *next* and *previous* buttons on the remote control would be used to page through the screens one at a time. Finally, after a word was selected, a screen with the definition would be shown. This would require the laborious preparation of 1000 screens for the definitions and more than 100 menu screens to access them. A more powerful system than DVD could simply read the text of a definition from a database file and display it on a generic definition screen.

The use of DVD-Video for education, productivity, games, and the like is disappointingly limited. The feature set was clearly designed from a limited goal of on-screen menus, simple branching, and karaoke. Clever use of the rudimentary interactive features of DVD can get around some restrictions, but most producers will be hard pressed to put in the extra time and effort required, thus resulting in reduced usability. A DVD-Video cookbook, for instance, might provide a simple index search of ingredients or dishes that would include *chickpeas* and *stew* but would frustrate someone looking for *garbanzo beans* or *goulash* and might not even include the carrots that are in the stew.

To make things worse, the DVD-Video feature set is incompletely or improperly implemented on first-generation and even second-generation players. Early developers had to scale back their plans after discovering that their ingenious discs worked differently or not at all on different players.

Limited Graphics

The subpicture feature of DVD could be extended far beyond simple captions, menus, and animation if it weren't limited to four colors and four contrast levels at a time. Much richer visual interaction could be achieved with more colors and with features such as sprites and rudimentary 3D capabilities.

The designers obviously chose to limit the subpicture format to save cost and bandwidth, but even a small improvement of 16 simultaneous colors would have made for better-looking subtitles, more sophisticated highlighting, and a superior graphic overlay environment.

Too Small

Part of the appeal of DVD is its small, convenient size. But, ironically, this is also a drawback. People are psychologically averse to paying the same amount for something smaller. Even though the smaller item may be better, the larger item somehow seems worth more.

DVD's small size also limits the cover art. Gone are the days of innovative art on LP jackets or good-sized movie art and descriptive text on laserdisc covers. Liner notes are also limited, but this shortcoming can be compensated for by including still pictures, short clips, and other material in video form on the disc itself.

No Bar Codes

One of the most powerful features of laserdisc players used in training and education is bar codes. Printed bar codes are scanned using a wand which sends commands to the player via the infrared remote interface, telling it to search to a specific picture or play a certain segment. A simple laserdisc player becomes a powerful interactive presentation tool when combined with a bar-code reader. Bar codes can be added to text-books, charts, posters, lesson outlines, storybooks, workbooks, and much more, enhancing them with quick access to pictures and movies.

Pioneer representatives have stated that they are developing an industrial/educational DVD player, but the lack of standard support for bar-code readers, even as add-ons, ultimately denies them to most player owners.

No External Control

Most consumer laserdisc players include an external control connector, and all industrial laserdisc players include a serial port for connection to a computer. An entire genre of multimedia evolved during the 1980s, using laserdisc players to add sound and video to computer software. Admittedly this is less important today as the multimedia features of computers improve, but many applications of DVD such as video editing, kiosks, and custom installations are limited by lack of an external control standard.

Escalated Obsolescence

DVD is attached at the hip to the computer marketplace, which has a nasty habit of evolving faster than is comfortable for the average customer. For contrast, consider laserdisc, which in 1998 will have been around for 20 years. Laserdiscs made in 1978 still play in most players and look very good. Compare this to computers: the first microcomputers came out only a few years before laserdisc, but they have already proceeded through many generations. How usable is most DOS software from 10 years ago? How useful today are word processing files from a TRS-80 or games from an Apple II?

The greatest advantage of digital information—its flexibility—is in a way its greatest shortcoming. It's too easy to tinker with the formula. TV, radio, and other systems have lasted for years with only minor improvements because it was too hard to make major improvements without starting over. But the digital clay of the DVD format is so malleable that it's only a matter of too short a time before the temptation to revamp it becomes irresistible. This doesn't necessarily mean that existing discs will not play in newer players, but it does mean that new features will be added which will require new or updated equipment, much to the delight of those who sell new equipment.

The next generation of DVD is already under development. It will use blue lasers to achieve the higher data density required for HDTV. Discs in this "HDVD" format will not play on older DVD players.

Average American consumers replace their TVs every seven years. Let us hope that the phases of DVD last at least that long.

No Computer Compatibility Standards

The multimedia CD-ROM industry has long been plagued by incompatibility problems. In 1995, return rates of CD-ROMs were as high as 40 percent, mostly because customers were unable to get them to work on their computers. Compatibility problems were caused by incorrect hardware or software setups, defects in video and audio hardware, bugs in video and audio driver software, and by the basic problem that hardware such as CD-ROM drives and microprocessors often weren't powerful enough for the tasks demanded of them. DVD-ROMs could be in for even worse treatment. In addition to the same compatibility problems of CD-ROMs, DVD-ROMs will have to deal with defects in video and audio decoder hardware or software, playback software that can't keep up with full-rate movies, DVD-Video navigation software that doesn't correctly emulate a DVD-Video player, and so on. Not all computers with a DVD-ROM drive will play movies from a DVD-Video disc, but this may not be understood by the person buying the computer with exactly that goal in mind.

The Interactive Multimedia Association, which has since merged with the Software Publishers Association, is working on recommended practices for DVD developers, but there is no widespread support for these standards and there is no guarantee that they will significantly reduce compatibility problems.

Summary

The creators of DVD are aware of most of its limitations. Some were deliberate compromises to keep down cost and complexity. Some were simply more than they wanted to deal with.

There are solutions to most of DVD's shortcomings. These solutions perhaps will appear in proprietary enhanced versions of DVD or, better yet, officially supported in the next generation of DVD. See Chap. 10 for more perspective on the future evolution of DVD.

Considering that DVD was a compromise solution beaten into a form that was acceptable to hundreds of people from dozens of companies in the consumer electronics, movie, and computer industries, all with different priorities and different motivations—other than profit—it's amazing that DVD turned out as well as it did.

DVD is not the be-all and end-all of audio/video entertainment or of computer data storage (not that it was ever intended to be). Technology had reached the point where it was time to introduce a new standard, free of the drawbacks and dead ends of compact disc, videotape, and laserdisc. Detractors complain that DVD should have waited longer and taken advantage of new technology such as shorter-wavelength lasers in order to store even more data. Or, that DVD-Video is not sufficiently improved over laserdisc, or that it should have waited and fully supported HDTV. But this kind of argument leaves one forever poised on the edge of a leap that is never taken, since something slightly better is always around the corner. Once blue lasers are commercially available, ultraviolet lasers will be in the labs, promising even greater storage density. And how much better is "enough"? Realistically, DVD-Video is already capable of more than most televisions can deliver. Improving the quality would have made DVD more expensive and less reliable for little or no visible gain. And HDTV, as promising as it is, will take many long years to establish a market able to sustain a major consumer electronics product such as DVD.

All in all, DVD is a major step forward in many areas. There is certainly room for improvement, but even the Brave Little Tailor killed only seven in one blow.

DVD Comparison

This chapter compares DVD to related consumer electronics and computer data storage products. Each section presents technical specifications as well as advantages and disadvantages. The charts are by necessity rather terse and technical, but most points are explained in the accompanying paragraphs or in Chaps. 3 and 4. Most terms and acronyms are also defined in the glossary.

Some specifications such as signal-to-noise ratio and dynamic range are technical maximums that are usually lower in practice. For example, both DVD video and audio at 24 bits per sample have a theoretical signal-to-noise ratio of 144 dB, but MPEG compression creates variable video noise. And in any case, current digital-to-analog converters are incapable of reproducing such a clean signal.

While some technologies may be considered competitors to DVD, they may also complement each other. For example, videotape and DVD can coexist much like audio cassette tape and audio CD. And digital videotape (DV) is likely to be very popular in producing video for DVD.

Laserdisc and CDV

Laserdisc is the most obvious competitor to DVD-Video, since it's a high-quality video format on optical disc. Some DVD player manufacturers expect their initial primary customers to be videophiles and home theater aficionados, many of whom own laserdisc players.

DVD may eventually replace laserdisc, but it will be a very long process. Laserdisc is well established as a videophile format. There are almost 10,000 laserdisc titles in the United States and over 35,000 titles worldwide that can be played on over 7 million laserdisc players. It will take DVD many years to reach this point. Until then, laserdisc has the superiority of tenure and will continue to be a source of quality video, especially for rare titles that may not appear on DVD for a long while, if ever. Even laserdisc owners who buy DVD will not immediately replace their collection. Laserdisc and DVD will coexist for a long while. Unfortunately, anticipation of DVD is already hurting laserdisc. Player sales in 1996 were down 37 percent even though sales of VCRs and HiFi/surround systems were up. Disc sales were also down over 30 percent, but this was mostly due to poor sales of music titles and could also be attributed to a dearth of blockbuster movies.

CDV, sometimes called *Video Single* or *CD Video* (not to be confused with *Video CD*), is actually a hybrid of CD and laserdisc. Part of a CDV contains 20 minutes of digital audio playable on any CD player, DVD player, or CD-compatible laserdisc player. The other part of a CDV contains 5 or 6 minutes of analog video and digital audio in laserdisc format, playable only on CDV-compatible laserdisc systems.

See Table 6.1 for laserdisc and DVD-Video specifications.

TABLE 6.1

Laserdisc and DVD-Video Specifications

	Laserdisc	DVD-Video
Diameter	30 or 20 cm	12 or 8 cm
Thickness	2.4 mm	1.2 mm
Rotational velocity	600 to 1800 rpm	570 to 1600 rpm
Video	Composite analog NTSC	Component digital MPEG-2
Playing time	1 hour/side (CLV), 0.5 hours/side (CAV)	2+ hours/side (1 layer), 4+ hours/side (2 layer)
Widescreen support	Letterbox*	Anamorphic
Analog copy protection	None	Macrovision
Video S/N	~50 dB	~70 dB
NTSC resolution[†]	~272,160 pels (567×480); ~204,120 (567×360) letterboxed to 16:9	345,600 pels (720×480)
PAL resolution[†]	~326,592 pels (567×576); ~244,944 (567×432) letterboxed to 16:9	414,720 pels (720×576)
Audio	2 analog channels (FM), 2 digital channels (LPCM with optional Dolby Digital or DTS)	8 digital tracks of up to 8 channels each (LPCM/Dolby Digital/MPEG-2 with optional DTS or SDDS)
Uncompressed audio	16-bit 44.1 kHz PCM	16/20/24-bit 48/96 kHz PCM
Compressed audio	384 kbps Dolby Digital	64–448 kbps Dolby Digital
Optional compressed audio	1411 kbps DTS	32–1536 kbps DTS
Audio S/N	115 dB (PCM)	96–144 dB (PCM)
Dynamic range	96 dB (16-bit PCM)	96/120/144 dB (16/20/24-bit PCM), 120 dB (20-bit Dolby Digital)
Frequency (± 0.3 dB)	4–20,000 Hz	4–22,000 Hz (48 kHz), 4–44,000 Hz (96 kHz)

*There are rare anamorphic laserdiscs, but standard laserdisc players can't format them for 4:3 televisions.
[†]Analog laserdisc video doesn't actually have pixels, but the count can be approximated using TV lines of horizontal resolution (4:3 aspect ratio) and scan lines.

Advantages of DVD-Video over Laserdisc

FEATURES. DVD-Video has the same basic features as CLV laserdisc (scan, pause, search) plus most of those added by CAV laserdisc (freeze, slow, fast) and adds multistory branching, parental control, multiple camera angles, video menus, interactivity, and more.

CAPACITY. Programs on DVD can be over four times longer than on laserdisc. A single-layer DVD-Video holds over two hours of material per side and a dual-layer disc holds over four hours. A CLV laserdisc holds one hour per side, and a CAV laserdisc holds only half an hour.

DVD-Video supports still frames with audio, allowing for hundreds or thousands of pictures accompanied by as much as 20 hours of surround sound. Laserdisc still frames have no audio (unless specially produced discs are connected to expensive still-frame audio equipment).

CONVENIENCE. Laserdiscs are large and can be cumbersome to handle. The disc size also makes the players large. DVD discs can be easily handled and can be sent through the mail cheaply. DVD players can be portable—the same size as CD players. DVD discs fit into standard-width drives designed for computers. One drawback of the smaller disc size is less space on the package for art and information.

Since laserdiscs can't hold more than an hour per side, the disc must be changed one or more times during a movie. Some laserdisc players can automatically flip the disc, which still causes a break of about 10 seconds and doesn't help for movies more than two hours long (except in the case of exotic two-disc players designed for viewers who are obsessed with cinematic continuity). Laserdisc sides often end where it's technically convenient rather than where it's unobtrusive. In comparison, a DVD can hold a four-hour movie on one side if both layers are used.

AUDIO. DVD-Video has up to eight audio tracks. Laserdisc has two stereo audio tracks: one analog and one digital.

DVD-Video uncompressed digital audio (PCM) allows sampling rates of 48 or 96 kHz with 16, 20, or 24 bits of precision. Laserdisc uncompressed digital audio uses 44-kHz sampling at 16 bits.

DVD-Video compressed audio uses Dolby Digital 5.1-channel surround sound at a typical data rate of 384 kbps, but can go up to 448 kbps for better quality. DVD-Video can optionally include compressed DTS or SDDS audio. DVD-Video can also use 5.1- or 7.1-channel MPEG-2 audio, although many players don't support it and few home theaters have eight speakers.

Laserdisc carries compressed Dolby Digital surround sound by preempting one of the analog audio channels. Laserdisc can optionally carry DTS surround sound by replacing both digital audio channels.

To be fair, it should be recognized that most movies on DVD use compressed Dolby Digital audio for the sound tracks, while most laserdiscs have an uncompressed PCM digital audio track. It's difficult to compare the two, given the subjective importance of 5.1-channel surround sound, but most tests show that the average listener can't tell the difference between uncompressed PCM audio and compressed Dolby Digital audio.

VIDEO. DVD has the potential for better video than laserdisc. Technically, the resolution of DVD-Video is approximately one-third better than laserdisc, two-thirds better in widescreen mode (see Table A.17). Laserdisc suffers from degradation inherent in analog format and in the composite NTSC or PAL video signal. DVD uses component digital video, and even though it's heavily compressed, it's virtually indistinguishable from studio masters when properly and carefully encoded. Analog laserdisc video is also compressed, since the color component of the video is reduced to less than one-sixth the resolution of the brightness component.

This doesn't mean that the video quality of DVD is always better than laserdisc. Only that it can and should be better. There are poorly made DVDs that look worse than well-made laserdiscs, and there are well-made DVDs that look better than poorly made laserdiscs. But any DVD which has had sufficient care taken in the process of film transfer and compression should look better than a laserdisc made with equal care.

It's worth noting that the average television is of insufficient quality to show much difference between laserdisc and DVD. Home theater systems—especially those with large or widescreen TV sets offering component video inputs—are needed to take best advantage of the improved picture quality of DVD.

Of course, just as with vinyl records and CDs, the arguments about analog laserdisc quality versus digital DVD quality will rage eternally. The only final answer is to compare them objectively, side by side, and form your own opinion.

NOISE. Most laserdisc players make a whirring noise that can be heard during quiet segments of a movie. This does not bother some people, but is quite annoying to others. The noise is due to the large size and higher spin rate of laserdiscs (600–1800 rpm compared to 600–1600 rpm for DVDs and 200–500 rpm for CDs). Many DVD players are as quiet as CD players.

SUBTITLES. When subtitles are included on a laserdisc they must be permanently added to the video picture. On letterboxed movies, they can be placed in the matte area so as not to cover up the picture, but they are still obtrusive, especially to those who don't prefer subtitles. DVD allows up to 32 different subtitles or graphic overlays which can be turned on or off at any time.

RELIABILITY. Laserdiscs were based on very advanced technology when they were introduced, and they still show signs of that heritage. Production is expensive, and stamping small precise pits in such a large surface continues to cause problems with clean mold separation. CDs and DVDs were based on better-established technology when they were introduced, leading to simpler and more reliable production.

Both laserdiscs and DVDs are made from two bonded substrates, but the thinner profile and smaller size of DVDs make them much more stable and subject to fewer warp problems.

Laserdiscs are subject to what is commonly called *laser rot:* the deterioration of the aluminum coating that can occur if the seal between disc sides is broken. Laserdiscs absorb moisture, which can penetrate the seal. The large size of laserdiscs makes them flexible, thus allowing more movement along the bond between sides, which can ruin the aluminum layer. DVDs are molded from material which absorbs about 10 times less moisture than laserdiscs, and DVDs are much more rigid.

Laserdiscs incorporate no error correction, although many newer players have noise-reduction circuitry. Noise in analog video is expected and accepted. Laserdisc video often suffers from *dropouts,* small white specks caused by minor imperfections and scratches. Severe flaws or large scratches can cause playback to skip or may cause the disc to be unplayable. Because DVD is a digital medium, errors are more drastic than on laserdisc. This is why the DVD format includes a very robust error correction system which can compensate for scratches as wide as 6 mm. Most imperfections or scratches on a DVD disc will not affect playback. Large flaws or scratches may cause the picture to skip or break up and may even render the disc unplayable. On the whole, DVD is more tolerant of physical flaws and surface damage than laserdisc.

AVAILABILITY AND SUPPORT. There are many more manufacturers of DVD players than of laserdisc players, without counting computers that can play DVD-Video. Dealers have been amazingly quick to clear out their inventories of laserdisc players and replace them with DVD players.

Titles are a different situation. Many studios expect to eventually release more DVD titles than laserdisc titles, but in the short run there will be a dearth of titles in DVD format. It will take the DVD market many years to reach the wealth of offerings available on laserdisc, but should DVD succeed, it will eventually surpass the number of titles available on laserdisc. Unfortunately, the expected rapid decline of the laserdisc market means that many new releases and rereleases will only be available on DVD.

PRICE. In the long run, DVD hardware and discs will be cheaper than laserdisc players and laserdiscs. The success of DVD-ROM and the rapidly expanding use of digital video and digital audio are driving down costs. DVDs are cheaper to replicate than laserdiscs, and though they are initially more expensive to produce and master than laserdiscs, these costs are dropping rapidly to the point where DVDs can be produced with a desktop computer and replicated for less than $1 a copy. Initial pricing for DVD movies was at the same level as VHS tapes, about 30 percent lower than laserdiscs. Some Hollywood studio representatives have indicated they intend to release older movies on DVD at even lower prices than videotape.

Laserdisc may have one advantage over new releases which are priced for rental on videotape and DVD, typically at $80 to $90. Laserdiscs are seldom released at rental prices and are thus available for about 60 percent less during the period before the videotape and DVD products are dropped to lower prices for retail sale.

Advantages of Laserdisc over DVD-Video

ESTABLISHED MARKET. Laserdisc has enjoyed almost 20 years of modest growth and has become established as the premiere videophile format. It will take DVD many years to catch up to laserdisc's 35,000 titles worldwide.

REVERSE PLAY. Because of the way MPEG-2 compressed video builds pictures by using the differences from key frames, it's impossible to play in reverse at normal speed without a large amount of memory in which to hold the set of previous frames. RAM for video and decoding is very expensive, so most DVD players can only play backward by jumping to key frames, which results in video playback about 15 times faster than normal or jerky playback at slower speeds. Laserdiscs can't play CLV discs backward at all, but they can play CAV discs backward and forward at various speeds.

NO REGIONAL CODES. DVD-Video discs can be coded so they won't play in certain geographical regions. Laserdiscs have no such codes. Any NTSC laserdisc will play in an NSTC laserdisc player, and any PAL laserdisc will play in a PAL player.

MULTISTANDARD PLAYERS. Both DVD and laserdisc support two incompatible television systems: NTSC and PAL. The video signal is different for each system, and they are not interchangeable. However, almost every laserdisc player sold outside of North America and Japan can play either type of laserdisc if connected to the proper television. A few multistandard DVD players have been introduced, but movie studios and distributors would prefer to limit their availability.

NO COPY PROTECTION. Laserdisc does not use Macrovision or any similar process which tampers with the video signal in an attempt to prevent copying, unlike DVD, where the superior video signal can be distorted by copy protection schemes. Ironically the lack of copy protection has hindered the growth of laserdisc since many studios are reluctant to release movies on laserdisc, especially new blockbuster hits before they have achieved worldwide release.

Compatibility of Laserdisc and DVD-Video

No normal DVD player will play a laserdisc. No standard laserdisc player will play a DVD. Laserdisc uses analog video, DVD uses digital video; they are very different formats. However, some manufacturers such as Pioneer and Samsung have developed combination players that accept DVDs and laserdiscs (as well as CDVs and audio CDs).

There will probably never be an option to modify or upgrade a laserdisc player to play DVD. DVD circuitry is completely different, the pickup laser is a different wavelength, the tracking control is more precise, the motor speeds are different, and so on. No such hardware upgrades have been announced, and, in any case, they would probably be more expensive than buying a DVD player to put next to the laserdisc player.

As for CDV, the audio portion will play on any DVD player, but the video portion will only be viewable with players which include laserdisc compatibility.

Videotape

When DVD was introduced, there were over 175 million VCRs in U.S. households—a coverage of over 86 percent—and there were over 400 million VCRs worldwide. In terms of market targets for DVD, this is the broad side of a barn. But until—if ever—DVD is recordable it could miss the barn completely. In spite of the fact that 70 percent of VCR owners have supposedly never recorded anything with their VCRs, consumers demand the ability to record. It's like buying a convertible automobile; people in sunny climates take down the top all the time, and people in rainy locales still want the option in case they get a few days of sun. Until at least the year 2000, a DVD player can only serve as an addition to the home entertainment system for those who desire higher quality and want to create a long-lasting video library. A DVD player can be a replacement for the CD player, but not the VCR.

The Betamax videotape format provides a slightly better picture than VHS, but is not covered here since it is not widely used. S-VHS and Super-Beta (ED Beta) are even more improved, but are likewise not covered here for the same reason.

In quantitative terms, DVD has over twice the resolution of VHS. In terms of perceived quality on a sufficiently good monitor, there is a stunning difference between the two. Table 6.2 compares VHS with DVD.

Advantages of DVD-Video over Videotape

CAPACITY. For typical use, such as prerecorded movies, both VHS and DVD have sufficient capacity. But for anything requiring longer playing times such as training videos or video libraries, a double-sided, dual-layer DVD can hold over 8 hours of high-quality video or over 33 hours at VHS quality.

FEATURES. Beyond the basic VCR features of play, pause, step, slow, fast, fast forward, and rewind, DVD adds instant rewind, high-speed scan, instant search, multistory branching, parental control, multiple camera angles, video menus, interactivity, and more.

Not all players support these features, and not all discs include them, but they are part of the basic DVD format.

CONVENIENCE. Discs can be more compactly stored and can be sent through the mail more easily and cheaply. DVD players can be portable and battery-powered, at a size only slightly larger than the disc itself.

TABLE 6.2

VHS and DVD-
Video Specifications

	VHS videotape	DVD-Video
Video	Composite analog NTSC	Component digital MPEG-2
Playing time	2 hours/tape (SP) or 6 hours/tape (EP) (8 hours EP with T-160 tapes)	2+ hours/side (1 layer), 4+ hours/side (2 layer)
Widescreen support	Letterbox*	Anamorphic
Analog copy protection	Macrovision	Macrovision
Video S/N	~45 dB	~70 dB
NTSC resolution[†]	~153,600 pels (320 × 480)	345,600 pels (720 × 480)
PAL resolution[†]	~185,600 pels (320 × 580)	414,720 pels (720 × 576)
Audio	1 analog mono track or 1 analog HiFi stereo track	8 digital tracks, each with up to 8 channels of surround sound
Audio S/N	~40 dB (mono), ~90 dB (HiFi)	96—144 dB
Dynamic range	90 dB (HiFi)	96/120/144 dB (16/20/24-bit PCM), 120 dB (Dolby Digital)
Frequency (±0.3 dB)	70—10,000 Hz (mono), 20—20,000 Hz (HiFi)	4—22,000 Hz (48 kHz), 4—44,000 Hz (96 kHz)

*Anamorphic video can be recorded on any video system, but standard VCRs can't format it for 4:3 televisions.

[†]Analog VHS video doesn't actually have pixels, but the count can be approximated using TV lines of horizontal resolution (4:3 aspect ratio) and scan lines.

DURABILITY. Videotapes are subject to degradation from wear and stretching, erasure from magnetic fields, and damage from heat. DVD discs never wear out, are impervious to magnetic fields, and are less susceptible to heat damage. Discs can be scratched, but as with CDs only large scratches will cause noticeable playback problems.

"Tape-eating" VCRs may eventually become something to reminisce about, like the hazards of being covered with soot after a train ride. It's possible that loose material or a defect in a DVD player could scratch a DVD, but this has been very infrequent with millions of CD players.

VCR owners who rent videos subject their machines to tapes of dubious history covered with unknown substances, thus requiring more frequent head cleanings. Oft-rented tapes are easily recognized by their excessive glitches and tracking problems. Since the laser head in a DVD player never touches the surface of a disc, the condition of the disc doesn't affect the player as long as the disc is not broken or warped. It remains to be seen how well DVD does in the rental market, weighing its overall durability against its susceptibility to scratches.

VCRs generally break down because of mechanical failure exacerbated by rewinding. DVD players have much simpler mechanisms and never need to rewind.

AUDIO. Videotape audio is analog. The amount of tape dedicated to the audio track in monophonic VHS and linear stereo VHS is only one-half of 1 percent. HiFi VHS uses more tape and a helical scan to get close to CD-quality audio. Dolby Surround encoding can be used to mix surround sound into the videotape stereo signal. In comparison, DVD includes up to eight audio tracks of CD-quality audio with Dolby Digital discrete surround sound and a subwoofer channel. The extra audio tracks can be used for foreign language, commentary, additional music, and more.

VIDEO. The video quality of VHS tape is much lower than broadcast or cable signals. Tape dropouts (poor or missing magnetic particles) cause dots and small flashes in the picture. Wear and stretching from the kids playing their favorite tape twice a day causes the picture to degrade quickly, not to mention the requirement of more frequent head cleanings. Head alignment differences cause tracking problems and additional loss of quality. DVD uses digital video, and even though it's compressed, properly produced discs look almost as good as studio masters. Discs never wear out from repeated playing, and servo-controlled laser tracking keeps everything in perfect alignment.

Prerecorded videotapes are copied in high-speed duplicating machines; they don't nearly match the quality of the duplication master. DVDs are stamped into plastic using metal plates; they contain virtually the same data as the master.

Each generation of a videotape copy loses quality. If recordable home DVD is developed, it will be able to make perfect copies. Once the video is encoded in MPEG-2 digital format, each successive copy will be a perfect replica. Of course, this assumes that the original copy is not protected. But copies of home videos sent to Grandma will no longer be so blurry that she can't tell the grandkids apart.

PRICE. Discs are cheaper than tapes and can be mass-produced faster and more easily. Whether this savings ever gets passed on to the consumer remains to be seen, since it never seemed to happen with CDs.* Some movie studio executives have stated that they plan to make DVDs as cheap or cheaper than videotape; especially older movies which have already made back their original cost.

SUBTITLES.   When subtitles are included on a videotape, they must be permanently added to the video picture. DVD allows up to 32 different subtitles or graphic overlays which can be turned on or off at will.

Advantages of Videotape over DVD-Video

RECORDABLE.   This is the killer difference. Recordable DVD-Video will not be available in the home before the year 2000, if ever. Recordable DVD-Video technology will have to improve significantly and become much cheaper before this can happen. Copy protection issues, which have seriously hampered other digital recording formats such as DAT and DV, may also delay this vital feature.

ESTABLISHED MARKET.   VHS has been around for just over 20 years. There are supposedly more than 30,000 different VHS titles in the United States and over 50,000 worldwide. It will take DVD a very long time, if ever, to reach this point. Many titles available on tape may never appear on DVD.

VHS also has a well-established rental market. There are approximately 27,000 video stores in the United States, visited each week by over 65 million people, who, in 1996, rented more than 3 billion videotapes and purchased more than 580 million. DVD must penetrate this market while it's being eroded by video-on-demand and pay-per-view programming.

NO REGIONAL CODES.   A code can be added to a DVD disc so that it won't play in players or computers from certain geographical regions. Videotapes have no such codes. The only limitation is among television systems, but an NTSC videotape will play in any NSTC VCR, and a PAL videotape will play in any PAL VCR.

---

*Consumers have long complained that CDs have not dropped in price as was often promised. However, neither have they gone up in price to match inflation. CD prices haven't changed much from the $15 level they reached shortly after introduction. But $15 in 1984 is equivalent to about $9.50 in 1997.

MULTISTANDARD PLAYERS. Both DVD and videotape must support two incompatible television systems: 525/60 (NTSC) and 625/50 (PAL). The video signal is stored differently for each system and they are not interchangeable. However, multistandard VCRs are available which can play either type of tape if connected to a multistandard monitor. Standards-converting VCRs are also available which use digital processing to convert between formats. The future widespread availability of multistandard and standards-converting DVD players is uncertain and is complicated by Japan (NTSC) and Europe (PAL) sharing the same DVD region code.

AVAILABILITY AND SUPPORT. Until DVD-Video becomes well established in the home market, if ever, it may be difficult to buy or rent discs. Finding repair shops and qualified technicians may also be difficult at first.

Compatibility of VHS and DVD-Video

As ludicrous as it seems, people have done stranger things than to try and put a disc in a tape player. A videotape player will not play a DVD. No DVD player will play a videotape. However, some manufacturers have developed dual models which contain both a DVD deck and a VHS deck in a single unit.

Digital Videotape (DV and D-VHS)

Digital videotape systems are generally aimed at the professional production and prosumer markets. However, it's worth taking a look at them since they are the closest digital video competitors to DVD. There are essentially two systems, DV (or DVC) and D-VHS. Purely professional systems such as Digital-S, Betacam SX, Digital Betacam, and D1 are not covered.

Like DVD, DV has gained unified industry support. The original proposal from Matsushita, Philips, Sony, and Thomson was endorsed in 1993 by Hitachi, JVC, Mitsubishi, Sanyo, Sharp, and Toshiba, and since then has been supported by many other companies. Unfortunately, there have already been nonstandard enhancements to the format: Matsushita's DVCPro and Sony's DVCam use different physical formats or recording densities which make the tapes incompatible, but they use the same data formats in order to connect to other DV equipment.

DV camcorders appeared in 1995, but DV recording decks were delayed in the United States primarily by concerns that they might be able to make perfect copies of DVDs. DV recorders appeared in 1997 after a copyright protection system was added.

DV uses I-MPEG compression. I-MPEG is based on DCT and quantization similar to MPEG, but it compresses each frame separately (similar to MPEG's I frames or motion-JPEG) and uses interfield compression to take advantage of redundancy within a frame. Because there is no interframe compression, I-MPEG is less efficient than MPEG but is better for editing since frames can be moved and combined without requiring decoding and recoding of a group of dependent frames.

As with DAT, the DV format specifies a computer data storage variation intended for backup and archiving.

D-VHS was developed by JVC and is ostensibly supported by Hitachi, Matsushita, and Philips. D-VHS is oriented more toward the consumer market than DV, and it is backward-compatible with VHS, meaning it can read and write VHS tapes as well as read and write digital data using special D-VHS tapes. D-VHS was announced in April of 1995, but after two years has yet to appear as a commercial product outside of Japan. *D-VHS* originally stood for *Digital-VHS,* but now stands for *Data-VHS.* Unlike other digital tape formats, D-VHS does not convert or record analog video—it only records and reads bitstreams. This means D-VHS can record from a digital source such as DBS, digital cable, HDTV, and DVD (assuming each of these has a compressed digital bitstream output), but the D-VHS player has to send the data back out to a compatible decoder in order to display it. This requires a television with a built-in decoder or a bitstream input on a digital video device such as a DVD player. At the time DVD was introduced, such digital bitstream connections were not available on any consumer products.

Because of its bitstream capability, D-VHS is also being positioned for computer data backup in the home. Analog video sources are recorded and reproduced by D-VHS decks in analog form, not digital. D-VHS systems as planned are unable to do any conversion between analog and digital formats.

See Table 6.3 for DV and DVD-Video specifications.

Advantages of DVD-Video over Digital Videotape

CAPACITY.   MiniDV cassettes can hold 1 hour of video, standard DV cassettes can hold 4½ hours. An 8-cm DVD can hold approximately ¾ to 2½ hours; a 12-cm DVD can hold approximately 2 to 8 hours.

D-VHS has higher capacity than DVD (see the following section). Even though the areal bit capacity of DV is significantly higher than D-VHS, DV tape is more narrow.

FEATURES. Beyond DV and D-VHS features of play, pause, slow, fast, step, fast forward, and rewind, DVD adds instant access, search, menus, interactivity, and more. However, these features may not be provided by all discs or supported by all DVD players.

DURABILITY. Videotapes are subject to degradation from wear and stretching, erasure from magnetic fields, and damage from heat. Even though the very small tape width of DV makes it susceptible to stretching and dropouts, the digital data format and error correction largely compensate. In comparison, discs never wear out, are impervious to magnetic fields, and are less susceptible to heat damage. Discs can be scratched, but as with CDs only large scratches will cause noticeable playback problems.

Even high-precision, semiprofessional videotape equipment can occasionally eat a tape. It's possible that a DVD player could scratch a disc, but this is very rare.

Videotape equipment is quite complex, with DV heads spinning at 9000 rpm and hundreds of small components which can break down because of mechanical failure. DVD players have much simpler mechanisms.

VIDEO. In VHS mode, D-VHS provides VHS video. In digital bitstream mode, the video depends entirely on the digital source and may be better or worse than DVD.

AUDIO. DV provides one stereo track at high quality (48 kHz, 16-bit) or two stereo tracks at slightly lower quality (48 kHz, 12-bit). DVD provides one stereo track at super-high quality (96 kHz, 24-bit), one 8-channel track at high quality (48 kHz, 16-bit), or up to 8 tracks of 5.1-channel Dolby Digital surround or 5.1/7.1-channel MPEG-2 surround.

In VHS mode, D-VHS provides standard VHS HiFi audio. In digital bitstream mode, the audio depends entirely on the digital source.

PRICE. Discs are cheaper than tapes and can be mass-produced faster and more easily than tapes. It's unlikely that DV will ever be used for prerecorded commercial video.

At the time DVD was introduced, DV cameras and decks cost $3000 to $5000, and the professional DVCPro cameras and decks were more than $15,000. The prices of DV cassette tapes were $10 to $25. It's expected that recordable DVD discs will start at around $40 and eventually drop to $5 or

TABLE 6.3

DV and DVD-Video Specifications

	DV	D-VHS	DVD-Video
Video	Component digital	Composite analog or digital bitstream	Component digital
Playing time	0.5 to 1 hours/tape (mini), 4.5 hours/tape (standard)	2 to 6 hours/tape (VHS), 3.5 (28.2 Mbps) to 49 (2 Mbps) hours/tape (D-VHS)	2+ hours/side (1 layer), 4+ hours/side (2 layer)
Data capacity	5.5G to 50G bytes	31.7G bytes (300m tape), 44.4G bytes (420m tape)	4.7G to 17G bytes
Digital compression	I-MPEG, ~5:1 (from 8-bit 4:1:1 or 4:2:0)	None (external)	MPEG-1 or MPEG-2, ~30:1 (from 8-bit 4:2:0)
Data rate	25.146 Mbps CBR video, up to 1.536 Mbps audio, ~35.5 Mbps max.	28.2 Mbps (HD), 14.1 Mbps (STD), 2 to 7 Mbps (LP)	Up to 9.8 Mbps combined VBR/CBR video and audio
Error correction	RS-CIRC	RS (inner/outer)	RS-PC
Coded frame rate	29.97* (525/60), 25* (625/50)	n/a	29.97* or 24† (525/60), 25* or 24† (625/50)
Widescreen support	Anamorphic‡	Letterbox (VHS)	Anamorphic
Analog copy protection	None	Macrovision (VHS)	Macrovision
Copy management	CGMS	CGMS	CGMS

Encryption	Yes	No (external)	Yes, CSS
525/60 resolution	345,600 pels (720 × 480)	~153,600 pels (320 × 480) (VHS)	345,600 pels (720 × 480)
625/50 resolution	414,720 pels (720 × 576)	~185,600 pels (320 × 580) (VHS)	414,720 pels (720 × 576)
Audio	2 tracks of 2 channels (32 kHz, 12-bit nonlinear PCM) or 1 track of 2 channels (32/44.1/48 kHz, 16-bit linear PCM)	Analog VHS stereo HiFi or digital bitstream	8 tracks of up to 8 channels each (LPCM/Dolby Digital/MPEG-2)
Audio S/N	72 dB (12-bit), 96 dB (16-bit)	~40 dB (mono VHS), ~90 dB (HiFi VHS)	96–144 dB
Dynamic range	96 dB	~90 dB (HiFi VHS)	96/120/144 dB (16/20/24-bit PCM), 120 dB (20-bit Dolby Digital)
Frequency (±0.3 dB)	4–15,000 Hz (32 kHz), 4–20,000 Hz (44.1 kHz), 4–22,000 Hz (48 kHz)	70–10,000 Hz (mono VHS), 20–20,000 Hz (HiFi VHS)	4–22,000 Hz (48 kHz), 4–44,000 Hz (96 kHz)

*Interlaced.
†Progressive.
‡Special feature on some equipment only.

217

less. DV hardware and tape prices will also come down, but without the advantage of a mass-market computer counterpart such as DVD-ROM, they will not drop nearly as far as DVD hardware and disc prices.

Essentially no D-VHS equipment was available when this book was written. Decks are expected to be about the same price as DVD players, and tapes will be much cheaper when measured in cost per gigabyte (see the following section). Separate digital audio/video equipment with digital connections—such as IEEE 1394 FireWire—will be required to take advantage of D-VHS's digital bitstream capability.

Advantages of Digital Videotape over DVD-Video

CAPACITY.   D-VHS has a much greater capacity than DVD, with a digital tape holding almost 50 gigabytes of data.

RECORDABLE.   As with VCRs, this is the difference that makes all the difference. Recordable DVD may make an appearance in the professional video industry before it trickles down to the consumer, but the high compression required by DVD-Video makes it an unsuitable candidate for shooting and editing. Recordable DVD will more likely be the final destination of digital video files from DV cameras and editing systems. Since it's possible to store DV-format (I-MPEG) video on a DVD-ROM, this may become popular for quick-access archiving.

D-VHS can record from a digital source, but a digital decoder must also be available for playback.

EDITING.   A significant advantage of DV is that each frame is compressed individually, so they can be inserted, deleted, and combined in any order. This is especially useful for nonlinear digital editing systems. Because DVD's MPEG-2 P and B frames rely on nearby frames, they must be decompressed and recompressed to make an edit within a group of pictures. This can degrade picture quality.

VIDEO.   DV uses the same component digital format as DVD-Video, the only difference being the sampling system. DV uses 4:1:1 sampling for NTSC and 4:2:0 sampling for PAL. DVD-Video uses 4:2:0 sampling for both NTSC and PAL. Both sampling methods record the same amount of information but in slightly different ways, and there are endless arguments over which is better. DV's I-MPEG compression removes much less information than DVD's MPEG-2 compression, but is correspondingly less efficient. DV video quality is superior to DVD's average video data rate of 3.5 Mbps, but is not noticeably different when DVD rates are increased to more than 5 or 6 Mbps.

D-VHS can record a digital video bitstream at up to 28 Mbps, which is more than adequate for even high-quality digital video formats such as those used for HDTV.

PRICE. D-VHS tapes may cost more than DVD discs, even more than recordable discs in the long term, but they are much more cost-effective when measured in price per gigabyte.

Compatibility of Digital Videotape and DVD-Video

DV and DVD-Video are not directly compatible. DV's intraframe compression technique is similar to MPEG's, but is technically not the same. Certain key low-level differences make them incompatible and cause many headaches for implementors of hardware and software intended to support both formats. As long as these differences are accounted for, DV's I-MPEG compression format can be easily converted to MPEG-2. Both are component digital formats, and other than errors introduced in converting between sampling systems, and possible minor artifacts introduced by the differences in compression techniques, there will be almost no loss of quality when transferring from one to the other.

D-VHS and DVD-Video are not directly compatible. But it's possible that until recordable DVD is cheaply available, D-VHS could become a favorite method of recording from DVD. In this case, both the DVD player and the D-VHS recorder must have a digital connection, such as FireWire. In addition, either the DVD player or some other device such as an HDTV display must be able to decode the DVD-specific MPEG-2/Dolby Digital bitstream when connected to the D-VHS deck. Features of DVD-Video such as seamless branching, camera angles, and so on would no longer be available from a sequential bitstream.

It is expected that both DV and D-VHS recorders will respect the copy generation management information sent by the DVD player.

Audio CD

The official DVD-Audio format has yet to be defined, but in the meantime, the audio capabilities of the DVD-Video format pack quite a wallop.

DVD-Video discs can be produced with or without video, and some hardware manufacturers have audio-only DVD players in the works. See Table 6.4 for a comparison of specifications.

Advantages of DVD-Video over Audio CD

QUALITY. Many people feel that CD is sufficiently perfect. Others claim it isn't even close. In any case, DVD has it beat. DVD-Video specifies three different audio formats: linear PCM (Pulse Code Modulation, the same as audio CD), 5.1-channel Dolby Digital surround, and 5.1/7.1-channel MPEG-2 surround.

CD audio is sampled 44,100 times a second using 16 digital bits to hold each value. DVD PCM audio is sampled at either 48,000 or 96,000 times a second and uses 16, 20, or 24 bits to hold the values. The reproducible frequency is just below half the sampling rate, which gives CD a limit of about 20 kHz and DVD a limit of about 44 kHz. Since the average human hearing range doesn't extend beyond about 20 kHz, it might seem that DVD holds an advantage only for dogs, but higher sampling rates have been shown to result in improved sound reproduction. The sampling size determines the dynamic range (approximately 6 dB per bit), but it also has benefits for noise shaping and other digital signal processing techniques which can take advantage of the extra bits of precision.

CD audio uses two channels: left and right stereo. At lower sample rates and bit rates, DVD PCM can have up to 8 channels. Dolby Digital uses 5.1 channels: left, right, center, left-rear, right-rear, and subwoofer. MPEG-2 can optionally add left-center and right-center channels.

TABLE 6.4

Audio CD and DVD-Video Specifications

	Audio CD	DVD-Video
Audio	16-bit 44.1-kHz PCM	16/20/24-bit 48/96-kHz PCM, 20-bit 48-kHz Dolby Digital/MPEG-2 5.1/7.1-channel surround sound
Audio S/N	105 dB	96—144 dB
Dynamic range	96 dB (16-bit PCM)	96/120/144 dB (16/20/24-bit PCM), 120 dB (Dolby Digital)
Frequency (±0.3 dB)	4—20,000 Hz (44.1-kHz PCM)	4—22,000 Hz (48 kHz), 4—44,000 Hz (96 kHz)
Playing time	~80 minutes	~27 hours of surround sound, ~7 hours of 20-bit 48-kHz stereo, ~138 minutes of 24-bit 96-kHz stereo*

*All times are for a single 4.4-gigabyte layer. Times for a dual-layer disc are almost twice as long.

Both of DVD-Video's surround-sound formats are compressed from 16-, 18-, or 20-bit 48-kHz source. Psychoacoustic processing is used to remove imperceptible sounds and redundant information. Occasional compression artifacts may be heard, but the resulting surround-sound experience is similar to that of a theater—assuming the DVD player is hooked up to a sufficiently good home sound system.

A few CDs are available with DTS surround sound. These CDs are not playable on regular CD players. DVD allows DTS as an option, and with its larger capacity DVD can contain standard PCM audio, a Dolby Digital version for those with Dolby Digital Decoders, and a DTS version for those with DTS decoders.

CAPACITY. By squeezing the tracks tightly together, an audio CD can be made to hold as much as 84 minutes of audio, rather than the specified 72 or 74 minutes. DVD, even at its highest level of uncompressed stereo sound quality on a single-layer disc, holds over two hours of audio. Using all 5.1 channels of Dolby Digital audio, a single-sided, single-layer DVD can play for over 27 hours. And using only two channels of Dolby Digital, more than 54 hours fit on a single layer, and a mind-boggling 197 hours can be packed onto a double-sided, dual-layer disc.

VIDEO. It may seem strange to list video as an advantage of DVD over audio CD, but there have been many attempts to add video to music CDs, including CDV, CD+G, and Enhanced CD (see the sections on laserdisc and other CD formats in this chapter for details).

Given the achievements of MTV, the success of music performance videos, and the amount of existing music video footage with no retail channel, it's expected that DVD-Video's combination of high-quality video with the convenience and audio quality of CD will tap a larger market of music listeners who are interested in the visual aspects of the performance. DVD music video will also appeal to the karaoke market, especially with its multilingual subtitle capabilities.

Advantages of Audio CD over DVD-Video

ESTABLISHED BASE. By the end of 1996, there were over 600 million audio CD players and another 100 million or so CD-ROM drives capable of playing audio CDs. Over 10 billion audio CDs have been produced since 1982. Since DVDs may not play in CD players, but CDs will play in DVD players, there's no compelling reason for publishers to release music titles in DVD format. Especially not before the DVD-Audio standard is finalized.

DVD-Video makes sense for music with video and for high-end music titles where the publisher wants to take advantage of higher PCM sampling rates and bit rates. But for standard music titles, publishers will stick with a market of 700 million CD units which will continue to grow with CD-capable DVD units.

Compatibility of Audio CD and DVD-Video

In general, all DVD-Video players and DVD-ROM drives can play an audio CD. This is not actually required by the DVD standard, but so far all manufacturers have designed their DVD hardware to read CDs.

No CD player or CD-ROM drive can play audio from a DVD. It's possible that the DVD-Audio format may include a *legacy* variation containing music in CD format on one layer of the disc and in DVD format on another, or CD data sandwiched between the DVD lead-in and an outer ring of DVD data. However, there are certain technical obstacles which make either approach difficult or expensive.

See the "Other CD Formats" section which follows for details on compatibility between DVD and variations of the CD format which include music.

CD-ROM

See Table 6.5 for a listing of CD-ROM and DVD-ROM specifications.

TABLE 6.5

CD-ROM and DVD-ROM Specifications

	CD-ROM	DVD-ROM
Capacity	650.4 megabytes	4.38 to 15.9 gigabytes
Error correction	RS-CIRC	RS-PC
Error correction overhead	34%	13%
Modulation	EFM (8/14)	EFMPlus (8/16)
Transfer rate*	150 KB/s (1×)	1353 KB/s (1×)
File system	ISO-9660, HFS, other	UDF, UDF Bridge, other†

*Reference rates for single-speed drives. The transfer rate for double speed drives is 300 KB/s for CD-ROM and 2705 KB/s for DVD-ROM, and so on.

†Technically, DVD-ROM discs are supposed to stick with the UDF Bridge format, but this kind of restriction has often been historically ignored.

Advantages of DVD-ROM over CD-ROM

CAPACITY. A CD-ROM holds about 650 megabytes. This can be pushed to about 730 megabytes by squeezing the tracks tighter together. A single-layer DVD holds 4.4 gigabytes, which is 7 times what a CD-ROM holds. A dual-layer DVD holds 8.0 gigabytes, 12.5 times more than a CD-ROM. A double-sided, single-layer DVD holds 8.8 gigabytes, 14 times more than a CD-ROM. A double-sided, dual-layer DVD holds 15.9 gigabytes, which is 25 times what a CD-ROM holds. (See page 133 for an explanation of the improvements from CD to DVD that account for the increased capacity.)

SPEED. The CD-ROM specification requires a minimum transfer rate of 150 kilobytes/second. Caches and multispeed CD-ROM drives can raise the transfer rate much higher, even above that of a standard DVD-ROM drive. Multispeed drives spin the disc at higher multiples of the standard velocity to increase the rate at which data is read off the CD. However, producers of CD-ROM—based software must often deal with the huge installed base of single-speed and double-speed CD-ROM drives.

The DVD-ROM specification requires a minimum transfer rate of 11.08 million bits/second (1353 kilobytes/second), which is 9 times faster than a single-speed CD-ROM drive at 1.23 million bits/second or roughly equivalent to a 9× CD-ROM drive. As with CD-ROM drives, the manufacturers will continually increase the speed of DVD-ROM drives to improve performance.

Some DVD-ROM drives read CDs and DVDs at the same scanning velocity, and therefore transfer CD-ROM data about as fast as a 3× (triple-speed) CD-ROM drive. Other DVD-ROM drives increase the speed to achieve higher data rates when reading CD-ROMs, some higher than 20×.

RELIABILITY. Even though DVD-ROM reduces the amount of space taken up for error correction to 13 percent versus CD-ROM's 34 percent, DVD-ROM uses a more advanced technique which is about 10 times more effective at correcting errors.

Because DVDs are made of two thin substrates glued together, they are more rigid than a solid CD-ROM. The improved rigidity makes them spin more smoothly, resulting in better reading accuracy. Disc bonding technology has become well developed for use with laserdiscs (which are also made of two sides glued together) and is quite reliable, although the hot-melt glue method may be inadequate for discs left on a car dashboard in July; the bond could begin to slip at temperatures above 150°F (70°C).

The data layer of a CD is at the top of the disc (which is read in the player from the bottom), and is protected by only a thin layer of lacquer. Deep scratches can physically damage the metallic layer or expose it to oxidation. DVD's data layers are at the center, on the inside surface of the substrates, and are consequently more protected.

IMPROVED STANDARDS.   CD-ROM is an afterthought added three years later to the CD-Audio standard. Other variations such as CD-ROM XA, multisession, CD-R, Video CD, and CD-RW are afterthoughts built on afterthoughts. Many incompatibilities exist in the CD family. Enhanced CD (including CD Plus which was a replacement for CD Extra, which allows computer data to be added to a disc with music tracks that can be played in an audio CD player) was not standardized until 1995 and is incompatible with early CD-ROM drives and driver software. The erasable CD-RW standard established at the end of 1996 is not compatible with any CD-ROM drive built before 1997, nor with most built after. The ISO-9660 file system went through several iterations under such names as High Sierra, Rockridge, and Frankfurt, and didn't adequately support Macintosh and UNIX file systems. Full support for these file systems had to be added as incompatible extensions.

DVD, on the other hand, was designed from the ground up to be computer-compatible. DVD-Video and DVD-Audio are layers on top of the DVD-ROM standard. The recordable and erasable versions of DVD were anticipated and mostly accounted for. The UDF file system, developed by OSTA (Optical Storage Technology Association) supports all major operating systems and provides for recordability and erasability.

Unfortunately, DVD-RAM wasn't finalized until long after the first DVD-ROM drives were built and is incompatible with them.

Advantages of CD-ROM over DVD-ROM

ESTABLISHED BASE.   In 1996, there was an installed base of about 100 million CD-ROM drives. Another 50 million drives are expected to be sold in 1997. Forecasts for DVD-ROM drive sales in 1997 range from 500 thousand to 10 million (the lower number being much more realistic). Even the most optimistic projections don't expect the installed base of DVD-ROM drives to exceed CD-ROM drives before the year 2000, although more than one forecast expects CD-ROM drive production to have ceased by then. It will take several years for DVD-ROM drives to reach the point of critical mass where publishers begin to require them for their software. And it will take much longer before publishers begin to abandon CD-ROM, especially since DVD-ROM drives are backward-compatible.

CD production systems are in place and well established, both at the desktop development level and the manufacturing and replication level. CD-ROM replication plants can be upgraded for DVD production in a relatively easy manner, since much of the equipment is the same. Development of DVD-ROM content which does not rely on the higher data rate or specific video features of DVD, is almost exactly the same as for CD-ROM. Development of DVD-Video content or DVD-Video—based multimedia software, on the other hand, requires new equipment and techniques, especially for desktop production.

RECORDABLE. Although the DVD format includes provisions for recordable and rewritable versions, the standards were not finalized when DVD was released at the end of 1996. CD-R, the recordable version of CD-ROM, is well established and has become quite inexpensive. CD-RW, the rewriteable version of CD-ROM, was introduced at the same time as DVD-ROM, but may not establish itself before being replaced by DVD-RAM.

NO REGIONAL CODES OR ENCRYPTION. Technically, regional codes and encryption are not part of the DVD-ROM standard. However, the importance placed on computers being able to play DVD-Video discs in DVD-ROM drives has dragged them into the equation. The result: long delays in the introduction of DVD, longer delays in the release of DVD-ROM drives, initial added cost to DVD-ROM hardware for authentication, added complexity for operating system and application support of DVD-ROM drives, and general muddling of the elementary distinction between computer data on DVD-ROM and movies on DVD-Video. CD-ROM has been largely free of this type of extraneous influence.

Compatibility of CD-ROM and DVD-ROM

In general, all DVD-ROM drives can read CD-ROMs. However, there are many variations of the CD format which are detailed in the "Video CD and CD-i" and the "Other CD Formats" sections. Some of these variations are compatible with DVD-ROM drives and some are not. The most notable exception is that about half of the first generation of DVD-ROM drives are unable to read CD-R discs.

No CD-ROM drive can read a DVD-ROM disc. It's possible that a dual-layer *legacy* format will be developed, with one layer readable in a DVD-ROM drive and the other layer readable only in a CD-ROM drive, but these may be more trouble than they are worth.

Video CD and CD-i

Video CD, sometimes called *VCD* and not to be confused with *CDV*, is a standard for storing audio and video using the CD format. In many ways it can be considered the precursor to DVD. Because of the capacity and speed limitations of the CD format, Video CD quality is limited; it is considered to be near that of VHS videotape.

The Philips CD-i format was created as a specialized interactive (that's what the *i* stands for) application of CD for custom players that connect to a TV. New models of CD-i players can play Video CDs; older models require a motion video adapter.

See Table 6.6 for a listing of the Video CD and DVD-Video specifications.

Advantages and Disadvantages of CD-i

Compared to DVD, CD-i has a few advantages and disadvantages not shared by Video CD. These are covered first, followed by the remaining comparisons with Video CD.

FEATURES. The interactivity of CD-i goes far beyond that of DVD-Video. CD-i players are actually special-purpose computers. They contain a Motorola 68000 processor, the same one that powered early Macintosh computers. Additional specialized processors provide support for graphics and video. CD-i players have memory for data storage, optional keyboards, and even optional modems for connecting to the Internet. CD-i supports fully interactive multimedia programs and can generate text and graphics in response to user input. DVD-Video has limited interactivity using only premade text and graphics. CD-i was the first consumer device to use MPEG-1 video. CD-i players can decode multiple MPEG-1 video channels from a single multiplexed stream for multiple video windows of selectable sizes and aspect ratios and up to 16 audio tracks for up to 18 hours of audio per disc. Full- or partial-screen images can be overlaid with

TABLE 6.6

Video CD and
DVD-Video
Specifications

	White Book (Video CD 2.0)	DVD-Video
Video	Component digital MPEG-1	Component digital MPEG-2
Playing time	74 minutes	2+ hours/side (single layer), 4+ hours/side (dual layer)
Widescreen support	Letterboxed*	Anamorphic
Compression	~90:1 (from 8-bit 4:2:0)	~30:1 (from 8-bit 4:2:0)
Analog copy protection	None	Macrovision, CGMS-A
Digital copy management	None	CGMS-D
525/60 (NTSC) resolution	84,480 pels (352 × 240)	345,600 pels (720 × 480)
625/50 (PAL) resolution	101,376 pels (352 × 288)	414,720 pels (720 × 576)
Coded frame rate[†]	29.97[‡] or 23.976[‡] (525/60), 25[‡] (625/50)	29.97[§] or 24[∥] (525/60), 25[§] or 24[∥] (625/50)
Still picture (I frame)	704 × 480 (525/60), 704 × 576 (625/50)	720 × 480 (525/60), 720 × 576 (625/50)
Audio	16 stereo or mono tracks (MPEG-1 layer II)	8 tracks of up to 8 channels each
Uncompressed audio	16-bit 44.1-kHz LPCM (if no video)	16/20/24-bit 48/96-kHz LPCM
Compressed audio	224 kbps MPEG-1 layer II (44.1 kHz)	64–448 kbps Dolby Digital (48 kHz) or 64–912 kbps MPEG-2 (48 kHz) or 64–384 kbps MPEG-1 layer II (44.1 kHz)
Audio S/N	96 dB	96–144 dB
Dynamic range	96 dB	96/120/144 dB (16/20/24-bit PCM), 120 dB (Dolby Digital)
Frequency (±0.3 dB)	4–20,000 Hz (44.1 kHz)	4–22,000 Hz (48 kHz), 4–44,000 Hz (96 kHz)
Data rate	Maximum 1.1519291 kbps	Maximum 9.8 Mbps

*Anamorphic video could be put on Video CDs, but the players can't format it for 4:3 televisions.

[†]MPEG-1 allows any coded frame rate to be displayed at either 29.97 or 25 fps when decoded. MPEG-2 requires the pulldown rate to be determined at encoding time.

[‡]Noninterlaced (each frame shown twice).

[§]Interlaced.

[∥]Progressive.

transparency on motion video with hardware-rendered transition effects such as dissolves, wipes, slides, and scrolls. Text overlay can be generated on the fly, including up to 32 stored subpicture streams, memory resident pop-up menus, and real-time graphics. A computerlike graphical interface with an on-screen cursor is controlled by a wireless remote control.

On the other hand, once DVD is supported by video game consoles, the level of interactivity may meet or exceed that of CD-i.

AVAILABILITY AND SUPPORT. CD-i hardware and software is almost entirely produced or funded by Philips and Korea's LG Electronics with a handful of independent hardware and software licensees on the side. About half a million players have been sold in the United States and about 1.5 million worldwide.

More than a dozen manufacturers produce DVD-Video players, not counting manufacturers of DVD-capable computers. Dozens of producers are creating interactive DVD-Video titles in spite of its limited capabilities.

Advantages of DVD-Video over Video CD

FEATURES. The DVD-Video format includes the same basic features as Video CD (menus, pause, search, freeze, slow, fast, scan) and adds seamless branching, parental control, multiple camera angles, and more.

CAPACITY. Programs on DVD can be over four times longer than on Video CD. A single-layer DVD-Video holds over two hours of material per side and a dual-layer disc holds over four hours. A Video CD holds 74 minutes and has only one side.

Both DVD and Video CD support still frames with audio, but DVD has the potential for hundreds more pictures and hours more of surround sound.

CONVENIENCE. Since Video CDs can't hold much more than an hour, the disc must be changed one or more times during a movie. A DVD-Video can easily hold a four-hour movie on one side.

AUDIO. DVD-Video has up to eight digital audio tracks. Each track can hold uncompressed audio with quality better than audio CD or compressed 5.1-channel surround sound in Dolby Digital or MPEG-2 format. Video CD normally has one track of compressed, 2-channel audio in MPEG-1 format.

VIDEO. The quality of DVD-Video vastly exceeds that of Video CD, with 4 times the resolution in normal mode and 5½ times in widescreen mode (compared to letterboxed Video CD). DVD-Video uses MPEG-2 compression, which is more efficient than the MPEG-1 compression used by Video CD. Video in MPEG-2 looks better than in MPEG-1, even at the same resolution and data rate and especially if variable bitrate is used. MPEG-1 video is better only at data rates below 2 Mbps. DVD-Video supports both MPEG-1 and MPEG-2.

PRICE. Currently, Video CD has the price advantage over DVD-Video. Video CD movies sell for an average of $20 in the United States and for as little as $5 in Asian countries. Video CD players typically cost $200 to $300. If DVD-Video succeeds, DVD movies may become cheaper than Video CDs since the production and manufacturing costs will be equivalent while the market will be larger. DVD-Video player prices will likewise be lowered significantly by the larger market.

Advantages of Video CD over DVD-Video

WORLDWIDE STANDARD (SORT OF). Video CD solved the problem of compatibility between 525/60 television systems (NTSC) and 625/50 television systems (PAL) in a rather procrustean manner. Video is stored internally in one of two formats designed for best display on one of the two television systems. Each format is converted for display on the other television system by repeating or dropping frames and by adding extra black lines to the top and bottom or chopping lines off the top and bottom.

DVD-Video likewise stores video in a format corresponding to the intended display system, but uses two different audio formats (Dolby Digital for 525/60 and MPEG-2 for 625/50). Only special multistandard DVD players can play both types of disc, and only if connected to the correct television. This not a problem on computers, since they already have to manipulate the video in order to display it on the monitor.

The DVD-Video standard includes codes that producers can use to prevent playback in certain geographical regions. Video CDs have no such codes.

ESTABLISHED BASE. Six million Video CD players were sold in 1996, creating an established base of over 11 million players, mostly in Asia and Europe. Video CDs can also be played on most CD-i players and on almost any computer with a CD-ROM drive and the proper MPEG-1 decoding hardware or software. Over 15 million computers in the United States alone are capable of playing Video CDs.

Over 7000 Video CD titles exist worldwide, with about 500 available in the United States. Video CDs generally cost about the same or slightly less than videotapes.

Compatibility of CD-i and DVD

No DVD drive or player can play a CD-i disc (Green Book format). A DVD-ROM drive can read data only from a CD-i bridge disc and requires special hardware and a specific operating system to make use of the CD-i data.

No CD-i player can play a DVD. However, Philips, the inventor of CD-i, has announced that it will make a DVD player that will include a CD-i adapter for playing existing CD-i discs. Some people expect Philips to create a "DVD-i" format in attempt to breathe a little more life into CD-i (and recoup a bit more from its investment of more than $1 billion).

Compatibility of Video CD and DVD

Many DVD-Video players and DVD-ROM drives can play audio and video from a Video CD. Compatibility with the White Book Video CD standard is not required by the DVD specification, but it's trivial from an engineering standpoint since any MPEG-2 decoder can also decode MPEG-1. Most manufacturers have announced that their DVD players will play Video CDs, but anyone purchasing a DVD player with Video CDs in mind is advised to check the player specifications since some players do not play Video CDs. This is more of a marketing decision than a technical decision and may be influenced by the problem of pirated movies being cheaply available on Video CD.

Other CD Formats

Many variations of the basic CD standard have been created to address limitations of the original design or to add new features. Most of these features have now been integrated into DVD, but DVD-ROM drives and DVD-Video players are generally backward-compatible with common mutations of CD. The details follow.

Compatibility of CD-R and DVD

Not all DVD-ROM drives can read recordable CDs (Orange Book Part II).
Most DVD-Video players can't read CD-Rs, but the primary reason to use
a CD-R in a DVD-Video player would be for homemade music CDs or
homemade video CDs, which are rare.

The problem is that CD-Rs are invisible to the wavelength of laser
required by DVD because the dye used in CD-Rs doesn't properly reflect
the laser beam. This problem has been addressed in many ways. Sony and
Samsung have both developed twin-laser pickups in which one laser is
used for reading DVDs and the other for reading CDs and CD-Rs. These
solutions provide complete backward-compatibility with the millions of
extant CD-R discs. A new Type II CD-R has been proposed that will work
with CD-ROM drives and all DVD units, but in the increasingly remote
event that new Type II blanks make it to market, they will cost more than
current CD-Rs and will take far too long to supplant the existing CD-R
supply. The new format would probably become established just in time to
be incompatible with the next generation of blue-laser DVD technology.

Compatibility of CD-RW and DVD-ROM

DVD drives and players supposedly can read new rewriteable CDs
(Orange Book Part III). CD-RW discs can't be read by CD-ROM drives and
CD players manufactured before 1997. Even newer drives generally must
sport the MultiRead mark before they can be assumed to be CD-RW
compatible.

CD-RW has a lower reflectivity difference than specified by the CD
standard, thus requiring Automatic Gain Control (AGC) circuitry. Most
DVD-ROM drives and DVD players contain AGC circuitry which is also
able to read CD-RW discs. The CD-RW format does not have the invisibil-
ity problem of CD-R (see the previous section).

The new MultiRead standard guarantees CD-RW compatibility, and
some DVD manufacturers have committed to support it.

Compatibility of Photo CD and DVD

Most DVD-ROM drives will read Kodak Photo CDs since they already
support the requisite CD-ROM XA and multisession standards. However,
the operating system or the application must specifically support the

Photo CD file format in order for the data to be of any use. Since Photo CDs are usually produced using CD-R media, they may suffer from the CD-R problem (see the previous sections).

At the time this book was written, no DVD-Video players were able to play Photo CDs. The CD-R problem aside, DVD-Video players could support Photo CDs with a few extra chips and a license from Kodak, but it seems that no manufacturer is interested.

Compatibility of Enhanced CD (CD Extra) and DVD

DVD-Video players will play music from Enhanced CDs (which contain music tracks followed by computer data tracks). Most DVD-ROM drives will play music and read data from Enhanced CDs, unless they are of the track-zero (pregap) type which is not properly supported by all software drivers.

Compatibility of CD+G and DVD

A few DVD-Video players support CD+G (music with additional graphics); specifically those with karaoke features. Most players sold in the United States do not.

Most DVD-ROM drives can read CD+G discs, but require proper software to reconstruct the graphics.

MovieCD

MovieCD is a new computer movie playback system introduced in February of 1997 by Sirius Publishing and based on its own proprietary video-encoding technology: Motion Pixels. MovieCDs are intended solely for playback on computers—there are no stand-alone players.

MovieCD titles are stored on standard CD-ROMs and can be played back on a 486 DX2 66-MHz or faster computer using the Microsoft Windows operating system. At least 8 MB of RAM and a double-speed CD-ROM drive are required. Video quality, according MovieCD's creators, is slightly better than VHS videotape. MovieCD's primary competitor is

Video CD (see the previous sections), which has never succeeded in the United States. Reviewers consider MovieCD video quality to be just below that of Video CD. In early 1997, about 50 movies were released in MovieCD format, none of which were new releases and many of which were not big sellers in the theater or on videotape.

Since most new computers with DVD-ROM drives are capable of playing audio and video at much higher quality, MovieCD can be thought of as a "poor man's DVD" and will likely be outclassed as more computers become DVD-capable. It's possible that a higher-quality DVD-based version of MovieCD will be developed, but it will still be confined to playback on computers.

MiniDisc (MD) and DCC

MiniDisc was introduced in 1991 by Sony as a replacement for cassette tapes (not CDs, as many have mistakenly assumed). MiniDiscs are 64-mm erasable magneto-optical discs in a plastic shell similar to that of small floppy disks. Prerecorded discs can be stamped like CDs or DVDs. The MiniDisc format uses ATRAC audio compression, a 52-band perceptual coding technique also used by Sony's theatrical SDDS format. A variation of MiniDisc for computer use, called MD-Data, is capable of holding 140 megabytes.

MiniDisc competed fiercely with Digital Compact Cassette (DCC), a format that was introduced in 1992 by Philips. DCC had the advantageous capability of playing and recording standard compact cassette tapes, but did not do well in the marketplace and was officially abandoned by Philips in late 1996. DCC used PASC compression, which is essentially the same as MPEG-1 Layer II. See Table 6.7 for specifications of MD and DCC.

Advantages of DVD-Video over MiniDisc

QUALITY. MiniDisc was rushed to market because of rival DCC, and the flaws in the first version of its audio compression system were not well received. Since then, the ATRAC compression technology has gone through four generations and has improved significantly, slowly overcoming initial bad impressions. Still, many audio purists feel that MiniDisc's compression adversely affects audio quality. DVD-Video's PCM

TABLE 6.7

MiniDisc and DVD-
Video Specifications

	MiniDisc	DVD-Video
Diameter	64 mm	80 or 120 mm
Thickness	1.2 mm	1.2 mm (two 0.6-mm substrates)
Audio	20-bit 44.1-kHz ATRAC compressed, 2 channels	16/20/24-bit 48/96-kHz PCM, 16-bit 48-kHz Dolby Digital/ MPEG-2 5.1/7.1-channel surround sound
Data rate	292 kbps CBR	64—448 kbps CBR (Dolby Digital), 64—912 kbps VBR (MPEG)
Error correction	RS-CIRC	RS-PC
Modulation	EFM (8/14)	EFMPlus (8/16)
Audio S/N	120 dB	96—144 dB
Dynamic range	105 dB (20-bit PCM)	96/120/144 dB (16/20/24-bit PCM), 120 dB (20-bit Dolby Digital)
Frequency (±0.3 dB)	4—20,000 Hz (44.1 kHz)	4—22,000 Hz (48 kHz), 4—44,000 Hz (96-kHz PCM)
Playing time	74 minutes	~27 hours of surround sound, ~7 hours of 20-bit 48-kHz stereo, ~138 minutes of 24-bit 96-kHz stereo*
Data capacity	140 MB	4.4 to 15.9 GB

*All times are for a single 4.4-gigabyte layer. Times for a dual-layer DVD are almost twice as long.

format uses no compression and is technically much superior. DVD-Video's two compressed audio formats Dolby Digital and MPEG-2, use a higher data rate than MiniDisc (384 kbps average compared to 292 kbps), but they contain six channels of audio as compared to MiniDisc's two channels. Of course, the same audio purists who dislike MiniDisc's compression turn up their noses at Dolby Digital and MPEG-2 audio as well.

CAPACITY. A MiniDisc holds 74 minutes of audio, or 140 MB of data. DVD, using uncompressed stereo sound on a single-layer disc, holds over two hours of audio. Using all 5.1 channels of Dolby Digital audio, a single-sided, single-layer DVD can play for over 27 hours. DVD holds over 8 GB of data per side, about 60 times more than MD-Data.

SUPPORT. MiniDisc is supported primarily by Sony, while DVD had already garnered the support of over 100 companies at its introduction.

Advantages of MiniDisc over DVD-Video

DURABILITY.   The optical disc used by the MiniDisc system is more vulnerable than a DVD disc, but it's encased in a plastic shell to protect it. DVDs are unprotected and subject to scratches.

Unfortunately, the MiniDisc shell adds significantly to the production cost. The designers of DVD rejected a mandatory shell, but allow caddies or shells as an option.

CONVENIENCE.   Because MiniDiscs are in a shell, they can be easily handled without fear of fingerprints and scratches.

MiniDiscs are about 3 inches across, making them very easy to use and to store. Standard DVD discs are over 5 inches across, but the DVD format also includes a 3-inch version, which may become the preferred size of DVD-Audio discs.

Compatibility of MiniDisc and DVD-Video

No DVD player can play a MiniDisc, and no MiniDisc player can play a DVD. It's not likely that a dual-format player will be developed, since the systems are quite different.

The ATRAC encoding system used to store audio on a MiniDisc is proprietary to Sony. The SDDS format, which is an option on DVD-Video discs, is based on ATRAC; but no current DVD players support SDDS, no discs have been announced with SDDS audio tracks, nor are any external SDDS decoders available (as of 1997).

Magneto-optical Drives (MO)

A *magneto-optical* drive, also called a *rewriteable optical* drive, is essentially a hybrid of optical disc technology and magnetic disc technology. Magneto-optical systems rely on a property of certain materials that allows their magnetic state to be changed when heated to a certain temperature. A low-power polarized laser is used to read the data by detecting the magnetic orientation of spots on the disc. A high-power laser is used to heat spots that are changed by a local magnetic field.

There are essentially two standard formats of MO discs and drives. The 3½-inch format first appeared with 128-MB capacity, moved up to 230 MB, and recently became available in 640-MB sizes. The 5¼-inch format is currently available in 1.2- and 2.6-GB capacities. The 2.6-GB version holds 1.3 GB on each side of the disc.

There are proprietary versions of magneto-optical drives which can store as much as 4.6 GB, but these do not follow the ISO standards, and although they can read discs from other drives, their high-density formatted discs do not work in other drives. See Table 6.8 for MO specifications.

Advantages of DVD-ROM over MO

COST. At the time DVD was introduced, 3½-inch MO drives cost $600 to $800, with blank cartridges priced around $60. The 5¼-inch drives cost around $2000, with blank discs in the $150 range. DVD-ROM drives and discs are much cheaper, but of course are not rewritable. DVD-R and DVD-RAM drives are expected to initially be more expensive but eventually drop to the same price range. DVD-R and DVD-RAM media will start out cheaper than MO media and will undoubtedly drop much lower.

DVD discs can be stamped quickly and cheaply. MO discs are generally not used for prerecorded data since they are expensive and must be individually recorded.

CAPACITY. DVD-ROM discs hold much more than MO discs. Even DVD-R discs hold 4G bytes, and DVD-RAM discs hold 2.6G bytes, slightly more than the largest standard MO disc. The next generation of MO technology is expected to have storage capacities of about 7G bytes per side, close to the 8G bytes of dual-layer DVD discs.

SUPPORT. MO technology is supported by several companies such as Sony, Fujitsu, and Pinnacle. DVD-ROM already has much broader industry support which should be extended to DVD-R and DVD-RAM as well.

TABLE 6.8

MO and DVD-ROM Specifications

	MO	DVD
Capacity	128 MB to 2.6 GB	4.38 to 15.9 GB (DVD-ROM), 3.95 GB (DVD-R), 2.58 GB (DVD-RAM)
Sector size	512 or 1024 bytes	2048 bytes
Transfer rate*	Up to 3.9 MB/s	1.3 MB/s

*Reference rates for single-speed drives.

Advantages of MO over DVD-ROM

RECORDABLE. Until DVD-R and DVD-RAM are available, MO has the advantage of being erasable. However, once the recordable and erasable DVD formats are available, they will have the significant advantage of millions of new DVD-ROM drives which can read them.

DURABLE. MO discs are more vulnerable than DVD discs, but they are encased in a plastic shell for protection. DVDs are unprotected and subject to scratches. Some variations of DVD-RAM also use shells. Unfortunately the shell adds to the production cost.

Compatibility of MO and DVD-ROM

Since MO discs are encased in a shell, they are incompatible with DVD. However, a new version of MO technology—MO7—is under development and promises to provide drives that can read DVD discs as well as MO cartridges.

Both media store digital information. A computer with both types of drives connected can transfer data between the two formats.

Digital Audio Tape (DAT)

Digital Audio Tape was developed by Sony and Philips for digital storage of music and data. Sadly, DAT was an early casualty of copy protection battles and was delayed for years while serial copy management schemes and legislation were produced. The format achieved little success in the home audio market, but has become a standard for professional audio recording and computer data archiving.

Most computer DAT drives include lossless hardware data compression in order to store more data on a tape. See Table 6.9 for DAT specifications.

Advantages of DVD over DAT

COST. The cheapest DAT decks cost around $500, with professional units beginning in the $1000 price range. Computer DAT drives are generally in the $700 to $1200 range. DVD players are priced at similar levels;

TABLE 6.9

DAT and DVD-
Video Specifications

	DAT	DVD
Audio	16-bit 44.1/48-kHz linear PCM, 12-bit 32-kHz nonlinear PCM; 2 channels	16/20/24-bit 48/96-kHz linear PCM, 20-bit 48-kHz Dolby Digital/ MPEG-2 multichannel
Audio S/N	~92–96 dB	~96–144 dB
Dynamic range	92–96 dB (16-bit PCM)	96/120/144 dB (16/20/24-bit PCM), 120 dB (20-bit Dolby Digital)
Frequency (±0.3 dB)	4–14,500 kHz (32 kHz), 4–22,000 Hz (44.1/48 kHz)	4–22,000 Hz (48 kHz), 4–44,000 Hz (96 kHz PCM only)
Playing time	2 hours (44.1/48 kHz), 4 hours (32 kHz)	~27 hours of surround sound, ~7 hours of 20-bit 48-kHz stereo, ~138 minutes of 24-bit 96-kHz stereo[*]
Copy management	SCMS	CGMS, CSS
Data capacity	2 to 4 GB[†]	4.4 to 15.9 GB
Data rate	~2–5 Mbps	11.08 Mbps

[*]All times are for a single 4.4-gigabyte layer. Times for a dual-layer disc are almost twice as long.
[†]Uncompressed.

DVD-ROM drives are cheaper. Recordable DVD units will start out much more expensive, but should fall to the same price levels as DAT recorders and drives within a year or two.

DVD-ROM discs, of course, are much cheaper to produce than DAT cassettes. Surprisingly, recordable DVD media will be cheaper than DAT before the end of 1998 (and perhaps even before the end of 1997).

CAPACITY AND SPEED. DVD-ROM discs hold much more than DAT cassettes. Recordable DVD capacities are close to DAT capacities.

All versions of DVD have higher data transfer rates than DAT. Obviously, access times are not even close.

DURABILITY. Tape is subject to degradation from wear and stretching, dropouts, erasure from magnetic fields, and damage from heat. DAT error correction can compensate for most raw data errors. In comparison, discs never wear out, are impervious to magnetic fields, and are less susceptible to heat damage. DVD error correction is much more robust. Discs can be scratched, but only large scratches will cause noticeable playback problems or data loss.

DAT decks and drives eat tapes. It's possible that a DVD player could scratch a disc, but this is rare.

DAT equipment includes helical scanning heads, tape loading mechanisms, and hundreds of small components which can easily break down. DVD players have much simpler mechanisms.

Advantages of DAT over DVD

SUPPORT.   In the audio recording industry, DAT equipment is widely used and well supported. In the computer industry, DAT is popular for data backup, but DVD-ROM and its recordable variations will eventually eclipse it.

RECORDABLE.   Once again, until DVD-R and DVD-RAM are available, DVD is at a disadvantage.

Compatibility of DAT and DVD

DAT tapes and decks are not physically compatible with DVD discs and players.

DAT and DVD-Video share the same 48-kHz PCM digital audio signal format. In fact, most PCM audio on DVD-Video discs was recorded using DAT.

Both DAT and DVD-ROM carry digital data. A computer with a DAT drive and a DVD-ROM drive connected to it can interchange data between the two media.

DVD-Video at Home

The primary focus of DVD hype and marketing is home entertainment. Even though copy protection and lack of titles delayed the introduction of DVD players, the same problems have delayed DVD-ROM in the computer industry. Initial interest in DVD was high, with many stores selling out their entire allotment of players within a few days of receiving them.

This chapter talks about how to use a DVD player at home—how to hook it up to a television, stereo system, or complete home theater system for the best sound and picture. This chapter also focuses on the process of deciding to buy a DVD and includes a buying-decision quiz.

How to Hook Up a DVD Player

The DVD format is designed around some of the latest advances in digital audio and video, yet the players are also designed to work with TVs and video systems of all varieties. Therefore, the back of a DVD player can have a confusing diversity of connectors producing a potpourri of signals.

This section discusses the advantages and disadvantages of each kind of output signal, what the connectors are like, and how to hook them up to typical home/video equipment.

Refer to the "Video interface" and "Audio interface" sections of Chap. 4 for technical details.

Signal Spaghetti

Most DVD players produce the following output signals:

- *Analog stereo audio.* The standard two-channel audio signal, which can include Dolby Surround encoding.

- *Digital audio.* Raw digital signal for connecting to an external digital-to-analog converter or digital audio decoder. There are two different signal interface formats for digital audio. Both formats can carry PCM audio, multichannel Dolby Digital (AC-3) encoded audio, multichannel MPEG-2 encoded audio, and additional optional digital audio data.

- *Composite baseband video.* The standard video signal for connecting to a TV with direct video inputs or an A/V receiver.

- *Y/C (s-video).* A higher-quality video signal in which the luminance and chrominance portions travel on separate wires.

Some players may produce additional signals:

- *Six-channel analog surround.* Six audio signals from the internal audio decoder, for connecting to a multichannel amplifier or a Dolby-Digital-ready (AC-3-ready) receiver.

- *AC-3 RF audio.* The Dolby Digital frequency-modulated (FM) audio signal from a laserdisc, for connecting to an audio processor or receiver with an AC-3 demodulator and decoder.

- *RF audio/video.* Old-style combined audio and video signals modulated onto a VHF radio-frequency carrier for connection to the antenna leads of a TV tuner.

- *Component analog video.* Three video signals (RGB or YUV) for connecting to a high-end television monitor or video projector.

Connector Soup

The different audio and video signals may be presented on the following types of connectors:

- *RCA phono.* (Fig. 7.1) This is the most common connector, used for analog audio, digital audio, composite video, and component video. The term *cinch* is also used for this connector.

- *BNC.* (Fig. 7.2) This connector carries the same signals as RCA connectors, but is more popular on high-end equipment.

Figure 7.1
RCA phono
connector.

Figure 7.2
BNC connector.

- *Phono or miniphono.* (Fig. 7.3) This connector carries stereo analog audio signals and may be used by portable DVD players. It may also appear on the front of a DVD player for use with headphones.

- *S-video DIN-4.* (Fig. 7.4) This connector, also called Y/C, carries separated video signals on a special 4-conductor cable.

- *Toslink fiber optic.* (Fig. 7.5) This connector, developed by Toshiba, uses a fiber-optic cable to carry digital audio. One advantage of the fiber-optic interface is that it's not affected by external interference and magnetic fields. The cable should not be more than 30 to 50 feet (10 to 15 meters) long.

- *Digital.* (Fig. 7.6) The IEEE 1394/FireWire connector is not yet available on DVD players. Once the format has been adopted, it will carry all the combined audio and video signals on a single cable.

- *DB-25.* (Fig. 7.7) This 25-pin connector, adapted from the computer industry, is used by some audio systems for multichannel audio input.

- *SCART.* (Fig. 7.8) This 20-pin multipurpose connector, used primarily in Europe, carries many audio and video signals on a single cable: analog audio, composite RGB video, component video, and RF.

- *Type-F.* (Fig. 7.9) This connector typically carries a combined audio and video RF signal over a 75-ohm cable. A 75-ohm to 300-ohm converter may be required.

Audio Hookup

A DVD player must be connected to an *audio system:* a receiver, a control amp or preamp, a digital-to-analog converter, an audio processor, an audio decoder, an all-in-one stereo, a TV, a boombox, or other equipment designed to process or reproduce audio.

For simplicity, the following sections will occasionally use the term *multichannel audio* to refer to Dolby Digital (AC-3) audio or MPEG-2 audio. This does not refer to Dolby Surround audio, which has only a two-channel signal. If your system provides both Dolby Digital and Dolby Pro Logic, connect the DVD player to the Dolby Digital inputs for the best result.

Discs for NTSC players are required to provide at least one audio track using either Dolby Digital or PCM audio. Discs for PAL players are required to provide at least one MPEG or PCM audio track. Most NTSC players are unable to play MPEG audio tracks. Many PAL players are able to play both MPEG and Dolby Digital audio tracks. Dolby Digital is becoming the dominant multichannel audio standard for DVD and other

Figure 7.3
Phono/miniphono connector.

Figure 7.4
DIN-4 (s-video) connector.

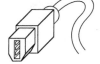

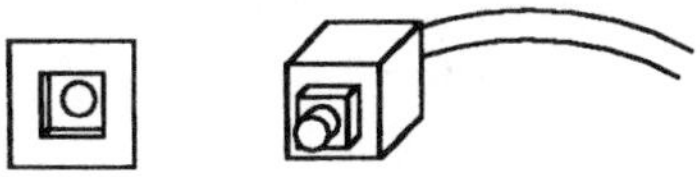

Figure 7.5
Toslink connector.

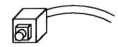

Figure 7.6
IEEE 1394 connector.

Figure 7.7
DB-25 connector.

Figure 7.8
SCART connector.

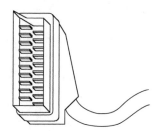

Figure 7.9
Type F connector and adapters.

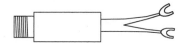

digital video formats, and it's not clear that MPEG-2 will ever see much use. DVD also supports optional multichannel formats including DTS and SDDS. See Chap. 4 for details on different audio formats, including the difference between Dolby Surround/Pro Logic and Dolby Digital.

Most DVD players provide two or three audio hookup options. These options are detailed in the following sections.

DIGITAL AUDIO.   The digital audio outputs provide the highest quality audio signal. This is the preferred connection for audio systems which are capable of it. Almost all DVD players have digital audio outputs for PCM audio and multichannel audio. These outputs carry either the raw digital audio signal directly from the digital audio track or the two-channel downmixed PCM signal from the internal Dolby Digital or MPEG-2 multichannel decoder.

For multichannel audio output, the encoded digital signal bypasses the player's internal decoder. The appropriate decoder is required in the receiver or as a separate audio processor.

For PCM audio output, the PCM signal from an audio track is sent directly to the digital audio output. Or, alternately, the multichannel decoder in the player produces a PCM signal. In either case, a receiver with built-in digital-to-analog converter (DAC) or an outboard digital-to-analog converter is required. Some players provide separate outputs for multichannel audio and for PCM audio. Other players have either a switch on the back or a section in the on-screen setup menu where you can choose between multichannel or PCM output. The multichannel output menu option will usually be labeled *AC-3* or *Dolby Digital.*

Most NTSC DVD players have only a Dolby Digital decoder, so they can produce PCM audio only from a Dolby Digital sound track (or a PCM sound track), not an MPEG-2 sound track. However, the MPEG-2 sound track can usually be sent to an external decoder. Most PAL DVD players include both Dolby Digital and MPEG-1 decoders and can produce PCM output from either format.

The digital audio output is also used for PCM audio from a CD. Players which can play Video CDs may also produce PCM audio output converted from the MPEG-1 audio signal. Combination laserdisc/DVD players will also use this output for the laserdisc's PCM audio track (but not the AC-3 track; see the following).

The direct output from PCM tracks on a DVD is at a 48- or 96-kHz sampling rate with either 16, 20, or 24 bits. The converted PCM output from multichannel audio tracks is at 48 kHz and up to 20 bits. The PCM output from a CD is at 44.1 kHz and 16 bits. The PCM output from a laserdisc player is also at 44.1 kHz and 16 bits. The connected audio component does not need to be able to handle all these variations, but the more the better. A system capable of 16 and 20 bits at sample rates of 48 and 96 kHz is recommended. Some DVD players are incapable of properly formatting a PCM signal for output at high sampling rates or bit sizes. If you have an external system capable of 24 bits or 96 kHz, make sure the player can correctly produce the digital audio signal.

The digital audio output must be connected to a system designed to accept either PCM digital audio, Dolby Digital (AC-3), or both.

Some players include a dynamic range compression setting which boosts soft audio. This setting should be turned off for home theaters and turned on for environments where the dialogue can't be clearly heard.

DTS and SDDS are not used on most DVD discs. They are optional multichannel surround formats that are allowed in the DVD format but not directly supported by most players. Each requires the appropriate decoder in the receiver or a separate audio processor.

DIGITAL AUDIO CONNECTIONS.   There are two different standards for digital audio connection interface: *coax* and *optical.* There are many arguments about which one is better, but they are both digital signal transports, and, with good-quality cables and connectors they will deliver the exact same data. Some players have one or the other type of connector, though many have both.

Coax digital audio connections use the IEC-958 II standard, also known as S/P DIF (Sony/Philips Digital Interface Format). Most players use RCA phono connectors, but some use BNC connectors. Use a 75-ohm cable to connect the player to the audio system. Multichannel connectors will usually be labeled *Dolby Digital* or *AC-3.* PCM audio connectors will usually be labelled *PCM, digital audio, digital coax, optical digital,* or so on. Dual-purpose connectors may be labeled *PCM/AC-3, PCM/Dolby Digital,* or something similar. Make sure you use a video-quality cable; a cheap RCA patch cable may degrade the digital signal to the point that it does not work.

NOTE   *Hooking a coax cable to the AC-3 RF input of your audio system may not work since DVD's digital audio is not in RF format (see the following).*

Optical digital audio connections use the EIAJ CP-340 standard, also known as Toslink. Connect an optical cable between the player and the audio receiver or audio processor. The connectors will be labeled *Toslink, PCM/AC-3, optical, digital, digital audio,* or the like.

If the connection (either coax or optical) is made to a multichannel audio system, select *AC-3* (or *MPEG-2*) audio output from the player's setup menu or via the switch on the back of the player. If the connection is to a standard digital audio system (including those with Dolby Pro Logic processors), select *PCM* audio output from the player's setup menu or via the switch on the back.

In cases where the player has an optical (Toslink) connection but the audio system has a coax (S/P DIF) connection, or vice versa, a converter can be purchased for about $100.

COMPONENT AUDIO.   A component multichannel audio connection can be as good as a digital audio connection. However, these outputs use the digital-to-analog converters that are built into the player, and they may not always be of the best quality, especially on a low-cost player. If you have an amplifier with multichannel inputs or a Dolby-Digital-ready receiver, component audio connections are an appropriate choice, since an expensive Dolby Digital decoder is no longer required.

All DVD players include a built-in multichannel audio decoder. Not all players include the digital-to-analog converters and external connectors necessary to make the decoded audio available.

COMPONENT AUDIO CONNECTIONS.   The player will typically have six RCA or BNC jacks, one for each channel. A receiver/amplifier with six audio inputs—or more than one amplifier—is required. Hook six audio cables to the connectors on the player and to the matching connectors on the audio system. The connectors will typically be labeled for each speaker position: *L, LT,* or *Left; R, RT,* or *Right; C* or *Center; LR, Left Rear, LS,* or *Left Surround; RR, Right Rear, RS,* or *Right Surround;* and *Subwoofer* or *LFE.*

Some receivers use a single DB-25 connector instead of separate connectors. An adapter cable is required to convert from DB-25 on one end to six RCA connectors on the other.

STEREO/SURROUND AUDIO.   A two-channel audio connection is the most widely used option, but it does not have the quality and discrete channel separation of a digital or multichannel audio connection. All DVD players include at least one pair of RCA (or perhaps BNC) connectors for stereo output. Any disc with multichannel audio will automatically be downmixed by the player to Dolby Surround output for connection to a regular stereo system or a Dolby Surround/Pro Logic system.

STEREO/SURROUND AUDIO CONNECTIONS.   Connect two audio cables with RCA or BNC connectors to the player. Connect the other ends to a receiver, an amplifier, a TV, or other audio system. Connectors may be labeled audio, left, or right. The connector for the left channel is usually white, and the connector for the right channel is usually red.

In some cases, the audio input on the stereo system (such as a boom box, if it can be rightly called a stereo system) will be a phono or miniphono jack instead of two RCA jacks. An adapter cable must be used.

If the player is a portable player with a miniphono connector, a phono to RCA adapter cable is usually required to connect the player to the audio system.

If the player includes a phono or miniphono connector for headphones, it's generally not recommended that the headphone output be used to connect the player to a stereo system, since the line levels are not appropriate.

AC-3 RF DIGITAL AUDIO. This digital audio output is provided by combination laserdisc/DVD players only. The AC-3 digital audio signal from the FM audio track of a laserdisc is presented at this output. Laserdisc AC-3 audio does not appear at the standard PCM/AC-3 output (although the stereo PCM audio track does). Audio from a DVD does not come out of the AC-3 RF output. In other words, this is a special output designed solely for the AC-3 signal from a laserdisc, which is in a different format from DVD's AC-3 signal.

Hook a coax cable from the AC-3 RF output of the player to the AC-3 RF input of the receiver or AC-3 processor. Make sure the receiving end is set to RF mode or can automatically adapt to an RF signal.

In order to receive all audio signals from a combination laserdisc/DVD player, three separate audio hookups are required: a PCM/AC-3 connection (for DVD digital audio and laserdisc PCM digital audio), an AC-3 RF connection (for laserdisc AC-3 audio), and an analog stereo connection (for the laserdisc analog channels, which often contain supplemental audio).

Video Hookup

A DVD player must be connected to a *video system:* a television, a video projector, a flat-panel display, a video processor, an A/V receiver or video switcher, a VCR, a video capture card, or other equipment capable of displaying or processing a video signal. If you have a widescreen TV, the details can be confusing. See Chap. 3 for information about aspect ratios and widescreen display modes.

Most DVD players provide two or three video hookup options, detailed in the following sections.

COMPONENT VIDEO.   Until digital connections are available, this is the preferred method of connecting a DVD player to a video system. Component video output provides three separate video signals in RGB or YUV (Y, B-Y, R-Y) format. These are two different formats that are not directly interchangeable.

Unlike composite or s-video connections, component signals do not interfere with each other and are thus not subject to the slight picture degradation caused by crosstalk. Since the video is stored in three component parts on the disc, this provides the cleanest path from disc to display.

Unfortunately, not all DVD players provide component video output, there are very few televisions with component video connections, and there are very few receivers or A/V controllers which can switch between component inputs.

COMPONENT VIDEO CONNECTIONS.   Some DVD players, notably U.S. and Japanese models, have YUV component video output in the form of three RCA or BNC connectors. The connectors may be labeled Y, U, and V; or Y, P_b, and P_r; or Y, B-Y, and R-Y. The connectors may be colored green, blue, and red, respectively.

Some DVD players, notably European models, have RGB component video output via a 20-pin SCART connector or via three RCA or BNC connectors. The RGB connectors are generally labeled R, G, and B, and may be colored to match. Hook a SCART cable from the player to the video system or hook three video cables from the three video outputs of the player to the three video inputs of the video system.

NOTE   *Connecting YUV to RGB (or RGB to YUV) will not work; a transcoder is required, which generally costs $200 or more.*

S-VIDEO.   Almost all players have s-video (Y/C) output, which generally gives a better picture than composite video output unless the s-video cable is very long. The advantage of s-video is that the luma (Y) and chroma (C) signals are carried separately. They are stored independently on the disc, so it's best that they not have to be combined by the player and then separated by a comb (or similar) filter in the TV.

S-video may be erroneously referred to as *S-VHS*, since it was popularized by S-VHS VCRs.

S-VIDEO CONNECTIONS.   Hook an s-video cable from the player to the video system. The round, 4-pin connectors may be labeled *Y/C*, *s-video*, or *S-VHS*.

COMPOSITE VIDEO. This is the most common but lowest-quality connection. All DVD players have standard baseband video connectors. This is the same type of video output provided by most VCRs, camcorders, and video game consoles.

This signal is also called CVBS (composite video baseband signal).

COMPOSITE VIDEO CONNECTIONS. Hook a standard video cable from the player to the video system. The connectors are usually yellow and may be labeled video, CVBS, composite, baseband, and so on.

RF AUDIO/VIDEO. This is the worst way to connect a DVD player to a television and is only provided by a few players for compatibility with older televisions which have only an antenna connection. The RF signal carries both audio and video modulated onto a VHF carrier frequency. This type of output is provided by many VCRs and cable boxes.

RF CONNECTIONS. Connect a coax cable with Type-F connectors from the player to the antenna input of the TV. The connectors may be labeled RF, TV, VHF, antenna, Ch. 3/4, or so on. If the TV antenna connection has two screws rather than a screw-on terminal, a 75-ohm to 300-ohm adapter is needed. Set the switch near the connector on the back of the player to either channel 3 or 4; whichever is not used for broadcast in your area. Tune the TV to the same channel.

Digital Hookup

When DVD players were introduced, none included digital video connections or digital bitstream connections. This is partly because the copyright protection and encryption systems for digital video had not yet been established and partly because almost no other consumer equipment provided digital connections at that time. There is also no standard format for streaming compressed audio/video over digital connections. Once the standards are developed, new DVD players must convert their playback information into the proper format.

It's expected that the copyright and standards issues will be resolved and that eventually most consumer electronics equipment will be interconnected via IEEE 1394/FireWire or a similar format.

See the "Digital connections" section of Chap. 10 for more information.

How to Get the Best Picture

If possible, use component video connections. If this is not an option, an s-video connection is better than a composite video connection.

Turn the sharpness control on the TV all the way down. Video from DVD is much clearer than from traditional analog sources. The TV's sharpness feature adds an artificial high-frequency boost. If the sharpness control is not turned down, it exaggerates the high frequencies and causes distortion, just as the treble control set too high for a CD causes it to sound harsh. This can create a shimmering or "ringing" effect. DVD video has exceptional color fidelity, so muddy or washed out colors are almost always a problem in the display, not in the DVD player or disc.

Get your TV calibrated or calibrate it yourself. A correctly calibrated TV is adjusted to proper color temperature, visual convergence, and so on, resulting in accurate colors and skin tones, straight lines, and a more accurate video reproduction than is generally provided by a television when it comes out of the box. Organizations such as the Imaging Science Foundation (ISF) train technicians to calibrate televisions. This typically costs from $175 to $600. Another option is to use ISF's *Video Essentials* DVD, based on the *Video Essentials* laserdisc and its predecessor, *A Video Standard*. The disc provides instructions, test pictures, and other resources to calibrate both audio and video systems.

Connect the DVD player to a good sound system. This may sound like a strange way to improve the picture, but numerous tests have shown that when viewers are presented with identical pictures and two different quality levels of audio, they perceive the picture that is accompanied by high-quality audio to be better than the picture associated with low-quality audio.

THX Certification

Lucasfilm THX was developed in 1983 with the goal of assuring that theatergoers experience quality picture and sound presentation as intended by the filmmaker. THX technologies and standards were then extended to the living room. The Home THX program work with leading manufacturers to incorporate proprietary designs into certified home theater components such as receivers, speakers, and laserdisc players. The THX Digital Mastering program offers studios the certification of picture and audio quality during film-to-video transfer, mastering, and replication of laserdiscs and tapes. Lucasfilm is now adapting these two programs for DVD.

Software Certification

A large part of the THX software certification process for DVD is the same as for laserdisc. This includes calibrating the video and sound equipment, monitoring the transfer from film to video master tape, and adding a special THX test signal in the vertical blanking interval. The same video master is generally used for laserdisc, videotape, and DVD.

The new and critical aspect of THX certification for DVD involves the MPEG-2 video encoding process. Part of the task is simply understanding the potential problems and paying attention to the many details. The MPEG encoding process attempts to reduce redundant information; the lower the entropy of the signal, the better the compression. Entropy can be increased by many characteristics of the source video such as lack of stability (weave), random noise (film grain), edge sharpness, and so on. These cause the encoder to require a higher bit rate, and may affect the quality if the needed bit rate is higher than can be allowed. For example, the first DVD movie to be THX-certified—*Twister*—contains considerable hand-held camera work. The shakiness of the picture requires a higher bit rate and careful attention to difficult sequences to make sure they are cleanly encoded.

The primary difficulty is that there are no tools for objectively measuring the output of an MPEG encoder. There are no machines or software algorithms that can simulate human visual response. Therefore, THX relies on trained viewers to monitor the output from a reference decoder connected to the MPEG encoder. The viewers are trained to look for digital compression artifacts such as *macroblocking* (visible squares) and *mosquitoes* (fuzzy dots around sharp edges). The encoding process is adjusted and repeated as many times as needed to eliminate problem areas. In some cases where the nature of the transfer or print causes special encoding problems, a new video transfer or even a different print may be requested.

THX verifies that a preliminary check disc plays as expected on a wide range of players. One advantage of DVD is that there is little chance for errors to be introduced after the digital premaster is created. The mastering and replication operations deal with a bitstream, not an analog video signal which might be degraded by improperly adjusted equipment.

Because multichannel theater audio has only recently become widespread, many older movies were released in stereo even though they had four- or six-track masters. To make the most of DVD's capabilities with these older films, a new sound track is mixed from the original multitrack masters. THX was initially developed for audio, and this is still its forte. THX engineers supervise the mixing process, test the equipment, and even adjust the audio signal to match the characteristics of new speaker technology that did not exist when the original sound track recording was created.

Although DVD supports 5.1-channel Dolby Digital audio, the vast majority of viewers will hear the downmixed stereo on a standard stereo system or a system based on Dolby Pro Logic surround sound. Therefore, the audio encoding process is monitored with a decoder connected to a Dolby Pro Logic processor. Trained listeners audition the result in a calibrated THX listening room, checking primarily that the dialogue—which was originally designed for a discrete center speaker—remains audible, even when played on only two speakers or on multiple speakers through Pro Logic decoding. Most modern action movies require that the audio mix be slightly adjusted to boost the dialogue or reduce the sound effects. This is a delicate process, since the balance and accuracy of the 5.1-channel version must be preserved along with the artistic decisions of the original audio editor. In a few cases, no amount of tweaking can achieve a satisfactory result, so a separate Dolby Surround track is added to the disc.

Hardware Certification

THX is developing a DVD test disc to be used internally for certifying the audio and video performance of DVD players.

After further evaluation of current DVD players, THX will work with manufacturers of next-generation DVD players to develop criteria for THX-certified models. These players will be held to a high level of performance. This can be measured using test signals in the same way THX-certified laserdisc players are tested. The most critical component is the analog video encoder. The numerical output of MPEG decoders varies little from player to player. On the other hand, the circuits that produce the composite and s-video signals have the most significant effect on the visual signal quality, and therefore must be given the closest attention.

THX's quality assurance and certification programs for audio and video will help bring out the best of DVD. Many people feel that THX engineers have raised the quality of laserdisc close to the level of studio master tapes that were the standard only 10 years ago. THX will likewise be working to help DVD live up to its potential to approach the quality of today's D-1 studio masters.

To Buy or Not to Buy

This section is intended to help someone who is thinking of buying DVD or someone who is selling DVD. *Selling* applies to much more than retail salespeople. Husbands might need some help selling their wives on the idea, or you might even need help convincing yourself that you absolutely cannot live another day without a DVD player. Accordingly, this section is written for the person buying the player. If you're doing the selling, adjust as needed.

One caveat: DVD is like the proverbial camel in the tent. In order to make the most of the picture quality and widescreen format you need a large TV or even a widescreen TV. And, to best reproduce DVD's surround sound you need a Dolby Digital sound system with five speakers and a subwoofer. If you've already got this gear, you're in great shape. And, according to the Consumer Electronics Manufacturers Association, 12 million of you are in great shape on the audio side and in pretty good shape on the video side. If you can easily afford the necessary equipment for turning your living room into a theater, then you probably don't need much convincing to add a DVD player. If you can't easily afford it, then perhaps you should downplay that part of the deal and think about it later when your pocketbook recovers from the DVD player. (And, in any case, it's beyond the intent of this book to hawk widescreen TVs and surround-sound systems.)

DVD may seem like an extravagance, but when you come right down to it, how much does anyone really *need* a TV, a stereo system, and a VCR or two? Some people would probably be happier and more productive without such indulgences. So, ask yourself how important it is to be entertained (or informed) and how important the quality of that entertainment (or information) is. The quiz at the end of this chapter may help.

Extol the Virtues

When you begin adding up all its features, DVD presents a very compelling face. (See the beginning of Chap. 3 for more details.)

- *Better video quality than anything else available.* On a good TV, the picture from DVD is truly impressive. On a widescreen TV, it will knock your socks off. But even on an average TV, you get a crisp picture with true colors and perfect freeze-frame.

- *Exceptional multichannel surround sound.* The spatial definition of 5.1-channel Dolby Digital audio must be experienced to be believed. But if you only have a Dolby Surround or Dolby Pro Logic system, all DVD players will provide 4-channel surround sound. Even with only a two-speaker stereo system, DVD sound quality is in the same league as audio CD.

- *Goodies and special editions.*   Movie studios are already spending a surprising amount of time and money to enhance DVD movies with extra features such as running commentary, behind-the-scenes footage, storyboards, script pages, production stills, director's-cut versions, alternate endings, screen tests, outtakes, theatrical trailers, interviews with cast and crew, and even Internet links (if you have the right kind of hybrid DVD player or DVD-Video—enabled computer). This extra material will only be available on DVD, not on tape.

- *Quick access.*   Do you ever want to jump straight to a favorite scene? Or, perhaps you can't remember exactly how that line you want to quote to your friends went? With a VCR, it's hardly worth the bother of fast forward and rewind. But on a DVD, you can jump quickly to a chapter or scan at high speed through the disc. And, with most movies, if you know the time code of the scene you want, just enter it into the remote control to jump directly there in less than a second or two.

- *Think of the children.*   DVD should have a certain appeal to parents. The parental control features are nice, and the discs can be played over and over without wear. The expected low prices should also be a plus. Moreover, publishers are taking advantage of the interactive features to develop education and "edutainment" products on DVD-Video for home learning.

- *Compatibility with CD.*   DVD players work with existing audio CDs. Most DVD players have digital audio outputs, a feature usually found only on deluxe-model CD players.

- *Compatibility with the future of audio.*   Many people in the music industry are very excited about high-quality, multichannel audio. Imagine listening to an orchestra as if you were the conductor or even the bassoon player, being able to pinpoint the locations of the instruments all around you. Or, picture a carefully recorded jazz session which recreates the echoes and ambiance of a cozy nightclub. Some amazing things will be done with audio recordings, and DVD will be the premiere medium (in audio-only format or along with video). There are those who object that hardly anyone will go to that much effort to record and mix all six channels, but people said the same thing when stereo came along; consider how many TV shows and movies now routinely use surround sound.

- *Compatibility with the future of TV.* In a way, DVD is halfway between standard TV and HDTV. It doesn't have the resolution of HDTV, but it's a digital format with widescreen capability. As good as DVD looks on a regular TV, it will look even better on an HDTV. If you're interested in this, make sure you get a DVD player with component video outputs. Or better yet, one with digital video output when they eventually appear.

- *Long-term compatibility.* Even when a new generation of "HDVD" players appears shortly after the turn of the century, the players will still play current DVD discs.

Beware of Bamboozling

A good way to undermine the case for DVD is to get carried away and overstate its capabilities or even unwittingly misrepresent its features. Make sure you read the "DVD Myths" section at the beginning of Chap. 3. Here are a few other points to keep in mind:

- *The audio of DVD-Video is generally not better than CD.* While it's true that DVD can include PCM audio at higher resolution than CD, most movies and other video on DVD will use Dolby Digital audio, which is compressed to a much lower data rate. Tests have shown that there's little difference between CD audio and Dolby Digital audio to the average listener, but a discerning ear can often pick out minor deficiencies in Dolby Digital. DVD does have the advantage of discrete surround sound.

- *Not every disc will use all the features.* Just because the DVD-Video system allows different aspect ratios, multiple audio tracks, subtitles, parental control, seamless branching, chapter jumps, production stills, and so on, doesn't mean these features will be available on every disc. In fact, until producers become accustomed to the capabilities of DVD and production techniques adapt to accommodate additional needs, many DVDs will use few or none of these options.

- *DVD is not HDTV.* DVD is standard definition TV (SDTV). The resolution of DVD is less than half that of HDTV (345,000 pixels versus 921,000 pixels or 2 million pixels). DVD players produce interlaced video, which is inferior to HDTV's progressive scan video (which effectively doubles the resolution). While it's true that DVD will look better on an HDTV set than almost any other consumer video format, it's not correct to classify DVD as high-definition. It's more accurate to present it as a bridge to HDTV.

- *DVD is not better simply because it's digital.* MiniDisc and Video CD are digital, but many people are unhappy with the fidelity of these formats. The output of first generation players is not digital—it's analog. Standard consumer displays have only analog inputs. Even component video output, although it provides a very clean signal, is not digital.

- *Laserdisc is not inferior because it's analog.* Laserdisc video is analog, but laserdiscs have both analog and digital sound tracks. Many newer laserdiscs also include an AC-3 (Dolby Digital) sound track that is essentially the same as that of DVD. Laserdisc video quality is only slightly below that of DVD.

DVD Is to Videotape What CD Is to Cassette Tape

A major disadvantage of DVD is that it can't record, but neither can CD players, and that hasn't stopped customers from buying over 600 million of them. Of course, it's more common to record from television than from radio, but most people have both a tape deck and a CD player, yet they think nothing of it. The same frame of mind should be cultivated for DVD—it's a companion to the VCR, not a replacement for it.

Unfortunately, the copy protection features of DVD can make it harder to copy from DVD to videotape than it is to copy from CD to audio tape.

Think of It as a CD Player That Plays Movies

If your CD player is getting old and cranky, or you're thinking of donating it to someone less fortunate than you and replacing it with a new model, consider a DVD player. As the price of DVD players drops, this makes ever more sense. Eventually, for less than a hundred dollars more than what you would pay for a decent CD player, you can get a DVD player which is a decent CD player and a great movie player to boot.

The Computer Connection

Just as many computers can play audio CDs in their CD drives, many new computers can play DVD-Videos in their DVD-ROM drives. It's not clear how many people actually want to watch movies or music videos on their computer, but the mere potential to do so may be a significant draw.

On the Other Hand

To be fair, perhaps you don't need a DVD player. If you are happy with the quality of your VCR or laserdisc player, and your desire is not kindled by the additional features, then DVD may not be in your cards.

If DVD succeeds, then four or five years down the road it will be cheaper and have a much better selection of programs. You can always wait and reevaluate.

There's also the consideration that DVD might not become all that it has been made out to be. After all of the hype, DVD has quite the set of promises to live up to. If DVD does not establish a sufficiently large presence in the home, it may never generate a large catalog of titles. DVD must compete with digital satellite, digital cable, and eventually with HDTV broadcasts. And, it's possible that movie studios could decide that pay-per-view distribution is more lucrative than DVD. As with any new format, there's an element of risk in buying into it during the first few years.

DVD is not perfect (see Chap. 5). The first players weren't even on the shelves before the designers were at work on the next generation. It's inevitable that new and improved versions of DVD will follow. At some point, an improved version of DVD designed for HDTV will be introduced. These new players will be compatible with existing discs, but new discs with new features may not work—or may only partially work—on older players. Even if there are no major changes, the quality of players and discs will steadily improve. The early bird may get the worm, but the biggest worms don't come out until evening.

The DVD-Video Buying Decision Quiz

This quiz can help you decide whether or not to get a DVD-Video player. Each answer will lead you to the next appropriate question. As you progress, you will accrue points. If you have strong feelings one way or the other, feel free to increase or decrease the suggested number of points. If you are a laserdisc owner, you may not wish to add points for features your laserdisc player already has. Your score at the end will give you an idea of how important the features and advantages of DVD are to you.

This isn't a scientifically certified quiz, and some of the questions may not be especially valid, but the mere process of thinking about each question should help you evaluate DVD technology.

1. Is audiovisual entertainment important to you?
   - ☐ No — Go to question 1a.
   - ☐ Yes — Go to question 2.

   1a. Is audiovisual education or information important to you?
   - ☐ No — DVD probably isn't for you. Stick with what you have (or don't have). Your score is 0. Go to the end.
   - ☐ Yes — Go to question 2.

2. Do you value high-quality video?
   - ☐ No — Go to question 3.
   - ☐ Yes — Go to question 2a.

   2a. Do you have a widescreen TV?
   - ☐ No — Go to question 2b.
   - ☐ Yes — DVD is practically a necessity. Add 10 points. Go to question 3.

   2b. Are you thinking of getting a widescreen TV?
   - ☐ No — Go to question 2c.
   - ☐ Yes — DVD would be a perfect match for your widescreen TV. Get models with component video inputs for best picture. Add 8 points. Go to question 3.

   2c. Do you have a 25-inch or larger TV?
   - ☐ No — Go to question 2d.
   - ☐ Yes — DVD will look better on your TV than videotape or laserdisc. Add 3 points. Go to question 2e.

   2d. Would you consider getting a larger TV?
   - ☐ No — Are you sure high-quality video is important to you? If so, add 1 point. Go to question 2e.
   - ☐ Yes — DVD will look better on your new TV than videotape or laserdisc. Get at least a 27-inch TV with s-video or component video inputs for best picture. Add 2 points. Go to question 3.

2e. Do you want to see movies in their original widescreen aspect ratio?

☐ No — Most DVD movies have a full-screen pan & scan option. Add 1 point. Go to question 3.

☐ Maybe — Most DVD movies give you a choice of full-screen or widescreen (letterbox). Add 1 point. Go to question 2f.

☐ Yes — Go to question 2f.

2f. Do you dislike letterbox format? (Black bars at the top and bottom.)

☐ No — Most DVD movies can be watched in widescreen letterbox format. Add 2 points. Go to question 3.

☐ Yes — Go to question 2g.

2g. You ought to get a widescreen TV.

☐ No — Sorry, you're stuck with letterbox or pan & scan. Go to question 3.

☐ OK — Good choice. You should get a DVD player to match it. Add 6 points (not 10, since you had to be talked into it). Go to question 3.

3. Do you enjoy high-quality audio?

☐ No — Go to question 4.

☐ Yes — Go to question 3a.

3a. Do you have a high-end audio system?

☐ No — Go to question 3b.

☐ Yes — DVD can provide better-than-CD audio (20 or 24 bits at 48 or 96 kHz) for exceptionally pure sound recordings. Add 4 points. Go to question 3b.

3b. Do you have a Dolby Digital (AC-3) audio processor or receiver?

☐ No — Go to question 3c.

☐ Yes — Almost all DVD movies have Dolby Digital sound tracks, so DVD will make the most of your investment. Add 8 points. Go to question 4.

3c. Would you consider getting a Dolby Digital system or an add-on for your current system?	☐ No ☐ Yes	Go to question 3d. Good choice, since this is the wave of the future. Most DVD movies have Dolby Digital sound tracks, so DVD is a perfect match for your new audio system. Add 7 points. Go to question 4.
3d. Do you have a Dolby Surround or Dolby Pro Logic sound system?	☐ No ☐ Yes	Go to question 3e. DVD will automatically create Dolby Surround output from Dolby Digital sound tracks. Most DVD movies will sound very good on your system. Add 3 points. Go to question 4.
3e. Would you consider getting a surround-sound processor and speakers?	☐ No ☐ Yes	Go to question 3f. This is cheaper than Dolby Digital, but will still bring your TV room much closer to a theater. Almost all DVD movies have surround audio, so DVD is a perfect match for your new surround system. Add 3 points. Go to question 4.
3f. Do you have a stereo system with external inputs?	☐ No ☐ Yes	Go to question 3g. You can hook a DVD player to your stereo for CD-quality stereo sound. Add 2 points. Go to question 4.
3g. Do you have a stereo TV with external audio inputs?	☐ No ☐ Yes	If high-quality audio is important to you, you ought to get a better sound system. Add 1 point. Go to question 4. You can connect a DVD player to your TV for CD-quality stereo sound. Add 1 point. Go to question 4.

4. Do you have a laserdisc player?	☐ No ☐ Yes	Go to question 5. Go to question 4a.
4a. Do you hate changing disc sides in the middle of a movie?	☐ No ☐ Yes	Go to question 4b. DVD movies fit on one side. Add 2 to 4 points, depending on how much you hate it. Go to question 4b.
4b. Does the whirring noise of your player bother you?	☐ No ☐ Yes	Go to question 4c. Most DVD players are as quiet as CD players. Add 2 to 4 points depending on how much it bothers you. Go to question 4c.
4c. Do you think laserdisc prices are too high?	☐ No ☐ Yes	Go to question 5. DVDs are generally as cheap or cheaper than videotapes. Add 3 points. Go to question 5.
5. Do you buy prerecorded videotapes?	☐ No ☐ Yes	Go to question 6. DVDs may be cheaper. DVDs are more versatile and often contain goodies such as extra footage and audio commentary. DVDs are easier to store and will never wear out. Add 4 points. Go to question 5a.
5a. Do you buy used videotapes?	☐ No ☐ Yes	Go to question 6. As long as it's not scratched, a used disc will look exactly as good as when it was new. Add 2 points. Go to question 6.
6. Do you rent videotapes?	☐ No ☐ Yes	Go to question 7. DVDs won't have a degraded picture from being rented over and over (although they may have occasional glitches caused by dirt or scratches). DVDs don't need

to be rewound. Add 1 point.
Go to question 7.

7. Do you want to choose   ☐ No   Go to question 8.
   from a large selection of   ☐ Yes   It will take a while for
   movies on video?   DVD to match the selection
                                         of videotape or laserdisc.
                                         Subtract 3 or 4 points
                                         depending on how old
                                         this book is. Go to
                                         question 8.

8. Do you want to watch a   ☐ No   Go to question 9.
   lot of old or rare movies   ☐ Yes   It will take time for some
   on video?   movies to appear on DVD,
                                         if ever. Subtract 2 to 4
                                         points depending on how
                                         rare your tastes are and
                                         how limited the current
                                         DVD selection is. Go to
                                         question 9.

9. Do you use your VCR   ☐ No   Go to question 10.
   for recording?   ☐ Yes   Go to question 9a.

   9a. Do you want to   ☐ No   Good, since you'll have to
       replace your VCR   use your VCR to record.
       with a DVD player?   Subtract 1 point. Go to
                                         question 10.
                               ☐ Yes   You can't do that yet, unless
                                         you never record (or this
                                         book is more than 4 years
                                         old). Subtract 10 points. Go
                                         to question 10.

10. Do you enjoy perfor-   ☐ No   Go to question 11.
    mance audio and video   ☐ Yes   DVD gives you the best pic-
    (concerts, music videos,   ture and excellent audio,
    opera, ballet, etc.)?   often in multichannel sur-
                                         round. Add 2 to 4 points,
                                         depending on how much
                                         of a fan you are. Go to
                                         question 11.

11. Do you watch foreign films?

☐ No   Go to question 12.

☐ Yes   DVD's multilingual features allow a single version to serve multiple foreign markets, making foreign films more available. Add 3 points. Go to question 11a.

11a. Do you watch foreign tapes or discs that must be imported?

☐ No   Go to question 11b.

☐ Yes   DVD's regional codes may prevent you from watching discs released in other countries. Subtract 2 to 5 points, depending on the number of imported discs you would want to watch. (If you watch many imported discs, consider buying a player from the same country as the discs.) Go to question 11b.

11b. Do you prefer subtitles?

☐ No   Subtitles can be turned off. Add 1 point. Go to question 11c.

☐ Yes   Films on DVD can have subtitles in many languages. Subtitles can be turned on or off. Add 2 points. Go to question 11c.

11c. Do you prefer the original language sound track?

☐ No   If you favor a dubbed sound track, DVD movies may let you switch between up to eight languages. Add 2 points. Go to question 12.

☐ Yes   Some foreign films on DVD have a dubbed main sound track but let you switch to the original dialogue. Add 2 points. Go to question 12.

12. Would you like to watch a mature film but have your children (or your parents) watch the edited version?

☐ No   Go to question 13.

☐ Yes   Multiple versions of a movie can be put on a single DVD. The parental control feature allows you to set a password to prevent viewing unedited versions. Add 2 points. Go to question 13.

13. Have you ever erased a tape (accidentally or from a magnetic field) or had one become warped from heat?

☐ No   Go to question 14.

☐ Yes   Optical discs can't be erased, are unaffected by magnetic fields, and have much higher heat tolerance than tapes. Add 2 points. Go to question 14.

14. Does your VCR ever eat tapes?

☐ No   Consider yourself lucky. Go to question 15.

☐ Yes   DVD players are mechanically simpler and much less likely to damage discs. Add 1 point. Go to question 15.

15. Do you like to freeze video or step through it a frame at a time?

☐ No   Go to question 16.

☐ Yes   Most DVD players give you perfect digital still pictures and let you step forward or back a frame at a time. And they don't suddenly start playing if you leave them on pause for more than 5 minutes. Add 2 points. Go to question 16.

16. Do you wish your VCR could instantly jump directly to any spot on a tape?

☐ No   Go to question 17.

☐ Yes   DVD players can search to any chapter or timecode in a second or two. Add 3 points. Go to question 17.

17. Do you long for more
    control of what you watch
    (change viewpoints,
    choose endings, edit a
    music video your way)?

    ☐ No   Go to question 18.
    ☐ Yes   On properly prepared discs,
            the multiple camera angles,
            seamless branching, and
            interactivity of DVD can
            make you an active viewer.
            Add 3 points. Go to
            question 18.

18. Would you like to play
    interactive movies or
    multimedia games with-
    out buying a multimedia
    computer?

    ☐ No   Go to question 19.
    ☐ Yes   Some games that depend
            heavily on video will have
            editions for home DVD-
            Video players. Add 3 points.
            Go to question 19.

19. Must you be one of the
    first to have the latest,
    greatest gadget?

    ☐ No   Go to the end.
    ☐ Yes   DVD is extremely cool and
            is guaranteed to impress
            your friends. Add 5 points.

PENCILS DOWN. Wasn't that fun? Add up your points and see where
you stand.

45–61   You're starving for DVD. Get it now.

35–44   You will definitely enjoy DVD. Start saving up.

15–34   You may need some more convincing, or you may want to wait
           until DVD is more established.

Below 15   You probably don't need DVD. Or you'll have to be convinced by
           less practical excuses.

DVD-Video
in Business

DVD-Video may see its first business success in the education and training area. The effectiveness of video has long been recognized for instruction and learning, and the advantages of DVD-Video are sufficient in many cases to warrant the complete replacement of existing video equipment with DVD equipment. DVD is also a natural fit for business marketing and communications.

The Appeal of DVD

DVD has many advantages over other media, including videotape, print, CD-ROM, and the Internet. Even in the case of CD-ROM multimedia, the capacity of DVD to carry large amounts of full-screen video makes it more compelling, more effective, and more entertaining.

- *Low cost.* Production and replication costs of DVD-Video and DVD-ROM will quickly drop below that of videotape and CD-ROM, especially when cost calculations take the larger capacity into account. Corporate and government databases currently filling dozens or hundreds of CD-ROMs can be put on fewer DVD-ROMs, with one DVD-ROM taking the place of twenty-five CD-ROMs. Businesses spending millions of dollars on videotapes can reduce the cost of duplication and inventory by a factor of four or more once DVD-players become widespread and disc production costs drop. Just as cheap CD players can now be found for less than $75 and CD-ROM drives can be had for less than $50, the economy of scale will eventually drive the price of DVD hardware below $100. At this point, it becomes cost-effective to equip entire groups of recipients with bare bones players or with DVD-ROM upgrades for their computers, simply to reap the benefits of the medium.

- *Simple, inexpensive, reliable distribution.* Five-inch discs are easier and cheaper to mail than tapes or books. Optical discs are not susceptible to damage from magnetic fields, X rays, or even cosmic rays, which can damage tapes or magnetic discs in transit.

- *Ubiquity.* An apparent drawback to DVD—especially DVD-Video—is the lack of an installed base of players. But regardless of how long it takes DVD-Video players to begin showing up in place of VCRs, many businesses will soon have at least one DVD-equipped computer. As DVD-ROM overtakes CD-ROM, it will greatly amplify the audience for DVD-based material. Various forecasts indicate that between 2002 and 2010 the number of installations capable of playing DVD-Video will exceed the number of VCRs. This will occur in the business world much sooner than in the home, possibly before the year 2000.

■ *High capacity.* A double-sided, dual-layer DVD-Video disc can hold over 8 hours of video, and over 28 if compressed at videotape quality. Eight hours of video would require two bulky and expensive video-cassettes or would take more than 25 hours to transmit over the Internet with a high-speed T1 connection. Many hours of video and hundreds of gigabytes of data can be sent anywhere in the world by slipping a few discs into an overnight express mailer.

■ *Self-contained ease of use.* DVD-ROM programs can obviously include integrated instruction. The features of DVD-Video are also sufficient to provide instruction, tutorials, and pop-up help. A disc can start with a menu of programs, how-to sections, and background information. Rather than being tied to a linear taped presentation, the viewer can select appropriate material, instantly repeat any piece, or jump from section to section.

■ *Portability.* Video presentations no longer require a VCR. A portable DVD-Video player—the size of a portable CD player—can be slipped into a briefcase and hooked up to any television or video monitor. For small presentations, there will be all-in-one units with an integrated LCD video screen. For large audiences there will be portable video projectors with built-in DVD-Video players. Notebook computers with DVD-ROM drives and audio/video decoding capabilities can be used for both DVD-Video and DVD-ROM multimedia presentations.

■ *Desktop production.* Just as printed publications can be created with a desktop computer and a laser printer, DVD will enable video production to be done from beginning to end with inexpensive desktop equipment. A complete setup will be remarkably affordable within several years of the introduction of DVD: a digital video camera (under $2000) can be plugged into a digital video editing computer (under $6000) and the final product can be assembled and recorded onto a DVD-R disc with DVD authoring software and recording hardware (less than $2000). An entire video production studio on a desktop for under $10,000.

■ *Merged media.* DVD bridges the gap between many different information sources. A single disc can contain all the information normally provided by such disparate sources as videotapes, newspapers, computer databases, audio tapes, printed directories, and information kiosks. Training videos can be accompanied with printable manuals, product demonstrations can include spec sheets and order forms, databases can include Internet links for updated information, product catalogs can include video demonstrations, and so on.

The Appeal of DVD-Video

The conveniences of DVD-Video—which in the home are enjoyable but not essential—are translated in the office into efficiency and effectiveness. DVD-Video also brings computers into the picture. Unlike in the home, where the value of being able to play a video disc on a computer is questionable, the usefulness of computers doing double duty as video players is apparent.

The natural inclination when working with computers is to take advantage of additional features of computers such as keyboard entry, graphical interactivity, and so on; but in many cases this is counterproductive and inefficient. Simpler may be better.

In the first few developmental years of DVD-ROM, the integration of DVD-Video features into a computer will not be straightforward. It will take time to develop the authoring environments and the delivery systems. (See Chap. 9 for a few details.) Even after the wrinkles are smoothed out and the learning curve is eased, developing a computer-based multimedia project may be more difficult and expensive than developing a similar project using only DVD-Video.

There are certain advantages of standard DVD-Video over DVD-ROM–based multimedia:

- *Easier development at a lower cost.*   There are fewer programming and design requirements.
- *Easier for the customer.*   The limited interface is simple to learn and is usually accessible using a remote control. Hooking a player to a TV is much simpler than getting a multimedia computer to work.
- *Familiar interface.*   Menus and remote controls are similar.
- *Larger audience and no cross-platform worries.*   Macintosh computers, Windows computers, workstations, DVD players, and even video game consoles can all play standard DVD-Video discs.

There are certain kinds of programs which lend themselves better to DVD-Video. These include programs with large amounts of video, programs intended for users who may not be comfortable with computers, programs with still pictures accompanied by extensive audio, and so on. Here are a few examples of material appropriate for DVD-Video:

- Employee orientation
- Company press kit
- Corporate report or newsletter
- Product demonstration

- Product catalog
- Information kiosk, including product/service searches, traveler's aid, and way-finding
- Product training
- Video tour or video brochure
- "Video billboards"
- Testing, including drivers' licenses and professional certification (e.g., real estate broker's license)
- Automobile navigation system
- Ambient video and music
- Emergency response information systems
- Lecture support resources
- Repair and maintenance manual
- Medical informed consent information
- Patient information systems, home health special needs instruction
- Language translation assistance

Of course, DVD-Video also has its disadvantages when compared to other media. (The disadvantages of DVD-Video compared to DVD-ROM are covered in the next section.) Following are a few examples of material that may not be appropriate for DVD-Video:

- *Documentation.* (Not searchable, not easily read on TV.)
- *Video games.* (Require dynamic interface with quick response.)
- *Databases.* (DVD-Video is not well suited for large amounts of text.)
- *Productivity applications.* (Word processing, checkbook balancing, and so on can't be supported by DVD players.)
- *Network applications.* (DVD data rate is higher than what the average 10-Mbps network can support.)
- *Text entry.*
- *Constantly changing databases.*

The Appeal of DVD-ROM

DVD-ROM has its own advantages over DVD-Video. Because a DVD-ROM can contain any sort of computer data and software, the possibilities are practically endless. DVD-ROM is appealing because of its increased capacity. There is little question that it will supersede CD-ROM as the medium of choice for computers. Some of the advantages of DVD-ROM over DVD-Video include:

- *Flexibility.*　Any application or content can be used. The only limitation is the target computer platform.

- *Compatibility.*　Existing software can be put onto DVD-ROM with little or no change.

- *Familiar development tools.*　There is no need to switch from a programming language or multimedia authoring package already in use. And most will support the improved audio/video capabilities of DVD in future versions.

- *Memory.*　Unlike DVD players, computers can store information such as preferences, scores, updates, and annotations.

- *Interface.*　Computers allow keyboard entry, point-and-click graphical interface.

- *Connectivity.*　Computers can be connected to networks, Internet, hard disk drives, and so on.

Additional advantages and applications of DVD-ROM are covered in Chap. 9.

Sales and Marketing

DVD-Video can be an excellent sales and presentation tool. Imagine a complete sales presentation system contained in a portable DVD-Video player. For example, home sales presentations could be greatly enhanced by professional video supplements provided on DVD. The presenter would simply plug a portable player into the customer's TV (or put a disc in the customer's player). Unlike videotape, which must be watched straight through, a DVD can contain different segments for different scenarios, answers to common questions, and so on. The need to train sales and marketing representatives up front can be reduced by having them rely on carefully prepared presentations that can be called up as needed.

Product catalogs with thousands of photographs and video vignettes can be put on a single disc for a fraction of the cost of printed catalogs. The drawback, of course, is that a video catalog can't be read at the kitchen table.

A DVD can contain literally hundreds of hours of audio, any part of which can be accessed in seconds, making it the perfect vehicle for instructional audio programs.

Training and Business Education

Once sufficient numbers of DVD players and DVD-equipped computers are established in businesses, there is no question that DVD will become a leading delivery format for business training. The Internet has certain advantages such as low cost and timeliness, but the demand for high-quality multimedia far exceeds the capabilities of the Internet for the near future. DVD is better suited to deliver such multimedia and can easily be integrated with the Internet to provide the best of both worlds.

DVD-Video is strictly defined and fully supported by DVD players and by DVD-Video navigation software on most DVD-equipped computers. As with all authoring systems, the ease of development is inversely proportional to the flexibility of the tools (see Fig. 8.1). As the parameters of the system are constrained, the complexity of the task is reduced. Since DVD-Video is quite constrained, it is relatively easy to develop for it, given the proper tools. Those considering video training programs should decide if the features of DVD-Video meet their requirements. A very simple product containing mostly menus, pictures, and movies may be developed in less time and for less money than with a complex computer authoring system.

DVD-Video will work so well for certain corporate education and training applications that the content will sell the hardware. Player purchases will be an insignificant part of the deal. When the price of a player reaches $200 or $300, companies spending millions of dollars on video-based education and training programs should not think twice about equipping their employees or labs with players. Many companies that today buy specialized systems such as study kiosks or CD-i players should evaluate switching to DVD players.

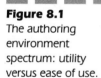

Figure 8.1
The authoring environment spectrum: utility versus ease of use.

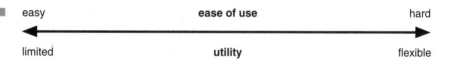

easy   **ease of use**   hard

limited   **utility**   flexible

DVD-ROM, on the other hand, covers the entire spectrum, from custom-programmed software to fill-in-the blank lesson templates. Practically any authoring or software development system can produce material to be delivered on DVD-ROM. The main advantage of DVD-ROM over other media is space, data transfer speed, and cost per byte. A significant advantage of DVD-ROM over CD-ROM is responsiveness. DVD-ROM access times and transfer rates are much better than the current CD-ROM platform, which consists primarily of 2× to 6× drives and often requires painstaking optimization in order to achieve acceptable levels of performance. DVD-ROM drive transfer rates are similar to hard disks. Although their access rates are slower, in most cases DVD-ROM's higher capacity and lower cost more than compensate.

Communications

Companies spend billions of dollars a year producing printed information, much of which requires unwieldy indexes and other reference material merely to make it accessible. And much of it quickly becomes out of date in a very short time. Companies are learning to use CD-ROM and the Internet, but for very large publications, or those which benefit from a graphical or video ingredient, DVD-ROM and DVD-Video provide an extremely cost-effective means of distribution coupled with improved access to the content.

DVD for Computers

The wall dividing home entertainment from computers used to be solid and unbreached. In recent years, it began to crumble; then along came DVD which knocked an enormous hole in it. DVD enriches both sides by bringing them closer together. Lamentably, each side brings to the other a new set of problems and old bad habits.

Just as CD-ROM is used for purposes as diverse as databases, multimedia, software distribution, backup, document archiving, publication, photographic libraries, and so on, DVD-ROM will be used for all of that and more. It's when DVD's audio and video features enter the picture that things may become confused.

Understanding how DVD relates to computers can become very complicated. On the one hand, there is DVD-ROM, which can be thought of as nothing more than an improved version of CD-ROM; but on the other hand, there is DVD-Video, which can stand completely on its own or can be tightly integrated with computers. The details get very tangled up in between the two hands. This chapter may help sort things out.

NOTE   *Many technical details of information provided in this chapter are explained in Chap. 4.*

DVD-Video Sets the Standard

Ironically, the MPEG-2 video and Dolby Digital audio features of DVD-Video were selected and implemented for home video players, but because of the enormous influence of DVD, they are becoming the de facto video and audio standards on computers as well. Computer graphic display boards are appearing with additional circuitry to handle motion compensation and other processor-intensive features of digital video decoding. Audio card manufacturers are scrambling to include support for Dolby Digital audio. Companies that specialize in simulating multispeaker surround sound from two computer speakers are jumping on the DVD bandwagon and ensuring that their systems work with Dolby Digital audio tracks. Operating systems developers such as Microsoft and Apple are building support for DVD audio and video into their core multimedia layers. And the MMX feature of Intel's latest CPU as well as the TriMedia coprocessor in MacOS computers are being used extensively to handle DVD-style video and audio.

Multimedia: Out of the Frying Pan...

The most high-profile use of CD-ROM has been for multimedia: computer software which combines text, graphics, audio, motion video, and more. To battle-weary multimedia CD-ROM developers, DVD either seems like a breath of fresh air or more of the same old been-there-done-that. Multimedia CD-ROM products are expensive and difficult to produce. There is a huge disparity of computer capabilities among customers and a frustrating inconsistency of support for audio and video playback, especially on the popular Windows platform. Hundreds of multimedia CD-ROM titles are produced each year, but only a handful of them make money, in part because customers have been burned too many times by CD-ROMs that don't work on their computers.

DVD-ROM may be perceived as a new area for multimedia development without the stigma of CD-ROM and with the cachet of digital movies and surround-sound capabilities. Given the lessons learned from CD-ROM, DVD-ROM could be an opportunity to finally get it right: a ubiquitously easy-to-use, high-performance multimedia format. On the other hand, DVD-ROM might inherit all the problems of CD-ROM on top of its own new set of problems.

Influential companies such as Microsoft, Apple, and Intel and organizations such as the Software Publishers Association and the OpenDVD Consortium are promoting guidelines and standards in hopes of ensuring compatibility and interoperability between hardware and software. But it remains to be seen if anyone bothers to stay within the ropes during the mad rush for DVD gold.

DVD by Any Other Name

The confusing part about DVD and computers is where the DVD-Video ends and the computer begins. The only constant is the DVD-ROM drive itself. Some computer upgrade kits include a drive and an entire DVD player on a card. Other upgrade kits or DVD-Video–enabled computers include complete DVD audio and video decoding hardware. Others include only small amounts of extra circuitry to accelerate DVD-Video playback. Some systems rely entirely on software. Still other systems contain only a DVD-ROM drive and are incapable of playing video or audio. It's clear that a text database on DVD-ROM, for example, has nothing to do with the DVD-Video standard. And it's mostly clear that a blockbuster Hollywood movie that can be viewed on the computer monitor relies heavily on the DVD-Video standard. But what if the disc containing the blockbuster movie includes additional computer-only bonuses such as a screen saver or a computer game based on the movie?

The following classifications of DVD products may shed some light on the variety of options. A summary is provided in Table 9.1. Note that the classifications cover both DVD-ROM and DVD-Video.

Pure DVD-Video

A *pure* DVD-Video is one which is designed entirely for use on a standard DVD-Video player. It can also be played on a DVD-Video–enabled computer, but nothing is different (other than the tiny computer screen and the chair that's not as comfortable as the living-room couch). In this case, the computer serves merely as an expensive DVD-Video player. The computer's DVD-Video navigation software is all that is needed or used.

The target audience for this type of product is movie and video viewers. Note that the flexibility of the DVD-Video format allows a pure DVD-Video to contain still images, screens of text, additional footage, supplementary audio, and other enhancements generally associated with special editions.

Examples of pure DVD-Videos include movies, product demo videos, and instructional videos.

TABLE 9.1

DVD Product Classifications for Computers

Classification	Content	Ice cream analogy
Pure	DVD-Video only	Vanilla
Bonus	DVD-Video plus computer supplements	Vanilla with sprinkles
Augmented	DVD-Video plus computer enhancements or framework	Caramel swirl
Split	Independent DVD-Video and computer versions	Neapolitan
Multimedia	DVD-ROM for computer, any format of audio and video	Sundae
Data	DVD-ROM for computer data or applications only	Frozen yogurt

Computer Bonus DVD-Video

Just as there are Enhanced CDs which contain both music to be played on a CD audio player and additional goodies to be used on a computer, there are DVD-Video products with extra material designed for a computer. The disc can be played normally on a DVD-Video player. The video part of the disc can also be played with the computer's DVD-Video navigation software. The primary audience is similar to that of pure DVD-Video. The difference is that the disc also contains computer software or computer data that the producer thinks will make the disc more appealing: movie scripts, searchable databases of supplemental information, still pictures in computer format, short video clips in computer video format, screen savers, icons, computer games, Internet Web links, and so on.

Computer-augmented DVD-Video

This type of product can be played on a DVD-Video player, but it is amplified and changed when played on a computer. The viewer might have more control over the sequence of the video, or the video might respond to the actions of the viewer. There may be interludes in the video where the computer offers a game or puzzle. Or, perhaps, the video is subsumed entirely by a computer-based game or environment in which the video plays a supplemental or reward role. In this case, the computer might present video segments in different order or generate additional graphics and create a composite image.

For example, a murder mystery could be played and enjoyed in a straightforward way on a DVD-Video player and perhaps even have multiple endings. But when the same disc is put into a computer, the user can choose to become a character in the drama. If the user chooses to play the role of the detective, that person can interrogate characters, search for records, collect and manipulate objects, answer questions, and become an interactive participant controlling the environment and outcome of the game.

Split DVD-Video/DVD-ROM

This type of disc can be used in a player or in a computer, but there is no overlap between the two. The computer version is usually related to the video player version, but there is no shared content. It's basically a pure DVD-Video product on one part of the disc and a multimedia DVD-ROM on the other part (see the following paragraph).

Multimedia DVD-ROM

This product can't be played in a DVD-Video player. It's intended for use in a computer only, like a traditional multimedia CD-ROM. The disc may actually contain audio and video in the same MPEG and Dolby Digital format as for a DVD-Video disc, but it can be played back only on a computer. Or, the disc may contain video at higher resolutions and different aspect ratios than those supported by the DVD-Video format.

The multimedia DVD-ROM will be the most visible application of DVD technology on computers. Current CD-ROM multimedia producers will gravitate toward DVD-ROM depending on their needs and the changing platforms of their customers. Multimedia programs requiring more than one CD are early candidates. As soon as the installed base of DVD-ROM drives in a given market reaches critical mass, associated multimedia publishers can switch their existing content from CD-ROM to DVD-ROM. They may wish to take advantage of the increased capacity and higher minimum data rate of DVD-ROM to include more content and to improve the quality of audio and video.

The multimedia DVD-ROM could even become the primary application of DVD at home, if major computer companies such as Microsoft, Compaq, and Intel succeed with their plans of capturing the home market with a computer-based, multimedia, HDTV entertainment system.

Data Storage DVD-ROM

With all the audio and video hype swirling around DVD-ROM, it's easy to overlook it as a simple data storage solution. DVD-ROM can hold the same data as hard disks, floppy disks, and CD-ROMs, but in vastly greater quantity. Text documents, graphical documents, databases, catalogs, software applications, and so on can all be stored on DVD-ROM—the bigger the better. Most CD-ROMs are not multimedia products, and multidisc sets are common.

DVD-ROM for Computers

The simplest support for DVD on a computer is a DVD-ROM data drive. Support for the audio, video, subpicture, and navigation features of DVD-Video is provided as an additional layer (see "DVD-Video for Computers," which follows).

A DVD-ROM drive (sometimes referred to as a DVD *logical unit*) is supported by the operating system as a random-access, block-oriented input-output device. It can be considered simply a large, read-only data storage device.

Features

A single-speed DVD-ROM drive transfers data at 11.08 Mbps (1.321 MB/s),* which is just over nine times the 1.229 Mbps (150 KB/s) data rate of a single-speed CD-ROM drive. Although 10× and faster CD-ROM drives achieve a higher data transfer rate than 1× DVD-ROM drives, they push the limits of CD technology and suffer from spin stability problems and read errors. A double-speed DVD-ROM drive transfers data at 22.16 Mbps (2.642 MB/s), equivalent to an 18× CD-ROM drive. Most drives include read-ahead RAM buffers to allow burst data rates of over 100 Mbps (12 MB/s) as long as the connection between the drive and the computer is fast enough.

DVD-ROM average seek times are around 150 ms, with average access times of about 200 ms.

As with CD-ROM drives, most DVD-ROM drives include stereo output for reproducing audio from CDs. For internal drives, the audio signals are usually mixed into the computer's own audio circuitry. For external drives, the output can be connected to a pair of headphones or speakers. This feature is only for audio CDs, not DVDs. Very few DVD-ROM drives include the decoders necessary to directly play audio or video from a DVD-Video. Because of cost, complexity, and copy protection issues, the audio/video decoding and playback systems are almost always in the computer rather than in the drive.

Compatibility

All first-generation DVD-ROM drives are able to read CDs, and all future drives are expected to do so as well. Most drives are able to read variations of the CD format including CD-DA, CD-ROM, CD-ROM XA, CD-i, Video CD, and Enhanced CD. In the case of Video CD and CD-i, specific hardware or software may be required to make use of the data after it's read from the disc. Many first-generation DVD-ROM drives, such as those from Pioneer and Toshiba, are not able to read CD-Rs.

See Chap. 6 for more details of DVD-ROM compatibility.

---

*The oft-used figure of 1.385 refers to millions of bytes per second, not megabytes per second.

Interface

DVD-ROM drives are available with E-IDE/ATAPI or SCSI-2 interfaces. The SFF 8090 (Mt. Fuji) standard extends the ATAPI and SCSI command sets to provide support for DVD-ROM, including physical format information, copyright information, regional management, decryption authentication, burst-cutting area (BCA), disc identification, and manufacturing information (see Table 9.2).

TABLE 9.2

DVD (SFF 8090) Interface Command Information

Physical	
DVD book type and version	DVD-ROM, 1.0
Disc size	120 or 80 mm
Minimum read rate	2.52, 5.04, 10.08 Mbps
Number of layers	1 or 2
Track path	PTP or OTP
Layer type	Read-write
Linear density	0.267 or 0.293 µm/bit
Track density	0.74 µm/track
BCA present	Yes or no
Copyright	
Protection system	Yes or no
Region management	8 bits, set = playable, cleared = not playable
Authentication	
Disc key	2048-byte authentication key
BCA (optional)	
BCA information	12 to 188 bytes
Manufacturing	
Manufacturing info	2048 bytes of manufacturing information from lead-in area

Disk Format and I/O Drivers

System-level driver software is required to allow the computer to read blocks of data from a DVD disc. DVD is designed around the UDF file system, but includes an ISO-9660 bridge format for backward-compatibility. (See Chap. 4 for details.) Of course, at the lowest level, a DVD-ROM is simply a block-oriented data storage medium and can be formatted for almost any file system: Apple HFS, Windows FAT16, and so on. However, since UDF provides explicit cross-system support, standardization via UDF is strongly recommended. Technically, the UDF Bridge format is required on all DVD-ROM discs by the official DVD-ROM specification.

The ISO-9660 file system is readable by almost any computer with a CD-ROM drive. However, file system access is usually tightly coupled with the CD-ROM I/O driver. Since the basic DVD media format is not compatible with existing CD drive units, a new I/O driver may be required, depending on how well the DVD-ROM drive supports older drive command sets. Because of this, most operating system developers and driver developers are bringing out new drivers that support UDF along with the new hardware.

WINDOWS. Microsoft plans to support DVD-ROM only in the upcoming version of Windows (Memphis—the version following Windows 95) by providing an updated CD-ROM class driver. DVD-ROM support is also planned for version 5.0 of Windows NT in the form of a Win32 Driver Model (WDM) device driver. The UDF file system will be supported in both OSs by an installable file system (ISF) package.

Microsoft has no plans to support DVD-ROM in earlier versions of its system software such as Windows 3.11, Windows NT 4.0, or even Windows 95. Support for older Windows operating systems will be provided by manufacturers of DVD hardware upgrade kits. Different manufacturers will supply different drivers. Most such drivers will be closely tied to the hardware. Some DVD-ROM drives emulate CD-ROM hardware. This allows new drivers to be quickly and easily developed by simply modifying old drivers, but it sacrifices the full range of DVD-ROM capabilities. Such approaches may not support the UDF file system. Other DVD-ROM drives provide a full interface as defined by the SFF 8090 standard and require more extensive software driver development.

It's probable that Microsoft will develop extensions to the DVD-Video format, but little is currently being done in this area. The standard *autorun.inf* file can be used to create DVD-ROM products which automatically begin execution when they are inserted into a drive.

MAC OS.   Apple plans to ship Macintosh computers with DVD-ROM drives in the second half of 1997. Other MacOS computer makers have similar plans. New versions of the Mac operating system will provide support for UDF. Apple is developing a file system extension that will probably be made available for earlier versions of the operating system. This extension, similar to that for the ISO 9660 file system, will extend the operating system to recognize volumes formatted for UDF.

Almost any new or existing MacOS computer can be upgraded to support DVD-ROM by connecting an external drive to the built-in SCSI port. DVD-ROM volumes with the UDF Bridge format will be recognized by the existing 9660 file system extension. Full support for UDF discs can be enabled by installing the appropriate new file system extensions.

DVD-Video for Computers

From a certain point of view, DVD movies on a computer seem almost an oxymoron. Why take an audio-visual experience originally designed for maximum sensory impact on a large screen with a theatrical sound system and reproduce it on a small computer screen with midget computer speakers? The answer is that computers are steadily becoming more like entertainment systems, even to the point that some home computers are designed to be installed in the living room. Not all computers will sprout remote controls and channel tuners, but there is much more to DVD-Video than movies. There are educational videos, business presentations, training films, product demos, computer multimedia, DVD/Internet combinations, and more.

Computer hardware and software companies are eagerly anticipating the convergence of PCs and TVs, or at least the development of TVs to the point that they have PC-like features and PC-like operating systems, or the development of PCs to the point that they can be sold as replacements for TVs. This has motivated them to cooperate amazingly well with the entertainment and consumer electronics industries. Computer companies also recognize that the issues of protecting artistic ownership rights in a digital environment must be dealt with sooner or later. It might as well be sooner; and DVD has been chosen as the first battleground. Earlier skirmishes occurred with DAT and MiniDisc, but had little to do with computers. Since then, the importance of entertainment to the computer industry has increased significantly. TVs and PCs won't merge overnight, and in a certain sense they will always be differentiated. But their commingling will continue, with DVD squarely in the center. The sooner the legal, political, and business issues are put to rest, the sooner the technical details can be tackled.

In the short term, DVD-Video for computers is important both for customer perception and as a source of content. Many customers do not understand the difference between DVD-ROM and DVD-Video. Making sure that DVD in all its variations is supported by a DVD computer goes a long way toward alleviating customer confusion and dissatisfaction. As for something to play on the new computer, it will take at least a year or two before significant new DVD-based computer software is available. In the interim, DVD-Video titles can help fill the gap.

The DVD-Video—enabled Computer

Not just any computer can play a DVD-Video disc. Of course, a DVD-ROM drive is required, but a drive alone is insufficient for the first three classifications listed in Table 9.2, and possibly the fourth and fifth. Specific hardware and software are needed. For video playback using only software, the computer must be fast enough and have enough display horsepower to keep up with full-motion, full-screen video. Otherwise, specialized hardware must be added to take on the task of decoding and playing the audio and video.

SOFTWARE DVD-VIDEO PLAYBACK. Only the very fastest computers with the latest graphics hardware can play standard DVD-Video discs by using only software. See Table 9.3. The minimum system is a 233-MHz Pentium MMX or a 300-MHz PowerPC, and even these are not fast enough to keep from dropping frames. For completely smooth playback, a 300-MHz Pentium MMX, a 400-MHz Alpha workstation, a 400-MHz PowerPC, or a PowerPC with a TriMedia coprocessor is required. In the case of a Pentium, only accelerated graphics port (AGP) hardware is able to supply the needed video display performance.

Since MPEG video uses YC_bC_r colorspace (as opposed to RGB) with 4:2:0 sampling and interlaced scanning, a graphics card with native support for these formats is advantageous.

The allocation of processor capacity is shown in Fig. 9.1. For a typical 233-MHz Pentium system, the processor is at close to 100 percent utilization the entire time. Heavy video motion requires even more processing power, but since the CPU obviously can't give more than 100 percent,

TABLE 9.3

Target Platform
for Software DVD-
Video Playback

	Windows	MacOS
CPU	Pentium MMX	PowerPC 604
Minimum speed	233 MHz	300 MHz
Memory	16–32 MB SD-RAM	16 MB
Video bus	AGP	n/a
Video memory	2–4 MB EDO/SD-RAM	n/a
Bus	PCI or PCI/ISA	PCI
Drive controller	ATAPI (SFF 8090) IDE/SCSI, bus master DMA, 12 Mbps minimum	Built-in SCSI (SFF 8090)
Audio	AC '97 chipset, 48 kHz	Standard built-in
Software	Audio/video decoder, DVD-Video navigator	QuickTime, DVD-Video navigator

video frames must be dropped, resulting in jerky playback. On faster processors, the utilization numbers are proportionately smaller. This leaves headroom for handling more complex video and also allows the computer to perform other tasks while the video is playing. Clearly, until the speed of the average computer increases, it will be sorely taxed to reproduce DVD-Video in software. And, it will have little or no capacity left over for other simultaneous tasks commonly required by interactive multimedia software.

Figure 9.1
Nominal CPU
utilization for
software DVD
playback.

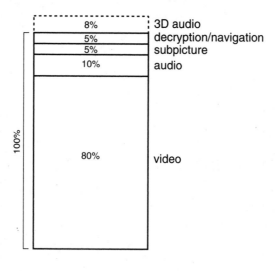

8%	3D audio
5%	decryption/navigation
5%	subpicture
10%	audio
80%	video

100%

Of course, nothing's ever this cut and dried. Some DVD-Video discs contain only MPEG-1 video and audio, which is much less demanding than MPEG-2 video and Dolby Digital audio. In this case, a 133-MHz 486 or any PowerPC is generally sufficient to play the disc. In other words, any computer able to play a Video CD should also be able to play DVD-Video that contains MPEG-1 data instead of MPEG-2.

DVD-Video playback software is often bundled with a DVD-ROM computer or a DVD-ROM upgrade kit. See App. B for a list of companies that make DVD-Video playback software.

HARDWARE DVD-VIDEO PLAYBACK. In order to play standard DVD-Videos on any computer sold before 1997, and most sold after, a hardware upgrade is required. This generally includes a DVD-ROM drive, possibly a new IDE or SCSI interface card, a new display card, and special chips for decoding MPEG-2 video and Dolby Digital audio. The reason a new display adapter is required is that the data bus of most computers is not fast enough to carry 30 full frames of video each second. Video data is much larger after it's decoded. For example, a 640×480 display at 16 bits per pixel requires a data rate of 147 Mbps to maintain 30 frames/sec. This is over 15 times the maximum 9.8 Mbps data rate of compressed DVD video. A 1024×768 display at 24 bits/pixel, even at a slower movie frame rate of 24 per second, requires over 450 Mbps. When the display card is coupled to the decoder, the data can be routed directly to video RAM, completely avoiding the bottleneck of the bus. In most cases, both Intel (Windows) and Motorola/PowerPC (MacOS) computers require a PCI bus to handle even the compressed data, although it's possible that NuBus cards will be developed for hardware DVD-Video playback on older Macintosh computers.

Another approach is to use the minimum amount of specialized hardware. For example, motion compensation is one of the most data-intensive parts of MPEG-2. If a small amount of hardware is made available to handle this task, the central processor and memory bus can be freed up to perform the rest of the decoding. Many new graphics cards take this approach. These cards provide *hardware accelerated* DVD-Video playback by dedicating a small portion of the graphics circuitry (usually the accelerator chip) to handle MPEG decoding tasks. This usually involves giving over a few thousand gates on a chip with millions of gates and essentially provides a hardware speedup of about 35 percent for free.

Other options include decoding the video in hardware, and decoding the audio in software, since audio decoding requires much less processor time.

See App. B for a list of companies selling DVD hardware upgrades.

PROGNOSIS FOR HARDWARE AND SOFTWARE PLAYBACK.
DVD-Video playback on computers is being delayed by copy protection
issues and encryption licensing roadblocks (see the next section). Fully
hardware-based systems will begin to trickle out in 1997, but it will probably take until early 1998 for software licensing problems to be resolved and
for many DVD-Video—enabled computers to begin to appear. For the first
year or so, hardware or a combination of hardware and software will be
required for high-quality video playback. By the end of 1998 or so, CPU
power will have increased to the point where high-quality software-only
playback is realistic. By then most new graphics controllers will include
DVD acceleration circuitry to free up the CPU for other tasks.

The DVD-Video format supports MPEG-1 video, which can be played
using only software on a reasonably fast computer such as a Pentium or
PowerMac. In some cases, MPEG-1 may actually look better than MPEG-
2 because the computer doesn't have to drop video frames in order to
keep up. Many computers have MPEG-1 decoder hardware built in. By
end of 1996, there were over 15 million computers in the United States
capable of playing MPEG-1 video. MPEG-1 material is more widely available, MPEG-1 encoders are highly optimized and can produce better quality video than ever, and MPEG-1 audio/video encoders are much cheaper
than MPEG-2 video encoders and Dolby Digital audio encoders. Many
early DVD titles, especially those in DVD-ROM format, will use MPEG-1
video instead of MPEG-2.

Copyright Protection and CSS Licensing

Copyright information is stored in every sector of the disc, indicating if the
sector is allowed to be copied or not. If a DVD-ROM drive encounters "no
copies allowed" information on a recordable disc, it will refuse to play it.

If a disc contains encrypted data, a corresponding decryption key is
stored in an area of the disc that is readable only by the drive. The computer cannot directly read this information. When an encrypted sector is
encountered, the drive and the decoder exchange a set of keys, further
encrypted by *bus obfuscation* keys to prevent eavesdropping by other programs. This authentication process eventually produces the key used by
the descrambler to decrypt the data. Until an authentication success flag
is set in the drive, it will not read encrypted sectors. The drive itself does
not decrypt the data, it merely participates in the two-way process of
establishing an authenticated key, then sends the encrypted data to the
descrambler. (See Fig. 9.2.)

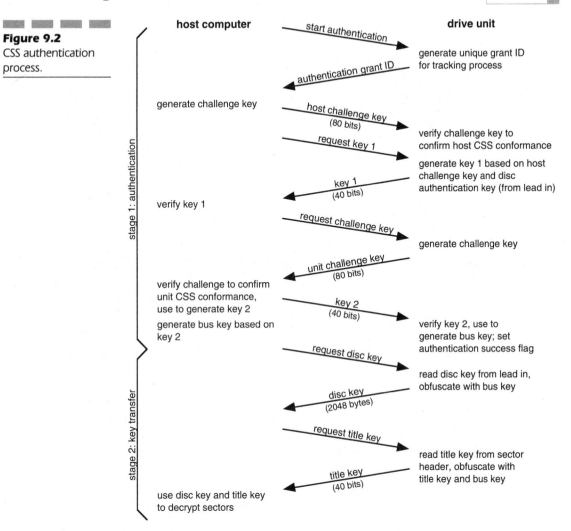

Figure 9.2
CSS authentication
process.

Figure 9.2
CSS authentication
process.

NOTE *In the context of CSS,* scrambling *and* encryption *mean the same thing.*

All components participating in this process must be licensed to use the DVD content scrambling system (CSS). Although regional management is technically independent of copy protection, it's generally included as a requirement of CSS-compliant components. CSS also requires that analog output of descrambled video be covered by an analog protection system (APS) such as Macrovision or similar. Digital output, such as USB or IEEE 1394 (FireWire) must be protected by a digital copy prevention or copy management system (DPS). The standards for these systems are currently under development.

Scrambled video must be descrambled before it can be processed by the MPEG video decoder. The descrambler may be part of the same circuitry as the video decoder, or it may be independent. The descrambler and the decoder can be implemented in hardware or software.

After the video is descrambled and decoded, the video is sent to the display. The system is expected to protect the descrambled data from being copied. This includes copies of the digital data by software in the computer (to a hard disk, for example), copies of the digital data via external connection (to a bitstream recorder, for example), and copies of the video signal by external video recorders.

CSS COMPLIANCE. CSS-compliant computers are required to have the following:

- A CSS-licensed DVD-ROM drive with authentication hardware
- CSS-licensed decoding hardware/software, including authenticator and descrambler
- CSS-licensed video components
- Regional management support
- Protection of digital output
- Protection of analog video output
- Prevention against copying descrambled files
- Rejection of "no copies allowed" material on a recordable disc (may be provided by drive or by system)

The CSS license is royalty-free. Licensing and management of keys is currently done by Matsushita, but will be handed over to an independent entity once the entity is created. Any computer industry segment involved in the production or integration of hardware or software components which are affected by CSS may be required to obtain a license and abide by its restrictions, as follows.

OPERATING SYSTEM MAKERS. A CSS license is not officially required, but the operating system should protect descrambled data so that it can't be copied either as files or as data streams. For example, a video *T* filter must not be allowed to split off a stream of decrypted video during playback. The OS must also not allow complete bit-image copies of DVD-Video discs.

The OS must support regional management for DVD-Video discs if not handled elsewhere. The OS must provide for, or not interfere with, DPS and APS information in the video output.

APPLICATION DEVELOPERS. A CSS license may be required if the application directly manipulates DVD-Video files. The application is subject to the same restrictions as an OS (see the preceding section).

DISC MANUFACTURERS. Companies which master and replicate encrypted discs must have a CSS license in order to apply disc keys and to scramble sectors. They are responsible for maintaining the secrecy of the keys and the scrambling algorithms.

DRIVE MAKERS. A CSS license is required only if the drive supports CSS authentication. If so, the drive must perform authentication handshaking and key obfuscation.

COMPONENT MAKERS. A CSS license is required for any hardware or software component, such as a descrambler or a decoder, that directly deals with the descrambled data stream. Descrambling components are strictly licensed since they use the "secret" descrambling algorithm and the "secret" keys. The components must safeguard the algorithm, the keys, and the descrambled data. Licensed components can only be sold to other CSS-licensed integrators or OEMs.

A CSS license is also required for DVD add-in cards that incorporate DVD-Video playback features. The hardware must protect descrambled digital outputs and analog outputs.

A CSS license is not required for graphic cards and other video display components, but other licensed components are not allowed to be connected to display components which include television video output unless analog protection is provided. If a method is devised for protecting RGB outputs, it may be required as well.

SYSTEM INTEGRATORS AND OEMS. A CSS license is required for companies that produce or assemble DVD-Video–enabled computers. The final system must comply with all requirements, including video output protection, digital output protection, descrambled file protection, and regional management. No hardware or software may be added which allows circumvention of any license requirements. Partly assembled subsystems must be distributed only to licensed integrators or resellers.

RETAILERS AND RESELLERS.   A CSS license is required only for retailers who do additional assembly or integration. The restrictions are the same as for system integrators.

USERS.   No license is required, although users who desire to assemble their own systems might not be able to legally purchase licensed components. The goal is to make DVD-Video a plug-and-play system, with the end user unaffected by CSS entanglements.

A RECIPE FOR RESISTANCE.   The DVD Copy Protection Technical Working group worked very hard to make the licensing process as simple and unrestrictive as possible, but anything with this many rules and requirements can easily go awry. Strenuous objections on the part of computer hardware and software companies had to be overcome, but the golden glow of Hollywood movies on computers was apparently a strong incentive to compromise.

Most of the computer industry had no say in these negotiations. This is an industry notorious for its lack of regard for regulations and artificial barriers. Computer software developers long ago gave up the fight for copy-protected software, since it did little to slow down those determined to make copies but sorely inconvenienced honest users who were unable to make legal backup copies or had problems simply installing or uninstalling the software they had purchased. It's possible that the DVD copy protection system will suffer the same fate.

The CSS algorithm and keys are supposed to be a "very big secret," but anyone who thinks it will remain a secret for long is delusional. It's inevitable that the algorithm will be broken, the keys will be compromised, and the entire system will be laid out in detail on the Internet, perhaps next to the instructions on how to build nuclear weapons.

A worse problem is the potentially onerous restrictions on computer retailers and computer owners. Many "Mom & Pop" computer stores assemble low-cost systems from diverse components. How happy will they be with the licensing requirements demanded of them? How many of them will simply turn to the inevitable gray market for supplies? And what about the computer owner who simply wants to upgrade to a new video card? Even a lowly computer owner who purchases a system assembled from licensed components by a licensed integrator is presumably barred from buying a new licensed component, since these components can only be sold to licensed integrators. Of course, there is nothing to prevent end users from swapping in different video boards without APS and making copies to their hearts' content. But clearly, the same factors of cost and convenience that keep consumers from engaging in mass duplication of audio CDs and videotapes apply to DVD as well, with or without complex technical copy protection schemes.

When this book was written, these potential nightmares were nebulously looming. It remains to be seen if the CSS licensing process works as smoothly and unrestrictively as its creators hope, or if it succeeds only in smothering the potential for DVD-Video on computers, or if the entire system is castrated by workarounds, compromises, hacks, and gray markets and in short order rendered moot and inoffensive.

DVD-Video Drivers

Driver software is required for video and audio and possibly for DVD file I/O. When DVD-ROM computers are first released, the drivers will not be built into the operating system and must be specially written for the hardware or software decoding system and supplied with the computer or the upgrade kit. For Windows, the drivers will be written for MCI (Multimedia Command Interface) or DirectShow. For MacOS, the drivers will be written for QuickTime. There's a definite danger that different drivers will work in slightly different ways and that they may have compatibility problems with programs written for other drivers. This has been the dismal state of affairs in the past. In spite of better operating system support and better cooperation between vendors, it's overly optimistic to hope for much better this time around.

Eventually, the operating systems will catch up to the hardware. Then the authoring tools and applications will eventually catch up to the operating systems. Part of the problem is that the multimedia content of DVD is *streaming data*. Unlike traditional computer data—which can be read into memory in its entirety or in small chunks—audio and video data is continuous and time-critical. In the case of DVD, a constant stream of data must be fed from the DVD-ROM, split into separate streams, fed to decryptors, decoders, and other processors, combined with graphics and other computer-generated video, possibly combined with computer-generated audio, and then fed to the video display and audio hardware. This data stream, which can be monstrous when decompressed, may pass through the CPU and the bus many times on its trip from the disc to the display and the speakers. In order to make this process as efficient as possible, optimized low-level operating support is essential. Some operating systems such as Apple's MacOS with QuickTime already support streaming data. Others, such as Microsoft Windows, only support streaming data properly in the newest versions.

MICROSOFT WINDOWS ARCHITECTURE. Microsoft will not use its aging MCI interface to support DVD-Video, but instead is relying exclusively on the shiny new Win32 Driver Model (WDM) Streaming class driver, designed for the next generation of Windows (code-named Memphis) and Windows NT 5.0. The WDM Streaming class driver interconnects device drivers to handle multiple data streams. The driver handles issues such as synchronization, direct memory access (DMA), internal and external bus access, and separate bus paths (for example, sending the video display data over a specialized channel to avoid overwhelming the system bus). Microsoft has implemented a generic design that allows hardware manufacturers to develop a single minidriver to interface their component to the WDM Streaming class driver. For example, an MPEG-2 video decoder maker, a Dolby Digital audio decoder vendor, or an IEEE 1394/FireWire interface card developer each have to write only one minidriver that conforms to a single driver model in order to operate with each other. (See Fig. 9.3.)

DVD-Video playback and navigation is supported by DirectShow versions 2.0 and newer. Video display is supported by the DirectDraw API. Because full frame-rate decoded video has too high a bandwidth to be passed back and forth on most current implementations of the PCI bus, it often must travel on a separate path to the display adapter. Intel has designed the Advanced Graphics Port (AGP) architecture to support this. Microsoft's DirectDraw hardware abstraction layer (HAL) and video port extensions (VPE) provide hardware-independent support for AGP and similar parallel bus or parallel memory access architectures.

Figure 9.3
Microsoft Windows DVD architecture.

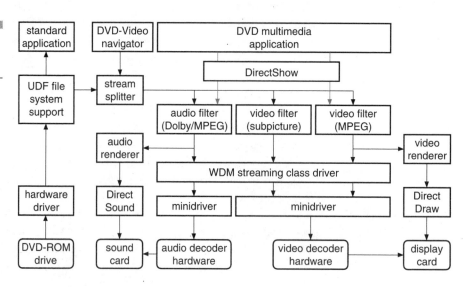

Regionalization is supported by the class driver in cooperation with the Windows operating system. One of the six regional codes is built into each copy of the OS. The code is hidden so that it is difficult to change. The class driver, which may also include its own regional coding, checks the codes on the disc. If the disc does not contain a code that matches the code in the class driver and/or the code from the OS, the driver will refuse to play it.

Copy protection is also supported by the OS. Microsoft will not provide a decryptor, but will develop software to act as an agent for facilitating the exchange of authentication keys between the DVD-ROM drive and the hardware or software decryption module.

NOTE   *For details of regional management and copy protection, see Chap. 4.*

Older versions of Windows will not be able to play movies from DVD-Video discs or even use DVD-Video—based multimedia software unless the DVD-Video media is supported by add-on hardware and software. DVD upgrade kits intended for use with DVD-Video must include separate navigation software for playing movies and other DVD-Video titles. For additional DVD-Video functionality, such as playing MPEG-2—encoded video and Dolby Digital—encoded audio, they also must include MCI or Active-Movie drivers. Some efforts are underway to standardize the command set of such drivers, but given historical precedent, it's likely that each will be slightly different. The differences will result in a huge headache for software publishers who must then design and test their products for myriad combinations of hardware and drivers.

DVD-Video will also be supported by Apple's QuickTime for Windows. Refer to the next section.

APPLE QUICKTIME ARCHITECTURE. The existing stream-oriented architecture of QuickTime easily supports DVD-Video media types on Macintosh and other MacOS-based computers, as well as on Microsoft Windows computers. MPEG-1 software playback was provided by the QuickTime MPEG Extension, which was released in February of 1997. Codecs for MPEG-2 video, Dolby Digital audio, and other DVD-Video streams are being developed by Apple and other hardware and software vendors to work with QuickTime versions 2.0 and newer. This allows makers of DVD upgrade kits and DVD-Video playback boards to provide either open or proprietary support for applications to work with their hardware. Apple plans to fully incorporate standardized support for DVD-Video media types beginning in QuickTime version 3.0. A player library will provide modules to support various features of DVD-Video playback, including navigation, audio/video decoding, hardware interface, and so on. As DVD-Video playback support gradually migrates from add-in hardware boards to components on the logic board, and finally to software and media processors, the QuickTime interface should remain consistent. Apple's plans for initial DVD-Video support include custom hardware decoding boards as well as add-in boards with TriMedia processors. These will be developed by other companies and possibly by Apple as well.

Because the QuickTime Media Layer (QTML) provides a standardized open architecture, it's probable that existing applications and development tools will not require any changes to support DVD-Video. Once the QuickTime modules are in place, some applications will work right out of the box with DVD-Video.

Regional management and decryption will be supported at the QuickTime module level. An application can have proprietary QuickTime codecs, which can only be registered by the application and which are unregistered when the application quits. This allows a DVD-Video playback application to use a QuickTime descrambling module to play protected movies without making the video stream available to other applications. Apple has applied for a CSS license and is in the process of evaluating ways of supporting CSS at the system software or hardware level.

According to Apple, two-thirds of all multimedia CD-ROM titles are developed on MacOS computers, including some which are designed to be used only on the Windows platform. Apple intends to provide a high level of standardized support for both DVD content development and DVD applications.

CHAPTER **10**

The Future of DVD

In the spring of 1997, as this book was being finished, DVD-Video had just begun to appear worldwide. Interest was high, but no measure of even the initial success of DVD was available. Nevertheless, much has been forecast about DVD, and educated guesses may be of some use to many readers. At the very least it should prove entertaining and informative to reread this chapter four or five years hence.

It's widely anticipated that DVD-ROM will be a huge success. The insatiable demand for more computer storage space and the growing sophistication of multimedia require bigger and faster media. Backward-compatibility of DVD-ROM with CD-ROM makes it the prime contender.

The success of DVD-Video is less of a sure bet. It's possible that without the computer market to support development, drive down costs, and hold open the window of acceptance, DVD-Video would fail. Even standing on the shoulders of DVD-ROM, DVD-Video could still fail. After all, how many of the people who don't mind watching worn-out rental tapes on poorly adjusted 19-inch televisions with tinny speakers care about picture quality, aspect ratios, and surround sound? How many of the people watching broadcast or cable TV wish they had a DVD player with no recording capability so they couldn't use it to timeshift their favorite fatuous sitcoms? On the other hand, the Electronics Industry Association (EIA) claims there are more than 12 million home theaters, less than a third of which have laserdisc players and all of which could benefit from DVD-Video. And the explosive growth of 18-inch DBS satellite systems, one of the most successful consumer video products of all time, can't be attributed entirely to popular dislike of cable companies or to the variety of premium channels and pay-per-view programs. Obviously, quality and features are important to some extent.

The success of DVD-Audio is even less assured than that of DVD-Video. Most consumers are perfectly happy with their CD players and have no compelling reason to upgrade. Likewise, the industry doesn't seem to be in any hurry to create a DVD-Audio format.

Even if the entire DVD format is a roaring success, it will still take time to become established. "This will probably take three to five years to get to the general consumer," says Mike Fidler, senior vice president for new technology at Pioneer. In some sense the physical limitations will be the shortest leash holding back DVD. There are simple constraints on the number of factories that can pump out DVD hardware and discs. Some predictions for the number of movies that would be available within a year of DVD's release turned out on close inspection to require more than three new titles a day—quite beyond the capacity of all the disc pressing plants and video compression centers combined. Pioneer's first release of players in the United States, after spending months making as many of them as they could, still provided enough for only 20 units to major outlets in big cities; and in many cases every single player was spoken for before reaching the store, and almost all stores were sold out within a week or two.

The variables involved in predicting the road of DVD are extremely complex. But this has not deterred many people from making plentiful predictions from the sensible to the outrageous.

The Prediction Gallery

The DVD format was announced in December of 1995. In the 11 months between then and the appearance of the first DVD players for sale in Japan, the only people making money from DVD were journalists and analysts. Considering the disparity between their forecasts, some of them were making more money than they deserved. Here is an interesting pot-pourri of prognostications, all made in 1996. (See Fig. 10.1.)

Philips: 25 million DVD-ROM drives worldwide by the year 2000 (10 percent of projected 250 million optical drives).

Pioneer: 500,000 DVD-ROM drives sold in 1997, 54 million sold in 2000.

Toshiba: 120 million DVD-ROM drives in 2000 (80 percent penetration of 150 million PCs). Toshiba projects that it will no longer make CD-ROM drives in the year 2000.

International Data Corporation (IDC): 10 million DVD-ROM drives sold in 1997, 70 million sold in 2000 (surpassing CD-ROM), 118 million sold in 2001. Over 13 percent of all software will be available on DVD-ROM in 1998. DVD recordable drives will make up more than 90 percent of the combined CD/DVD recordable market in 2001, with DVD drive units installed in 95 percent of computer systems with fixed storage. IDC later revised its figures to 3.7 million in 1997, 10.8 million in 1998, 36.5 million in 1999, and 95 million in the year 2000.

AMI: Installed base of 7 million DVD-ROM drives by 2000.

Intel: 70 million DVD-ROM drives by 1999 (sales will surpass CD-ROM drives in 1998).

InfoTech: 1.1 million DVD-V players in 1997, 10 million by 2000. 1.2 million DVD-ROM drives in 1997, 39 million by 2000. 250,000 interactive (video game or cable TV set-top) DVD players in 1997, 6 million by 2000. InfoTech revised its DVD-Video predictions in January of 1997 to a slightly lower 820,000 units in the first year, with an installed base of 80 million by 2005.

Dataquest: One-year sales of 15 million DVD-Video players in 2000. DVD optical drive market of $35 million by 1996 and $4.1 billion by 2000.

Paul Kagan Associates: 12 million DVD-Video players in the United States after 5 years. Total DVD-Video business of $6 billion per year by the year 2000.

Simba: Annual DVD software sales of up to $35 million by 1997 and $100 million by 1999.

Freeman Associates: DVD-ROM drive sales of 89 million by 2001, accompanied by zero sales of CD-ROM drives.

Electronic Industry Association of Japan (EIAJ): Combined U.S. and Japanese DVD-Video and DVD-ROM market of $23.6 billion by 2005, with a DVD-ROM drive in about 80 percent of all new PCs.

Microsoft: As many as 100 million PC-based digital TV sets by 2005. (Predicted in March 1997.)

Intel: By the year 2000, all PCs shipped will be DTV receivers. (Predicted in March 1997.)

Figure 10.1
Comparison of
DVD predictions.

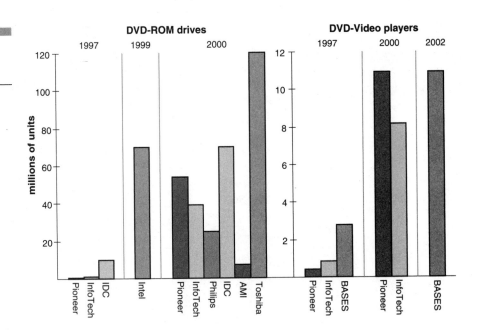

For comparison, there was an installed base of about 600 million CD players and about 100 million CD-ROM drives worldwide at the end of 1996. Annual CD industry sales are over $50 billion. The number of CD units to be sold in 1997 is estimated at 100 million players and 50 million drives. CD-ROM drives are projected to increase to 143 million in 1997, 190 million in 1998, 224 million in 1999, and 203 million by 2000.

There are about 400 million VCRs and 1.2 billion televisions worldwide. There are over 500,000 widescreen TVs in Europe. In 1996, American consumers spent $16 billion to rent about 3 billion videotapes and purchase more than 580 million tapes. Over 87 percent of America's 96 million television households have at least one VCR. The home theater market, with over $15 billion in annual sales, saw HiFi VCR sales of over $1 billion in 1996. Over 7 million 27-inch or larger TVs were sold in 1997. About 3 million digital satellite systems were shipped by the end of 1996. Almost 7 million Video CD players were sold worldwide in 1996.

U.S. domestic box office total for 1996 was $5.9 billion. The video game industry is over $3 billion.

It's enlightening and quite sobering to compare the DVD projections with the success rate of previous consumer products. See Fig. 10.2.

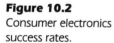

Figure 10.2
Consumer electronics success rates.

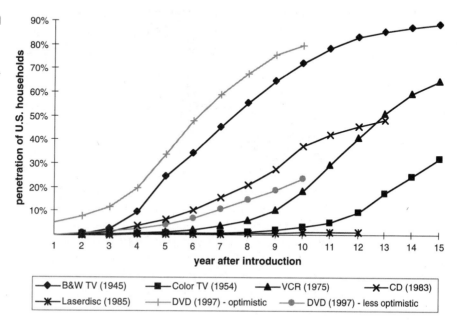

New Generations of DVD

The development of DVD was planned to proceed in stages. DVD-Video was released first as a consumer entertainment product, closely followed by DVD-ROM for computers. Record-once DVD-R is targeted for the second half of 1997, with erasable DVD-RAM coming in 1998. DVD-Audio was originally expected to appear along with DVD-Video, but it soon became clear that it was better to wait and create a well-considered and well-supported audio standard for DVD.

Early ambitions to make all versions of DVD physically compatible were derailed by late additions to DVD-RAM, which made it incompatible with first-generation DVD-ROM drives.

Also planned from early on, but in more nebulous terms, was an improved high-density DVD format for HDTV and even more capacious data storage. Deep thinkers are undoubtedly envisioning third and fourth generations of DVD for digital film, three-dimensional video, and the always growing computer storage demands.

Recordable DVD

As explained elsewhere in more detail (see the "DVD Myths" section of Chap. 3), a version of DVD for home video recording will take years to be developed, if ever. But recordable DVD-ROM, like recordable CD-ROM, is expected to sell like hotcakes once the price drops below the magic points of $1000 and $500.

DVD-R. The record-once format, DVD-R, is championed by Pioneer and is expected to appear in the second half of 1997. The recorder is tentatively priced at $17,000 but may debut at an even higher price. Discs are expected to start at $40 to $50. Since much of the DVD-R technology is borrowed from CD-R, which has already paved the way in establishing consumer demand and distribution channels, the price of DVD-R products will drop even faster. Within a year the cost of recordable drives should drop below $5000, passing below the $1000 mark barely one or two years later. Acceptance might be held up by a crucial shortcoming: DVD-R discs can only hold 3.7 gigabytes (4 billion bytes) compared to DVD-ROM's 4.4 gigabytes (4.7 billion bytes). Many of the early purchasers of CD-R recorders were CD-ROM developers who wanted to have a reliable way to test their new software before committing to having thousands of discs pressed, and who also wanted a simple way to send the finished product to the replication plant. Unfortunately, the boost of DVD-R to 4.4 gigabytes is expected to take a few years. In the meantime, the less-than-optimal and less-than-affordable solution may be to connect multiple DVD-R drives into a single virtual volume or use multi-gigabyte hard drives and digital linear tape (DLT).

DVD-RAM. The erasable, rerecordable format—DVD-RAM—was once promised for summer of 1997 but will probably not appear until sometime in 1998. As DVD players and discs were being released in early 1997, two competing proposals were finally combined to create the final sanctioned erasable format. Toshiba promised that drives would be available by the end of 1997 for as little as $350, but most industry observers had heard the cry of "wolf" too many times and set their sights on the middle of 1998, accompanied by prices in the $800 range. Philips and Sony abstained from approving the format, raising the specter of a competing, incompatible, magneto-optical version.

DVD-RAM discs were originally supposed to be readable by all DVD-ROM drives and DVD-Video players, but the new format requires support for defect lists which were not covered in the initial DVD spec. Therefore, first-generation DVD drives and players won't read DVD-RAM discs.

FUTURE COMPATIBILITY. When the next incarnation of DVD readers is developed, using smaller wavelength lasers, the readers will probably face the same problem that DVD readers had with CD-R discs—that the dyes used in the DVD-R polymer recording material do not properly reflect other wavelengths of light. As before, the solution might require dual lasers in the optical pickup assembly or improved material in the DVD-R that works with lasers of both wavelengths.

DVD Players, Take 2

Manufacturers will continue to improve DVD players in the endless race to best the competition. Future players may include digital connections for video, audio, and direct bitstream output; video processing circuitry to improve picture quality; progressive scan circuitry to make discs with interlaced video look better on new digital TVs; improved interactivity; and other features such as smooth reverse play.

It's also feasible that future generations of DVD players will include phone or Internet connections to make pay-per-view discs possible.

DIGITAL CONNECTIONS. The first few generations of DVD players lack digital video connectors, primarily because copy protection standards and digital interchange protocols are still under development. But at some point, DVD players will benefit from the new digital interconnection standards being developed for consumer electronics and computers. Once the standards are developed, new DVD players must convert playback information into the proper format. This should be trivial for encoded MPEG audio/video and encoded Dolby Digital audio, but may be more complicated for subpictures. Obviously, the menus and random-access features of DVD will not be available if the outgoing digital bitstream is recorded for later playback. But the primary purpose of a digital connection is to provide a pristine signal for the decoder in the digital television or the digital media center equipment.

The IEEE 1394 external serial bus system is the best candidate for digital connection. It uses a foolproof connector adopted from video game consoles. Apple Computer's original design for the product was called FireWire, a name that stuck even after the IEEE adopted it as standard number 1394. Its first major support was from Sony with its digital video cameras, although Sony chose to call it the *DV connector.* Other companies are also beginning to support the IEEE 1394/FireWire/DV system in their products. Initial implementations support data rates of 100 to 400 Mbps, and new versions under development can support data rates over 1 Gbps. At these speeds, even some uncompressed digital video signals can be accommodated.

Intel's Universal Serial Bus (USB) standard is intended primarily for computer peripherals such as mice and keyboards. But standards are inevitably stretched beyond their original purview, and USB's 12-Mbps bandwidth is capable of carrying compressed audio and video information.

The advantages of digital connections are as follows:

- *A single cable to carry audio, video, and even power.* (Sony's DV connector does not carry power.) DVD players can fairly bristle with a ludicrous number of connectors to cover all possible scenarios: 2 audio connectors for stereo sound, 1 or 2 coax digital audio connectors, 1 or 2 optical digital audio connectors, 6 audio connectors for 5.1-channel sound, a composite video connector, an s-video connector, and 3 connectors for component video. Of course, a digital connector is yet one more, but in theory it will be the last new connector ever needed, since it will be able to accommodate all future signals.

- *Daisy chaining.* IEEE 1394 allows dozens of devices to talk to each other with only one cable connected between each of them. Other star configurations can also be used. (See Fig. 10.3.)

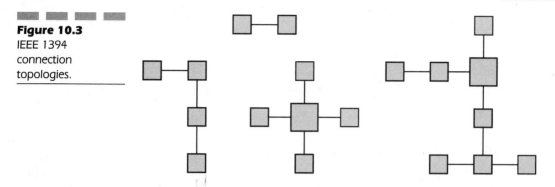

Figure 10.3
IEEE 1394
connection
topologies.

- *Little or no electronic interference.* Because the signals are digital, they are practically immune to degradation from external sources.
- *Long cable lengths.* Cables can be up to 15 feet (4.5 meters) long.

Many new computers will have both USB and IEEE 1394 interfaces. In some cases the digital audio and video from the computer's DVD-ROM drive will be available to external digital devices, possibly even DVD recorders.

Hybrid Systems

The ways in which the DVD format will be combined with other products and systems are intriguingly diverse. DVD-ROMs will be integrated with the Internet. Home DVD players will add Internet connections, or home Internet-TV products will add DVD-Video players or DVD-ROM drives. New pay-per-view systems may be built around DVD players; discs might appear for free in the mail to be viewed or purchased by having the player make a quick phone call to authorize the charge to an account or credit card. Both home and commercial video game systems will include DVD-Video and DVD-ROM units. Public information kiosks will incorporate DVD technology. Car navigation systems will take advantage of DVD storage capacity for maps and graphics and might even pipe DVD movies to a monitor in the back seat. As MPEG video and Dolby Digital audio become more common, the digital decoder may move into the television or the stereo system, making the player an inexpensive transport which along with other devices, such as a digital satellite receiver, digital cable box, digital TV tuner, or video phone connection, would simply feed compressed signals to the video display.

The living room of the cost-conscious consumer may be the primary focus for splicing DVD into other formats. These possibilities are explored further in the section entitled "The Changing Face of Home Entertainment," which follows.

HDVD

Before DVD players had even hit the streets in most countries, DVD developers began talking about and demonstrating new high-density or high-definition versions. HD-DVD, often called HDVD for short, is expected to be a reality in the year 2000 or 2001. Given the typical gap between expectations and their fulfillment, products based on HDVD will more likely appear around the year 2003.

The essential advancement is a blue laser, which has a smaller wavelength than the visible red lasers of DVD and can therefore read smaller pits. This has been projected to yield an increase in data density of four to ten times that of DVD.

In February of 1997, Toshiba announced a prototype player with a storage capacity of 7 gigabytes, about 1.5 times that of standard DVD. The data rate had been increased to an average of 14 Mbps, about three times the current rate, sufficient for high-resolution video images with 1125 scan lines. Toshiba planned to increase the capacity to 14 gigabytes per layer, allowing a total of 50 gigabytes on a dual-layer, double-sided disc.

A new format of this type will require new players. HDVD discs will not be playable in older players, but the new players will undoubtedly play older discs. They will probably even make the video from older discs look better with improved circuitry, new digital signal processing, and progressive scan output.

There has been speculation that a double-headed player reading both sides of the disc at the same time could double the data rate for applications such as HDTV. This is currently impossible since the layer 0 track spirals go in opposite directions. The DVD standard would have to be amended to allow reverse spirals on the second side. This still might not get the idea off the ground, since large buffers or precise alignment in both the radial and angular dimensions would be required to keep both sides in sync.

NO LD-SIZED DVD. Inevitably, rumors appear of DVD technology being applied to the larger 12-inch (30-cm) form factor of laserdiscs. Variations of laserdisc technology have been used for high-definition television, such as the HDLD format for the Japanese HiVision system, but it's quite improbable that such a format will be adopted for commercial digital video, given the disadvantages of larger discs. Existing CD production lines can be easily adapted to higher-density formats as long as the physical diameter does not change. Large discs require larger molds, which are more difficult to inject molten polycarbonate into and which can be much more difficult to separate from the pressed discs, especially with the tiny pit sizes used by DVD. Large discs are more subject to warping and create more stress and slippage at the bonding layer, which can damage the reflective data layer. Large discs require larger players and stronger motors (which make battery-powered portable players more difficult) and have more noise and stability problems because of the higher velocity at the outer edge.

Twelve-inch discs are dinosaurs. Development of new high-density optical media is oriented toward the more practical 5-inch (12-cm) format.

DVD for Computer Multimedia

During the development and introduction of DVD, many people were confused by the difference between DVD-Video and DVD-ROM. As computers evolve from data processors to media processors this distinction will become mostly irrelevant. Eventually, a DVD movie will play equally well in a movie player or a computer.

Currently, the power of general-purpose processors in computers is insufficient to fully reproduce digital video at the level provided for by the DVD-Video format; additional hardware is needed to achieve full quality. But computers, faithful to Moores' law, double in processing power every 18 months. Within a short time of the introduction of DVD, all new computers will be able to play audio and video from DVDs at full quality and still have enough processing capacity left for other tasks. Computer display subsystems will be designed for displaying graphics and video at 30 frames/second or higher and will no longer be a bottleneck for live video. Digital I/O connections such as IEEE 1394/FireWire will be common, allowing the computer to capture, process, combine, and generate high-quality digital video and audio.

Of course, HDTV will come along and raise the stakes, probably once again requiring specialized video hardware for a year or so while CPUs and software catch up. The game of leapfrog between hardware and software has been played out many times before; they will no doubt continue hopping past each other throughout their future development.

It's possible that the approach taken by Apple Computer with the Tri-Media chip will prove to be the winner. It's a given that future computers will incorporate multiple processors, so making one or more of those processors optimized for media makes sense. The traditional processors are free to crunch data and handle general tasks, while the media processors manipulate video and generate 3D graphical worlds. On the other hand, Intel may have the upper hand with its approach of counting on its general-purpose processors to eventually become fast enough and powerful enough to handle formerly specialized tasks.

The Death of CD-ROM

As evidenced in the preceding "Prediction Gallery," the range of dates given for the disappearance of CD-ROM would make a fine office pool, but they all agree that CD-ROM will become obsolete. Not overnight, to be sure, since CD-ROM had a 100 million-unit lead on DVD-ROM when it was introduced, but it's conceivable that no more CD-ROM drives will be made after the year 2000, and it's a pretty sure bet that the last production lines will have changed over before 2005.

The insatiable demand for storage space will quickly propel DVD-ROM into the computer mainstream. Because DVD-ROM drives can read CDs, the only real barriers are support and price. DVD-ROMs will be supported in upcoming operating system upgrades, as well as by hardware upgrade kits. And prices should very quickly drop to CD-ROM levels because of economies of scale and because most of the mechanisms and components are based on existing CD technology.

Just as Microsoft has pushed acceptance of new operating systems by ensuring that desirable new software was only available on the new platform, and just as software publishers have driven acceptance of CD-ROM drives by making products available only on CD, the establishment of DVD-ROM drives will be hastened by the desire of software publishers for a bigger vessel in which to distribute their products.

THE BRIEF EXISTENCE OF CD-RW. Rewritable CD, finalized at the end of 1996 and introduced shortly after DVD-ROM, has a tough row to hoe. It finally brings the Holy Grail of erasability to the basic CD format, but only by being incompatible with all existing CD drives and players. It will have a very short window of opportunity before being eclipsed by DVD-RAM or even by new magneto-optical drives that can read DVD discs. It has its supporters, who say that it will fill an important niche until DVD-RAM is standardized and affordable, but it also has its detractors who wonder why anyone bothered to bring it to market. Ironically, some success of CD-RW will be provided by DVD-ROM drives, which were the first units on the market able to read CD-RW discs.

Standards, Anyone?

Computer standards often develop like meandering cowpaths which later become so well traveled that they end up being paved into meandering roads. DVD offers both promise and hardship: as a new format which can be done well or a new jungle through which too many crooked paths can be blazed.

Take, for instance, DVD's predecessor, MPEG-1 video on CD, which was a standards nightmare. Each hardware and software implementation of MPEG-1 was slightly different, with companies designing their own different MCI interfaces and data formats. The market for MPEG-1 video hardware decoding, which at first looked so promising as an alternative to quarter-screen, low-resolution video codecs, took a nosedive before it ever got off the ground. Software publishers discovered that their movies might play fine on one card but not on another. The OpenMPEG Consortium was created in an attempt to resolve the problems, but did not receive sufficient industry support and was never able to accomplish much.

Some of the members of the OpenMPEG Consortium, now sadder and wiser, formed the OpenDVD Consortium with more pragmatic goals: no attempt is being made to define a standard, instead the organization provides a common meeting ground for computer DVD developers and serves as a clearinghouse for information. It's hoped that by sharing details of implementations, both hardware makers and software developers will be able to better ensure that their products work with as broad a range of other products as possible.

The Interactive Multimedia Association (IMA), with slightly loftier goals, established numerous technical working groups (TWGs) in December of 1996 to deal with issues such as standardized architectures, cross-platform interactive media formats, hybrid Internet-DVD applications, data interchange formats for DVD authoring and production, technical safeguards, and compliance testing.

Mr. Computer Goes to Hollywood

As digital technology steadily improves, the computer will become as much a media machine as a computation machine. Today's distinction between DVD-Video and DVD-ROM is important yet confusing. When the next wave of computers fully incorporates high-fidelity audio and video, the distinction between DVD-Video and DVD-ROM will disappear, resulting in thoroughly amazing applications as the interactive power of Silicon Valley and the sensory impact of Hollywood coalesce on desktop computers.

The Changing Face of Home Entertainment

The year 1996 was one that presaged the digital revolution of home entertainment. Direct broadcast digital satellite (DBS) systems were introduced and purchased by the millions. DVD was unveiled, though it didn't manage to appear anywhere but in Japan before the end of the year. And, in December of 1996, the FCC approved the U.S. DTV* standard, which ushered in 1997: "The Year of Waiting for Digital TV."†

DBS and DVD each have one foot in the past and one foot in the future. They use digital signal recording and compression methods to squeeze the most quality into their limited transmission and storage capacities, but convert the signal to analog format for display on conventional televisions. But as digital televisions slowly begin to push their creaky predecessors out of living rooms and offices, the pure digital signal of DVD and similar technologies will be ready and waiting for them. Video from existing discs and players will look better than ever on widescreen digital televisions. New-generation DVD players will enhance existing discs by generating progressive-scan video and supplying it via digital connectors, leaving behind the flicker and flutter of interlaced video and freeing all television personalities everywhere to wear pinstriped fabrics and sit in front of miniblinds.

It will take many years for digital television to even establish a foothold, yet this period will also witness the computerization of television. This doesn't mean that every television will sprout a floppy disk drive, a mouse, and system crash error messages, but it does mean that as consumer electronics companies and home computer makers endeavor to

---

*DTV is a set of broadcast standards for digital HDTV transmission in the U.S. Other countries may develop different HDTV standards, such as DVB in Europe.

†Followed by 1998: "The Year No One Can Afford Digital TV."

make their products more suitable to the basic entertainment needs, communication needs, and productivity needs of home users, features from computers such as on-screen menus, pointers, multiple windows, and even an Internet connection will become commonplace. DVD is the perfect format for this environment, able to carry content for both the television and the computer and all the variations in between.

In the meantime, the traditional television is getting better with each passing year. The term *big screen TV* applies to ever larger sizes: 35-inch sets are now the price of 25-inch sets a few years ago, and of 19-inch sets a few years before that. Widescreen TV's have been available for a few years, but have not caught the attention of most American buyers. Widescreen popularity in Europe and in Japan—where over 50 percent of new television purchases are widescreen—is helping to drive prices down, and the introduction of widescreen DTV will help even further. The biggest impediment has been a lack of movies and other video source in widescreen format. DVD will begin to fill this hole with its native support for wide aspect ratio displays.

Convergence will happen with systems other than the computer and the TV. Prime candidates are cable set-top boxes, satellite receivers, video game consoles, Internet TV boxes, even telephones, cellular phones, hand-held computers, and, of course, DVD players. See Fig. 10.4. Engineers are already at work designing new boxes that combine the features of digital satellite receivers and DVD players, since they share many of the same MPEG-2 digital video components. Digital cable boxes will combine the features of cable TV tuners and DVD players, and will top it off with an Internet connection. Program listings from the Internet can be shown on the TV screen so that shows can be marked for recording with the click of a remote control, and the system will automatically compensate for delays caused by ball games or newsbreaks. Video game consoles will include DVD-ROM drives for game play, giving them the ability to double as DVD movie players. In short, because of the flexibility and interconnectability of inexpensive digital electronics, all the independent pieces we have grown accustomed to can be tossed in a big hat, shaken around, and pulled back out as new, mixed-and-matched systems with more features at lower prices.

Major computer companies, led by Microsoft, Intel, and Compaq, have already announced plans for PC-based digital television (DTV) sets which will support a subset of the ATSC DTV recommendations. The planned base format will use MPEG-2 video at 1280×720 progressive scan along with Dolby Digital audio. This matches well with the DVD-Video format and can be easily supported by any DVD-ROM drive at a data rate of about 6 or 7 Mbps.

Figure 10.4
Media convergence
in the digital age.

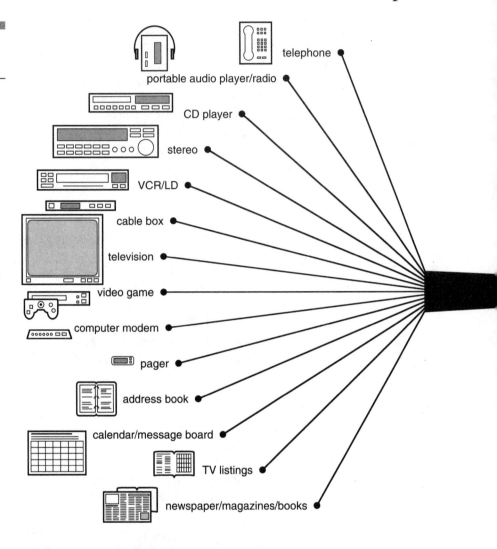

telephone

portable audio player/radio

CD player

stereo

VCR/LD

cable box

television

video game

computer modem

pager

address book

calendar/message board

TV listings

newspaper/magazines/books

DVD in the Classroom

Unlike the home entertainment market, where laserdiscs never gained more than a tiny videophile niche, the education market adopted laserdisc technology early on and in a big way. Over 200,000 laserdisc players have been sold to schools in the United States, almost one for every building. So, the big question is, will DVD replace laserdisc? And the answer is no, not directly.

Most of the appeal of DVD-ROM is lost in a classroom environment. Lessons usually never last more than 45 minutes, so there's no pressing

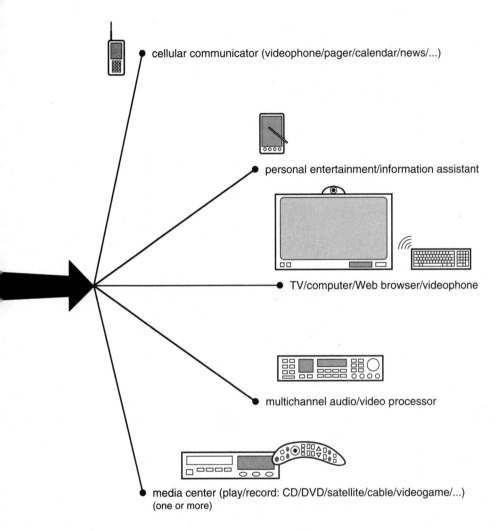

cellular communicator (videophone/pager/calendar/news/...)

personal entertainment/information assistant

TV/computer/Web browser/videophone

multichannel audio/video processor

media center (play/record: CD/DVD/satellite/cable/videogame/...)
(one or more)

need for hours of uninterrupted video. Surround-sound audio is point-less, especially since most laserdiscs and VCRs use the cheap speakers in the television. Laserdisc video quality is already as good or better than most of the classroom televisions it's shown on. Multilingual audio tracks and subtitles are nice, but it's already possible to put four audio tracks on a laserdisc by using both channels of analog audio and both channels of digital audio. DVD's menus and interactivity are an improvement over passive laserdiscs, but most educators would prefer to make the jump to computers and gain significantly more power and flexibility.

Laserdisc players maintain advantages over DVD players. Any still picture or movie can be accessed almost instantly by entering a 5-digit frame number on the remote control, or easier yet, by scanning a printed bar code. The biggest advantage is established content. Over 3000 educational laserdiscs have been developed over the past 15 years or so. Many of these are still just as effective and useful as they were when they were first developed. It's improbable that such a wealth of visual resources will ever be developed for DVD-Video, especially since educational publishers will wait for schools to buy players while schools wait for the publishers to make DVD-Video products.

Educational media publishers have already been spread thin by too many new formats, many of which seem as much a step backward as forward. Videotape appeared shortly after laserdisc; and though it could record, it had poor picture quality, no decent still-frame capability, and no random access. The subsequent "advance" was digitized video—ala QuickTime and Video for Windows—playing from a CD. It was flexible and could be integrated with computers, but lost vital detail with its quarter-screen fuzzy picture and required a TV converter box or a video projector for full-class presentation. Publishers were next asked to support Video CD, which provided full-screen digital video but still lacked quality and had almost no installed base of players. Then came the Internet, which was highly interactive and timely, but essentially precluded motion video. It's little wonder that gun-shy publishers are not eager to embrace yet another newfangled medium.

But the failure of DVD-Video to unseat laserdisc in the classroom hardly means that laserdisc's days are unnumbered. Beginning in 1996, educational sales of players and discs dropped almost as quickly as in the home market. Competition from computers, and especially the Internet, is finally proving too much for the reliable but no longer glamorous workhorse, which will slowly decline over the next decade. The end of the heyday of laserdiscs signals the decline of all stand-alone audio/visual players.

DVD will succeed in the educational environment, but almost surely via computers rather than DVD-Video players. Long before educational DVD discs are plentiful enough and players are cheap enough to justify their purchase, new computers being purchased by schools will be able to play DVD-Video discs as well as educational DVD-ROM software. Ironically, this promises to provide the market that educational publishers need in order to embrace DVD-Video. Cleverly designed products will work in both DVD-Video—enabled computers at school and in DVD-Video players at home. Home education, both formal and informal, will drive the demand for this kind of product.

In the long run, multimedia PCs will replace classroom TVs, VCRs, overhead projectors, and laserdiscs, just as these have replaced filmstrip projectors and 16mm movies. Most lightweight content will come from the Internet, but the necessary graphics, audio, and video will be provided by DVD. Inasmuch as technology adoption in schools typically lags behind business and home use by several years, the process may take some time. This is unfortunate, since the case for computer and media integration in education is more compelling than almost anywhere else. Technology is not a magic elixir that will cure the ills of the education system, but it is a very powerful tool that when wielded properly can be truly effective. DVD-Video as currently implemented does not seem to be well suited as an educational tool, but computers combined with DVD in both -ROM and -Video form promise to substantially advance the state of the art by providing the kind of high-capacity knowledge bases and high-impact sensory environments that foster more effective learning.

The Far Horizon

In the very long term, the Internet will merge with cable TV, broadcast TV, radio, telephones, satellites, and eventually even newspapers and magazines. In other words, the Internet will take over the communications world. News, movies, music, advertising, education, games, financial transactions, e-mail, and most other forms of information will be delivered via this giant network. Internet bandwidth, currently lagging far behind the load being demanded of it, will eventually catch up as did other systems such as intercontinental telephone networks and communications satellites. Discrete media such as DVD will then be relegated to niches such as software backup, archiving, time-shift "taping," and collector's editions of movies. Why go to a software store to buy a DVD-ROM or to a movie rental store to rent a DVD when you can have it delivered right to your computer or your TV or even your digital video recorder? But in the intervening years, DVD in all its permutations and generations promises to be the definitive medium for both computers and home entertainment.

APPENDIX A

Quick Reference

TABLE A.1

Meanings of Prefixes

Prefix	Name	Common use	Computer use	Difference (%)
k or K	Kilo	1,000 (10^3)	1,024 (2^{10})	2.4
M	Mega	1,000,000 (10^6)	1,048,576 (2^{20})	4.9
G	Giga	1,000,000,000 (10^9)	1,073,741,824 (2^{30})	7.4
T	Tera	1,000,000,000,000 (10^{12})	1,099,511,628 (2^{40})	10

Figure A.1 DVD-Video conversion formulas.

formula	example
time (hours) = $\frac{\text{space (G bytes) x 8000}}{\text{data rate (Mbps) x 3600}}$	$\frac{4.7}{4.69}$ x 2.22= 2.2 hours
data rate (Mbps) = $\frac{\text{space (G bytes) x 8000}}{\text{time (hours) x 3600}}$	$\frac{8.5}{3}$ x 2.22= 6.3 Mbps
space (G bytes) = $\frac{\text{data rate (Mbps) x time (hours) x 3600}}{8000}$	5 x 2 x 0.45 = 4.5 G bytes

for gigabytes (instead of billions of bytes) replace 8000 with 8590 (or replace 2.22 with 2.39, and 0.45 with 0.42)

TABLE A.2
Capacities of DVD

Format	Width (cm)	Sides/layers	Giga-bytes	Million bytes	×CD-ROM	Typical hours (minutes)[a]	Minimum to maximum hours[b]	Typical audio hours (minutes)[c]	Minimum to maximum audio hours[d]
DVD-ROM	12	SS/SL[e]	4.38	4.70	6.9	2.2 (133)	1.0–9.0	2.7 (163)	1.7–163
DVD-ROM	12	SS/DL	7.95	8.54	12.5	4.0 (242)	1.9–16.5	4.9 (296)	3.1–296
DVD-ROM	12	DS/SL	8.75	9.40	13.8	4.4 (267)	2.1–18.1	5.4 (326)	3.4–326
DVD-ROM	12	DS/DL	15.90	17.08	25.0	8.0 (485)	3.8–33.0	9.8 (593)	6.2–593
DVD-ROM	8	SS/SL	1.36	1.46	2.1	0.6 (41)	0.3–2.8	0.8 (50)	0.5–50
DVD-ROM	8	SS/DL	2.48	2.66	3.9	1.2 (75)	0.6–5.1	1.5 (92)	1.0–92
DVD-ROM	8	DS/SL	2.72	2.92	4.3	1.3 (82)	0.6–5.6	1.6 (101)	1.1–101
DVD-ROM	8	DS/DL	4.95	5.32	7.8	2.5 (151)	1.2–10.2	3.0 (184)	1.9–184
DVD-R	12	SS/SL	3.68	3.95	5.8	1.8 (112)	0.9–7.6	2.2 (137)	1.4–137
DVD-R	12	DS/SL	7.36	7.90	11.6	3.7 (224)	1.7–15.2	4.5 (274)	2.9–274
DVD-R	8	SS/SL	1.15	1.23	1.8	0.6 (34)	0.3–2.3	0.7 (42)	0.4–42
DVD-R	8	DS/SL	2.29	2.46	3.6	1.1 (69)	0.5–4.7	1.4 (85)	0.9–85
DVD-RAM	12	SS/SL	2.40	2.58	3.8	1.2 (73)	0.6–4.9	1.4 (85)	0.9–89
DVD-RAM	12	DS/SL	4.80	5.16	7.6	2.4 (146)	1.1–9.9	2.9 (179)	1.9–179
CD-ROM[f]	12	SS/SL	0.635	0.682	(1)	0.3 (19)	0.2–1.3	0.3 (23)	0.2–23

[a]Approximate video playback time, given an average data rate of 4.7 Mbps (1 video track at 3.5 Mbps, 3 audio tracks at 1.152 Mbps total, and 4 subpicture tracks at a combined average of 0.04 Mbps). Actual playing times can be much longer or shorter (see next column).

[b]Minimum video playback time at the highest data rate of 10.08 Mbps. Maximum playback time at the MPEG-1 data rate of 1.15 Mbps.

[c]Typical audio-only playback time at the 2-channel PCM audio rate of 96 kHz and 20 bits (3,840 Mbps).

[d]Minimum audio-only playback time at the highest single-stream PCM audio rate of 6,144 Mbps. Maximum audio-only playback time at the lowest Dolby Digital or MPEG-2 data rate of 64 kbps.

[e]SS = single side, DS = double side, SL = single layer, DL = dual layer.

[f]Mode 1; 74 minutes (333,000 sectors). Audio/video times are for comparison only.

TABLE A.3

DVD-Video Stream
Data Rates

	Minimum (kbps)	Typical (kbps)	Maximum (kbps)	Combined maximum
MPEG-2 video	1500	3500	9800	n/a
MPEG-1 video	1150	1150	1856	
PCM	768	1536	6144	
Dolby Digital	64	384	448	9800
MPEG-1 audio	64	192	384	
MPEG-2 audio	64	384	912	
Subpicture	n/a	10	3360	9800

TABLE A.4

Playing Times for
Various Data Rates

Data rate (Mbps)			Playing time per disc in minutes (hours)			
Video average	Audio (no. of tracks)	Total[1]	SS/SL[2]	SS/DL	DS/SL	DS/DL
3.5	1.152 (3)[3]	4.69	133 (2.2)	242 (4.0)	267 (4.4)	485 (8.0)
3.5	0.768 (2)[3]	4.31	145 (2.4)	264 (4.4)	290 (4.8)	528 (8.8)
3.5	0.384 (1)[3]	3.92	159 (2.6)	290 (4.8)	319 (5.3)	580 (9.6)
3.5	3.072 (8)[3]	6.61	94 (1.5)	172 (2.8)	189 (3.1)	344 (5.7)
3.5	1.536 (1)[4]	5.08	123 (2.0)	224 (3.7)	246 (4.1)	448 (7.4)
8.9	1.152 (3)[3]	10.08	62 (1.0)	112 (1.8)	124 (2.0)	225 (3.7)
9.7	0.384 (1)[3]	10.08	62 (1.0)	112 (1.8)	124 (2.0)	225 (3.7)
7.0	0.768 (2)[3]	7.81	80 (1.3)	145 (2.4)	160 (2.6)	291 (4.8)
6.0	0.768 (2)[3]	6.81	92 (1.5)	167 (2.7)	184 (3.0)	334 (5.5)
5.0	0.768 (2)[3]	5.81	107 (1.7)	196 (3.2)	215 (3.5)	392 (6.5)
4.0	0.768 (2)[3]	4.81	130 (2.1)	236 (3.9)	260 (4.3)	473 (7.8)
3.0	0.768 (2)[3]	3.81	164 (2.7)	299 (4.9)	329 (5.4)	598 (9.9)
2.0	0.192 (1)[5]	2.23	280 (4.6)	510 (8.5)	561 (9.3)	1020 (17.0)
1.15[6]	0.192 (1)[5]	1.38	453 (7.5)	823 (13.7)	906 (15.1)	1647 (27.4)
1.15[6]	0.064 (1)[7]	1.25	499 (8.3)	908 (15.1)	999 (16.6)	1816 (30.2)

[1]Total data rate includes 4 subpicture streams (0.04 Mbps).
[2]SS = single side (4.7G), DS = double side (8.5G), SL = single layer (9.4G), DL = dual layer (17G).
[3]5.1-channel Dolby Digital audio
[4]16-bit/48-kHz PCM audio
[5]2-channel Dolby Digital or MPEG audio
[6]MPEG-1 video
[7]1-channel Dolby Digital or MPEG audio

TABLE A.5
Audio Playing Times at Various Data Rates

Format	kbps	No video				+ Average 3.54 Mbps video			
		SS/SL*	SS/DL	DS/SL	DS/DL	SS/SL	SS/DL	DS/SL	DS/DL
DD mono (1 ch)	64	163.0	296.4	326.3	592.9	2.8	5.2	5.7	10.5
DD stereo (2 ch)	192	54.3	98.8	108.7	197.6	2.7	5.0	5.5	10.1
DD multi (5.1 ch)	384	27.1	49.4	54.3	98.8	2.6	4.8	5.3	9.6
DD maximum (5.1 ch)	448	23.2	42.3	46.6	84.7	2.6	4.7	5.2	9.5
2 DD multi (2 × 5.1 ch)	768	13.5	24.7	27.1	49.4	2.4	4.4	4.8	8.8
MPEG maximum (7.1 ch)	912	11.4	20.8	22.9	41.6	2.3	4.2	4.6	8.5
3 DD multi (3 × 5.1 ch)	1152	9.0	16.4	18.1	32.9	2.2	4.0	4.4	8.0
PCM 16/48 stereo (2 ch)	1536	6.7	12.3	13.5	24.7	2.0	3.7	4.1	7.4
PCM 20/48 stereo (2 ch)	1920	5.4	9.8	10.8	19.7	1.9	3.4	3.8	6.9
8 DD multi (8 × 5.1 ch)	3072	3.3	6.1	6.7	12.3	1.5	2.8	3.1	5.7
PCM 20/96 stereo (2 ch)	3840	2.7	4.9	5.4	9.8	1.4	2.5	2.8	5.1
PCM 24/96 stereo (2 ch)	4608	2.2	4.1	4.5	8.2	1.2	2.3	2.5	4.6
PCM 16/48 multi (8 ch)	6144	1.6	3.0	3.3	6.1	1.0	1.9	2.1	3.9

Playing time per disc (hours)

*SS = single side, DD = Dolby Digital, DS = double side, SL = single layer, DL = dual layer.

Figure A.2
Data rate versus
playing time.

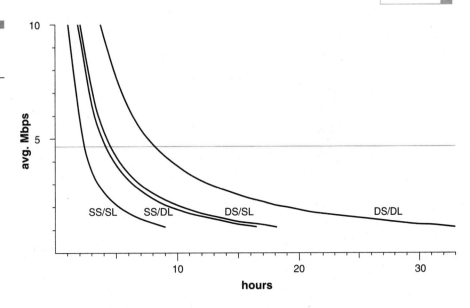

Figure A.3
Data rate versus
capacity.

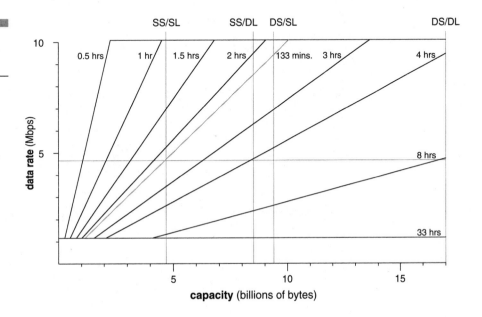

TABLE A.6

Physical
Characteristics
of DVD

Thickness	1.2 mm (+0.3/−0.06) (2 bonded substrates)
Substrate thickness	0.6 mm (+0.043/−0.030)
Spacing layer thickness	55 μm (±15)
Mass (12 cm)	13 to 20 g
Mass (8 cm)	6 to 9 g
Diameter	120 or 80 mm (±0.30)
Spindle hole diameter	15 mm (+0.15/−0.0)
Clamping area diameter	22 to 33 mm
Inner guardband diameter	33 to 44 mm
Burst cutting area diameter	44.6 (±0.8) to 47 (±0.10) mm
Lead-in diameter	45.2 to 48 mm
Data diameter (12 cm)	48 (+0/−0.4 mm) to 116 mm
Data diameter (8 cm)	48 to 76 mm
Lead-out diameter	70 to 117 mm (approximately 2 mm wide, 1 mm min.)
Outer guardband diameter	117 to 120 mm or 77 to 80 mm
Reflectivity	45 to 85% (SL), 18 to 30% (DL)[*]
Readout wavelength	650 or 635 nm (red laser)
Polarization	Circular
Numerical aperture	0.60 (objective lens)
Optical spot diameter	0.58 to 0.60 μm
Refractive index	1.55 (±0.10)
Tilt margin (radial)	±0.8°
Track spiral (outer layer)	Clockwise
Track spiral (inner layer)	Clockwise or counterclockwise
Track pitch	0.74 μm (±0.01 avg.)
Pit length	0.400 to 1.866 μm (SL), 0.440 to 2.054 μm (DL)
Data bit length (avg.)	0.2667 μm (SL), 0.2934 μm (DL)
Channel bit length (avg.)	0.1333 μm (SL), 0.1467 μm (DL)
Correctable burst error	6.0 mm (SL), 6.5 mm (DL)
Maximum local defects	100 μm (air bubble), 200 μm (black spot)
Rotation	Counterclockwise (to readout surface)
Rotational velocity[†]	570 to 1630 rpm (574 to 1528 rpm in data area)
Scanning velocity[†]	3.49 m/s (SL), 3.84 m/s (DL) (±0.03)
Environmental temperature	−25 to 70°C

[*]SL = single layer, DL = dual layer.
[†]Reference value for a single-speed drive.

TABLE A.7

DVD and CD
Characteristics
Comparison

	DVD	CD
Thickness	1.2 mm (2 × 0.6)	1.2 mm
Mass (12 cm)	13 to 20 g	14 to 33 g
Diameter	120 or 80 mm	120 or 80 mm
Spindle hole diameter	15 mm	15 mm
Lead-in diameter	45.2 to 48 mm	46 to 50 mm
Data diameter (12 cm)	48 to 116 mm	50 to 116 mm
Data diameter (8 cm)	48 to 76 mm	50 to 76 mm
Lead-out diameter	70 to 117 mm	76 to 117 mm
Outer guardband diameter (12 cm)	117 to 120 mm	117 to 120 mm
Outer guardband diameter (8 cm)	77 to 80 mm	77 to 80 mm
Reflectivity (full)	45 to 85 percent	70 percent minimum
Readout wavelength	650 or 635 nm	780 nm
Numerical aperture	0.60	0.38 to 0.45
Focus depth	0.47	1
Track pitch	0.74 μm	1.6 μm
Pit length	0.400 to 1.866 μm (SL),* 0.440 to 2.054 μm (DL)	0.833 to 3.054 μm (1.2 m/s), 0.972 to 3.560 μm (1.4 m/s)
Data bit length	0.2667 μm (SL), 0.2934 μm (DL)	0.6 μm (1.2 m/s), 0.7 μm (1.4 m/s)
Channel bit length	0.1333 μm (SL), 0.1467 μm (DL)	0.3 μm
Modulation	8/16	8/14 (8/17 with merge bits)
Error correction	RS-PC	CIRC
Error correction overhead	13 percent	23/34 percent‡
Correctable error (1 layer)	6 mm (SL), 6.5 mm (DL)	2.5 mm
Speed (rotational)†	570 to 1600 rpm	200 to 500 rpm
Speed (scanning)†	3.49 m/s (SL), 3.84 m/s (DL)	1.2 to 1.4 m/s
Channel data rate†	26.16 Mbps	4.3218 Mbps
User data rate†	11.08 Mbps	1.41/1.23 Mbps‡
User data:channel data	2048:4836 bytes	2352:7203/2048:7203‡
Format overhead	136 percent	206/252 percent‡
Capacity	1.4 to 8.0 GB per side	0.783/0.635 GB‡

*SL = single layer, DL = dual layer.

†Reference value for a single-speed drive.

‡CD-DA/CD-ROM Mode 1. Nominal 74 minutes (333,000 sectors).

TABLE A.8

Comparison of
MMCD, SD,
and DVD

	MMCD	SD	DVD
Diameter	120 mm	120 mm	120 mm
Thickness	1.2 mm	2×0.6 mm	1.2 mm
Sides	1	1 or 2	1 or 2
Layers	1 or 2	1 or 2	1 or 2
Data area (diameter)	46–116 mm	48–116 mm	48–116 mm
Minimum pit length	0.451 μm	0.400 μm	0.400 μm
Track pitch	0.84 μm	0.74 μm	0.74 μm
Scanning velocity	4.0 m/s	3.27 m/s	3.49 m/s
Laser wavelength	635 nm	650 nm	650 or 635 nm
Numerical aperture	0.52	0.60	0.60
Modulation	8/16	8/15	8/16
Channel data rate	26.6 Mbps	24.54 Mbps	26.16 Mbps
Maximum user data rate	11.2 Mbps	10.08 Mbps	11.08 Mbps
Average user data rate	3.7 Mbps	4.7 Mbps	4.7 Mbps
Capacity (single layer)	3.7 billion bytes	5.0 billion bytes	4.7 billion bytes
Capacity (dual layer)	7.4 billion bytes	9.0 billion bytes	8.54 billion bytes
Sector size	2048 bytes	2048 bytes	2048 bytes
Error correction	CIRC+	RS-PC	RS-PC
Stated playing time	135 minutes	140 minutes	133 minutes
Video encoding	MPEG-2 VBR	MPEG-2 VBR	MPEG-2 VBR
Audio encoding	MPEG-2 Layer II	AC-3	AC-3, MPEG-2, PCM, etc.

TABLE A.9

Data Storage
Characteristics
of DVD

Modulation	8/16 (EFMPlus)
Sector size (user data)	2048 bytes
Logical sector size	2064 bytes (2048 + 12 header + 4 EDC)
Recording sector size	2366 bytes (2064 + 302 ECC)
Unmodulated physical sector	2418 bytes (2366 + 52 sync)
Physical sector size	4836 (2418 × 2 modulation)
Error correction	Reed-Solomon product code (208,192,17) × (182,172,11)
Error correction overhead	15% (13% of recording sector: 308/2366)
ECC block size	16 sectors (32,768 bytes user data, 37,856 bytes total)
Format overhead	16% (37,856/32,768)
Maximum random error	≤280 in 8 ECC blocks
Channel data rate*	26.16 Mbps
User data rate*	11.08 Mbps
Capacity (per side, 12 cm)	4.38 to 7.95 gigabytes (4.70 to 8.54 billion bytes)
Capacity (per side, 8 cm)	1.36 to 2.48 gigabytes (1.46 to 2.66 billion bytes)

*Reference value for a single-speed drive.

TABLE A.10

DVD-Video Physical
Data Units

Unit	Maximum
Video Title Set (VTS)	99 per disc
Video Object Set (VOBS)	99 per VTS
Video Object (VOB)	
Cell	
Video Object Unit (VOBU)	
Pack (PCK)	
Packet (PKT)	

TABLE A.11

DVD-Video Logical
(Presentation) Data
Units

Unit	Maximum
Title	99 per disc
Program chain (PGC)	999 per title, 16 per parental block
Part of title (PTT)	999 per title
Program (PG)	99 per PGC
Cell pointer	255 per PGC

TABLE A.12

DVD-Video Format

Multiplexed data rate	Up to 10.08 Mbps
Video data	1 stream
Video data rate	Up to 9.8 Mbps (typical average 3.5)
TV system	525/60 (NTSC) or 625/50 (PAL)
Video coding	MPEG-2 MP@ML/SP@ML VBR/CBR or MPEG-1 VBR/CBR
Coded frame rate	24 fps* (film), 29.97 fps† (525/60), 25 fps† (625/50)
Display frame rate	29.97 fps† (525/60), 25 fps† (625/50)
MPEG-2 resolution	720×480, 704×480, 352×480 (525/60); 720×576, 704×576, 352×576 (625/50)
MPEG-1 resolution	352×240 (525/60); 352×288 (625/50)
MPEG-2 GOP maximum	36 fields (525/60), 30 fields (625/50)
MPEG-1 GOP maximum	18 frames (525/60), 15 frames (625/50)
Aspect ratio	4:3 or 16:9 anamorphic‡

*Progressive (decoder performs 3-2 or 2-2 pulldown).
†Interlaced (59.94 or 50 fields per second).
‡Anamorphic only allowed for 720 and 704 resolutions.

TABLE A.13

Dolby Digital Audio

Sample frequency	48 kHz
Sample size	Up to 20 bits
Bitrate	64 to 448 kbps, 384 typical
Channels (front/rear)*	1/0, 2/0, 3/0, 2/1, 2/2, 3/1, 3/2
Karaoke modes	L/R, M, V1, V2

*LFE channel can be added to all variations.

TABLE A.14

MPEG Audio

Sample frequency	48 kHz only
Sample size	Up to 20 bits
MPEG-1	Layer II only
MPEG-1 bitrate	64 to 192 kbps (mono), 64 to 384 kbps (stereo)
MPEG-2	BC (matrix) mode only
MPEG-2 bitrate[*]	64 to 912 kbps
Extension streams[†]	5.1-channel, 7.1-channel
Channels (front/rear)[‡]	1/0, 2/0, 2/1, 2/2, 3/0, 3/1, 3/2, 5/2
Karaoke channels	L, R, A1, A2, G

[*]MPEG-1 Layer II stream + extension stream(s).
[†]AAC (unmatrix, NBC) not allowed.
[‡]LFE channel can be added to all variations.

TABLE A.15

PCM Audio

Sample frequency	48 or 96 kHz
Sample size	16, 20, or 24 bits
Channels	1, 2, 3, 4, 5, 6, 7, or 8
Karaoke channels	L, R, V1, V2, G

TABLE A.16

Subpicture

Data	0 to 32 streams
Data rate	Up to 3.36 Mbps
Unit size	53,220 bytes (up to 32,000 bytes of control data)
Coding	RLE (maximum 1440 bits/line)
Resolution[*]	Up to 720×478 (525/60) or 720×573 (625/50)
Bits per pixel	2 (defining one of 4 types)
Pixel types	Background, foreground, emphasis-1, emphasis-2
Colors[*]	4 out of 16 (from 4-bit palette,[†] one per type)
Contrasts[*]	4 out of 16[†] (one per type)

[*]Area, content, color, and contrast can be changed for each field.
[†]Color palette and contrast can be changed every PGC.

TABLE A.17
Video Resolution Chart

Format		VHS (1.33)	VHS (1.78)	VHS (2.35)	LD (1.33)	LD (1.78)	LD (1.85)	LD (2.35)	VCD (1.33)	VCD (1.78)	VCD (2.35)
NTSC	TVL	250	250	250	425	425	425	425	264	264	264
	H pixels	333	333	333	567	567	567	567	352	352	352
	V pixels	480	360	272	480	360	346	272	240	180	136
	Total pixels	159,840	119,880	90,576	272,160	204,120	196,182	154,224	84,480	63,360	47,872
PAL	TVL	240	240	240	450	450	450	450	264	264	264
	H pixels	320	320	320	600	600	600	600	352	352	352
	V pixels	576	432	327	576	432	415	327	288	216	163
	Total pixels	184,320	138,240	104,640	345,600	259,200	249,000	196,200	101,376	76,032	57,376

Format		DVD (1.33/1.78)	DVD (1.85)	DVD (2.35)	DTV3 (1.33)	DTV3 (1.78)	DTV3 (2.35)	DTV4 (1.78)	DTV4 (2.35)
NTSC	TVL	540/405	540/405	540/405	720	720	720	1080	1080
	H pixels	720	720	720	1280	1280	1280	1920	1920
	V pixels	480	461	363	960	720	545	1080	817
	Total pixels	345,600	331,920	261,360	1,228,800	921,600	697,600	2,073,600	1,568,640
PAL	TVL	540	540	720					
	H pixels	720	720	720					
	V pixels	576	554	436					
	Total pixels	414,720	398,880	313,920					

NOTES:
1. DTV is neither PAL nor NTSC. The values are placed in the NTSC rows for convenience.

2. Wide aspect ratios (1.78 and 2.35) for VHS, LD, and VCD assume letterbox. For comparison, letterboxed 1.66 aspect ratio resolution is about 7 percent higher than 1.78. Letterbox is also assumed for DVD and DTV at 2.35 aspect ratio. DVD's native aspect ratio is 1.33; it uses anamorphic mode for 1.78. DTV's native aspect ratio is 1.78.

3. The very rare 1.78 anamorphic LD has the same pixel count as 1.33 LD. Anamorphic LD letterboxed to 2.35 has almost the same pixel count as 1.78 LD (567×363). The mostly nonexistent 1.78 anamorphic VHS has the same pixel count as 1.33 VHS. Anamorphic VHS letterboxed to 2.35 has almost the same pixel count as 1.78 VHS (333×363). There is no commercial 2.35 anamorphic format and no corresponding stretch mode on widescreen TVs.

4. TVL is lines of horizontal resolution per picture height. For analog formats, the customary value is used; for digital formats, it's derived from the actual horizontal pixel count adjusted for aspect ratio. DVD's horizontal resolution is lower for 1.78, since the pixels are wider. "Pixels" for VHS and LD are approximations based on TVL and scan lines.

5. Resolutions refer to the medium, not the display. If a DVD player performs automatic letterboxing on a 1.85 movie (stored in 1.78) the displayed vertical resolution on a standard 1.33 TV is the same as from a letterboxed LD (360 lines).

TABLE A.18

Video Resolution Comparison Chart

Format	VCD* (16:9)	VCD (4:3)	VHS* (16:9)	VHS (4:3)	LD* (16:9)	LD (4:3)	DVD (16:9/4:3)	DTV3 (16:9)	DTV4 (16:9)
Horizontal pixels	352	352	333	333	567	567	720	1280	1920
Vertical pixels	180	240	360	480	360	480	480	720	1080
Total pixels	63,360	84,480	119,880	159,840	204,120	272,160	345,600	921,600	2,073,600
× VCD (16:9)‡		*1.33†*	1.89	2.52	3.22	*4.30*	5.45	14.55	*32.73*
× VCD (4:3)			*1.42*	1.89	2.42	3.22	4.09	*10.91*	*24.55*
× VHS (16:9)				*1.33*	1.70	2.27	2.88	7.69	*17.30*
× VHS (4:3)					*1.28*	1.70	2.16	*5.77*	*12.97*
× LD (16:9)						*1.33*	1.69	4.51	10.16
× LD (4:3)							1.27	*3.39*	*7.62*
× DVD (16:9/4:3)								2.67	6.00
× DTV3 (16:9)									2.25

*16:9 aspect ratios for VHS, LD, and VCD are letterboxed in a 4:3 picture.

†Comparisons between different aspect ratios are not as meaningful. These are shown in *italics*.

‡Comparisons at 1.85 or 2.35 aspect ratios are essentially the same as at 16:9 (1.78).

TABLE A.19

Compatibility Chart

Disc	DVD-Video player	DVD-ROM drive	DVD/LD player	LD player	CD player	CD-ROM drive	Video CD player
DVD-Video	Yes	Depends[a]	Yes	No	No	No	No
DVD-ROM[b]	No	Yes	No	No	No	No	No
LD	No	No	Yes	Yes	No	No	No
Audio CD	Yes	Yes	Yes	Yes[c]	Yes	Yes	Yes
CD-ROM[d]	No	Yes	No	No	No	Yes	No
CD-R[e]	Few[f]	Some[f]	Few[f]	Yes[c]	Yes	Yes	Yes
CD-RW[e]	Yes	Yes	Yes	No	No	Some[g]	No
CDV	Part[h]	Part[h]	Usually[c]	Usually[c]	Part[h]	Part[h]	Part[h]
Video CD	Some[i]	Depends[a]	Some[i]	No	No	Depends[a]	Yes
Photo CD	No	Depends[f,j]	No	No	No	Depends[j]	No
CD-i	No	Depends[k]	No	No	No	Depends[k]	No

[a]Computer requires hardware or software to decode and display audio/video.

[b]DVD-ROM containing data other than standard DVD-Video files.

[c]Most newer LD players can play audio from a CD and both audio and video from a CDV.

[d]CD-ROM containing data other than standard CD digital audio.

[e]Containing CD digital audio data.

[f]DVD units require an additional laser tuned for CD-R readout wavelength.

[g]Only new MultiRead CD-ROM drives can read CD-RW discs.

[h]CD digital audio part of disc only (no video).

[i]Not all DVD players can play Video CDs.

[j]Computer requires software to read and display Photo CD graphic files.

[k]Computer requires hardware or emulation software to run CD-i programs.

TABLE A.20

ISO 639 Language Codes

aa	Afar	ga	Irish	mg	Malagasy	sl	Slovenian
ab	Abkhazian	gd	Scots Gaelic	mi	Maori	sm	Samoan
af	Afrikaans	gl	Galician	mk	Macedonian	sn	Shona
am	Amharic	gn	Guarani	ml	Malayalam	so	Somali
ar	Arabic	gu	Gujarati	mn	Mongolian	sq	Albanian
as	Assamese	ha	Hausa	mo	Moldavian	sr	Serbian
ay	Aymara	hi	Hindi	mr	Marathi	ss	Siswati
az	Azerbaijani	hr	Croatian	ms	Malay	st	Sesotho
ba	Bashkir	hu	Hungarian	mt	Maltese	su	Sudanese
be	Byelorussian	hy	Armenian	my	Burmese	sv	Swedish
bg	Bulgarian	ia	Interlingua	na	Nauru	sw	Swahili
bh	Bihari	ie	Interlingue	ne	Nepali	ta	Tamil
bi	Bislama	ik	Inupiak	nl	Dutch	te	Telugu
bn	Bengali; Bangla	in	Indonesian	no	Norwegian	tg	Tajik
bo	Tibetan	is	Icelandic	oc	Occitan	th	Thai
br	Breton	it	Italian	om	(Afan) Oromo	ti	Tigrinya
ca	Catalan	iw	Hebrew	or	Oriya	tk	Turkmen
co	Corsican	ja	Japanese	pa	Punjabi	tl	Tagalog
cs	Czech	ji	Yiddish	pl	Polish	tn	Setswana
cy	Welsh	jw	Javanese	ps	Pashto, Pushto	to	Tonga
da	Danish	ka	Georgian			tr	Turkish
de	German	kk	Kazakh	pt	Portuguese	ts	Tsonga
dz	Bhutani	kl	Greenlandic	qu	Quechua	tt	Tatar
el	Greek	km	Cambodian	rm	Rhaeto-Romance	tw	Twi
en	English	kn	Kannada	rn	Kirundi	uk	Ukrainian
eo	Esperanto	ko	Korean	ro	Romanian	ur	Urdu
es	Spanish	ks	Kashmiri	ru	Russian	uz	Uzbek
et	Estonian	ku	Kurdish	rw	Kinyarwanda	vi	Vietnamese
eu	Basque	ky	Kirghiz	sa	Sanskrit	vo	Volapuk
fa	Persian	la	Latin	sd	Sindhi	wo	Wolof
fi	Finnish	ln	Lingala	sg	Sangro	xh	Xhosa
fj	Fiji	lo	Laothian	sh	Serbo-Croatian	yo	Yoruba
fo	Faeroese	lt	Lithuanian	si	Singhalese	zh	Chinese
fr	French	lv	Latvian, Lettish	sk	Slovak	zu	Zulu
fy	Frisian						

TABLE A.21

ISO 3116 Country
Codes and
DVD Regions

Country	ISO codes		DVD region	Country	ISO codes		DVD region
Afghanistan	AF	AFG	004	5	Brazil	BR	BRA	076	4
Albania	AL	ALB	008	2	British Indian Ocean Territory	IO	IOT	086	5
Algeria	DZ	DZA	012	5					
American Samoa	AS	ASM	016	1	Brunei Darussalam	BN	BRN	096	3
Andorra	AD	AND	020	2	Bulgaria	BG	BGR	100	2
Angola	AO	AGO	024	5	Burkina Faso	BF	BFA	854	5
Anguilla	AI	AIA	660	4	Burundi	BI	BDI	108	5
Antarctica	AQ	ATA	010		Cambodia	KH	KHM	116	3
Antigua and Barbuda	AG	ATG	028	4	Cameroon	CM	CMR	120	5
					Canada	CA	CAN	124	1
Argentina	AR	ARG	032	4	Cape Verde	CV	CPV	132	5
Armenia	AM	ARM	051	5	Cayman Islands	KY	CYM	136	4
Aruba	AW	ABW	533	4					
Australia	AU	AUS	036	4	Central African Republic	CF	CAF	140	5
Austria	AT	AUT	040	2					
Azerbaijan	AZ	AZE	031	5	Chad	TD	TCD	148	5
Bahamas	BS	BHS	044	4	Chile	CL	CHL	152	4
Bahrain	BH	BHR	048	2	China	CN	CHN	156	6
Bangladesh	BD	BGD	050	5	Christmas Island	CX	CXR	162	4
Barbados	BB	BRB	052	4	Cocos (Keeling) Islands	CC	CCK	166	4
Belarus	BY	BLR	112	5					
Belgium	BE	BEL	056	2	Colombia	CO	COL	170	4
Belize	BZ	BLZ	084	4	Comoros	KM	COM	174	5
Benin	BJ	BEN	204	5	Congo	CG	COG	178	5
Bermuda	BM	BMU	060	1	Cook Islands	CK	COK	184	4
Bhutan	BT	BTN	064	5	Costa Rica	CR	CRI	188	4
Bolivia	BO	BOL	068	4	Côte d'Ivoire	CI	CIV	384	5
Bosnia and Herzegowina	BA	BIH	070	2	Croatia (Hrvatska)	HR	HRV	191	2
Botswana	BW	BWA	072	5	Cuba	CU	CUB	192	4
Bouvet Island	BV	BVT	074		Cyprus	CY	CYP	196	2

TABLE A.21
(Continued)

Country	ISO codes			DVD region	Country	ISO codes			DVD region
Czech Republic	CZ	CZE	203	2	Ghana	GH	GHA	288	5
Denmark	DK	DNK	208	2	Gibraltar	GI	GIB	292	2
Djibouti	DJ	DJI	262	5	Greece	GR	GRC	300	2
Dominica	DM	DMA	212	4	Greenland	GL	GRL	304	2
Dominican Republic	DO	DOM	214	4	Grenada	GD	GRD	308	4
					Guadeloupe	GP	GLP	312	4
East Timor	TP	TMP	626	3	Guam	GU	GUM	316	4
Ecuador	EC	ECU	218	4	Guatemala	GT	GTM	320	4
Egypt	EG	EGY	818	2	Guinea	GN	GIN	324	5
El Salvador	SV	SLV	222	4	Guinea-Bissau	GW	GNB	624	5
Equatorial Guinea	GQ	GNQ	226	5	Guyana	GY	GUY	328	4
Eritrea	ER	ERI	232	5	Haiti	HT	HTI	332	4
Estonia	EE	EST	233	5	Heard and McDonald Islands	HM	HMD	334	4
Ethiopia	ET	ETH	231	5					
Falkland Islands (Malvinas)	FK	FLK	238	4	Holy See (Vatican City State)	VA	VAT	336	2
Faroe Islands	FO	FRO	234	2	Honduras	HN	HND	340	4
Fiji	FJ	FJI	242	4	Hong Kong	HK	HKG	344	3
Finland	FI	FIN	246	2	Hungary	HU	HUN	348	2
France	FR	FRA	250	2	Iceland	IS	ISL	352	2
France, Metropolitan	FX	FXX	249	4	India	IN	IND	356	5
French Guiana	GF	GUF	254	4	Indonesia	ID	IDN	360	3
French Polynesia	PF	PYF	258	4	Iran (Islamic Republic of)	IR	IRN	364	2
French Southern Territories	TF	ATF	260		Iraq	IQ	IRQ	368	2
					Ireland	IE	IRL	372	2
					Israel	IL	ISR	376	2
Gabon	GA	GAB	266	5	Italy	IT	ITA	380	2
Gambia	GM	GMB	270	5	Jamaica	JM	JAM	388	4
Georgia	GE	GEO	268	5	Japan	JP	JPN	392	2
Germany	DE	DEU	276	2	Jordan	JO	JOR	400	2

TABLE A.21
(Continued)

Country	ISO codes		DVD region	Country	ISO codes		DVD region
Kazakhstan	KZ	KAZ	398	5	Martinique	MQ	MTQ	474	4
Kenya	KE	KEN	404	5	Mauritania	MR	MRT	478	5
Kiribati	KI	KIR	296	4	Mauritius	MU	MUS	480	5
Korea (North), Democratic People's Republic of	KP	PRK	408	5	Mayotte	YT	MYT	175	5
					Mexico	MX	MEX	484	4
					Micronesia	FM	FSM	583	4
Korea (South), Republic of	KR	KOR	410	3	Moldova	MD	MDA	498	5
Kuwait	KW	KWT	414	2	Monaco	MC	MCO	492	2
Kyrgyzstan	KG	KGZ	417	5	Mongolia	MN	MNG	496	5
Lao People's Democratic Republic	LA	LAO	418	3	Montserrat	MS	MSR	500	4
					Morocco	MA	MAR	504	5
Latvia	LV	LVA	428	5	Mozambique	MZ	MOZ	508	5
Lebanon	LB	LBN	422	2	Myanmar (Burma)	MM	MMR	104	3
Lesotho	LS	LSO	426	2	Namibia	NA	NAM	516	5
Liberia	LR	LBR	430	5					
Libyan Arab Jamahiriya	LY	LBY	434	5	Nauru	NR	NRU	520	4
					Nepal	NP	NPL	524	5
Liechtenstein	LI	LIE	438	2	Netherlands	NL	NLD	528	2
Lithuania	LT	LTU	440	5	Netherlands Antilles	AN	ANT	530	4
Luxembourg	LU	LUX	442	2	New Caledonia	NC	NCL	540	4
Macau	MO	MAC	446	3					
Macedonia, the Former Yugoslav Republic of	MK	MKD	807	2	New Zealand	NZ	NZL	554	4
					Nicaragua	NI	NIC	558	4
					Niger	NE	NER	562	5
Madagascar	MG	MDG	450	5	Nigeria	NG	NGA	566	5
Malawi	MW	MWI	454	5	Niue	NU	NIU	570	4
Malaysia	MY	MYS	458	3	Norfolk Island	NF	NFK	574	4
Maldives	MV	MDV	462	5	Northern Mariana Islands	MP	MNP	580	4
Mali	ML	MLI	466	5					
Malta	MT	MLT	470	2	Norway	NO	NOR	578	2
Marshall Islands	MH	MHL	584	4	Oman	OM	OMN	512	2

TABLE A.21
(Continued)

Country	ISO codes		DVD region	Country	ISO codes		DVD region
Pakistan	PK	PAK	586	5	Singapore	SG	SGP	702	3
Palau	PW	PLW	585	4	Slovakia (Slovak Republic)	SK	SVK	703	2
Panama	PA	PAN	591	4					
Papua New Guinea	PG	PNG	598	4	Slovenia	SI	SVN	705	2
					Solomon Islands	SB	SLB	090	4
Paraguay	PY	PRY	600	4					
Peru	PE	PER	604	4	Somalia	SO	SOM	706	5
Philippines	PH	PHL	608	3	South Africa	ZA	ZAF	710	2
Pitcairn	PN	PCN	612	4	South Georgia and the South Sandwich Islands	GS	SGS	239	4
Poland	PL	POL	616	2					
Portugal	PT	PRT	620	2	Spain	ES	ESP	724	2
Puerto Rico	PR	PRI	630	1	Sri Lanka	LK	LKA	144	5
Qatar	QA	QAT	634	2	St. Helena	SH	SHN	654	5
Réunion	RE	REU	638	5	St. Pierre and Miquelon	PM	SPM	666	1
Romania	RO	ROM	642	2					
Russian Federation	RU	RUS	643	5	Sudan	SD	SDN	736	5
					Suriname	SR	SUR	740	4
Rwanda	RW	RWA	646	5	Svalbard and Jan Mayen Islands	SJ	SJM	744	2
Saint Kitts and Nevis	KN	KNA	659	4					
					Swaziland	SZ	SWZ	748	2
Saint Lucia	LC	LCA	662	4	Sweden	SE	SWE	752	2
Saint Vincent and the Grenadines	VC	VCT	670	4	Switzerland	CH	CHE	756	2
					Syrian Arab Republic	SY	SYR	760	2
Samoa	WS	WSM	882	4					
San Marino	SM	SMR	674	2	Taiwan	TW	TWN	158	3
São Tomé and Príncipe	ST	STP	678	5	Tajikistan	TJ	TJK	762	5
					Tanzania	TZ	TZA	834	5
Saudi Arabia	SA	SAU	682	2	Thailand	TH	THA	764	3
Senegal	SN	SEN	686	5	Togo	TG	TGO	768	5
Seychelles	SC	SYC	690	5	Tokelau	TK	TKL	772	4
Sierra Leone	SL	SLE	694	5	Tonga	TO	TON	776	4

TABLE A.21
(Continued)

Country	ISO codes			DVD region	Country	ISO codes			DVD region
Trinidad and Tobago	TT	TTO	780	4	Uzbekistan	UZ	UZB	860	5
Tunisia	TN	TUN	788	5	Vanuatu	VU	VUT	548	4
Turkey	TR	TUR	792	2	Venezuela	VE	VEN	862	4
Turkmenistan	TM	TKM	795	5	Viet Nam	VN	VNM	704	3
Turks and Caicos Islands	TC	TCA	796	4	Virgin Islands (British)	VG	VGB	092	4
Tuvalu	TV	TUV	798	4	Virgin Islands (U.S.)	VI	VIR	850	1
Uganda	UG	UGA	800	5					
Ukraine	UA	UKR	804	5	Wallis and Futuna Islands	WF	WLF	876	4
United Arab Emirates	AE	ARE	784	2	Western Sahara	EH	ESH	732	5
United Kingdom	GB	GBR	826	2	Yemen	YE	YEM	887	2
United States	US	USA	840	1	Yugoslavia	YU	YUG	891	2
United States Minor Out-lying Islands	UM	UMI	581	1	Zaire	ZR	ZAR	180	5
					Zambia	ZM	ZMB	894	5
Uruguay	UY	URY	858	4	Zimbabwe	ZW	ZWE	716	5

APPENDIX B

Companies and Resources

The following companies provide DVD-related products or services. Industry organizations are also listed. This is by no means an exhaustive list, but includes most companies which are directly involved with DVD technology. Stock symbols are included for readers interested in investing in DVD companies.

* = One of the 10 founding members of the DVD Forum.

Manufacturers

Akai

DVD-Video players

www.akai.com, www.semi-tech.com

Akai is a subsidiary of the Semi-Tech Group, a major worldwide manufacturer and distributor of electronic and other products for the home and digital equipment for professional musicians. Akai's research and development operations are located primarily in Japan, and its manufacturing facilities are based primarily in other Asian countries.

Akai Electric Company, Ltd.
12—14, Higashi-Kojiya 2-chome, Ohta-ku
Tokyo 144, Japan
81-3-3745-9697, 81-3-3745-9880, (fax) 81-3-3745-9560
TOKYO:6802

Alpine

DVD-ROM car navigation system
Alpine Electronics of America, Inc.
19145 Gramercy Place
Torrance, CA 90501
310-326-8000, (fax) 310-533-0369

Altec Lansing

DVD-ROM car navigation system
www.altecmm.com
RR 6 Box 209
Milford, PA 18337-9807
717-296-6444, 800-648-6663, (fax) 717-296-1222

ATI
Decoding and display hardware
www.atitech.com

ATI Technologies, one of the largest suppliers of 3D graphics and multimedia technology in the world, designs, manufactures, and markets multimedia solutions and graphics components for personal computers. Founded in 1985, ATI employs more than 800 people at headquarters in Thornhill, Ontario, with offices in the United States, Germany, France, the United Kingdom, Ireland, and Japan.

ATI Technologies, Inc.
3761 Victoria Park Ave.
Carborough, Ontario M1W 3S2, Canada
416-756-0718, (fax) 416-756-0720
TOR:ATY

Axis
DVD-ROM jukebox servers
www.axis.com

Axis Communications is a leading provider of network and Web appliances, including CD-ROM and DVD-ROM jukebox servers. Founded in 1984 in Lund, Sweden, Axis employs 200 people.

Axis Communications, Inc.
4 Constitution Way
Woburn, MA 01801
800-444-AXIS, (fax) 617-938-6161

Brandt
See Thomson.

C-Cube
Encoder and decoder hardware
www.c-cube.com, info@c-cube.com

C-Cube Microsystems is an industry leader in the development and delivery of highly integrated digital video silicon solutions that address the consumer electronics, communications, and convergence markets. C-Cube is headquartered in Milpitas, California, with offices in North America, Europe, and Asia.

C-Cube Microsystems, Inc.
1778 McCarthy Blvd.
Milpitas, CA 95035
408-944-6300, (fax) 408-944-6314
NASDAQ: CUBE

Chartered Electronics Industries (CEI)
Playback hardware
210A Twin Dolphin Drive
Redwood City, CA 94065
415-591-6617, (fax) 415-591-8310

Chips and Technologies
Encoder, decoder, and display hardware
www.chips.com
Chips and Technologies develops semiconductor and software products including enhanced graphics, full-motion video, and other advanced display solutions for notebook and desktop computers.
2950 Zanker Rd.
San Jose, CA 95134
408-434-0600, fax 408-894-2082
NASDAQ: CHPS

Cirrus Logic, Inc.
Decoding and display hardware
www.cirrus.com
3100 West Warren Avenue
Fremont, CA 94539-6423
510-623-8300
NASDAQ: CRUS

Clarion
DVD-ROM car navigation system
www.clarionmultimedia.com
Leading supplier of audio systems and car multimedia to automobile manufacturers.
661 W. Redondo Beach Blvd.
Gardena, CA 90247
310-327-9100, (fax) 310-327-1999

CompCore
Decoding hardware and software, DVD-Video playback software
www.compcore.com
CompCore Multimedia is a subsidiary of Zoran.
3120 Scott Boulevard, 2d Floor
Santa Clara, CA 95054
408-567-0552, (fax) 408-567-0586

Creative Labs

DVD-ROM upgrade kits, audio and video hardware

www.creaf.com

Creative Technology is a leading maker of audio cards and multimedia upgrade kits, including the industry-standard Sound Blaster audio card series.

1901 McCarthy Boulevard
Milpitas, CA 95035
408-428-660, 800-998-5227, (fax) 408-432-6706
NASDAQ:CREAF

Denon

DVD-Video players

www.denon.com

Denon Electronics
222 New Road
Parsippany, NJ 07054
201-575-7810, (fax) 201-808-1608

Diamond

DVD-ROM upgrade kit

www.diamondmm.com

Diamond Multimedia Systems, Inc.
2880 Junction Avenue
San Jose, CA 95134-1922
408-325-7000, 800-468-5846, (fax) 408-325-7070
NASDAQ: DIMD

DynaTek

DVD-ROM servers

www.dynatek.ca, info@raider.dynatek.ca

Founded in 1988, DynaTek Automation Systems is a wholly owned Canadian company experienced in the development and production of high-capacity, secure information storage and retrieval systems. The head office is located in Bedford, Nova Scotia, with sales and distribution offices across Canada, the United Kingdom, and Israel.

902-832-3000

E4

www.elecede.com, info@elecede.com

E4 is a developer of video and graphics products for the PC and Macintosh. The company is a wholly owned subsidiary of Dooin Electronics, Korea's leading manufacturer of PC cards.

1731 Technology Drive, Suite 800
San Jose, CA 95110
408-441-6060, (fax) 408-441-6070

Envisioneering
3864 Bayberry Lane,
Seaford, NY 11783-1503
516-783-6244, fax 516-679-8167

Faroudja
DVD-Video players, video processors
www.faroudja.com
Faroudja Laboratories produces high-end video-processing equipment for professional broadcast and consumer markets. Founded in 1971, the company holds more then 60 patents in the field of video processing, including S-VHS.
750 Palomar Ave
Sunnyvale, CA 94086
408-735-1492, (fax) 408-735-8571

Ferguson
See Thomson.

Fisher
DVD-Video players
See also Sanyo.
www.audvidfisher.com

GE
See Thomson.

GoldStar
See LG Electronics.

Harman International (Harman Kardon/Infinity/JBL/...)
DVD-Video players
www.harman.com, www.harmankardon.com
Harman International is a leader in the design, manufacture, and marketing of a full range of consumer and professional audio products under the brands BSS, DOD, Harman Kardon, Infinity, JBL, Lexicon, Mark Levinson, Soundcraft, Studer, and others.
NYSE: HAR

HEURIS
Audio- and video-encoding systems
www.heuris.com
HEURIS provides video compression products and services for the interactive digital video marketplace.
2675 Scott Avenue, Suite G
St. Louis, MO 63103
314-534-1514, 800-923-9232, (fax) 314-534-4351

Hi-Val
DVD-ROM upgrade kits
www.hival.com
Hi-Val offers a wide range of multimedia solutions by combining DVD-ROM drives and CD-ROM drives with sound cards and software. Hi-Val also sells CD-recorders, CD changers, graphics accelerators, and wireless products.
Santa Ana, CA
714-953-3000

Hitachi*
DVD-Video players, DVD drives
www.hitachi.com, 800-448-2244
Hitachi, headquartered in Tokyo, is the world's leading electronics company. The company markets and manufactures a wide range of products, including computers, displays, telephones, semiconductors, RAM, consumer products, home appliances, elevators, industrial robots, industrial equipment, and industrial supplies

Hitachi Home Electronics
3890 Steve Reynolds Blvd.
Norcross, GA 30093
404-279-5600, (fax) 404-279-5699

Hitachi America, Ltd.
401 West Artesia Boulevard
Compton, CA 90220
213-605-2542, (fax) 213-515-6223

Hitachi America, Inc.
110 Summit Ave.
Montvale, NJ 07645
201-573-0774

Hitachi, Ltd.
American Business Development Department

6, Kanda Surugadai 4-chome
Chiyoda-ku
Tokyo 101, Japan
81-3-3258-2280, (fax) 81-3-3258-2104
NYSE:HIT

Hyundai
DVD-Video players
www.hea.com
Established in 1983, Hyundai Electronics America (HEA) is a U.S. subsidiary of Hyundai Electronics Industries Company, (HEI), part of Hyundai Business Group, one of the largest business groups in Korea. HEA develops, sells, markets, and distributes a wide variety of electronic devices, including semiconductors, mass storage systems, computer systems, liquid crystal displays, monitors, multimedia and digital video systems, and communications systems. Hyundai Business Group and Hyundai Electronics America are privately held companies. HEI completed a public offering in December 1996.

Hyundai Electronics America
3101 North First St.
San Jose, CA 95134
408-232-8000

IBM Microelectronics
Encoder and decoder hardware
www.chips.ibm.com
One of the top computer companies, IBM produces mainframes, minicomputers, microcomputers, peripherals, operating systems, networking systems, and applications software.

404 Wyman Street
Mailstop 504
Waltham, MA 02254
617-895-1339

1055 Joaquin Road, 1st Floor
Mountain View, CA 94043
415-855-4121, 415-694-3173
NYSE:IBM

InnovaCom
Authoring, premastering, encoder and decoder hardware, DVD PC/TV
www.innovacom-mpeg.com

InnovaCom, concurrently working on video compression using its single-chip MPEG-2 integrated circuit encoding capability, will establish a production facility near Hollywood, and will license the DVD authoring technology to feature-film producers, directors, editors, and their companies.
2855 Kifer Road, Suite 100
Santa Clara, CA 95051
408-727-2447, (fax) 408-727-6275
OTC/BB: MPEG

JVC (Victor)*
DVD-Video players
www.jvcinfo.com, www.victor.co.jp

JVC Information Products Company of America
17811 Mitchell Avenue
Irvine, CA 92714
714-261-1292, (fax) 714-261-9690

JVC Company of America
41 Slater Dr.
Elmwood Park, NJ 07407
201-794-3900, (fax) 201-523-3601

Kenwood
DVD-Video players
www.kenwoodusa.com, info@kenwoodusa.com
Founded in 1946, Kenwood Corporation provides home audio and car audio products, test and measuring instruments, and telephone and communications equipment.
2201 East Dominguez St.
Long Beach, CA 90810-1009
310-639-9000

Kodak
Recordable DVD discs
www.kodak.com

Eastman Kodak Company
Business Imaging Systems
901 Elmgrove Road
Rochester, NY 14653-6324
800-243-8811, (fax) 716-726-0818
MNYSE: EK

NEC
DVD-RAM video camera, DVD-ROM drives
www.nec.com, 800-338-9549
NEC offers a full spectrum of products and systems in computers, communications, and semiconductor devices. The NEC Technologies division is a leading manufacturer of computer peripherals and other technology products for the North American market, including desktop and presentation monitors, video projectors, printers, optical storage products, computers, and various technology products for the automotive market.

NEC Technologies, Inc.
1250 N. Arlington Heights Drive, Suite 500
Itasca, IL 60143-1248
630-775-7900, (fax) 630-775-7901

339 North Bernardo Avenue
Mt. View, California 94043
415-528-6000, (fax) 415-528-5400

LG Electronics (Goldstar)
DVD-Video players
www.lge.co.kr
LG Electronics (LGE) develops products such as DVDs, LCD TVs, CD-ROM drives, and network computers. Since its establishment in 1958 as Korea's pioneer consumer electronics company, LGE has expanded worldwide.

LG Electronics U.S.A., Inc.
1000 Sylvan
Englewood Cliffs, NJ 07632
201-816-2000, (fax) 201-816-0636
MON:LG.M, TOR:LG.TO

Liberty Systems
90 Carando Drive
Springfield, MA 01104
413-746-6734, (fax) 413-746-6743

LSI Logic
Decoder and playback hardware
www.lsil.com
1551 McCarthy Blvd.
Milpitas, CA 95035-7424
408-433-8000
NYSE: LSI

Magnavox
www.magnavox.com
See Philips.

Marantz
See Philips.

Matrox
Decoding and display hardware
www.matrox.com
For more than 20 years, Matrox Electronics Systems has been a technology leader in the development of computer-based digital video hardware and software development tools. A privately held company headquartered in Dorval, Quebec, Matrox employs more than 800 people in the design, development, manufacturing, and marketing of video, graphics, imaging, and networking products.

Matrox Electronics Systems, Ltd.
1055 St. Regis Blvd.
Dorval, Quebec H9P 2T4, Canada
514-685-2630, 800-361-4903, (fax) 514-685-2853

Matsushita (Panasonic/National/Technics/Quasar)*
DVD-Video players, DVD drives, DVD car navigation systems
www.panasonic.com, 800-742-8086
Established in Osaka, Japan in 1918, Matsushita Electric Industrial Company (MEI) is one of the world's leading producers of electronic and electric products for consumer, business, and industrial use, including TVs, VCRs, radios, computers, computer peripherals, telephones, semiconductors, air conditioners, batteries, bicycles, cameras, copiers, fax machines, pagers, and refrigerators. Overseas operations include 183 companies in 42 countries. Matsushita's products are marketed under the Panasonic, Technics, Quasar, and National brand names in 170 countries. Matsushita also controls JVC (Victor).

Matsushita Electric Industrial Company, Ltd.
2-15 Matsuba-cho, Kadoma
Osaka 571, Japan
81-6-905-4195, (fax) 81-6-905-1507

Panasonic Company
One Panasonic Way
Secaucus, NJ 07094
201-348-7000, 201-348-7016
NYSE:MC

Maxell
Recordable media
www.maxell.com, 800-325-771

Maxell Corporation of America
12880 Moore Street
Cerritos, CA, 90703
(fax) 310-404-3083

22-08 Route 208
Fair Lawn, NJ 07410
201-794-5900, (fax) 201-796-8790

MediaMatics
Decoding software, DVD-Video playback software
www.mediamatics.com
48430 Lakeview Boulevard
Fremont, CA 94538
510-668-4850, (fax) 510-668-4860

Meridian
DVD-Video players, audio systems
www.meridian-audio.com, www.meridian.co.uk
Meridian is a highly regarded producer of digital audio products.

Meridian Audio Ltd
Stonehill, Stukeley Meadows, Huntingdon
Cambridgeshire PE18 6ED, UK
44-1480-52144, (fax) 44-1480-459934

Meridian America Inc.
Building 2400, Suite 122
3800 Camp Creek Parkway
Atlanta, GA 30331
404-344-7111, (fax) 404-346-7111

Meridian Data, Inc.
DVD-ROM jukebox servers
www.meridian-data.com
Meridian Data is an industry-leading provider of network software and
servers for storing and accessing CD-ROM and DVD-ROM information.
5615 Scotts Valley Drive
Scotts Valley, CA 95066
408-438-3100, (fax) 408-438-6816
NASDAQ: NMS

Mitsubishi*

DVD-Video players

www.melco.co.jp

Mitsubishi Electric is a global leader in information technology, telecommunications, electronic systems and devices, as well as industrial and consumer products. Its operations in Japan comprise 60 facilities employing approximately 48,000 people. Outside of Japan, Mitsubishi Electric's international subsidiaries employ nearly 34,000 employees working in over 120 facilities around the world, including 30 that are operated by Mitsubishi Electric America, Mitsubishi Electric's largest subsidiary.

Mitsubishi Consumer Electronics of America, Inc.
2001 E. Carnegie Ave.
Santa Ana, CA 92705
714-261-3200, (fax) 714-250-3923

Mitsubishi Electric Corporation
6100 Atlantic Boulevard
Norcross, GA 30071
800-347-5724, (fax) 408-481-9488

Mitsubishi Chemical America, Inc.
445 Indio Way
Sunnyvale, CA 94086
800-347-5724, (fax) 408-481-9488

Motorola

Audio encoding and decoding hardware (DSP products)

www.mot-sps.com

Motorola Semiconductor Products Sector (SPS) is the largest U.S.-based broad-line supplier of semiconductor solutions, designing and manufacturing chips for communications, computing, and consumer products. Motorola SPS employs approximately 50,000 people at 31 major facilities around the world.

6501 William Cannon Drive West
Austin, TX
847-576-5000
NYSE: MOT

National

See Matsushita.

NEC Technologies, Inc.

DVD-ROM drives

www.nec-global.com

1250 North Arlington Heights Road, Suite 500
Itasca, IL 60143
630-775-7883, (fax) 630-775-6717

1255 Michael Dr.
Wood Dale, IL 60191
708-860-9500

Nordmende

See Thomson.

Oak Technology, Inc.

Decoder and display hardware, DVD-Video playback software
www.oaktech.com
139 Kifer Ct.
Sunnyvale, CA, 94086
408-737-0888, (fax) 408-737-3838
NASDAQ: OAKT

Oki

Video-encoding hardware
www.oki.com
Established in 1962, Oki America is a wholly owned U.S. subsidiary of Oki
Electric, Japan's first telecommunication manufacturer.

Oki America, Inc.
Three University Plaza
Hackensack, NJ 07601
201-646-0011, (fax) 201-646-9229

Oki Electric Industry Company, Ltd
10-3, Shibaura 4-chome, Minato-ku
Tokyo 108, Japan
81-3-5445-6417, (fax) 81-3-5445-6336

Onkyo

DVD-Video players
www.onkyo-america.com, www.onkyo.co.jp
3030 Barker Dr.
Columbus, IN 47201-9611
812-342-0332

PAGG

Decoder hardware
www.pagg.com
Established in 1981, PAGG Corporation is a leading electronics manufacturing services company providing electronics manufacturing ser-

vices to a variety of OEMs, including the manufacture of printed circuit board assemblies and the testing and assembly of electronic subsystems and systems.
425 Fortune Blvd.
Milford, MA 01757
508-478-8544, (fax) 508-634-2409

Panasonic
See Matsushita.

Philips (Magnavox/Marantz/Norelco)*
DVD-Video players, encoding and decoding hardware, DVD drives
www.philips.com
Philips is one of the world's biggest electronics companies. Philips was an early supporter of the development of television, invented the cassette tape, and has developed numerous other technologies in cooperation with Sony, including the compact disc. Philips makes CD players, VCRs, TVs, cassette tape players, and other consumer entertainment items, as well as shavers, hair dryers, lights, semiconductors, and more. The company owns most of Polygram.

Philips Consumer Electronics
One Philips Drive
PO Box 14810
Knoxville, TN 37914-1810
615-521-4316, (fax) 615-521-3252

Philips Semiconductors
2099 Gateway Place, Suite 100
San Jose, CA 95110
408-453-5129, (fax) 408-453-0680
NYSE: PHG

Pioneer*
DVD-Video players, DVD car navigation systems
www.pioneerusa.com, www.pioneer.co.jp, 800-444-6784
Pioneer Electronic Corporation is a world leader in electronics for the home, commerce, and industry. Products include laserdisc players, TVs, VCRs, optical storage drives, computers, audio equipment, and car navigation systems. Pioneer owns the Pioneer Music Group and Pioneer Entertainment labels.

Pioneer Electronic Corporation
Business Systems Company
15-5 Ohmorinishi 4-Chome

Ohta-ku, Tokyo 143, Japan
81-3-3763-2369, (fax) 81-3-3763-3104

Pioneer New Media Technologies, Inc.
2265 E. 220th St.
Long Beach, CA 90810
310-835-6177, 310-952-2111, (fax) 310-816-0472

Pioneer Electronics (Europe) N.V.
Haven 1087, Keetberglaan 1
9120 Melsele, Belgium
32-3-570-0511, (fax) 32-3-570-0894
NYSE:PIO

Plasmon Data

DVD-ROM jukebox servers

www.plasmon.com

Plasmon Data was founded in 1982. Plasmon is a pioneer in the optical media, jukebox technology, and removable and mass-storage industries. The Plasmon Group has manufacturing facilities and sales offices in the United States and United Kingdom and additional sales offices in France and Germany.

9625 West 76th St
Eden Prairie, MN 55344
612-946-4100, 800-451-6845, (fax) 612-946-4141

2045 Junction Avenue
San Jose, CA 95131
408-474-0100, (fax) 408-474-0111
London Stock Exchange: Plasmon Plc

Procom

DVD-ROM jukebox servers

www.procom.com

Procom Technology designs, manufactures, and markets enterprisewide intelligent storage devices for all major platforms, operating systems, and network protocols. Founded in 1987, the company employs more than 200 people. Procom has offices in Germany, France, and Canada, and services more than 90 countries through 50 distributors and resellers.

Procom Technology
2181 Dupont Drive
Irvine, CA 92715
714-852-100, 800-800-8600, (fax) 714-852-1221
NASDAQ: PRCM

Proscan
See Thomson.

Quadrant
Decoding hardware
www.qi.com
Quadrant International (QI), founded in 1994, is a leader in the convergence industry, where consumer electronics, telephony, entertainment, and computers intersect. QI's services include product technology licensing, software design and implementation, systems engineering consulting, and technological support services.

Quadrant International, Inc.
269 Great Valley Parkway
Malvern, PA 19355
610-251-9999, 800-700-0362, (fax) 610-695-2592

Quasar
See also Matsushita
1707 North Randall Road
Elgin, IL 60123
708-468-5600, (fax) 708-468-5656

Raytheon Semiconductor
Semiconductors (TV encoders)
www.raytheon.com/sd
Raytheon Company is an international, high-technology company that operates in four businesses: commercial and defense electronics, engineering and construction, aviation, and major appliances.
141 Spring St
Lexington, MA 02173
617-862-6600, 617-860-2172
NYSE: RTN

RCA
See Thomson.

Runco
DVD-Video players
www.runco.com
Runco International was founded in 1987 and was the first to coin the term *home theater.* Runco produces video-projection and -processing equipment.
2463 Tripaldi Way

Hayward, CA 94545
510-293-9154, (fax) 510-293-0201

S3
Decoder and display hardware
www.s3.com
S3 Incorporated, founded in 1989, is the world's largest supplier of multi-media acceleration hardware and associated software.

S3 Incorporated
2801 Mission College Blvd.
Santa Clara, CA 95052-8058
408-588-8000, (fax) 408-980-5444
NASDAQ: SIII

Saba
See Thomson.

Samsung
DVD-Video players, DVD drives, semiconductors
www.samsung.com
Samsung Electronics Company (SEC) develops, manufactures, and markets electronics products ranging from silicon to electronic systems, including telecommunication devices, systems, and peripherals. Samsung Electronics, with operations in more than 60 countries, is headquartered in Seoul, Korea, and is one of the major constituents of the Samsung Group, one of the 20 largest companies in the world.

Samsung Electronics America, Inc.
One Samsung Pl.
Ledgewood, NJ 07852
201-347-8004, (fax) 201-347-8650

Sanyo (Fisher)
DVD-Video players
www.sanyo.co.jp
Sanyo is a leading industrial corporation, maker of computers, audio/video equipment, telephones, displays, batteries, air conditioners, heating systems, and home appliances.

Sanyo Electric Company
1767 Sheridan Street
Richmond, IN 47374.
317-935-7574, (fax) 317-935-0174
NASDAQ:SANYY

SGS-Thomson Microelectronics
See Thomson.

Sharp
DVD-Video players
www.sharp-usa.com, www.sharpmeg.com
Founded in 1912 (as the maker of the Ever Sharp pencil), Sharp Corporation is a worldwide developer of digital technologies including liquid crystal display (LCD), optoelectronics, infrared and semiconductors, and flash memory. Sharp employs more than 64,400 people worldwide, with offices in 32 countries.

Sharp Electronics Corporation
Sharp Plaza
PO Box 650
Mahwah, NJ 07430
201-529-8200, (fax) 201-529-9597

SICAN Microelectronics Corporation
Decoder hardware
www.sican-micro.com, info@sican-micro.com
SICAN GmbH, headquartered in Hannover, Germany, is a microelectronics design and technology licensing company, specializing in communications, multimedia, and networking applications. SICAN Microelectronics Corporation is the parent company's North American subsidiary.
400 Oyster Point Blvd.
South San Francisco, CA 94080-1904
415-871-1494

Sigma Designs, Inc.
DVD-Video playback hardware
www.sigma-designs.com
45601 Landing Parkway
Fremont, CA 94538
510-770-0100, (fax) 510-770-2640
NASDAQ: SIGM

Sony*
DVD-Video players, DVD drives
www.sony.com
Sony is the best-known consumer electronics company in the world and is also a major media producer. Sony develops TVs, VCRs, telephones, cam-

corders, video games, audio equipment, professional audio/video equipment, semiconductors, lasers, computers, computer peripherals, and much more. Sony also owns Columbia Pictures and Tri-Star Pictures movie studios and Columbia and Epic record labels. Sony Electronics has nearly 20,000 North American employees.

Sony Electronics, Inc.
1 Sony Dr.
Park Ridge, NJ 07656-8003
201-930-1000, (fax) 201-930-7202

Sony Electronics Inc.
3300 Zanker Road
San Jose, CA 95134-1940
408-955-5240, (fax) 408-955-5171

Sony Corporation of America
550 Madison Avenue
New York, NY 10022-3211
212-833-8600
NYSE: SNE, TOKYO:6758

STB Systems
DVD-ROM upgrade kits, playback hardware
www.stb.com
1651 North Glenville
P.O. Box 850957
Richardson, TX 75085-0957
972-234-8750, 888-234-8750, (fax) 972-234-1306
NASDAQ: STBI

TDK Electronics
Recordable media
www.tdkonline.com
TDK Corporation is a worldwide organization that develops, manufactures, and markets electronic components, semiconductors, and recording media.

12 Harbor Park Drive
Port Washington, NY 11050
212-388-1400, 516-625-0100, (fax) 516-625-0651

1-13-1, Nihonbashi, Chuo-ku
Tokyo 103, Japan
NYSE: TDK

Techexport

Encoding and decoding hardware
www.techexport.com
Techexport, founded in 1971, is one of the largest international computer product distribution and marketing companies in the United States focusing on digital video and digital prepress.
One North Avenue
Burlington, MA 01803
617-229-6900, (fax) 617-229-7706

Technics

See Matsushita.

Telefunken

See Thomson.

Texas Instruments, Inc.

Decoding and playback hardware
www.ti.com
P.O. Box 6118
Temple, TX 76503-6118
800-842-2737, (fax) 817-774-6074
NYSE: TXN

Thomson*

(RCA/GE/Proscan/Ferguson/Nordmende/Telefunken/Saba/Brandt)
DVD-Video players, decoding hardware, TV encoders
SGS-Thomson is a leading supplier of semiconductors for various markets, including audio, video, telecommunications, computing, and automotive industries.

Thomson Consumer Electronics

10330 North Meridian Street
Indianapolis, IN 46290-1024
908-233-2040, 317-587-4450, (fax) 317-587-6708

Thomson Multimedia
9 Place des Vosges
92050 Paris La Defense
Cedex, France
31-1-49-04-93-40, (fax) 31-1-49-04-98-82
NYSE: STM

TiltRac Corporation

DVD jukeboxes (video on demand servers)

www.tiltrac.com, info@tiltrac.com
3353 Earhart Drive, Suite 212
Carrollton, TX 75006
972-980-6991, 800-601-6991, (fax) 972-980-6994

Toshiba*
DVD-Video players, DVD drives
www.toshiba.com
Toshiba Corporation, headquartered in Tokyo, is a world leader in high-technology products spanning information/communications systems, consumer electronics, power systems and industrial equipment, and electronic components and materials. Toshiba America Information Systems (TAIS) is an independent operating company, owned by Toshiba America, a subsidiary of the Toshiba Corporation, the fifth-largest computer and electronics manufacturer. Toshiba Corporation is a world leader in high-technology products with 173 major subsidiaries worldwide.

Toshiba America Consumer Products, Inc.
82 Totowa Rd.
Wayne, NJ 07470
201-628-8000, (fax) 201-628-1875

Toshiba America Information Systems, Inc.
9740 Irvine Boulevard,
Irvine, CA 92713-9124
714-587-6122, 714-583-3000, (fax) 714-587-6847

Toshiba America Electronic Components, Inc.
1060 Rincon Circle
San Jose, CA 95131

Toshiba Corporation
1-1, Shibaura 1-Chome, Minato-ku,
Tokyo 105, Japan
81-3-3457-2381, (fax) 81-3-5444-9214

Trident Microsystems
Decoding and playback hardware
www.tridentms.com
17951 Lyons Circle
Huntington Beach, CA 92647
714-843-9300, 800-867-7782, (fax) 714-843-9373

Wired
Playback hardware and software
www.wiredinc.com

Wired Inc.
1040-155 Grant Road Building 155
Mountain View, CA 94040
415-969-9300

Xing
Encoding and decoding software
www.xingtech.com
A pioneer in digital compression software, Xing Technology Corporation is the leading provider of multimedia Internet and intranet tools for creation and delivery of digital audio and video.

Xing Technology Corporation
810 Fiero
San Luis Obispo, CA 93401
805-473-0145, (fax) 805-473-0147

Yamaha
DVD-Video players, audio decoders
www.yamaha.com, www.yamahayst.com

Yamaha Electronics Corporation, U.S.A.
6660 Orangethorpe Ave.
Buena Park, CA 90620
714-522-9105, (fax) 714-670-0108

Yamaha Systems Technology, Inc.
100 Century Center Court
San Jose, CA 95112
408-467-230, (fax) 408-467-8791

Zenith
DVD-Video players
www.zenith.com
Zenith is a leading U.S. maker of TVs, VCRs, cable boxes, cable modems, and other home entertainment products, with sales mostly confined to the United States. Zenith is a major player in the U.S. HDTV initiative. LG Electronics owns more than half of the company.

Zenith Electronics Corporation
1000 Milwaukee Ave.
Glenview, IL 60025-2493
708-391-8181, 847-391-7000, (fax) 708-391-8334

Zenith Electronics Corporation
2150 East Lake Cook

Buffalo Grove, IL 60089
708-808-5000, (fax) 708-808-4434
NYSE: ZE

Zoran
Encoder and decoder hardware and software
www.zoran.com

Zoran Corporation
3235 Kifer Road #310
Santa Clara, CA 95051
408-736-226, (fax) 408-736-2826
NASDAQ: ZRAN

DVD Tool Providers

Astarte USA
DVD recording software
www.astarte.de
10044 Adams Avenue, Suite 331
Huntington Beach, CA 92646
714-963-703, (fax) 714-963-0529

Cambridge Multimedia Systems Plc
Encoding and authoring systems
www.cambridge-multimedia.co.uk
St. Andrews, North Street
Burwell, Cambridge CB5 0BB, UK
01638-743121, (fax) 01638-743572

Chromatic
Encoding and decoding hardware (DSP products)
www.chromatic.com
Employer of the world-famous Chad Fogg, author of the Internet
MPEG FAQ

Chromatic Research, Inc.
615 Tasman Drive
Sunnyvale, CA 94089-1707
408-752-9100

Cinax Designs, Inc.
DVD-Video editing and playback utility software
www.cinax.com
150-1152 Mainland Street
Vancouver, BC V6B 4X2, Canada
604-685-2364, (fax) 604-685-7998

Daikin

DVD-Video authoring systems

www.daikin-comtec.com

Based in Japan, Daikin Industries provides digital media hardware and software solutions, including sound systems from Sonic Solutions and Daikin's own product, the Scenarist authoring system for professional multimedia content developers. The company's diverse operations also cover fluoro-chemicals, oil hydraulic and lubrication equipment, defense products, computer graphics systems, vacuums, cryogenics, and medical equipment.

Daikin U.S. Comtec Laboratories
101 Rowland Way, Suite 110
Novato, CA 94945
415-893-7811, (fax) 415-893-7807

Digital Vision USA

Encoding systems
11835 W Olympic Blvd.
Los Angeles, CA 90064
310-914-5200, (fax) 310-914-0011

Doug Carson & Associates

DVD production utilities and equipment
www.dcainc.com
1515 East Pine
Cushing, OK 74023
918-225-0346, (fax) 918-225-1113

Elektroson, Inc.

DVD recording software
www.elektroson.com
21054 South Bascom Avenue, Suite 160
Campbell, CA 95008
408-371-480, (fax) 408-371-4895

Epecom Graphics

DVD-Video authoring software
epecom@singnet.com.sg
19 Kallang Ave, 06-153
Singapore 339410
65-2960607, (fax) 65-2960992

Minerva Systems

Authoring and encoding systems

www.minervasys.com
3801 Zanker Road
San Jose, CA 95134-1402
408-487-2001, (fax) 408-487-2013

Optibase, Inc.
Encoding systems
www.optibase.com, 800-451-5101
5000 Quorum Drive, Suite 700
Dallas, TX 75240
214-774-3800, (fax) 214-239-1273

Optical Disc Company
One-off DVD recording system
76712.3036@compuserve.com
12150 Mora Drive
Santa Fe Springs, CA 90670
310-946-3050, (fax) 310-946-6030

OptiVision Inc.
MPEG video recorders
www.optivision.com
3450 Hillview Avenue
Palo Alto, CA 94304
415-855-0200, 800-562-8934, (fax) 415-855-0222

Philips Electronics
Encoding systems
www.philips.com
2099 Gateway Place, Suite 100
San Jose, CA 95110
480-453-7373, (fax) 408-453-6444

Pioneer New Media
Authoring and encoding systems
www.pioneerusa.com, 800-444-6784

Pioneer New Media Technologies, Inc.
2265 E. 220th Street,
Long Beach, CA 90810
310-952-2111, (fax) 310-952-2990

Software Architects
UDF development software
www.softarch.com

Software Architects develops and publishes file interchange, backup, and storage management software for personal computers.
19102 North Creek Pkwy., Suite 101
Bothel, WA 98011
206-487-0122, (fax) 206-487-0467

Sonic Solutions

Authoring, premastering
www.sonic.com
Based in Novato, California, Sonic Solutions designs and manufactures tools to assist audio and other multimedia professionals in preparing music, video, film, graphics, and entertainment software. Products include SonicStudio for audio CD and Sonic DVD Creator for DVD-Video.

Sonic Solutions
101 Rowland Way, Suite 110
Novato, CA 94945
415-893-8000, (fax) 415-893-8008
NASDAQ: SNIC

Vitec Multimedia

Video-encoding software
www.vitecmm.com, info@vitecmm.com
99, rue Pierre Sémard
F-92324 Châtillion Cedex, France
33-1-46-73-06-06, (fax) 33-1-46-73-06-00

Zapex

Encoding systems
www.zapex.com
1927 Landings Drive
Mountain View, CA 94043
415-254-2380, (fax) 415-254-2399

DVD Services

AGI Inc.

Packaging
1950 North Ruby St.
Melrose Park, IL 60160
708-344-9100, (fax) 708-344-9113

AIX Entertainment

Authoring, premastering

www.itrax.com, 800-668-4249
AIX Entertainment has been working in the DVD format since late 1996
and offers complete DVD production services.
8455 Beverly Boulevard Suite 500
West Hollywood, CA 90048

All Post
Authoring, post production, premastering
1133 North Hollywood Way
Burbank, CA 91505
818-556-5700, 818-556-5756, (fax) 818-556-5748

CD Associates, Inc.
Testing and verification
www.cdassociates.com
15375 Barranca Pkwy.,
Suite I-101
Irvine, CA 92618
714-733-8580, (fax) 714-453-0868

Cinram
Authoring, post production, premastering, replication
Joint venture with Santa Monica—based Pacific Ocean Post (POP).

Cinram Ltd.
2255 Markham Road
Scarborough, ON, Canada
613-726-166, (fax) 613-726-1609

1600 Rich Rd.
Richmond, IN 47374
317-962-9511, (fax) 317-962-1564

Crest National
Authoring, premastering
www.crestnational.com
1000 N. Highland Ave.
Hollywood, CA 90038
213-466-0624, (fax) 213-461-8901

CRUSH Digital Video
Authoring, post production, premastering
info@crushdv.com
123 Watts Street, 2d Floor
New York, NY 10013
212-965-150, (fax) 212-965-1499

CKS|Pictures
Authoring, premastering
www.cks.com
10443 Bandley Drive
Cupertino, CA 95014
408-342-5009, 408-366-5100, (fax) 408-366-5120
NASDAQ: CKSG

Clear-Vu Products
Packaging
18 Sylvester St.
Westbury, NY 11590
516-333-8880, (fax) 516-333-7695

Complete Post
Authoring, premastering
www.completepost.com
6087 Sunset Blvd.
Hollywood, CA 90028
213-467-1244, (fax) 213-461-2561

D2 Productions
Authoring, premastering
www.d2prod.com, d2prod@d2prod.com
P.O. Box 1809
Rosemead, CA 91770
818-576-8113, (fax) 818-576-0516

Denon Active Media (DAM)
Authoring, premastering, replication
www.denon.com/DAM_home.htm
3343 Peachtree Rd. NE, Suite 333
Atlanta, GA 30326
404-240-2940, (fax) 404-240-2950

dHouse
Authoring, design
www.d-House.com
7120 Redwood Boulevard
Novato, CA 94945

Digital Video Compression Center (DVCC)
Authoring, premastering

100 Universal City Plaza, Suite 506/J
Universal City, CA 91608
818-777-6300, (fax) 818-866-3313

Disc Manufacturing (DMI)
Mastering, replication, packaging
www.discmfg.com, 1-800-433-DISC

Disc Manufacturing, Inc.
2030 Main Street 13th Floor
Irvine, CA 92614
714-260-476, (fax) 714-260-4779

1409 Foulk Rd., Suite 102
Wilmington, DE 19803
302-479-2500, (fax) 302-479-2427
NASDAQ: QUIX

The Duplication Group
Authoring, premastering
4910 W. Amelia Earhart Dr.
Salt Lake City, UT 84116
801-531-7555, 801-531-0740

EDS Digital Studios
Authoring, premastering
newmedia.varitel-eds.com
3575 Cahuenga Blvd. West, Suite 675
Los Angeles California 90068
213-850-1165, 213-850-6151

Electric Switch
Authoring, premastering
DVD@electric-group.co.uk
Electric Switch, U.K.–based digital video compression company, provides
DVD production, encoding, and authoring services in London, run in
association with Panasonic OWL, a U.K.–based subsidiary of Matsushita
Electric Industrial Company. The service will use Panasonic's DVD
Authoring system.
7-11 Lexington St.
London W1R 3HQ, UK
44-171-437-4402, (fax) 44-171-437-4403

EMS
Disc testing and verification

tim_landers@wmg.com
1657 Euclid Street
Santa Monica, CA 90404
310-581-5800, (fax) 310-581-5899

Gelardi Design
Packaging
P.O. Box 2757
Wildes District Rd.
Kennebunkport, ME 04046
207-967-0679, (fax) 207-967-2820

Harmonic Hall Optical Disc Ltd.
Authoring, premastering
www.hk.super.net/~harmonic
19/F Wharf Cable Tower
9 Hoi Shing Rd.
Tsuen Wan, Hong Kong
24-212-1388, (fax) 24-14-2333

IBM Interactive Media
Authoring, premastering
www.solutions.ibm.com/multimedia/media-home.html
3200 Windy Hill Road
Atlanta, GA 30339
770-835-6391, (fax) 770-835-7249

ICDI
Authoring, premastering
www.icdi.be
Route Nationale 5, 191
B-6041 Gosselies, Belgium
32-71-25-75-50, (fax) 32-71-25-75-75

Interactive Communications Corporation (ICC)
Packaging
P.O. Box 194690
San Francisco, CA 94119
415-284-9600, (fax) 415-284-9300

International Duplication Centre (IDC)
Authoring, premastering, mastering, replication, packaging
321 West 44th St, 9th Fl.

New York, NY 10036
212-581-3940, (fax) 212-581-3979

Imation (formerly 3M Optical Products)
Replication
www.imation.com
1185 Willow Lake Blvd
Vadnais Heights, MN 55110
612-704-5050, (fax) 612-704-5007

JVC Disc America
Authoring, premastering, replication
www.jvcdiscusa.com
9255 W Sunset, Suite 717
Los Angeles, CA 90069
310-274-2221, (fax) 310-274-4392

Kao Infosystems
Mastering, replication, packaging
www.kaoinfo.com, 800-525-6575
Kao Infosystems Company, a leading software manufacturing and distribution services company, is a wholly owned subsidiary of Kao Corporation of America. The parent company, Kao Corporation of Japan, is a global conglomerate established in 1887 that develops, manufactures, and markets personal care, chemical, and information products.

Kao Infosystems Company
40 Grissom Road
Plymouth, MA 02360
508-747-562, (fax) 508-747-5521

Fremont, California
510-657-8425

Laserfile
Packaging
7083 Hollywood Blvd., Suite 305
Hollywood, CA 90028
213-8567-7318, (fax) 213-856-7390

Laser Pacific Media
Authoring, premastering
www.laserpacific.com
809 N. Cahuenga Blvd.

Hollywood, CA 90038
213-462-6266, (fax) 213-464-3233

Maxell
Authoring, premastering, mastering, replication, packaging
Services provided by the Hitachi Maxell facility in Tsukuba, Japan; Santa
Clara, California; and Dublin, Ireland.
www.maxell.com, 800-325-771

Maxell Corporation of America
12880 Moore Street
Cerritos, CA 90703
(fax) 310-404-3083

Mayking Multi-Media
Replication
www.mayking.co.uk
250 York Rd.
Battersea, London SW11 3SJ, UK
44-171-924-6765, (fax) 44-171-801-0945

Metatec
Replication
www.metatec.com
7001 Metatec Blvd.
Dublin, OH 43017
614-761-2000, (fax) 614-798-5847
NASDAQ: META

NB Digital Solutions
Authoring, premastering
www.nbdig.com, 800-909-6230
2110 Priest Bridge Drive
Crofton, MD 21114
410-721-5725, (fax) 410-721-5726
OTC: ESVC

Nimbus Manufacturing
Authoring, encoding, mastering, replication, packaging
800-231-0778
Nimbus operates replication plants in Charlottesville, Virginia; Sunnyvale,
California; Provo, Utah; Cwmbran, Wales; and Luxembourg (operated by
EuroNimbus, S.A.).

623 Welsh Run Road
Ruckersville, VA 22968

804-985-1100, (fax) 804-985-4525
NASDAQ: NMBS

NOB Interactive
www.nob.nl
Centrum voor de Nieuwe Media
Sumatralaan 45, 1217 GP, Hilversum
The Netherlands
31-(0)35-677-5413, 31-(0)35-677-5409

Pacific Coast Sound Works
Authoring, premastering
www.pcsw.com, 800-871-6734

8455 Beverly Blvd., Suite 500
West Hollywood, California 90048
213-655-4771, (fax) 213-655-8893

2440 Camino Ramon, Suite 200
San Ramon, CA 94583
213-654-4771

Pacific Video Resources (PVR)
Authoring, premastering
2331 Third St.
San Francisco, CA 94107
415-864-5679, (fax) 415-864-3813

Phoenix Digital Facilities
Design, authoring, premastering
Unit 4 Maple Cross Ind Est
Denham Way
Maple Cross, Herts WD3 2AS, UK
44-1923-77-7782, (fax) 44-1923-77-2163

Pioneer Video Manufacturing
Replication and packaging
www.pioneerusa.com
1041 E. 230th Street
Carson, CA 90745
310-518-0710, (fax) 310-834-1477

PrismaGraphics Inc.
Packaging
P.O. Box 703
Milwaukee, WI 53201
414-342-6464, (fax) 414-342-0932

Queens Group, Inc.
Packaging
52-35 Barnett Avenue
Long Island, NY 11104
718-457-770, (fax) 718-457-9258

Rainmaker Digital Pictures Group
Authoring, premastering
50 West 2d Ave.
Vancouver, BC V5Y 1B3, Canada
604-874-8700, (fax) 604-874-1719

Richard Diercks Company
Authoring, premastering
420 N. 5th St., Suite 300
Minneapolis, MN 55401
612-334-5900, (fax) 612-334-5907

Rose Packaging & Design
Packaging
6444 South Quebec Street, Building 7
Suite 212
Englewood, CO 80111
303-773-1003, (fax) 303-773-1041

Sonopress
Replication
Carl-Bertelsmann Str, 161F
Postfach 300
Gutersloh 33311, Germany
49-5241-80-5200, (fax) 49-5241-73543

Sony Disc Manufacturing
Mastering, replication, packaging
www.sony.com
188 N. Fruitridge Ave.
Terre Haute, IN 47802
812-462-8100, (fax) 812-462-8760

Technicolor
Mastering, replication, packaging
5255 East Mission Oaks Blvd.
Camarillo, CA 93012
805-455-1122, (fax) 805-445-9875

Television Associates (TVA)
Design and encoding
www.tva-online.com
2410 Charleston Rd.
Mountain View, CA 94043
415-967-6040, (fax) 415-964-2453

Univenture
Packaging
P.O. Box 28398
Columbus, OH 43228-0398
614-529-2100, (fax) 614-529-211

Valkieser Multi Media
Design, authoring, post production, premastering
newmedia@valkieser.nl
Huizerstraatweg 117A
1411 GM Naarden, The Netherlands
31-35-6955900, (fax) 31-35-6955955

Vision Wise
Authoring, premastering
www.visionwise.com, 888-979-WISE
3400 Carlisle, Suite 340
Dallas, TX 75204
214-979-9473, (fax) 214-979-2462

Warner*
Design, authoring, premastering, Mastering, replication, packaging
www.wmg.com

Warner Advanced Manufacturing Operations (WAMO)
1400 East Lockawanna Avenue
Olyphant, PA 18448
717-383-3291, (fax) 717-383-7487

Warner Media Services
3601 West Olive Ave, Suite 210
Burbank, CA 91505
818-953-2941, (fax) 818-843-6510
NYSE: TWX

Windsor New Media
Authoring, premastering
8 West 38th St.

New York, NY 10018
212-944-9090, (fax) 212-840-0217

Zomax Optical Media
Mastering, replication, packaging
5353 Nathan Lane
Plymouth, MN 55442
612-553-9300, (fax) 612-553-0826

DVD-Video Producers and Distributors

Alliance Entertainment
Distributor (U.S.)
800-329-7664
4250 Coral Ridge Drive
Coral Springs, FL 33065

Baker & Taylor
Distributor (U.S.)
8140 North Leigh Ave.
Morton Grove, IL 60053
847-965-8060

CAV Distributing
Distributor (U.S.)
257 Utah Ave.
South San Francisco, CA 94080
415-588-2228

Image Entertainment, Inc.
Distributor (U.S.)
Image Entertainment is the largest laserdisc licensee and distributor in the United States and is rapidly building a DVD distribution business. The company obtains titles from major motion picture studios under exclusive and nonexclusive license and whole distribution agreements.
9333 Oso Ave.
Chatsworth, CA 91311
818-407-9100, (fax) 818-407-9151
NASDAQ: DISK

Imaging Science Foundation (ISF)/Joe Kane Productions
Publisher (test disc)
www.videoessentials.com, www.imagingscience.com

Joe Kane Productions
11136 Hesby Street, Suite 115
North Hollywood, California 91601-4284

Ingram Entertainment

Distributor (U.S.)
800-621-1333
2 Ingram Blvd.
LaVergne, TN 37089
615-793-500

Laser Movies

Distributor (U.S.)
www.lasermovies.com, info@lasermovies.com
217 Seal Boulevard #A
Seal Beach, CA 90740
562-596-2244, (fax) 562-598-6697

Lumivision

Publisher
Established in 1988, Lumivision publishes and distributes programming for laserdisc and DVD, focusing on special interest programs.
877 Federal Blvd.
Denver, CO 80204
303-446-0400, (fax) 303-446-0101

Major Video Concepts

Distributor (U.S.)
800-365-0150
7998 Georgetown Rd., Suite 1000
Indianapolis, IN 46268
317-875-8000

Metro Global Media

Publisher
Metro Global Media publishes and distributes adult video titles.
NASDAQ: MGMA

MS Distributors

Distributor (U.S.)
6405 Muirfield Drive
Hanover Park, IL 60103
630-582-2888

Norwalk Distributors
Distributor (U.S.)
800-877-6021
1193 Knollwood Circle
Anaheim, CA 92801

Paramount Home Video
Publisher
www.paramount.com

Paramount Pictures Studios
5555 Melrose Avenue
Hollywood, CA 90038-3197
213-956-5000

Pioneer Entertainment
Distributor (worldwide)
www.pioneer-ent.com
2265 E. 220th St.
Long Beach, CA 90810

PolyGram
Publisher (audio and video)
www.polygram.com
PolyGram is controlled by Philips.

PolyGram International
8 St. James's Square
London SW1Y 4JU
0171-747-4217, (fax) 0171-747-4490

PolyGram Holding, Inc.
Worldwide Plaza
825 Eighth Avenue
New York, NY 10019
212-333-8357, (fax) 212-333-8203
NYSE: PLG

Simitar
Publisher
www.simitar.com, 800-486-8273
3850 Annapolis Lane, Suite 140
Plymouth, MN 55447

Time Warner
Publisher
www.pathfinder.com
The Time Warner conglomerate includes leading TV/movie studios
Warner Bros. and Castle Rock; TV networks CNN, TNT, TBS, and WB;
cable services HBO and Time Warner Cable; and major publishing companies Time and Warner Books.

Warner Home Video
4000 Warner Boulevard
Burbank, CA 91522
818-954-6401, (fax) 818-954-6497
NYSE:TWX

Twentieth Century Fox
Publisher
www.fox.com, www.tcfhe.com

Twentieth Century Fox
10201 W. Pico Blvd.
Los Angeles, CA 90064-2651

Twentieth Century Fox Home Entertainment, Inc.
P.O. Box 900
Beverly Hills, CA 90213-0900
310-277-2211

Universal Home Video
Publisher
www.universalpictures.com
70 Universal City Plaza
Universal City, CA 91608-1085
818-777-1000

Viacom
Publisher
www.viacom.com
Viacom, one of the world's largest media companies, owns or controls tele-
vision channels such as MTV, Nickelodeon, Showtime, UPN, and the USA
Network, as well as TV/movie studio Paramount Pictures, video chain
Blockbuster, and publisher Simon & Schuster.
AMEX:VIA

Warner Home Video
See Time Warner.

DVD-ROM Software Publishers

2 Way Media
www.launchonline.com
1632 5th St.
Santa Monica, CA 90401-3312
310-260-7786

Activision
www.activision.com
Activision develops interactive entertainment software for Windows, MacOS, Nintendo, Sony Playstation, and other systems.
11691 Wilshire Blvd., Suite 300
Los Angeles, CA 90025
310-473-9200, (fax) 310-479-4005
NASDAQ: ATVI

Digital Directory Assistance
www.dda-inc.com, www.phonedisc.com
6931 Arlington Rd., Suite 405
Bethesda, MD 20814
301-657-8548

Byron Preiss Multimedia
Partner with Simon & Schuster Interactive
24 West 25th St.
New York, NY 10010
202-645-9870, (fax) 212-645-9874
BSE: BYP

Electronic Arts
www.easports.com
1450 Fashion Island Blvd.
San Mateo, CA 94404
415-571-7171
NASDAQ: ERTS

Grolier Interactive
www.grolier.com
Sherman Turnpike
Danbury, CT 06816
203-797-3500

GT Interactive
www.iab.com

16 E. 40th St., 5th Fl.
New York, NY 10016
212-726-6500
NASDAQ: GTIS

Imagination Pilots Entertainment
www.ipilots.com
640 North LaSalle Street, Suite 560
Chicago, IL 60610
312-944-9471, (fax) 312-642-0616

Interactual Technologies
2017 Landings Dr.
Mountain View, CA 94043
415-943-1440, (fax) 415-943-1430

Mechadeus
135 Mississippi St., 3F
San Francisco, CA 94107
415-865-2700, (fax) 415-865-2645

Multicom
www.multicom.com
Multicom Publishing, founded in 1991, creates and distributes interactive
multimedia products and services in the home/family/lifestyle category.
1100 Olive Way
Seattle, WA 98101
206-622-5530, (fax) 206-622-4380
NASDAQ: MNET

Pro CD
222 Rosewood Dr.
Danvers, MA 01923
508-750-0000, (fax) 508-750-0060

Readysoft
www.readysoft.com
Purchased by Malofilm. May change name to Behavior Interactive.

Simon & Schuster Interactive
Owned by Viacom. Partner with Byron Preiss.
1230 Ave. of the Americas
New York, NY 10020
212-698-7000, (fax) 212-698-7555

Sumeria

www.sumeria.com
329 Bryant St., Suite 3D
San Francisco, CA 94107
415-904-0800, (fax) 415-904-0888

Tsunami Media, Inc.

www.tsumedia.com
48677 Victoria Lane, Suite 201
Oakhurst, CA 93644
209-683-8266, (fax) 209-683-8288

The Learning Company

The Learning Company (formerly SoftKey), one of the largest consumer software makers in the world, sells productivity, entertainment, and leisure computer software. Recent acquisitions include educational publishers MECC and The Learning Company (from which it took its new name), and multimedia developer Aris Multimedia Entertainment.
NYSE: TLC

Westwood Studios

www.westwood.com
Subsidiary of Spelling Entertainment Group
2400 N. Tenya Way
Las Vegas, NV 89128
702-228-4040
NYSE: SP

Xiphias

www.xiphias.com
8758 Venice Boulevard
Los Angeles, CA 90034
310-841-2790, (fax) 310-841-2559

Other Companies

Apple Computer

DVD-ROM file system and OS, QuickTime
www.apple.com
20525 Mariani Ave.
Cupertino, CA 95014
408-996-1010, (fax) 408-974-2483
NASDAQ: AAPL

Blockbuster
Video and music rentals and sales
(*See* Viacom, in "DVD-Video Producers and Distributors" section.)
Blockbuster Entertainment Group is a global entertainment retailer with more than 5000 music and video stores in 50 states and 24 foreign countries.

Dolby Laboratories
Audio encoder technology
100 Potrero Ave.
San Francisco, CA 94103-4813
415-558-0200

Macrovision
Antitaping technology
Macrovision is majority owned by JVC, which is controlled by Matsushita.
1341 Orleans
Sunnyvale, CA 94089
408-743-860, (fax) 408-743-8610
NASDAQ: MVSN

Microsoft
DVD-ROM file system and OS
www.microsoft.com
1 Microsoft Way
Redmond, WA 98052-8300
206-882-8080
NASDAQ: MSFT

THX (Lucasfilm Ltd.)
Audio/video software and hardware certification
1023 Hollywood Way
Burbank, CA 91505
818-526-0451, (fax) 818-526-0458

West Coast Entertainment Corporation
Video rental chain
West Coast owns, operates, and franchises 531 video sales and rental stores.
9990 Global Rd.
Philadelphia, PA 19115
215-677-1000, (fax) 215-677-5804
NASDAQ: WCEC

Spatializer Audio Laboratories, Inc.
3D audio technology
20700 Ventura Blvd., Suite 134
Woodland Hills, CA 91364
818-227-3370, (fax) 818-227-9750
NASDAQ: SPAZ

Standards Organizations

Audio Engineering Society (AES)/AES Standards Committee (AESSC)
www.aes.org
60 E. 42nd St.
New York, NY 10165-2520
212-661-8528, (fax) 212-682-0477

American National Standards Institute (ANSI)
www.ansi.org
11 West 42nd Street
New York, NY 10036
212-642-4900, (fax) 212-398-0023

Commission Internationale de l'Éclairage/International Commission on Illumination (CIE)
ciecb@ping.at
IE Central Bureau, Kegelgasse 27
A-1030 Vienna, Austria
43 (01) 714 31 87/0, (fax) 43 (01) 713 0838/18

Deutsches Institut für Normung/German Institute for Standardization (DIN)
www.din.de, postmaster@din.de
Burggrafenstrasse 6, D-10787
Berlin, Germany
49 30 26 01-0, (fax) 49 30 26 01 12 31

European Telecommunications Standards Institute (ETSI)
www.etsi.fr
Route des Lucioles, F-06921
Sophia Antipolis, Cedex, France
33 4 92 94 42 00, (fax) 33 4 93 65 47 16

European Broadcasting Union (EBU)
www.ebu.ch

European Computer Manufacturers Association (ECMA)
www.ecma.ch, helpdesk@ecma.ch
114 Rue de Rhône,
CH-1204 Genève 20, Switzerland
41 22 735 3634

International Electrotechnical Commission (IEC)
www.iec.ch
3 rue de Varembé, Case postale 131
1211 Genève 20, Switzerland
41 22 919 02 11, (fax) 41 22 919 03 00

International Organization for Standardization (ISO)
www.iso.ch, central@iso.ch
1 rue de Varembé, Case postale 56
CH-1211 Genève 20, Switzerland
41 22 749 01 11, (fax) 41 22 733 34 30

International Telecommunication Union (ITU)
www.itu.int, sales@itu.int
Sales Service
Place de Nations
CH-1211 Genève 20, Switzerland
41 22 730 6141 (English), 41 22 730 6142 (French), 41 22 730 6143 (Spanish), (fax) 41 22 730 5194

National Committee for Information Technology Standards (NCITS)
(Formerly the Accredited Standards Committee X3, Information Technology)
www.ncits.org

Optical Storage Technology Association (OSTA)
www.osta.org
311 E. Carrillo St.
Santa Barbara, CA 93101
805-962-1541

Society of Motion Picture & Television Engineers (SMPTE)
www.smpte.org, smpte@smpte.org
595 W. Hartsdale Ave.
White Plains, NY 10607-1824
914-761-1100, (fax) 914-761-3115

Other Related Organizations

Acoustic Renaissance for Audio (ARA)

www.meridian.co.uk/ara, ara@meridian.co.uk, negishi@gcds.canon.co.jp

Business Software Alliance (BSA)

www.bsa.org
1150 18th Street N.W., Suite 700
Washington, DC 20036
202-872-5500, (fax) 202-872-5501

Computer and Business Equipment Manufacturer's Association (CBEMA)

1250 Eye St., Suite 200
Washington, DC 20005
202-737-8888, (fax) 202-638-4922

Consumer Electronics Manufacturers Association (CEMA)

CEMA, a sector of the EIA, represents U.S. manufacturers of audio, video, consumer information, accessories, mobile electronics, and multimedia products.
www.cemacity.org

Electronic Industries Association (EIA)

A 72-year-old trade association representing all facets of electronics manufacturing.
www.eia.org
2500 Wilson Boulevard
Arlington, VA 22201-3834
703-907-7600, (fax) 703-907-7601

Information Technology Industry Council (ITI)

www.itic.org

Interactive Multimedia Association (IMA)

Now part of the Software Publishers Association (SPA)

Motion Picture Association of America (MPAA)

The MPAA serves as the advocate of the American motion picture, home video, and television production industries.
www.mpaa.org

OpenDVD Consortium

www.opendvd.org

Optical Video Disc Association (OVDA)
www.ovda.org
309 Santa Monica Blvd., Suite 205
Santa Monica, CA 90401
310-319-9119, (fax) 310-319-9138

Recording Industry Association Of America (RIAA)
www.riaa.com
1330 Connecticut Avenue NW, Suite 300
Washington, DC 20036
202-775-0101

SFF (Small Form Factor) Committee
250-1752@mcimail.com
14426 Black Walnut Ct.
Saratoga CA 95070
408-867-6630x303, (fax) 408-867-2115

Software Publishers Association (SPA)
www.spa.org, www.spa-europe.org
1730 M St. NW, Suite 700
Washington, DC 20036-4510
202-452-1600, (fax) 202-223-8756

Video Software Dealers Association (VSDA)
www.vsda.org
16530 Ventura Blvd., Suite 400
Encino, CA 91436
818-385-1500, (fax) 818-385-0567

APPENDIX C

References and Information Sources

DVD Information and Licensing

DVD specification
(Requires non-disclosure agreement and $5000US.)
000092030295@tg-mail.toshiba.co.jp
Mr. Y. Mizutani
Toshiba Corporation
Toshiba BLDG. 13D
DVD Division
1-1 Shibaura 1-Chome, Minato-ku
Tokyo 105-01, Japan

DVD logo and format licensing
Toshiba Corporation
DVD Business Promotion and Support
DVD Products Division
81-3-5444-9580, (fax) 81-3-5444-9430

CSS Interim Licensing

Matsushita Corporation
81-6-905-4155, (fax) 81-6-901-9299

Newsletters and Industry Analyses

Adams Media Research
Market research
tomadams@ix.netcom.com
15B West Carmel Valley Rd.
Carmel Valley, CA 93924
408-659-3070, (fax) 408-659-4330

The CD-Info Company (CDIC)
Industry directories, newsletters, and other publications
www.cd-info.com, info@cd-info.com
4800 Whitesburg Drive #30-283
Huntsville, AL 35802-1600
205-650-0406, (fax) 205-882-7393

Dataquest
Market research
www.dataquest.com
251 River Oaks Parkway
San Jose, CA 95134-1913
408-468-8000, (fax) 408-954-1780
Nine Technology Drive
P.O. Box 5093
Westborough, MA 01581-5093
508-871-5555

InfoTech
Market research
www.infotechresearch.com
Box 150, Skyline Dr.
Woodstock, VT 05091-0150
802-763-2097, (fax) 802-763-2098

International Data Corporation (IDC)
Market research
www.idcresearch.com
5 Speen Street
Framingham, MA 01701
508-872-8200, (fax) 508-935-4015

Knowledge Industry Publications, Inc. (KIPI)
Newsletters, magazines, conferences
www.kipinet.com, 800-800-5474
701 Westchester Avenue
White Plains, NY 10604
914-328-9157, (fax) 914-328-9093

Market Vision
Market research
www.webcom.com/newmedia, mktvis@cruzio.com
326 Pacheco Avenue, Suite 200
Santa Cruz, CA 95062
408-426-4400, (fax) 408-426-4411

Paul Kagan Associates
Market research
126 Clock Tower Place
Carmel, CA 93923-8734
408-624-1536

Phillips Business Information Ltd.
Newsletters: Inside Multimedia, Multimedia Monitor, Multimedia Week, and more
editorial@omnicom.co.uk
Forum Chambers, The Forum
Stevenage SG1 1EL, UK
+44 1438 742 424, (fax) +44 1438 742 424

SIMBA Information Inc.
Market research, newsletters
www.simbanet.com, info@simbanet.com
11 River Bend Drive South
P.O. 4234
Wilton, CT 06907
203-358-0234, (fax) 203-358-5824

Total Research in Multimedia
trimm@mail.idt.net.
Scottsdale, AZ

Magazines

Digital Video Magazine
www.dv.com
411 Borel Ave., Suite 100
San Mateo, CA 94402
415-358-9500, 888-776-7002, (fax) 415-358-8891

EMedia Professional
(formerly CD-ROM Professional)
www.onlineinc.com/emedia
649 Massachusetts Ave., Suite 4
Cambridge, MA 02139
617-492-0268, (fax) 617-492-3159

Replication News
Miller Freeman PSN, Inc.
2 Park Avenue, Suite 1820
New York, NY 10016
415-905-2200, (fax) 415-905-2239

Books

The Art of Digital Audio (2d ed.)
John Watkinson
Butterworth-Heinemann, 1994
ISBN: 0240513207

Being Digital
Nicholas Negroponte, Marty Asher
Vintage Books, 1996
ISBN: 0679762906

Compression in Video and Audio
John Watkinson
Focal Press, 1995
ISBN: 0240513940

Digital Video: An Introduction to MPEG-2
Barry G. Haskell, Atul Puri, Arun N. Netravali
Chapman & Hall, 1996
ISBN: 0412084112

Digital Video and Audio Compression
Stephen J. Solari
McGraw-Hill, 1997
ISBN: 0070595380

An Introduction to Digital Audio
John Watkinson
Focal Press, 1994
ISBN: 0240513789

MPEG Video: Compression Standard
Joan L. Mitchell, William B. Pennebaker, Chad E. Fogg
Chapman & Hall, 1996
ISBN: 0412087715

Principles of Digital Audio (3d ed.)
Ken C. Pohlmann
McGraw-Hill, 1995
ISBN: 0070504695

A Technical Introduction to Digital Video
Charles A. Poynton
John Wiley & Sons, 1996
ISBN: 047112253X

Television Engineering Handbook: Featuring HDTV Systems (revised ed.)
K. Blair Benson
McGraw-Hill, 1992
ISBN: 007004788X

Video Demystified **(2d ed.)**
Keith Jack
Hightext Publications, 1996
ISBN: 187870723X

Internet Sites

(Internet addresses for companies and organizations are provided in App. B.)

alt.video.dvd FAQ
www.videodiscovery.com/vdyweb/dvd
A concise explanation of DVD, based on questions posted to the alt.video.dvd Internet newsgroup.

CyberTheater & Laser Scans Newsletter
cybertheater.com/laserscans_idx.html
An Internet journal of home theater. Includes Laser Scans, an electronic newsletter on DVD and laserdisc, published by Chris McGowan.

E/Town: The Home Electronics Guide (DVD Central)
www.e-town.com/dvd
A collection of articles on DVD technology and products.

Laser Rot
www.laserrot.com
An on-line source of information about DVD and laserdiscs.

Laserviews
www.laserviews.com
The Web page for *Laserviews Magazine* covering the DVD and laserdisc video industry.

MPEG Pointers and Resources
www.mpeg.org
A comprehensive index of MPEG resources on the Internet.

Robert's DVD Info page
www.unik.no/~robert/hifi/dvd
A thorough list of pointers to DVD information, news, articles, companies, and so on.

Secrets of Home Theater & High Fidelity
www.sdinfo.com
An electronic journal dedicated to the enjoyment of audio and video experiences.

GLOSSARY

2:2 pulldown The process of transferring 24-frame-per-second film to video by repeating each film frame as two video fields. (See Chap. 3 for details.) When 24-fps film is transferred via 2:2 pulldown to 25-fps 625/50 (PAL) video, the film runs 4 percent faster than normal.

2:3 pulldown See **3:2 pulldown.**

3:2 pulldown The process of transferring 24-frame-per-second film to video by repeating one film frame as three fields, then the next film frame as two fields. (See Chap. 3 for details.)

4:1:1 The component digital video format with one C_b sample and one C_r sample for every four Y samples. 4:1 horizontal downsampling with no vertical downsampling. This amounts to a subsampling of chroma by a factor of two compared to luma. Chroma is sampled on every line, but only for every four luma pixels (i.e., a 1×4 grid). DVD uses 4:2:0 sampling, not 4:1:1 sampling.

4:2:0 The component digital video format used by DVD, where there is one C_b sample and one C_r sample for every four Y samples (i.e., a 4×4 grid). 2:1 horizontal downsampling and 2:1 vertical downsampling. Every other line is sampled, with one set of chroma samples for each two luma samples on a line. This amounts to a subsampling of chroma by a factor of two compared to luma.

4:2:2 The component digital video format commonly used for studio recordings, where there is one C_b sample and one C_r sample for every four Y samples (i.e., a 1×2 grid). 2:1 horizontal downsampling with no vertical downsampling. This allocates the same number of samples to the chroma signal as to the luma signal. The input to MPEG-2 encoders used for DVD is typically in 4:2:2 format, but the video is subsampled to 4:2:0 before being encoded and stored.

4:4:4 A component digital video format for high-end studio recordings, where Y, C_b, and C_r are sampled equally.

525/60 The scanning system of 525 lines per frame and 60 interlaced fields (30 frames) per second. Used by the NTSC television standard.

625/50 The scanning system of 625 lines per frame and 50 interlaced fields (25 frames) per second. Used by PAL and SECAM television standards.

8/16 modulation The form of modulation block code used by DVD to store channel data on the disc. See **modulation.**

AAC   Advanced audio coder. An audio-encoding standard for MPEG-2 that is not backward-compatible with MPEG-1 audio.

AC   Alternating current. An electric current that regularly reverses direction. Adopted as a video term for a signal of non-zero frequency. Compare to **DC.**

AC-3   The former name of the Dolby Digital audio-coding system. AC-3 followed AC-1 and AC-2. Still used in some standards documents.

ActiveMovie   The former name for Microsoft's DirectShow technology.

ADPCM   Adaptive differential pulse code modulation. A compression technique which encodes the difference between one sample and the next. Variations are lossy and lossless.

AES   Audio Engineering Society.

AES/EBU   A digital audio signal transmission standard for professional use, defined by the Audio Engineering Society and the European Broadcasting Union. S/P DIF is the consumer adaptation of this standard.

AGC   Automatic gain control. A circuit designed to boost the amplitude of a signal to provide adequate levels for recording. Also see **Macrovision.**

aliasing   A distortion (artifact) in the reproduction of digital audio or video that results when the signal frequency is more than twice the sampling frequency. The resolution is insufficient to distinguish between alternate reconstructions of the waveform, thus admitting additional noise that was not present in the original signal.

analog   A signal of (theoretically) infinitely variable levels. Compare to **digital.**

angle   In DVD-Video, a specific view of a scene, usually recorded from a certain camera angle. Different angles can be chosen while viewing the scene.

ANSI   American National Standards Institute. (See App. B.)

apocryphal   Of questionable authorship or authenticity. Erroneous or fictitious. The author of this book is fond of saying that the oft-cited 133-minute limit of DVD-Video is apocryphal.

artifact   An unnatural effect not present in the original video or audio, produced by an external agent or action. Artifacts can be caused by many factors, including digital compression, film-to-video transfer, transmission errors, data readout errors, electrical interference, analog signal noise, and analog signal crosstalk. Most artifacts attributed to the digital compression of DVD are in fact from other sources. Digital compression artifacts will always occur in the same place and in the same way. Possible MPEG artifacts are mosquitoes, blocking, and video noise.

aspect ratio The width-to-height ratio of an image. A 4:3 aspect ratio means the horizontal size is a third again wider than the vertical size. Standard television ratio is 4:3 (or 1.33:1). Widescreen DVD and HTDV aspect ratio is 16:9 (or 1.78:1). Common film aspect ratios are 1.85:1 and 2.35:1. Aspect ratios normalized to a height of 1 are often abbreviated by leaving off the *:1.*

ATAPI Advanced Technology Attachment (ATA) Packet Interface. An interface between a computer and its internal peripherals such as DVD-ROM drives. ATAPI provides the command set for controlling devices connected via an IDE interface. ATAPI is part of the Enhanced IDE (E-IDE) interface, also known as ATA-2. ATAPI was extended for use in DVD-ROM drives by the SFF 8090 specification.

ATSC Advanced Television Systems Committee. In 1978, the Federal Communications Commission (FCC) empaneled the Advisory Committee on Advanced Television Service (ACATS) as an investigatory and advisory committee to develop information that would assist the FCC in establishing an advanced broadcast television (ATV) standard for the United States. This committee created a subcommittee, the ATSC, to explore the need for and to coordinate development of the documentation of Advanced Television Systems. In 1993, the ATSC recommended that efforts be limited to a digital television system (DTV), and in September 1995 issued its recommendation for a Digital Television System standard, which was approved with the exclusion of compression format constraints (picture resolution, frame rate, and frame sequence).

ATV Advanced television. TV with significantly better video and audio than standard TV. Sometimes used interchangeably with *HDTV,* but more accurately encompasses any improved television system, including those beyond HDTV. Also sometimes used interchangeably with the final recommended standard of the ATSC, which is more correctly called *DTV.*

authoring For DVD-Video, authoring refers to the process of designing, creating, collecting, formatting, and encoding material. For DVD-ROM, authoring usually refers to using a specialized program to produce multimedia software.

autoplay (or **automatic playback**) A feature of DVD players which automatically begins playback of a disc if so encoded.

bandwidth   Strictly speaking, the range of frequencies (or the difference between the highest and the lowest frequency) carried by a circuit or signal. Loosely speaking, the amount of information carried in a signal. Technically, bandwidth does not apply to digital information; the term *data rate* is more accurate.

BCA   Burst cutting area. A circular section near the center of a DVD disc where ID codes and manufacturing information can be inscribed in bar-code format. (See Fig. 4.4.)

bit   A binary digit. The smallest representation of digital data: zero/one, off/on, no/yes. Eight bits make one byte.

bitmap   An image made of a two-dimensional grid of pixels. Each frame of digital video can be considered a bitmap, although some color information is usually shared by more than one pixel.

bit rate   The volume of data measured in bits over time. Equivalent to data rate.

bits per pixel   The number of bits used to represent the color or intensity of each pixel in a bitmap. One bit allows only two values (black and white), two bits allows four values, and so on. Also called *color depth* or *bit depth*.

bitstream   Digital data, usually encoded, designed to be processed sequentially and continuously.

bitstream recorder   A device capable of recording a stream of digital data but not necessarily able to process the data.

block   In MPEG video, an 8×8 matrix of pixels or DCT values representing a small chunk of luma or chroma. In DVD MPEG-2 video, a *macroblock* is made up of 6 blocks: 4 luma and 2 chroma.

blocking   A term referring to the occasional blocky appearance of compressed video. Caused when the compression ratio is high enough that the averaging of pixels in 8×8 blocks becomes visible.

Blue Book   The document that specifies the CD Extra interactive music CD format (see also **Enhanced CD**). The original CDV specification was also in a blue book.

Book A   The document specifying the DVD physical format (DVD-ROM). Finalized in August 1996.

Book B   The document specifying the DVD-Video format. Mostly finalized in August 1996.

Book C   The document specifying the DVD-Audio format. Not expected to be finalized before the middle of 1998 at the earliest.

Book D The document specifying the DVD record-once format (DVD-R). Finalized in August 1997.

Book E The document specifying the rewritable DVD format (DVD-RAM). Finalized in August 1997.

B picture (or **B frame**) One of three picture types used in MPEG video. B pictures are bidirectionally predicted, based on both previous and following pictures. B pictures usually use the least number of bits. B pictures do not propagate coding errors since they are not used as a reference by other pictures.

bps Bits per second. A unit of data rate.

brightness Defined by the CIE as the attribute of a visual sensation according to which area appears to emit more or less light. Loosely, the intensity of an image or pixel, independent of color; that is, its value along the axis from black to white.

burst A short segment of the color subcarrier in a composite signal, inserted to help the composite video decoder regenerate the color subcarrier.

B-Y, R-Y The general term for color-difference video signals carrying blue and red color information, where the brightness (Y) has been subtracted from the blue and red RGB signals to create B-Y and R-Y color-difference signals. (See Chap. 3.)

byte A unit of data or data storage space consisting of eight bits, commonly representing a single character. Digital data storage is usually measured in bytes, kilobytes, megabytes, and so on.

caption A textual representation of the audio information in a video program. Captions are usually intended for the hearing impaired, and therefore include additional text to identify the person speaking, off-screen sounds, and so on.

CAV Constant angular velocity. Refers to rotating disc systems in which the rotation speed is kept constant, where the pickup head travels over a longer surface as it moves away from the center of the disc. The advantage of CAV is that the same amount of information is provided in one rotation of the disc. Contrast with **CLV.**

C$_b$, C$_r$ The components of digital color-difference video signals carrying blue and red color information, where the brightness (Y) has been subtracted from the blue and red RGB signals to create B-Y and R-Y color-difference signals. (See Chap. 3.)

CBEMA Computer and Business Equipment Manufacturers Association. (See App. B.)

CBR Constant bit rate. Data compressed into a stream with a fixed data rate. The amount of compression (such as quantization) is varied to match the allocated data rate, but as a result quality may suffer during high compression periods. In other words, data rate is held constant while quality is allowed to vary. Compare to **VBR.**

CCIR Rec. 601 A standard for digital video. The CCIR changed its name to ITU-R, and the standard is now properly called ITU-R BT.601.

CD Short for *compact disc,* an optical disc storage format developed by Philips and Sony.

CD-DA Compact disc digital audio. The original music CD format, storing audio information as digital PCM data. Defined by the Red Book standard.

CD+G Compact disc plus graphics. A variation of CD which embeds graphical data in with the audio data, allowing video pictures to be displayed periodically as music is played. Primarily used for karaoke.

CD-i Compact disc interactive. An extension of the CD format designed around a set-top computer that connects to a TV to provide interactive home entertainment, including digital audio and video, video games, and software applications. Defined by the Green Book standard.

CD-Plus A type of Enhanced CD format using stamped multisession technology.

CD-R An extension of the CD format allowing data to be recorded once on a disc by using dye-sublimation technology. Defined by the Orange Book standard.

CD-ROM Compact disc read-only memory. An extension of the Compact disc digital audio (CD-DA) format that allows computer data to be stored in digital format. Defined by the Yellow Book standard.

CD-ROM XA CD-ROM extended architecture. A hybrid version of CD allowing interleaved audio and video.

CDV A combination of laserdisc and CD which places a section of CD-format audio on the beginning of the disc and a section of laserdisc-format video on the remainder of the disc.

cell In DVD-Video, a unit of video anywhere from a fraction of a second to hours long. Cells allow the video to be grouped for sharing content among titles, interleaving for multiple angles, and so on.

CEMA Consumer Electronics Manufacturers Association. A subsidiary of the Electronics Industry Association (EIA). (See App. B.)

CGMS   Copy guard management system. A method of preventing copies or controlling the number of sequential copies allowed. CGMS/A is added to an analog signal (such as line 21 of NTSC). CGMS/D is added to a digital signal, such as IEEE 1394.

challenge key   Data used in the authentication key exchange process between a DVD-ROM drive and a host computer, where one side determines if the other side contains the necessary authorized keys and algorithms for passing encrypted (scrambled) data.

channel   A part of an audio track. Typically there is one channel allocated for each loudspeaker.

channel data   The bits physically recorded on an optical disc after error-correction encoding and modulation. Because of the extra information and processing, channel data is larger than the user data contained within it.

chapter   In DVD-Video, a division of a title. Technically called a *part of title* (*PTT*).

chroma (C')   The nonlinear color component of a video signal, independent of the luma. Identified by the symbol C' (where ' indicates nonlinearity) but usually written as C because it's never linear in practice.

chroma subsampling   Reducing color resolution by taking fewer color samples than luminance samples. (See **4:1:1** and **4:2:0**.)

chrominance (C)   The color component (hue and saturation) of light, independent of luminance. Technically, chrominance refers to the linear component of video, as opposed to the transformed nonlinear chroma component.

CIE   Commission Internationale de l'Éclairage/International Commission on Illumination. (See App. B.)

CIRC   Cross-interleaved Reed Solomon code. An error-correction coding method which overlaps small frames of data.

clamping area   The area near the inner hole of a disc where the drive grips the disc in order to spin it.

closed caption   Text captions for video which are not normally visible, as opposed to *open captions*, which are a permanent part of the picture. In the United States, the official NTSC Closed Caption standard requires that all TVs larger than 13 inches include circuitry to decode and display caption information stored on line 21 of the video signal. DVD-Video can provide closed caption data, but the subpicture format is preferred for its versatility.

CLV   Constant linear velocity. Refers to a rotating disc system in which the head moves over the disc surface at a constant velocity, requiring that the motor vary the rotation speed as the head travels in and out. The further the head is from the center of the disc, the slower the rotation. The advantage of CLV is that data density remains constant, optimizing use of the surface area. Contrast with **CAV.**

codec   Coder/decoder. Circuitry or computer software that encodes and decodes a signal.

colorburst   See **burst.**

color depth   The number of levels of color (usually including luma and chroma) that can be represented by a pixel. Generally expressed as a number of bits or a number of colors. The color depth of MPEG video in DVD is 24 bits, although the chroma component is shared across 4 pixels (averaging 12 actual bits per pixel).

color difference   A pair of video signals that contain the color components minus the brightness component, usually B-Y and R-Y (G-Y is not used, since it generally carries less information). The color-difference signals for a black-and-white picture are zero. The advantage of color-difference signals is that the color component can be reduced more than the brightness (luma) component without being visually perceptible.

colorist   The title used for someone who operates a telecine machine to transfer film to video. Part of the process involves correcting the video color to match the film.

component video   A video system containing three separate color component signals, either red/green/blue (RGB) or chroma/color difference (YC_bC_r, YP_bP_r, YUV), in analog or digital form. The MPEG-2 encoding system used by DVD is based on color-difference component digital video. Very few televisions have component video inputs.

composite video   An analog video signal in which the luma and chroma components are combined (by frequency multiplexing), along with sync and burst. Also called *CVBS.* Most televisions and VCRs have composite video connectors, which are usually colored yellow.

compression   The process of removing redundancies in digital data to reduce the amount that must be stored or transmitted. Lossless compression removes only enough redundancy so that the original data can be recreated exactly as it was. Lossy compression sacrifices additional data to achieve greater compression.

constant data rate or **constant bit rate**   See **CBR.**

contrast   The range of brightness between the darkest and lightest elements of an image.

control area   A part of the lead-in area on a DVD containing one ECC block (16 sectors) repeated 192 times. The repeated ECC block holds information about the disc.

CPU   Central processing unit. The integrated circuit chip that forms the brain of a computer or other electronic device. DVD-Video players contain rudimentary CPUs to provide general control and interactive features.

crop   To trim and remove a section of the video picture in order to make it conform to a different shape. Cropping is used in the pan & scan process, but not in the letterbox process.

DAC   Digital-to-analog converter. Circuitry that converts digital data (such as audio or video) to analog data.

DAT   Digital audio tape. A magnetic audio tape format that uses PCM to store digitized audio or digital data.

data area   The physical area of a DVD disc between the lead in and the lead out (or middle area) which contains the stored data content of the disc.

data rate   The volume of data measured over time; the rate at which digital information can be conveyed. Usually expressed as bits per second with notations of kbps (thousand/sec), Mbps (million/sec), and Gbps (billion/sec). Digital audio date rate is generally computed as the number of samples per second times the bit size of the sample. For example, the data rate of uncompressed 16-bit, 48-kHz, two-channel audio is 1536 kbps. Digital video bit rate is generally computed as the number of bits per pixel times the number of pixels per line times the number of lines per frame times the number of frames per second. For example, the data rate of a DVD movie before compression is usually $12 \times 720 \times 480 \times 24 = 99.5$ Mbps. Compression reduces the data rate. Digital data rate is sometimes inaccurately equated with bandwidth.

DBS   Digital broadcast satellite. The general term for 18-inch digital satellite systems.

DC   Direct current. Electrical current flowing in one direction only. Adopted in the video world to refer to a signal with zero frequency. Compare to **AC.**

DCC   Digital compact cassette. A digital audio tape format based on the popular compact cassette. Abandoned by Philips in 1996.

DCT Discrete cosine transform. An invertible, discrete, orthogonal transformation. Got that? A mathematical process used in MPEG video encoding to transform blocks of pixel values into blocks of spatial frequency values with lower-frequency components organized into the upper-left corner, allowing the high-frequency components in the lower-right corner to be discounted or discarded.

decimation A form of subsampling which discards existing samples (pixels, in the case of spatial decimation, or pictures, in the case of termporal decimation). The resulting information is reduced in size but may suffer from aliasing.

decode To reverse the transformation process of an encoding method. Decoding processes are usually deterministic.

decoder 1) A circuit that decodes compressed audio or video, taking an encoded input stream and producing output such as audio or video. DVD players use the decoders to recreate information that was compressed by systems such as MPEG-2 and Dolby Digital; 2) a circuit that converts composite video to component video or matrixed audio to multiple channels.

delta picture (or **delta frame**) A video picture based on the changes from the picture before (or after) it. MPEG P pictures and B pictures are examples. Contrast with **key picture.**

deterministic A process or model whose outcome does not depend upon chance, and where a given input will always produce the same output. Audio and video decoding processes are mostly deterministic.

digital Expressed in digits. A set of discrete numeric values, as used by a computer. Analog information can be digitized by sampling.

digital signal processor (DSP) A digital circuit that can be programmed to perform digital data manipulation tasks such as decoding or audio effects.

digitize To convert analog information to digital information by sampling.

DIN Deutsches Institut für Normung/German Institute for Standardization. (See App. B.)

directory The part of a disc that indicates what files are stored on the disc and where they are located.

DirectShow A software standard developed by Microsoft for playback of digital video and audio in the Windows operating system. Replaces the older Video for Windows software.

disc key   A value used to encrypt and decrypt (scramble) a title key on DVD-Video discs.

disc menu   The main menu of a DVD-Video disc, from which titles are selected. Also called the *system menu* or *title selection menu*. Sometimes confusingly called the *title menu,* which more accurately refers to the menu within a title from which audio, subpicture, chapters, and so forth can be selected.

discrete cosine transform (DCT)   An invertible, discrete, orthogonal transformation. A mathematical process used in MPEG video encoding to transform blocks of pixel values into blocks of spatial frequency values with lower-frequency components organized into the upper-left corner, allowing the high-frequency components in the lower-right corner to be discounted or discarded.

discrete surround sound   Audio in which each channel is stored and transmitted separate from and independent of other channels. Multiple independent channels directed to loudspeakers in front of and behind the listener allow precise control of the soundfield in order to generate localized sounds and simulate moving sound sources.

display rate   The number of times per second the image in a video system is refreshed. Progressive scan systems such as film or HDTV change the image once per frame. Interlace scan systems such as standard television change the image twice per frame, with two fields in each frame. Film has a frame rate of 24 fps, but each frame is shown twice by the projector for a display rate of 48 fps. 525/60 (NTSC) television has a rate of 29.97 frames per second (59.94 fields per second). 625/50 (PAL/SECAM) television has a rate of 25 frames per second (50 fields per second).

DLT   Digital linear tape. A digital tape archive standard, commonly used for submitting a premastered DVD disc image to a replication service.

Dolby Digital   A perceptual coding system for audio, developed by Dolby Laboratories and accepted as an international standard. Dolby Digital is the most common means of encoding audio for DVD-Video and is the mandatory audio compression system for 525/60 (NTSC) discs.

Dolby Pro Logic   The technique (or the circuit which applies the technique) of extracting surround audio channels from a matrix-encoded audio signal. Dolby Pro Logic is a decoding technique only, but is often mistakenly used to refer to Dolby Surround audio encoding.

Dolby Surround   The standard for matrix encoding surround-sound channels in a stereo signal by applying a set of defined mathematical functions when combining center and surround channels with left and right channels. The center and surround channels can then be extracted by a decoder such as a Dolby Pro Logic circuit which applies the inverse of the mathematical functions. A Dolby Surround decoder extracts surround channels, while a Dolby Pro Logic decoder uses additional processing to create a center channel. The process is essentially independent of the recording or transmission format. Both Dolby Digital and MPEG audio compression systems are compatible with Dolby Surround audio.

downmix   To convert a multichannel audio track into a two-channel stereo track by combining the channels with the Dolby Surround process. All DVD players capable of playing NTSC are required to provide downmixed audio output from Dolby Digital audio tracks.

downsampling   See **subsampling**.

DRC   See **dynamic range compression**.

DSD   Direct Stream Digital. An uncompressed audio bitstream coding method developed by Sony. An alternative to PCM.

DSI   Data search information. Navigation and search information contained in the DVD-Video data stream. DSI and PCI together make up an overhead of about 1 Mbps.

DSP   Digital signal processor (or processing).

DTS   Digital Theater Sound. A perceptual audio-coding system developed for theaters. A competitor to Dolby Digital and an optional audio track format for DVD-Video.

DTV   Digital television. In general, any system that encodes video and audio in digital form. In specific, the Digital Television System proposed by the ATSC or the digital TV standard proposed by the Digital TV Team founded by Microsoft, Intel, and Compaq.

duplication   The reproduction of media, such as producing thousands of optical discs with a stamping process. (See also **replication**.)

DV   Digital Video. Usually refers to the digital videocassette standard developed by Sony and JVC.

DVB   Digital video broadcast. A European standard for broadcast, cable, and digital satellite video transmission.

DVC   Digital video cassette. Early name for DV.

DVCAM   Sony's proprietary version of DV.

DVCPro   Matsushita's proprietary version of DV.

DVD An acronym that officially stands for nothing, but is often expanded as *Digital Video Disc* or *Digital Versatile Disc.* The audio/video/data storage system based on 12- and 8-cm optical discs.

DVD-Audio (DVD-A) The planned audio-only format of DVD. Still undefined in 1997.

DVD-R A version of DVD on which data can be recorded once. Uses dye sublimation recording technology.

DVD-RAM A version of DVD on which data can be recorded more than once. Uses phase-change recording technology.

DVD-Recordable Generally refers to both DVD-R and DVD-RAM.

DVD-ROM The base format of DVD. ROM stands for *read-only memory,* referring to the fact that standard DVD-ROM and DVD-Video discs can't be recorded on. A DVD-ROM can store essentially any form of digital data.

DVD-Video (DVD-V) A standard for storing and reproducing audio and video on DVD-ROM discs, based on MPEG video, Dolby Digital and MPEG audio, and other proprietary data formats.

dye-sublimation Optical disc recording technology that uses a high-powered laser to burn readable marks into a layer of organic dye. Other recording formats include magneto-optical and phase-change.

dynamic range The difference between the loudest and softest sound in an audio signal. The dynamic range of digital audio is determined by the sample size. Increasing the sample size does not allow louder sounds; it increases the resolution of the signal, thus allowing softer sounds to be separated from the noise floor (and allowing more amplification with less distortion).

dynamic range compression A technique of reducing the range between loud and soft sounds in order to make dialogue more audible. Used in the downmix process of multichannel DVD sound tracks.

EBU European Broadcasting Union. (See App. B.)

ECC See **Error correction code.**

ECD Error-detection and correction code. See **error-correction code.**

ECMA European Computer Manufacturers Association. (See App. B.)

EDC A short error-detection code applied at the end of a DVD sector.

EDTV Enhanced-definition television. A system which uses existing transmission equipment to send an enhanced signal which looks the same on existing receivers but carries additional information to improve the picture quality on new enhanced receivers. PALPlus is an example of EDTV. (Contrast with **HDTV** and **IDTV.**)

EFM   Eight-to-fourteen modulation. A modulation method used by CD. The 8/16 modulation used by DVD is sometimes called *EFM plus.*

EIA   Electronics Industry Association. (See App. B.)

E-IDE   Enhanced Integrated Drive Electronics. Extensions to the IDE standard providing faster data transfer and allowing access to larger drives, including CD-ROM and tape drives, using ATAPI. E-IDE was adopted as a standard by ANSI in 1994. ANSI calls it *Advanced Technology Attachment-2 (ATA-2)* or *Fast ATA.*

elementary stream   A general term for a coded bitstream such as audio or video. Elementary streams are made up of packs of packets.

encode   To transform data for storage or transmission, usually in such a way that redundancies are eliminated or complexity is reduced. Most compression is based on one or more encoding methods. Data such as audio or video is encoded for efficient storage or transmission and is decoded for access or display.

encoder   1) A circuit or program that encodes (and thereby compresses) audio or video; 2) a circuit that converts component digital video to composite analog video. DVD players include TV encoders to generate standard television signals from decoded video and audio; 3) a circuit that converts multichannel audio to two-channel matrixed audio.

Enhanced CD   A general term for various techniques that add computer software to a music CD, producing a disc which can be played in a music player or read by a computer. Also called *CD Extra, CD Plus, hybrid CD, interactive music CD, mixed-mode CD, pre-gap CD,* or *track-zero CD.*

entropy coding   Variable-length, lossless coding of a digital signal to reduce redundancy. MPEG-2 applies entropy coding after the quantization step.

error-correction code   Additional information added to data to allow errors to be detected and possibly corrected. See Chap. 3.

ETSI   European Telecommunications Standards Institute. (See App. B.)

field   A set of alternating scan lines in an interlaced video picture. A frame is made of a top (odd) field and a bottom (even) field.

file   A collection of data stored on a disc, usually in groups of sectors.

file system   A defined way of storing files, directories, and information about them on a data storage device.

filter (*verb*) To reduce the amount of information in a signal. (*noun*) A circuit or process that reduces the amount of information in a signal. Analog filtering usually removes certain frequencies. Digital filtering (when not emulating analog filtering) usually averages together multiple adjacent pixels, lines, or frames to create a single new pixel, line, or frame. This generally causes a loss of detail, especially with complex images or rapid motion. See **letterbox filter.** Compare to **interpolate.**

Firewire A standard for transmission of digital data between external peripherals, including consumer audio and video devices. The official name is *IEEE 1394,* based on the original Firewire design by Apple Computer.

fixed rate Information flow at a constant volume over time. See **CBR.**

forced display A feature of DVD-Video allowing subpictures to be displayed even if the player's subpicture display mode is turned off. Designed for showing subtitles in a scene where the language is different from the native language of the film.

fps Frames per second. A measure of the rate at which pictures are shown for a motion video image. In NTSC and PAL video, each frame is made up of two interlaced fields.

frame The piece of a video signal containing the spatial detail of one complete image; the entire set of scan lines. In an interlaced system, a frame contains two fields.

frame doubler A video processor that increases the frame rate (display rate) in order to create a smoother-looking video display. Compare to **line doubler.**

frame rate The frequency of discrete images. Usually measured in frames per second (fps). Film has a rate of 24 frames per second, but usually must be adjusted to match the display rate of a video system.

frequency The number of repetitions of a phenomenon in a given amount of time. The number of complete cycles of a periodic process occurring per unit time.

G Giga. An SI prefix for denominations of 1 billion (10^9).

GB Gigabyte.

Gbps Billions (10^9) of bits per second.

G byte One billion (10^9) bytes. Not to be confused with *GB* or *gigabyte* (2^{30} bytes).

gigabyte 1,073,741,824 (2^{30}) bytes. See the end of Chap. 1 (p. 12) for more information.

GOP   Group of pictures. In MPEG video, one or more I pictures followed by P and B pictures. A GOP is the atomic unit of MPEG video access. GOPs are limited in DVD-Video to 18 frames for 525/60 and 15 frames for 625/50.

gray market   Dealers and distributors who sell equipment without proper authorization from the manufacturer.

Green Book   The document developed in 1987 by Philips and Sony as an extension to CD-ROM XA for the CD-i system.

HDTV   High-definition television. A video format with a resolution approximately twice that of conventional television in both the horizontal and vertical dimensions, and a picture aspect ratio of 16:9. Used loosely to refer to the U.S. DTV System. Contrast with **EDTV** and **IDTV**.

Hertz   See **Hz**.

HFS   Hierarchical file system. A file system used by Apple Computer's Mac OS operating system.

High Sierra   The original file system standard developed for CD-ROM, later modified and adopted as ISO 9660.

horizontal resolution   See **lines of horizontal resolution**.

HRRA   Home Recording Rights Association.

HSF   See **High Sierra**.

HTML   Hypertext markup language. A tagging specification, based on SGML (standard generalized markup language), for formatting text to be transmitted over the Internet and displayed by client software.

hue   The color of light or of a pixel. The property of color determined by the dominant wavelength of light.

Huffman coding   A lossless compression technique of assigning variable-length codes to a known set of values. Values occurring most frequently are assigned the shortest codes. MPEG uses a variation of Huffman coding with fixed code tables, often called *variable-length coding (VLC)*.

Hz   Hertz. A unit of frequency measurement. The number of cycles (repetitions) per second.

IDE   Integrated Drive Electronics. An internal bus, or standard electronic interface between a computer and internal block storage devices. IDE was adopted as a standard by ANSI in November 1990. ANSI calls it *Advanced Technology Attachment (ATA)*. Also see **E-IDE** and **ATAPI**.

IDTV Improved-definition television. A television receiver that improves the apparent quality of the picture from a standard video signal by using techniques such as frame doubling, line doubling, and digital signal processing.

IEC International Electrotechnical Commission. (See App. B.)

IED ID error correction. An error-detection code applied to each sector ID on a DVD disc.

IEEE Institute of Electrical and Electronics Engineers. An electronics standards body.

IEEE 1394 A standard for transmission of digital data between external peripherals, including consumer audio and video devices. Also known as FireWire.

I-MPEG Intraframe MPEG. An unofficial variation of MPEG video encoding that uses only intraframe compression. I-MPEG is used by DV equipment.

interframe Something that occurs between multiple frames of video. Interframe compression takes temporal redundancy into account. Contrast with **intraframe.**

interlace A video scanning system in which alternating lines are transmitted, so that half a picture is displayed each time the scanning beam moves down the screen. An interlaced frame is made of two fields. (See Chap. 3.)

interleave To arrange data in alternating chunks so that selected parts can be extracted while other parts are skipped over, or so that each chunk carries a piece of a different data stream.

interpolate To increase the pixels, scan lines, or pictures when scaling an image or a video stream by averaging together adjacent pixels, lines, or frames to create additional inserted pixels or frames. This generally causes a softening of still images and a blurriness of motion images because no new information is created. Compare to **filter.**

intraframe Something that occurs within a single frame of video. Intraframe compression does not reduce temporal redundancy, but allows each frame to be independently manipulated or accessed. (See **I picture.**) Compare to **interframe.**

inverse telecine The reverse of 3:2 pulldown, where the frames which were duplicated to create 60-fields/second video from 24-frames/second film source are removed. MPEG-2 video encoders usually apply an inverse telecine process to convert 60-fields/second video into 24-

frames/second encoded video. The encoder adds information enabling the decoder to recreate the 60-fields/second display rate.

I picture (or **I frame**)   In MPEG video, an *intra* picture that is encoded independent from other pictures (see **intraframe**). Transform coding (DCT, quantization, and VLC) is used with no motion compensation, resulting in only moderate compression. I pictures provide a reference point for dependent P pictures and B pictures and allow random access into the compressed video stream.

ISO   International Organization for Standardization. (See App. B.)

ISO 9660   The international standard for the file system used by CD-ROM. Allows filenames of only 8 characters plus a 3-character extension.

ITU   International Telecommunication Union. (See App. B.)

ITU-R BT.601   The international standard specifying the format of digital component video. Currently at version 5 (identified as 601-5).

Java   A programming language with specific features designed for use with the Internet and HTML.

JCIC   Joint Committee on Intersociety Coordination.

JEC   Joint Engineering Committee of EIA and NCTA.

jewel box   The plastic clamshell case that holds a CD or DVD.

JPEG   Joint Photographic Experts Group. The international committee which created its namesake standard for compressing still images.

k   Kilo. An SI prefix for denominations of one thousand (10^3). Also used, in capital form, for 1024 bytes of computer data (see **kilobyte**).

karaoke   Literally *empty orchestra*. The social sensation from Japan where sufficiently inebriated people embarrass themselves in public by singing along to a music track. Karaoke was largely responsible for the success of laserdisc in Japan, thus supporting it elsewhere.

KB   Kilobyte.

kbps   Thousands of bits per second (1000).

k byte   One thousand (10^3) bytes. Not to be confused with *KB* or *kilobyte* (2^{10} bytes).

key picture (or **key frame**)   A video picture containing the entire content of the image (intraframe encoding), rather than the difference between it and another image (interframe encoding). MPEG I pictures are key pictures. Contrast with **delta picture.**

kHz   Kilohertz. A unit of frequency measurement. One thousand cycles (repetitions) per second or 1000 hertz.

kilobyte   1024 (2^{10}) bytes. See p. 12 for more information.

laserdisc   A 12-inch (or 8-inch) optical disc that holds analog video (using an FM signal) and both analog and digital (PCM) audio. A precursor to DVD.

layer   The plane of a DVD disc on which information is recorded in a pattern of microscopic pits. Each substrate of a disc can contain one or two layers. The first layer, closest to the readout surface, is layer 0; the second is layer 1.

lead in   The physical area 1.2 mm or wider preceding the data area on a disc. The lead in contains sync sectors and control data including disc keys and other information.

lead out   On a single-layer disc or PTP dual-layer disc, the physical area 1.0 mm or wider toward the outside of the disc following the data area. On an OTP dual-layer disc, the physical area 1.2 mm or wider at the inside of the disc following the recorded data area (which is read from the outside toward the inside on the second layer).

legacy   A term used to describe a hybrid disc that can be played in both a DVD player and a CD player.

letterbox   The process or form of video where black horizontal mattes are added to the top and bottom of the display area in order to create a frame in which to display video using an aspect ratio different than that of the display. The letterbox method preserves the entire video picture, as opposed to pan & scan. DVD-Video players can automatically letterbox a widescreen picture for display on a standard 4:3 TV.

letterbox filter   Circuitry in a DVD player that reduces the vertical size of anamorphic widescreen video (combining every 4 lines into 3) and adds black mattes at the top and bottom. Also see **filter.**

level   In MPEG-2, levels specify parameters such as resolution, bit rate, and frame rate. Compare to **profile.**

linear PCM   A coded representation of digital data that is not compressed. Linear PCM spreads values evenly across the range from highest to lowest, as opposed to nonlinear (*companded*) PCM which allocates more values to more important frequency ranges.

line doubler   A video processor that doubles the number of lines in the scanning system in order to create a display with scan lines that are less visible. Some line doublers convert from interlaced to progressive scan.

lines of horizontal resolution   A common but subjective measurement of the resolution of an analog video system, measured in half-cycles per picture height. Each cycle is a pair of lines, one black and one white. Sometimes abbreviated as *TVL*. The measurement is usually made by viewing a test pattern to determine where the black and white lines blur into gray. The resolution of VHS video is commonly gauged at 240 lines of horizontal resolution, broadcast video at 330, laserdisc at 425, and DVD at 500 to 540. Because the measurement is relative to picture height, the aspect ratio must be taken into account when determining the number of vertical units (roughly equivalent to pixels) that can be displayed across the width of the display. For example, an aspect ratio of 4/3 multiplied by 540 gives 720 pixels.

locale   See **regional code.**

logical   An artificial structure or organization of information created for convenience of access or reference, usually different from the physical structure or organization.

logical unit   A physical or virtual peripheral device, such as a DVD-ROM drive.

lossless compression   Compression techniques that allow the original data to be recreated without loss. Contrast with **lossy compression.**

lossy compression   Compression techniques that achieve very high compression ratios by permanently removing data while preserving as much significant information as possible. Lossy compression includes perceptual coding techniques that attempt to limit the data loss to that which is least likely to be noticed by human perception.

LP   Long-playing record. An audio recording on a plastic platter turning at $33\frac{1}{3}$ rpm and read by a stylus.

LPCM   See **linear PCM.**

luma (Y′)   The brightness component of a color video image (also called the *grayscale, monochrome,* or *black-and-white* component). Nonlinear luminance. The standard luma signal is computed from nonlinear RGB as $Y' = 0.299\ R' + 0.587\ G' + 0.114\ B'$.

luminance (Y)   Loosely, the sum of RGB tristimulus values corresponding to brightness. May refer to a linear or nonlinear signal.

M   Mega. An SI prefix for denominations of one million (10^6).

Mac OS   The operating system used by Apple Macintosh computers.

macroblock   In MPEG MP@ML, the four 8×8 blocks of luma information and two 8×8 blocks of chroma information from a 16×16 area of a video frame.

macroblocking   An MPEG artifact. See **blocking.**

Macrovision An antitaping process that modifies a signal so that it appears unchanged on most televisions but is distorted and unwatchable when played back from a videotape recording. Macrovision takes advantage of characteristics of AGC circuits and burst decoder circuits in VCRs to interfere with the recording process.

magneto-optical Recordable disc technology using a laser to heat spots that are altered by a magnetic field. Other formats include dye-sublimation and phase-change.

main level (ML) A range of proscribed picture parameters defined by the MPEG-2 video standard, with maximum resolution equivalent to ITU-R BT.601 ($720 \times 576 \times 30$). (Also see **level.**)

main profile (MP) A subset of the syntax of the MPEG-2 video standard designed to be supported over a large range of mainstream applications such as digital cable TV, DVD, and digital satellite transmission. (Also see **profile.**)

master The metal disc used to stamp replicas of optical discs. The tape used to make additional recordings.

mastering The process of replicating optical discs by injecting liquid plastic into a mold containing a master. Often used inaccurately to refer to *premastering.*

matrix encoding The technique of combining additional surround-sound channels into a conventional stereo signal. Also see **Dolby Surround.**

matte An area of a video display or motion picture that is covered (usually in black) or omitted in order to create a differently shaped area within the picture frame.

MB Megabyte.

Mbps Millions of bits per second (1,000,000).

M byte One million (10^6) bytes. Not to be confused with *MB* or *megabyte* (2^{20} bytes).

megabyte 1,048,576 (2^{20}) bytes. See p. 12 for more information.

megapixel A term referring to an image or display format with a resolution of approximately 1 million pixels.

memory Data storage used by computers or other digital electronics systems. Read-only memory (ROM) permanently stores data or software program instructions. New data cannot be written to ROM. Random-access memory (RAM) temporarily stores data—including digital audio and video—while it is being manipulated, and holds software application programs while they are being executed. Data can be read from and written to RAM. Other long-term memory includes hard disks, floppy disks, digital CD formats (CD-ROM, CD-R, and CD-RW), and DVD formats (DVD-ROM, DVD-R, and DVD-RAM).

MHz   One million (10^6) Hz.

Microsoft Windows   The leading operating system for Intel CPU-based computers. Developed by Microsoft.

middle area   On a dual-layer OTP disc, the physical area 1.0 mm or wider on both layers, adjacent to the outside of the data area.

mixed mode   A type of CD containing both Red Book audio and Yellow Book computer data tracks.

MO   Magneto-optical rewriteable discs.

modulation   Replacing patterns of bits with different (usually larger) patterns designed to control the characteristics of the data signal. DVD uses 8/16 modulation, where each set of 8 bits is replaced by 16 bits before being written onto the disc.

mosquitoes   A term referring to the fuzzy dots that can appear around sharp edges (high spatial frequencies) after video compression. Also known as the *Gibbs Effect*.

motion compensation   In MPEG, the process of analyzing previous or future frames to identify blocks that have not changed or have only changed location. Motion vectors are then stored in place of the blocks. This is very computation-intensive and can cause visual artifacts when subject to errors.

motion estimation   The process of estimating motion vectors during MPEG encoding. The term is often used interchangeably with *motion compensation.*

motion vector   A two-dimensional spatial vector used for MPEG motion compensation to provide an offset from the encoded position of a block in a reference (I or P) picture to the predicted position (in a P or B picture).

MP@ML   Main profile at main level. The common MPEG-2 format used by DVD (along with SP@SL).

MPEG   Moving Pictures Expert Group. An international committee that developed the MPEG family of audio and video compression systems.

MPEG audio   Audio compressed according to the MPEG perceptual encoding system. MPEG-1 audio provides two channels, which can be in Dolby Surround format. MPEG-2 audio adds data to provide discrete multichannel audio. Stereo MPEG audio is the mandatory audio compression system for 625/50 (PAL/SECAM) DVD-Video.

MPEG video   Video compressed according to the MPEG encoding system. MPEG-1 is typically used for low data rate video such as on a Video CD. MPEG-2 is used for higher-quality video, especially interlaced video, such as on DVD or HDTV. (See Table 3.5 for a comparison of MPEG-1 and MPEG-2.)

Mt. Fuji   See **SFF 8090**.

multiangle   A DVD-Video program containing multiple angles allowing different views of a scene to be selected during playback.

multichannel   Multiple channels of audio, usually containing different signals for different speakers in order to create a surround-sound effect.

multilanguage   A DVD-Video program containing sound tracks and subtitle tracks for more than one language.

multimedia   Information in more than one form, such as text, still images, sound, animation, and video. Usually implies that the information is presented by a computer.

multiplexing   Combining multiple signals or data streams into a single signal or stream. Usually achieved by interleaving at a low level.

MultiRead   A standard developed by the Yokohama group, a consortium of companies attempting to ensure that new CD and DVD hardware can read all CD formats (see "Innovations of CD" in Chap. 2 for a discussion of CD variations).

multisession   A technique in write-once recording technology that allows additional data to be appended after data written in an earlier session.

mux   Short for *multiplex*.

mux_rate   In MPEG, the combined rate of all packetized elementary streams (PES) of one program. The mux_rate of DVD is 10.08 Mbps.

NAB   National Association of Broadcasters.

NCTA   National Cable Television Association.

noise   Irrelevant, meaningless, or erroneous information added to a signal by the recording or transmission medium or by an encoding/decoding process. An advantage of digital formats over analog formats is that noise can be completely eliminated (although new noise may be introduced by compression).

noise floor   The level of background noise in a signal or the level of noise introduced by equipment or storage media below which the signal can't be isolated from the noise.

NTSC   National Television Systems Committee. A committee organized by the Electronic Industries Association (EIA) that developed commercial television broadcast standards for the United States. The group first established black-and-white TV standards in 1941, using a scanning system of 525 lines at 60 fields per second. The second committee standardized color enhancements using 525 lines at 59.94 fields per second. NTSC refers to the composite color-encoding system. The 525/59.94 scanning system (with a 3.58-MHz color subcarrier) is identified by the letter *M,* and is often incorrectly referred to as *NTSC.* The NTSC standard is also used in Canada, Japan, and other parts of the world. NTSC is facetiously referred to as meaning *never the same color* because of the system's difficulty in maintaining color consistency.

NTSC-4.43   A variation of NTSC where a 525/59.94 signal is encoded using the PAL subcarrier frequency and chroma modulation. Also called *60-Hz PAL.*

numerical aperture (NA)   A unitless measure of the ability of a lens to gather and focus light. A numerical aperture of 1 implies no change in parallel light beams. The higher the number, the greater the focusing power.

operating system   The primary software in a computer, containing general instructions for managing applications, communications, input/output, memory and other low-level tasks. DOS, Windows, Mac OS, and UNIX are examples of operating systems.

opposite path   See **OTP.**

Orange Book   The document begun in 1990 which specifies the format of recordable CD. Three parts define magneto-optical erasable (MO) and write-once (WO), dye-sublimation write-once (CD-R), and phase-change rewritable (CD-RW) discs. Orange Book added multisession capabilities to the CD-ROM XA format.

OS   Operating system.

OSTA   Optical Storage Technology Association. (See App. B.)

OTP   Opposite track path. A variation of DVD dual-layer disc layout where readout begins at the center of the disc on the first layer, travels to the outer edge of the discs, then switches to the second layer and travels back toward the center. Designed for long, continuous-play programs. Also called RSDL. Contrast with **PTP.**

overscan The area at the edges of a television tube that is covered to hide possible video distortion. Overscan typically covers about 4 or 5 percent of the picture.

pack A group of MPEG packets in a DVD-Video program stream. Each DVD sector (2048 bytes) contains one pack.

packet A low-level unit of DVD-Video (MPEG) data storage containing contiguous bytes of data belonging to a single elementary stream such as video, audio, control, and so forth. Packets are grouped into packs.

packetized elementary stream (PES) The low-level stream of MPEG packets containing an elementary stream, such as audio or video.

PAL Phase Alternate Line. A video standard used in Europe and other parts of the world for composite color encoding. Various version of PAL use different scanning systems and color subcarrier frequencies (identified with letters B, D, G, H, I, M, and N), the most common being 625 lines at 50 fields per second, with a color subcarrier of 4.43 MHz. PAL is also said to mean "picture always lousy" or "perfect at last," depending on which side of the ocean the speaker comes from.

palette A table of colors that identifies a subset from a larger range of colors. The small number of colors in the palette allows fewer bits to be used for each pixel. Also called a color look-up table (CLUT).

pan & scan The technique of reframing a picture to conform to a different aspect ratio by cropping parts of the picture. DVD-Video players can automatically create a 4:3 pan & scan version from widescreen video by using a horizontal offset encoded with the video.

parallel path See **PTP**.

parental management An optional feature of DVD-Video that prohibits programs from being viewed or substitutes different scenes within a program depending on the parental level set in the player. Parental control requires that parental levels and additional material (if necessary) be encoded on the disc.

part of title In DVD-Video, a division of a title representing a scene. Also called a *chapter.* Parts of titles are numbered 1 to 99.

PCI Presentation control information. A DVD-Video data stream containing details of the timing and presentation of a program (aspect ratio, angle change, menu highlight and selection information, and so on). PCI and DSI together make up an overhead of about 1 Mbps.

PCM An uncompressed, digitally coded representation of an analog signal. The waveform is sampled at regular intervals and a series of pulses in coded form (usually quantized) are generated to represent the amplitude.

PC-TV   The merger of television and computers. A personal computer capable of displaying video as a television.

pel   See **pixel**.

perceived resolution   The apparent resolution of a display from the observer's point of view, based on viewing distance, viewing conditions, and physical resolution of the display.

perceptual coding   Lossy compression techniques based on the study of human perception. Perceptual coding systems identify and remove information that is least likely to be missed by the average human observer.

PES   Packetized elementary stream.

PGCI   Program chain information. Data describing a chain of cells (grouped into programs) and their sector locations, thus composing a sequential program. PGCI data is contained in the PCI stream.

phase-change   A technology for rewritable optical discs using a physical effect in which a laser beam heats a recording material to reversibly change an area from an amorphous state to a crystalline state, or vice versa. Continuous heat just above the melting point creates the crystalline state (an erasure), while high heat followed by rapid cooling creates the amorphous state (a mark). (Other recording technologies include dye-sublimation and magneto-optical.)

physical format   The low-level characteristics of the DVD-ROM and DVD-Video standards, including pits on the disc, location of data, and organization of data according to physical position.

picture   In video terms, a single still image or a sequence of moving images. Picture generally refers to a frame, but for interlaced frames may refer instead to a field of the frame. In a more general sense, picture refers to the entire image shown on a video display.

picture stop   A function of DVD-Video where a code indicates that video playback should stop and a still picture be displayed.

PIP   Picture in picture. A feature of some televisions that shows another channel or video source in a small window superimposed in a corner of the screen.

pit   A microscopic depression in the recording layer of a disc. Pits are usually $\frac{1}{4}$ of the laser wavelength so as to cause cancellation of the beam by diffraction.

pit art   A pattern of pits to be stamped onto a disc to provide visual art rather than data. A cheaper alternative to a printed label.

pixel   The smallest picture element of an image (one sample of each color component). A single dot of the array of dots that makes up a picture. Sometimes abbreviated to pel. The resolution of a digital display is typically specified in terms of pixels (width by height) and color depth (the number of bits required to represent each pixel).

pixel aspect ratio   The ratio of width to height of a single pixel. Often means sample pitch aspect ratio (when referring to sampled digital video). Pixel aspect ratio for a given raster can be calculated as $y/x \times w/h$ (where x and y are the raster horizontal pixel count and vertical pixel count, and w and h are the display aspect ratio width and height). Pixel aspect ratios are also confusingly calculated as $x/y \times w/h$, giving a height-to-width ratio. (See Table 4.17.)

pixel depth   See **color depth.**

POP   Picture outside picture. A feature of some widescreen displays that uses the unused area around a 4:3 picture to show additional pictures.

P picture (or **P frame**)   In MPEG video, a "predicted" picture based on difference from previous pictures. P pictures (along with I pictures) provide a reference for following P pictures or B pictures.

premastering   The process of preparing data in the final format to create a DVD disc image for mastering. Includes creating DVD control and navigation data, multiplexing data streams together, generating error-correction codes, and performing channel modulation. Often includes the process of encoding video, audio, and subpictures.

presentation data   DVD-Video information such as video, menus, and audio which is presented to the viewer. (See **PCI.**)

profile   In MPEG-2, profiles specify syntax and processes such as picture types, scalability, and extensions. Compare to **level.**

program   In a general sense, a sequence of audio or video. In a technical sense for DVD-Video, a group of cells within a program chain (PGC).

program chain   In DVD-Video, a collection of programs, or groups of cells, linked together to create a sequential presentation.

progressive scan   A video scanning system that displays all lines of a frame in one pass. Contrast with interlaced scan. See Chap. 3 for more information.

psychoacoustic   See **perceptual encoding.**

PTP   Parallel track path. A variation of DVD dual-layer disc layout where readout begins at the center of the disc for both layers. Designed for separate programs (such as a widescreen and a pan & scan version on the same disc side) or programs with a variation on the second layer. Also most efficient for DVD-ROM random-access application. Contrast with **OTP.**

quantization levels   The predetermined levels at which an analog signal can be sampled as determined by the resolution of the analog-to-digital converter (in bits per sample); or the number of bits stored for the sampled signal.

quantize   To convert a value or range of values into a smaller value or smaller range by integer division. Quantized values are converted back (by multiplying) to a value which is close to the original but may not be exactly the same. Quantization is a primary technique of lossless encoding.

QuickTime   A digital video software standard developed by Apple Computer for Macintosh (Mac OS) and Windows operating systems. QuickTime is used to support audio and video from a DVD.

RAM   Random-access memory.

raster   The pattern of parallel horizontal scan lines that makes up a video picture.

read-modify-write   An operation used in writing to DVD-RAM discs. Because data can be written by the host computer in blocks as small as 2 KB, but the DVD format uses ECC blocks of 32 KB, an entire ECC block is read from the data buffer or disc, modified to include the new data and new ECC data, then written back to the data buffer and disc.

Red Book   The document first published in 1982 that specifies the original compact disc digital audio format developed by Philips and Sony.

Reed-Solomon   An error-correction encoding system that cycles data multiple times through a mathematical transformation in order to increase the effectiveness of the error correction, especially for burst errors (errors concentrated closely together, as from a scratch or physical defect). DVD uses rows and columns of Reed-Solomon encoding in a two-dimensional lattice, called *Reed-Solomon product code* (*RS-PC*).

reference picture (or **reference frame**)   An encoded frame that is used as a reference point from which to build dependent frames. In MPEG-2, I pictures and P pictures are used as references.

reference player   A DVD player that defines the ideal behavior as specified by the DVD-Video standard.

regional code   A code identifying one of the six world regions for restricting DVD-Video playback. See Table A.21.

regional management   A mandatory feature of DVD-Video to restrict the playback of a disc to a specific geographical region. Each player and DVD-ROM drive includes a single regional code, and each disc side can specify in which regions it is allowed to be played. Regional coding is optional—a disc without regional codes will play in all players in all regions.

replication   1) The reproduction of media such as optical discs (see stamping); 2) a process used to increase the size of an image by repeating pixels (to increase the horizontal size) and/or lines (to increase the vertical size) or to increase the display rate of a video stream by repeating frames. For example, a 360 × 240 pixel image can be displayed at 720 × 480 size by duplicating each pixel on each line and then duplicating each line. In this case the resulting image contains blocks of four identical pixels. Obviously, image replication can cause blockiness. A 24-fps video signal can be displayed at 72 fps by repeating each frame three times. Frame replication can cause jerkiness of motion. Contrast with **decimation**. Also see **interpolate**.

resampling   The process of converting between different spatial resolutions or different temporal resolutions. This may be based on simple sampling of the source information at higher or lower resolution or may include interpolation to correct for differences in pixel aspect ratios or to adjust for differences in display rates.

resolution   1) A measurement of relative detail of a digital display, typically given in pixels of width and height; 2) the ability of an imaging system to make clearly distinguishable or resolvable the details of an image. This includes *spatial resolution* (the clarity of a single image), *temporal resolution* (the clarity of a moving image or moving object), and *perceived resolution* (the apparent resolution of a display from the observer's point of view). Analog video is often measured as a number of lines of horizontal resolution over the number of scan lines. Digital video is typically measured as a number of horizontal pixels by vertical pixels. Film is typically measured as a number of line pairs per millimeter; 3) the relative detail of any signal, such as an audio or video signal.

RGB   Video information in the form of red, green, and blue tristimulus values. The combination of three values representing the intensity of each of the three colors can represent the entire range of visible light.

ROM   Read-only memory.

rpm   Revolutions per minute. A measure of rotational speed.

RS   Reed-Solomon. An error-correction encoding system that cycles data multiple times through a mathematical transformation in order to increase the effectiveness of the error correction. DVD uses rows and columns of Reed-Solomon encoding in a two-dimensional lattice, called *Reed-Solomon product code* (*RS-PC*).

RS-CIRC   See **CIRC.**

RSDL   Reverse-spiral dual-layer. See **OTP.**

RS-PC   Reed-Solomon product code. An error-correction encoding system used by DVD employing rows and columns of Reed-Solomon encoding to increase error-correction effectiveness.

R-Y, B-Y   The general term for color-difference video signals carrying red and blue color information, where the brightness (Y) has been subtracted from the red and blue RGB signals to create R-Y and B-Y color-difference signals. (See Chap. 3.)

sample   A single digital measurement of analog information. A snapshot in time of a continuous analog waveform. See **sampling.**

sample rate   The number of times a digital sample is taken, measured in samples per second, or Hertz. The more often samples are taken, the better a digital signal can represent the original analog signal. Sampling theory states that the sampling frequency must be more than twice the signal frequency in order to reproduce the signal without aliasing. DVD PCM audio allows sampling rates of 48 and 96 kHz.

sample size   The number of bits used to store a sample. Also called resolution. In general, the more bits allocated per sample, the better the reproduction of the original analog information. Audio sample size determines the dynamic range. DVD PCM audio uses sample sizes of 16, 20, or 24 bits.

sampling   Converting analog information into a digital representation by measuring the value of the analog signal at regular intervals, called samples, and encoding these numerical values in digital form. Sampling is often based on specified quantization levels. Sampling may also be used to adjust for differences between different digital systems (see **resampling** and **subsampling**).

saturation   The intensity or vividness of a color.

scaling   Altering the spatial resolution of a single image to increase or reduce the size; or altering the temporal resolution of an image sequence to increase or decrease the rate of display. Techniques include *decimation, interpolation, motion compensation, replication, resampling,* and *subsampling.* Most scaling methods introduce artifacts.

scan line A single horizontal line traced out by the scanning system of a video display unit. 525/60 (NTSC) video has 525 scan lines, about 480 of which contain actual picture. 625/50 (PAL/SECAM) video has 625 scan lines, about 576 of which contain actual picture.

scanning velocity The speed at which the laser pickup head travels along the spiral track of a disc.

SCMS Serial copy management system. Used by DAT, MiniDisc, and other digital recording systems to control copying and limit the number of copies that can be made from copies.

SCSI Small Computer Systems Interface. An electronic interface and command set for attaching and controlling internal or external peripherals, such as a DVD-ROM drive, to a computer. The command set of SCSI was extended for DVD-ROM devices by the SFF 8090 specification.

SDDS Sony Dynamic Digital Sound. A perceptual audio-coding system developed by Sony for multichannel audio in theaters. A competitor to Dolby Digital and an optional audio track format for DVD.

SDTV Standard-definition television. A term applied to traditional 4:3 television (in digital or analog form) with a resolution of about 700 × 480 (about $\frac{1}{3}$ megapixel). Contrast with **HDTV**.

seamless playback A feature of DVD-Video where a program can jump from place to place on the disc without any interruption of the video. Allows different versions of a program to be put on a single disc by sharing common parts.

SECAM Séquential couleur avec mémoire/sequential color with memory. A composite color standard similar to PAL, but currently used only as a transmission standard in France and a few other countries. Video is produced using the 625/50 PAL standard and is then transcoded to SECAM by the player or transmitter.

sector A logical or physical group of bytes recorded on the disc—the smallest addressable unit. A DVD sector contains 38,688 bits of channel data and 2048 bytes of user data.

SFF 8090 Specification number 8090 of the Small Form Factor Committee, an ad hoc group formed to promptly address disk industry needs and to develop recommendations to be passed on to standards organizations. SFF 8090 (also known as the *Mt. Fuji* specification), defines a command set for CD-ROM— and DVD-ROM—type devices, including implementation notes for ATAPI and SCSI.

SI Système International (d'Unités)/International System (of Units). A complete system of units for fundamental quantities of length, time, volume, mass, and so on.

signal-to-noise ratio The ratio of pure signal to extraneous noise, such as tape hiss or video interference. Signal-to-noise ratio is measured in decibels (dB). Analog recordings almost always have noise. Digital recordings, when properly prefiltered and not compressed, have no noise.

simple profile (SP) A subset of the syntax of the MPEG-2 video standard designed for simple and inexpensive applications such as software. SP does not allow B pictures. See **profile.**

SMPTE The Society of Motion Picture and Television Engineers. An international research and standards organization. The SMPTE time code, used for marking the position of audio or video in time, was developed by this group. (See App. B.)

S/N Signal-to-noise ratio. Also called SNR.

spatial Relating to space, usually two-dimensional. Video can be defined by its spatial characteristics (information from the horizontal plane and vertical plane) and its temporal characteristics (information at different instances in time).

spatial resolution The clarity of a single image or the measure of detail in an image. See **resolution.**

S/P DIF Sony/Philips digital interface. A consumer version of the AES/EBU digital audio transmission standard. Most DVD players include S/P DIF coaxial digital audio connectors providing PCM and encoded digital audio output.

SP@ML Simple profile at main level. The simplest MPEG-2 format used by DVD. Most discs use MP@ML. SP does not allow B pictures.

squeezed video See **anamorphic.**

stamping The process of replicating optical discs by injecting liquid plastic into a mold containing a master or stamper. Also (inaccurately) called mastering.

stream A continuous flow of data, usually digitally encoded, designed to be processed sequentially. Also called a bitstream.

subpicture Graphic bitmap overlays used in DVD-Video to create subtitles, captions, karaoke lyrics, menu highlighting effects, and so on.

subsampling The process of reducing spatial resolution by taking samples that cover larger areas than the original samples or of reducing temporal resolutions by taking samples that cover more time than the original samples. See **chroma subsampling.** Also called downsampling.

substrate   The clear polycarbonate disc onto which data layers are stamped or deposited.

subtitle   A textual representation of the spoken audio in a video program. Subtitles are often used with foreign languages and do not serve the same purpose as captions for the hearing impaired. See **subpicture.**

surround sound   A multichannel audio system with speakers in front of and behind the listener to create a surrounding envelope of sound and to simulate directional audio sources.

S-VHS   Super VHS (Video Home System). An enhancement of the VHS videotape standard using better recording techniques and Y/C signals. The term *S-VHS* is often used incorrectly to refer to *s-video* signals and connectors.

s-video   A video interface standard that carries separate luma and chroma signals, usually on a four-pin mini-DIN connector. Also called Y/C. The quality of s-video is significantly better than composite video since it does not require a comb filter to separate the signals, but it's not quite as good as component video. Most high-end televisions have s-video inputs. S-video is often erroneously called *S-VHS.*

sync   A video signal (or component of a video signal) containing information necessary to synchronize the picture horizontally and vertically. Also, specially formatted data on disc which helps the readout system identify location and specific data structures.

syntax   The rules governing construction or formation of an orderly system of information. For example, the syntax of the MPEG video encoding specification defines how data and associated instructions are used by a decoder to create video pictures.

system menu   The main menu of a DVD-Video disc, from which titles are selected. Also called the title selection menu or disc menu.

T   Tera. An SI prefix for denominations of one trillion (10^{12}).

telecine   The process (and the equipment) used to transfer film to video. The telecine machine performs 3:2 pulldown by projecting film frames in the proper sequence to be captured by a video camera.

telecine artist   The operator of a telecine machine. Also called a colorist.

temporal Relating to time. The temporal component of motion video is broken into individual still pictures. Because motion video can contain images (such as backgrounds) that do not change much over time, typical video has large amounts of temporal redundancy.

temporal resolution The clarity of a moving image or moving object, or the measurement of the rate of information change in motion video. See **resolution**.

time code Information recorded with audio or video to indicate a position in time. Usually consists of values for hours, minutes, seconds, and frames. Also called SMPTE time code. Some DVD-Video material includes information to allow the player to search to a specific time code position.

title The largest unit of a DVD-Video disc (other than the entire volume or side). Usually a movie, TV program, music album, or so on. A disc can hold up to 99 titles, which can be selected from the disc menu.

title key A value used to encrypt and decrypt (scramble) user data on DVD-Video discs.

track 1) A distinct element of audiovisual information, such as the picture, a sound track for a specific language, or the like. DVD-Video allows one track of video (with multiple angles), up to 8 tracks of audio, and up to 32 tracks of subpicture; 2) the continuous spiral channel of information recorded on a disc.

track buffer Circuitry (including memory) in a DVD player that provides a variable stream of data (up to 10.08 Mbps) to the system decoders of data coming from the disc at a constant rate of 11.08 Mbps (except for breaks when a different part of the disc is accessed).

track pitch The distance (in the radial direction) between the centers of two adjacent tracks on a disc. DVD-ROM standard track pitch is 0.74 μm.

transfer rate The speed at which a certain volume of data is transferred from a device such as a DVD-ROM drive to a host such as a personal computer. Usually measured in bits per second or bytes per second. Sometimes confusingly used to refer to data rate, which is independent of the actual transfer system.

transform The process or result of replacing a set of values with another set of values. A mapping of one information space onto another.

trim See **crop**.

tristimulus A three-valued signal that can match nearly all colors of visible light in human vision. This is possible because of the three types of photoreceptors in the eye. RGB, YC_bC_r, and similar signals are tristimulus, and can be interchanged by using mathematical transformations (subject to possible loss of information).

TVL Television line. See **lines of horizontal resolution.**

TWG Technical working group. A usually ad hoc group of representatives working together for a period of time to make recommendations or define standards.

UDF Universal Disc Format. A standard developed by the Optical Storage Technology Association designed to create a practical and usable subset of the ISO/IEC 13346 recordable, random-access file system and volume structure format.

UDF Bridge A combination of UDF and ISO 9660 file system formats that provides backward-compatibility with ISO 9660 readers while allowing full use of the UDF standard.

user data The data recorded on a disc independent of formatting and error-correction overhead. Each DVD sector contains 2048 bytes of user data.

VBI Vertical blanking interval. The scan lines in a television signal that do not contain picture information. These lines are present to allow the electron scanning beam to return to the top and are used to contain auxiliary information such as closed captions.

VBR Variable bit rate. Data that can be read and processed at a volume that varies over time. A data compression technique that produces a data stream between a fixed minimum and maximum rate. A constant level of compression is generally maintained, with the required bandwidth increasing or decreasing depending on the complexity (the amount of spatial and temporal energy) of the data being encoded. In other words, data rate is held constant while quality is allowed to vary. Compare to **CBR.**

VBV Video buffering verifier. A hypothetical decoder that is conceptually connected to the output of an MPEG video encoder. Provides a constraint on the variability of the data rate that an encoder can produce.

VfW See **Video for Windows.**

VHS Video Home System. The most popular system of videotape for home use. Developed by JCV.

Video CD An extension of CD based on MPEG-1 video and audio. Allows playback of near-VHS-quality video on a Video CD player, CD-i player, or computer with MPEG decoding capability.

Video for Windows   The system software additions used for motion video playback in Microsoft Windows. Replaced in newer versions of Windows by DirectShow (formerly called ActiveMovie).

Video manager (VMG)   The disc menu. Also called the title selection menu.

videophile   Someone with an avid interest in watching videos or in making video recordings. Videophiles are often very particular about audio quality, picture quality, and aspect ratio to the point of snobbishness.

Video title set (VTS)   A set of one to ten files holding the contents of a title.

VLC   Variable length coding. See **Huffman coding.**

VOB   Video object. A small physical unit of DVD-Video data storage, usually a GOP.

volume   A logical unit representing all the data on one side of a disc.

VSDA   Video Software Dealers Association. (See App. B.)

White Book   The document from Sony, Philips, and JVC, begun in 1993 that extended the Red Book compact disc format to include digital video in MPEG-1 format. Commonly called *Video CD.*

widescreen   A video image wider than the standard 4:3 aspect ratio. When referring to DVD or HDTV, *widescreen* usually implies a 16:9 aspect ratio.

window   A usually rectangular section within an entire screen or picture.

Windows   See **Microsoft Windows.**

XA   See **CD-ROM XA.**

Y   The luma or luminance component of video: brightness independent of color.

Y/C   A video signal in which the brightness (luma, Y) and color (chroma, C) signals are separated. Also called s-video.

YC_bC_r   A component digital video signal containing one luma and two chroma components. The chroma components are usually adjusted for digital transmission according to ITU-R BT.601. DVD-Video's MPEG-2 encoding is based on 4:2:0 YC_bC_r signals. YC_bC_r applies only to digital video, but is often incorrectly used in reference to the YP_bP_r analog component outputs of DVD players.

Yellow Book   The document produced in 1985 by Sony and Philips that extended the Red Book compact disc format to include digital data for use by a computer. Commonly called CD-ROM.

YP$_b$P$_r$ A component analog video signal containing one luma and two chroma components. Often referred to loosely as *YUV* or *Y, B-Y, R-Y*.

YUV In the general sense, any form of color-difference video signal containing one luma and two chroma components. Technically, YUV is applicable only to the process of encoding component video into composite video. See **YC$_b$C$_r$** and **YP$_b$P$_r$**.

INDEX

Index

Index

SOFTWARE AND INFORMATION LICENSE

The software and information on this diskette (collectively referred to as the "Product") are the property of The McGraw-Hill Companies, Inc. ("McGraw-Hill") and are protected by both United States copyright law and international copyright treaty provision. You must treat this Product just like a book, except that you may copy it into a computer to be used and you may make archival copies of the Products for the sole purpose of backing up our software and protecting your investment from loss.

By saying "just like a book," McGraw-Hill means, for example, that the Product may be used by any number of people and may be freely moved from one computer location to another, so long as there is no possibility of the Product (or any part of the Product) being used at one location or on one computer while it is being used at another. Just as a book cannot be read by two different people in two different places at the same time, neither can the Product be used by two different people in two different places at the same time (unless, of course, McGraw-Hill's rights are being violated).

McGraw-Hill reserves the right to alter or modify the contents of the Product at any time.

This agreement is effective until terminated. The Agreement will terminate automatically without notice if you fail to comply with any provisions of this Agreement. In the event of termination by reason of your breach, you will destroy or erase all copies of the Product installed on any computer system or made for backup purposes and shall expunge the Product from your data storage facilities.

LIMITED WARRANTY

McGraw-Hill warrants the physical diskette(s) enclosed herein to be free of defects in materials and workmanship for a period of sixty days from the purchase date. If McGraw-Hill receives written notification within the warranty period of defects in materials or workmanship, and such notification is determined by McGraw-Hill to be correct, McGraw-Hill will replace the defective diskette(s). Send request to:

Customer Service
McGraw-Hill
Gahanna Industrial Park
860 Taylor Station Road
Blacklick, OH 43004-9615

The entire and exclusive liability and remedy for breach of this Limited Warranty shall be limited to replacement of defective diskette(s) and shall not include or extend to any claim for or right to cover any other damages, including but not limited to, loss of profit, data, or use of the software, or special, incidental, or consequential damages or other similar claims, even if McGraw-Hill has been specifically advised as to the possibility of such damages. In no event will McGraw-Hill's liability for any damages to you or any other person ever exceed the lower of suggested list price or actual price paid for the license to use the Product, regardless of any form of the claim.

THE McGRAW-HILL COMPANIES, INC. SPECIFICALLY DISCLAIMS ALL OTHER WARRANTIES, EXPRESS OR IMPLIED, INCLUDING BUT NOT LIMITED TO, ANY IMPLIED WARRANTY OF MERCHANTABILITY OR FITNESS FOR A PARTICULAR PURPOSE. Specifically, McGraw-Hill makes no representation or warranty that the Product is fit for any particular purpose and any implied warranty of merchantability is limited to the sixty day duration of the Limited Warranty covering the physical diskette(s) only (and not the software or in-formation) and is otherwise expressly and specifically disclaimed.

This Limited Warranty gives you specific legal rights; you may have others which may vary from state to state. Some states do not allow the exclusion of incidental or consequential damages, or the limitation on how long an implied warranty lasts, so some of the above may not apply to you.

This Agreement constitutes the entire agreement between the parties relating to use of the Product. The terms of any purchase order shall have no effect on the terms of this Agreement. Failure of McGraw-Hill to insist at any time on strict compliance with this Agreement shall not constitute a waiver of any rights under this Agreement. This Agreement shall be construed and governed in accordance with the laws of New York. If any provision of this Agreement is held to be contrary to law, that provision will be enforced to the maximum extent permissible and the remaining provisions will remain in force and effect.